MY

ROAD

FROM

DAMASCUS

MY
ROAD
FROM
DAMASCUS

— A MEMOIR —

Jamal Saeed

TRANSLATED BY CATHERINE COBHAM

Published by ECW Press
665 Gerrard Street East
Toronto, Ontario, Canada M4M 1Y2
416-694-3348 / info@ecwpress.com

Editor for the Press: Michael Holmes
Cover Design: James Jones
Artwork on Cover: Youssef Abdelke
Author Photo: Rufaida al-Khabbaz

LIBRARY AND ARCHIVES CANADA CATALOGUING
IN PUBLICATION

Title: My road from Damascus: a memoir / Jamal Saeed ; translated by Catherine Cobham.

Names: Saeed, Jamal, 1959- author. | Cobham, Catherine, translator.

Identifiers: Canadiana (print) 20220184437 | Canadiana (ebook) 20220192073

ISBN 978-1-77041-621-5 (softcover)
ISBN 978-1-77852-002-0 (ePub)
ISBN 978-1-77852-003-7 (PDF)
ISBN 978-1-77852-004-4 (Kindle)

Subjects: LCSH: Saeed, Jamal, 1959- | LCSH: Authors, Canadian—Biography. | LCSH: Political refugees—Syria—Biography. | LCSH: Political refugees—Canada—Biography. | LCGFT: Autobiographies.

Classification: LCC PS8637.A355 Z46 2022 | DDC C813/.6—dc23

We acknowledge the support of the Canada Council for the Arts. *Nous remercions le Conseil des arts du Canada de son soutien.* This book is funded in part by the Government of Canada. *Ce livre est financé en partie par le gouvernement du Canada.* We acknowledge the support of the Ontario Arts Council (OAC), an agency of the Government of Ontario, which last year funded 1,965 individual artists and 1,152 organizations in 197 communities across Ontario for a total of $51.9 million. We also acknowledge the support of the Government of Ontario through the Ontario Book Publishing Tax Credit, and through Ontario Creates.

PRINTED AND BOUND IN CANADA

PRINTING: MARQUIS   5   4   3   2   1

To my parents, Saleh Saeed and Najeebah Shabow, who waited a long time for me to come home.

My mother is still waiting, but my father has stopped waiting for anybody.

Our battered suitcases were piled on the sidewalk again; we had longer ways to go. But no matter, the road is life.

— Jack Kerouac, *On the Road*

And as he journeyed, he came near Damascus: and suddenly there shined round about him a light from heaven.

— Acts 9:3

In Damascus
The stranger sleeps
Standing on his shadow
Like a minaret in the bed of eternity
Not longing for a country
Not longing for anyone . . .

— Mahmoud Darwish, "The Damascene Ring of the Dove"

Footnote: I love the elegance and lyricism of Darwish's poem about Damascus and am amazed by the splendor and glory of Damascus in many poems and books. However, these elegant poems and books do not refer to the sobbing that tears you apart, the sobbing that I, along with most of the people and houses in Damascus, know all too well.

— Jamal Saeed, May 2021

CHAPTER I

SILVER CHARM AND
APPLE TREES

I was holding my grandfather's hand in the backyard, watching my grandmother as she helped our cow give birth in the open air. The cow was
bellowing in pain, and I felt really sorry for her. Sitti, my grandma, slipped a
silver ornament in the shape of a star on the cow's horn and prayed to Allah
to help her. After the cow had given birth to a lovely little calf, I asked my
Sitti about the strange object she'd hung on the horn.

"It is a hamili," she replied. "It makes giving birth easier."

I looked closely at the star-shaped silver charm and asked about the engravings on it. Jaddi, my grandfather, explained they were words and symbols.

"Jaddi, what do the words say?" I asked, looking up at him.

"They are the words of Allah," he said.

"Did Allah himself write these words?"

"No. He sent them in a message delivered by an angel. And people wrote
down the angel's words."

"Can I speak to Allah?" I asked.

Jaddi laughed. "Only the prophet Musa can speak directly to Allah."

"Where does Musa live? Can I visit him?"

"Why do you want to visit him?" Jaddi asked.

"I want to ask if I can go with him when he speaks to Allah. I'd like to
hear Allah's voice."

"Musa lived a very long time ago, and, anyway, he wouldn't take young
boys to visit the Almighty." Jaddi laughed again.

"Your mother had a difficult labor when she was giving birth to you," Sitti told me, "and so the midwife asked where the village hamili was. The neighbor's goat was giving birth for the first time, just like your mother, so your aunt rushed next door and snatched the hamili from where it still hung on the nanny goat's horn. The word of Allah helped your mother when you came into the world," she added, tenderly touching the amulet's engraving.

In the weeks before I was born, Najeebah Shabow prepared carefully for the arrival of her new baby. She gathered together pieces of cotton fabric saved from flour sacks and sewed a small swaddling blanket, as well as a pillow and some garments, which were traditionally the same for boys and girls. Najeebah lovingly embroidered the baby blanket, pillow, and clothes destined for her baby, and his many siblings to follow, and the crib was made by the village carpenter, Abu Hikmat. Abu means "father of" in Arabic, and if a man has a son, you always identify the man as father of his first son's name. As I was the first son, my father was called Abu Jamal, even though I had six other brothers and was the first of ten children. It's the same for a woman, where Umm means "Mother of . . ." To this day, Najeebah Shabow is greeted as Umm Jamal.

When my mother's time came, my father went to fetch the midwife to help with my birth but found she was assisting her daughter-in-law who was also in labor. It's a rare situation in a small village to have two children born on the same morning. I was my mother's first child. She was just nineteen years old, and I was born in my parents' bedroom. My mother told me that she was in the middle of a powerful contraction when the midwife finally arrived.

"This is the easy stage," the midwife assured her.

My mother was not at all happy to hear this. "Get away from me, you bitch! I'd rather have a whore for a midwife."

The midwife laughed and began her work.

"After you were born," my mother used to say, "your grandma put salt on your body and washed you in a small tub in the other room in the house. She rubbed you with olive oil and ground myrtle leaves, put kohl around your eyes, and dressed you in the clothes we had prepared. Then she brought you to me. You were very small, and many of our friends and relatives thought you wouldn't survive. But I whispered in your ear, 'You will live.'"

My mother told me the story of my birth many times over the years, but I was most touched by it when I was just out of prison the first time and she told it to me yet again. Perhaps it was because I could relate the story of the hours following my birth to the new life of freedom I was experiencing outside prison.

My father understood freedom in his own way.

"Be your own boss so you don't have to take orders from other people."

This was why he chose not to work in the asphalt company that was one of the main employers of our village, founded by the French in 1927. My father had another theory, which was that farming was the most honorable career because it provided food for everyone. He loved farming.

I thought of him on the plane to Canada when the flight attendant gave us a form to fill in. I looked at the flag at the top of the form and my eyes rested on the maple leaf, which I knew was the Canadian national symbol. I thought of all the different symbols that nations, companies, and

Kfarieh, the green village where I was born and spent the first seventeen years of my life.

individuals chose to represent them and decided that, if I were asked, I would choose the apple. Not because of the biblical story of Adam and Eve, but because of memories of my own life from many years before, and one memory in particular.

My father was a pioneer farmer in our village, Kfarieh, in Syria. He was the first farmer in the area to plant Golden Delicious and Red Delicious apple trees. When I was about four years old, I stood watching him as he dug a series of holes and began to plant seedlings in them.

"Plant me, Dad," I said.

"Why?" he asked.

Stepping into one of the holes, I explained, "I want to be an apple tree, and then Mom will gather apples from my hair."

My father laughed. "But then you couldn't move."

"Change me into a moveable apple tree," I said.

I felt like an old apple tree sitting on a plane. When the flight attendant offered us a drink, I asked for apple juice.

CHAPTER 2

DESPAIR WAS THE SECRET
OF MY COURAGE

A s the steel door swung open, seven soldiers, all shouting orders and obscenities, rushed into our cold, dark prison cell.

"Faces to the wall, you sons of bitches," they screamed at the three of us.

"Hands behind your backs, animals."

"Lower your shit-filled heads and shut your eyes, bastards!"

I knew from the twelve years I'd spent in half a dozen Syrian prisons that the presence of many soldiers meant that one, or perhaps all of us, were about to be taken to meet an important army officer. They bound our hands, covered our eyes, and roughly stuffed cotton wool in our ears to make sure we couldn't hear what was being said unless they wanted us to. Suddenly, I was being dragged along the floor, pulled tripping up a flight of stairs, then jerked to a stop. The cotton wool was yanked from my ears, and I heard what I assumed was an officer's voice.

"What did you do after you got out of prison, Jamal?" he asked quietly.

"The first time . . ."

"Was there a second time?" came the voice, detached from its body.

"They detained me a month ago."

"Do you call that being detained? You didn't even spend a week with us, not even enough time to warm the floor under your ass. The important thing is, Jamal, what did you do after you left us?"

"I helped my family on the farm and then came to Damascus at the beginning of winter to carry on with my university studies."

"I'll make it easier for you, you piece of shit," he said, his tone changing. "What was the printing you did?"

"Some designs for silk-screen printing in the Faihaa printing works. I still design for them and get paid by the piece."

"What kind of designs do you do?"

"Butterflies . . . birds, flowers, fruit."

"You're lying, you son of a whore!"

"Your mother is no better than mine," I answered boldly. "There's no need for street language."

At this point he went wild and began to shout like a maniac. "Take this insolent bastard away. Execute him. We've got seventeen million people in Syria. We don't need this dog."

I raised my head and said clearly, "I am not a dog."

He repeated his order, his voice almost hoarse from the strain. "Take him away. Execute him at once. We don't need these sons of whores." I thought of saying something but made do with a scornful smile. "You shit!" he shouted. "Are you laughing at me? I swear to Allah, I'll make dog food of you! Take him away!"

This wasn't the first time I'd received abuse from an officer or been accused of treason because I'd helped print or distribute political leaflets. But on this occasion, I wasn't protecting anyone by suffering torture and abuse. I didn't have anything to confess. I was genuinely busy with my studies and earning enough to survive. I wasn't lying.

A soldier took hold of my arm and dragged me down more stairs to what I imagined was the interrogation room, the place where my life was to end. He left me standing alone, expecting the inevitable. And then I heard the door lock, and it became very silent.

Suddenly, my memory released a host of images and smells — things from the past that felt so real I forgot I was about to die. Maybe this illogical response to what should have been a terrifying situation was a manifestation of the awful despair that had set in the moment I was once again arrested.

I pictured the line that the rubber tube had made on my forehead. I'd seen this mark on the heads of many after they returned to their cell after interrogation, if they did return. As I waited alone in a locked room for my death sentence to be carried out, scenes from the past continued to follow one after another with amazing clarity. I could almost touch the white lace collar and sleeves of Barbara's red dress. At five years old, I was fascinated by the elegance of Barbara, the youngest daughter of the asphalt quarry manager. I scratched my back with my bound hands. It's as if the barbed wire I'd crawled under to meet Barbara more than a quarter of a century earlier is again scratching my back. My mother used to smile when she saw us together, Barbara and me, and point out I was three months older than her to the day. I see my mother's expression when I was released for the first time after my prolonged absence of about eleven years. I revel in the flood of joy that made her walk around the house in a daze, turning back to hug me again the instant she left, saying a few more words, her brief utterances dominating all other sounds, clear and warm: "My heart was lying at the crossroads, waiting for your footsteps, and now you've returned, my heart has returned to my chest," and "The hard waiting is over," and "Thank Allah we're no longer behind bars," speaking as if she had just come out of prison too. She pulls me to her, and I smell her scent and feel the heat of her tears falling on my face. Later I see the gleam of delight in her eyes as she welcomes the neighbors who have flocked to congratulate us on my release. They crowd around to see whether I am still like other people, if I can talk and see and hear, and if I still have five fingers on each hand after my long spell of incarceration. I can tell from the looks in their eyes and the questions they asked me that they are keen to investigate the impact of prison on my mind and body. Some are not afraid to blame me and call me stupid, believing I've damaged both myself and my family. I can see the effect of the passing years on them. Gray hair, wrinkles, baldness, and fat bellies prevented me from recognizing a few of the old ones, and recognizing the young ones, whom I've not seen since they were children, is even more difficult.

Waiting to be executed, I remember as clearly as if I can see them, many of the other people I'd known in different Syrian towns: children, men, and women, old and young; relatives, friends, and those who'd shared in the painful experiences of prison; interrogators out of control in the interrogation branch in Latakia; doomsday in cellblock seven in the military's special investigation branch in Damascus; prisoners of conscience, murderers, thieves, drug dealers, cats, rats, and police in al-Qala'a prison; bodies exhausted by fear, faces distorted by terror, souls brutalized by humiliation in Tadmur Prison. The faces of women I'd loved and cried over when they left, and those of the ones who loved me and who cried when I left. Informers for the intelligence services who visited me diligently after my release on the pretext of asking after my health. A great gathering of people, birds, beasts, with their features crystal clear; springs, rivers, different places by the sea, rough tracks, paved roads, and even familiar rocky outcrops. I am completely absorbed by this throng of images, smells, and the sounds my memory yields, sharper and more delicate than I would have believed possible, and in that moment I really forget where I am. I don't think about how my brazen answers to the officer have just slammed the door on my future.

I am devouring life avidly as if it only existed in the past when the door of the interrogation room opens and footsteps approach. I brace myself for the end, but nothing. If only I could move my hand, I would pull the blindfold away from my eyes. Has the soldier who entered the room changed his mind and left again? Or is he standing close to me this very second? I picture the room full of instruments of torture: an old tire, electric cables, clubs, a German chair, water, and a packet of pins on the metal table where the interrogator usually sat. Big, strong torturers no more than twenty-five years old will show up at any moment.

Mudar al-Jundi was detained in 1987 and disappeared. Colonel Mazhar Faris was in charge of the branch at the time. Did he say to them, "Take him away and execute him"? How many people lived in Syria then? How much did Mudar suffer before he died? How did he die?

The door opens again and I hear the sound of something being moved on a metal table. The door shuts again. Have they taken something out of the room? The sound of footsteps in the corridor. People hurrying, and then the sound of shouting. The desperate voice of a man begging his torturers to stop beating him, a wailing sound in which pain, hope, and impotence mingle. I know that wailing well. I've heard it many times, sometimes coming out of my own mouth.

Bassam once said to me that prison was the practice of grief, wailing, anticipation, and masturbation. Bassam killed himself after he came out of prison. Bassam's voice resembled that of the man who continues to cry out in the next room: "For the sake of Allah, stop!"

The executioner beats him again and shouts angrily, "That one is for Allah!" The man screams louder, continuing to beg for mercy. I know this pain. Before you lose consciousness, you feel like the whip is splitting your head apart. Now the man shouts, "For the sake of President Hafez al-Assad, please stop!"

"Don't insult Mr. President's name with your filthy tongue!" shouts the executioner as he resumes the torture.

"Tongues need re-educating before they say Mr. President's name," I whisper to myself. I have the habit of immediately recounting my experiences as I live them. It is as if I am preparing to tell the stories to others.

Am I going to scream like him? There's nobody around to whom I could say, "You're going to die. Let's hope they get it over with quickly." It's as if I am reassuring myself. The face of a woman I'd been madly in love with fills my mind. I used to talk to her even when she wasn't there, about joys, sorrows, bloodstained shirts, smells, and everything that was going around in my head. This simple dream that was never realized comes back to haunt me: We are walking by the river that runs through a meadow below our village. The violets are blooming, their scent filling the air; we're walking hand in hand, and I imagine that we blend with the scent of the violets, the sky, and the clouds, our bodies entwining as we fall to the ground and dissolve into the color of a million little flowers. The pine trees are playing with the wind, singing to us about how our embrace will last forever. And at that moment when we blaze with love, our kisses grow wings, become flying kisses . . . The door of the interrogation room opens suddenly. Get ready. Blazing love? Violets? Flying kisses? I'll say to them before they execute me, "I will die clean and pure so that people can be free, while you'll live on, stained by your murderous crimes." They'll mock me for this declamation. I myself mock such rhetoric. I'm an object of scorn and derision for them in any case, just like any victim. All the same, this is the message I feel like sending to everyone who isn't in prison anywhere in the world. Somebody somewhere might pass it on or at least remember it. I hear footsteps approaching. I picture my body on the dissection table in the Faculty of Medicine at Damascus University. Will any of my friends in the medical school be there and recognize my features, or will I have been completely disfigured? They might just throw my body into the desert to be devoured by wild animals. I am ready to die as footsteps approach. When they go away again, I feel a strange mixture of disappointment and joy. It seems I am waiting for life and death at the same time. Expecting to die at any moment isn't the hard thing: death appears like nothing more than a long sleep. I am just hoping I don't have to undergo much torture in the course of my transformation from a living person to a dead one.

I subsequently found out the name of the officer who shouted like a mad bull and ordered my execution. When an officer or even a conscript in the intelligence services insults you, you're likely to take refuge in silence. Standing up to him could include an element of courage, or stupidity, and responding to a beating might lead to death. I didn't think of correcting a statement such as "We've got seventeen million people in Syria," even if there were no more than thirteen million people living in the country in 1992. And it wasn't out of place for an intelligence officer to make the statement that we, the Syrian people, were at the disposal of these outfits who serve what they called "those at the top" or "the leadership," pointing upwards with their index fingers.

The humiliating state I was in wasn't compatible with courage or defiance: my feet were bare, my hands tied behind my back, my eyes bound with a strip of black plastic, fastened tightly at the back of my head. On previous occasions in front of the interrogators, I'd been more pragmatic, saying to myself, "When the beast that inhabits his torturers breaks free from its chains, all a detainee can hope for is more torture."

I learned from the soldier who brought me back to the interrogation room that the officer shouting at me was Brigadier General Mustafa al-Tajir, head of Branch 235, known as the Palestine Branch. I'd encountered many officers from military intelligence before him, but they hadn't delighted in the same degree of obscenity. With a few exceptions, vulgarity usually increased as the rank went down. This man was known to Syrians for his uninhibitedly abusive behavior, and his reputation as somebody who would stop at nothing meant a lot of the rich avoided falling out with him. They even curried favor with him and then gave him what he wanted, taking advantage of the fact that he could be bought.

I met Mustafa al-Tajir roughly eight hours after being detained for the third time. An intelligence patrol raided the house where I was living in Jaramana, near Damascus, at dawn on March 14, 1992, breaking down the door and pulling me out of bed. I asked if I could put on warm clothes, but they tied my hands and blindfolded me. Then they dragged me to a car along with the three others from the house: Jaffan, a Christian friend; his brother, Irfan; and Abd al-Karim. All of us were barefoot and wearing light night-clothes, shivering with cold as we were transported to the Palestine Branch of the military intelligence service. There we were thrown into a bare, cold room as if we were sacks of potatoes being unloaded in a warehouse.

"What do you think's going on?" Jaffan asked me in a voice trembling with cold.

"They're playing with us," I said. "I can't see any reason for them to arrest us. Perhaps they want to send a message to society that when they release a political prisoner, it doesn't mean they are no longer interested in him. Why did they arrest us about a month ago, in fact exactly a month ago, and from the same house?"

They released Irfan in the morning. We learned this only later. The reason for our arrest was likely to be quite trivial, in our eyes at least. The previous time, they'd beaten us savagely, but we only found out why after the interrogation: Some friends had spent the evening in our house. What a terrible crime. On that occasion they arrested all those who had attended the party. Despite the fact that the confessions confirmed it was a party like any other, people were still held in custody. It occurred to me that there must be a surplus of thugs ready to beat up and arrest people, and they didn't want them to be unemployed now they'd managed to paralyze the opposition. The prison cells themselves seemed to me like wild beasts needing food, and they fed on the days of the lives of the inmates who withered away inside their walls. It also occurred to me that perhaps our previous detention had been in the context of training exercises for new elements in the raiding parties. These arrests began and ended in the space of two weeks; then everybody was released — everybody, without exception. This wasn't usually the case. They usually kept some, at least, who were "subject to investigation," without an investigation necessarily taking place. And here I was in detention again after exactly a month.

I suppose, by the time of my third arrest, I'd finally lost interest in a life where I was dragged to these rooms of humiliation whenever they wished, not knowing when that might be and unable to do anything against them. I was overcome with such a feeling of despair that my life no longer meant much to me. I didn't want to face more torture, either psychological or physical, or to witness my spirit shriveling in the face of more fear and humiliation. Despair was the secret of my courage, of my reckless attitude toward my fate. If I wanted to use one word to describe my attitude to life at that time it would be "exhausted." Nightmares wore us out, as did the patrols that raided our houses and dragged us from our beds. Like all the times Jaffan and I had joked about our respective religions, I said to him after our arrest, "Oh man, you're talking like a miserable preacher on the saddest of Good Fridays."

At that lowest point, I remembered the horrible day we were transferred from al-Qala'a Civil Prison in Damascus to the military interrogation branch, and then to Tadmur Prison in the desert on Monday, September 13, 1982. Ten years before. I'd said to Jaffan, "This Monday is sadder than Good Friday," and reminded him of the hymn that tells the story of Christ on the cross. Although these were times fraught with anticipation and fear, Jaffan laughed. I don't exactly know why the hymn that told of the ascent to Golgotha came to my mind then.

In the vehicle carrying us to Tadmur, there were four of us accused of belonging to the Communist Labor Party and twenty-three youths accused of belonging to the Muslim Brotherhood. We were all bound with a single chain. The twenty-three were muttering prayers that smelled of fear, the same smell exuded by our bursts of laughter and long silences. I found out from the one chained next to me that they were reciting the "prayer of fire." It was supposed to make the torture that was bound to come easier to bear. I felt great affection for that young man who was lost in his prayer. I learned he had been arrested when he was sixteen, and here he was at seventeen taking refuge in his faith to protect him from the hell of Tadmur. When these youths muttering prayers were arrested, they were at secondary school in Saraqib, in Idlib province.

"Ten years have gone by," said Jaffan, "since our ride to the desert hell of Tadmur. Ironic, how it was in a ZiL truck manufactured by our Soviet comrades."

"And imagine," I added, "here we are living in one prison, and when we take refuge in our memories, we find ourselves in another."

There were meat hooks hanging from the roofs of the ZiL trucks. Besides carrying prisoners, they were used to transport animal carcasses to military and prison kitchens.

Where was Jaffan now? If they'd released him, he would have gone straight to our house and told them that we'd been arrested together, but that he hadn't seen me since a few hours after our arrest.

The same thing happened when Mudar al-Jundi was arrested: plenty of people volunteered details, and then nothing. Mudar vanished. After years of his family and friends trying to find out what had become of him, Colonel Jalal advised Mudar's wife, Amira, to stop wasting her time because he was dead. He told her he couldn't provide her with a death certificate, and when Amira informed us and members of his family, we each walked alone in Mudar's funeral procession, not knowing the date of his death, and we each engraved in our imaginations a tombstone whose whereabouts was unknown. Jaffan's visit to my family would be the end of a thread leading nowhere, the end of a thread that didn't exist. It would be the beginning of the journey to discover my fate, and my family would say the phrase repeated by so many others, "All we want to know is whether he's still alive." My mother would be the one who repeated it more than anyone else, speaking for the family and for herself, while my father would chew on his grief in silence. It felt as if I was preparing to write an article about my mother's past, fraught with wishes and hopes, and about her future where these hopes would become more numerous, more oppressive, and would be accompanied by an even greater anguish. The dead cannot write their memoirs or tell stories. Their stories are buried with them or devoured by the same wild beasts that devour their corpses.

Suddenly, footsteps are moving closer. A soldier touches my hand and it's as if Azrael is taking me. I instinctively snatch my hand away.

"Don't worry, Jamal," a voice says gently.

Soldiers call detainees "animal," "fucker," or, if they're polite, the number of the prisoner's cell. The family doesn't call their son "number nine." The prison warden calls the prisoner by name only if he's being summoned for interrogation, or if the situation requires the warden to be sure that this particular inmate is the one he's looking for. Before the soldier arrived, I had been talking to myself about my death. When he called me by name for the first time since the order had been given for my execution, I prepared myself to confront a death that seemed both inevitable and imminent. An image of my mother frying potatoes crowded out all other thoughts. I wished I could be there eating those hot brown fries, as I often did while she was preparing lunch.

I'm astonished when he frees my wrists from the handcuffs and removes the blindfold. My eyes begin scooping up everything in the room, greedily fulfilling their normal, healthy function. The soldier looks at me and smiles.

"I respect your courage. Nobody else has dared talk to Mustafa al-Tajir like that." I hadn't known I was talking to the head of the branch. I scrutinize the soldier's face to see if he is making fun of me. He appears serious and calm, and even pats me affectionately on the shoulder, this handsome youth with a thick black mustache, green eyes, and a scar on his forehead. He asks me to scream while he flogs a worn car tire lying on the floor. "I'm Mahmud from Daraa," he says. "I'm doing my military service. Only a month to go."

I knew a lot of torturers and prison guards. A few of them showed some sympathy or even offered a few small kindnesses, but this was the first time one of them had trusted me.

"Aren't you afraid that some prisoner might report you?" I ask. "You'd be in big trouble."

"Not when the prisoner's brave like you," he replies.

The kindness of the guard left me in a state of confusion, maybe for half an hour, maybe more, maybe less. I don't know. But after he left me alone in that interrogation room, I was so aware of our common suffering as Syrians, I almost wept. The despair that was my strength started to fade. Mahmud had opened a window to the future. I would visit Daraa and look for this young man who hadn't gone through with the order to torture me.

I reflected on the hopes and dreams that had made me oppose the regime that had been in power since shortly after I was born, comparing the Syria I lived in with the Syria I dreamed of. I never imagined I would live an ocean away in Canada or write about my time in the interrogation room . . . a time when I sat in the jaws of death waiting to be swallowed whole.

CHAPTER 3

HOLY

I was one of many dreamers who made the pilgrimage to Hasiba's. Her home was one of three rooms in an old house, surrounding an open courtyard. Hasiba's room served as the kitchen, living room, and bedroom for her, her sister, and their parents. There was a table in one corner with a triple-burner gas stove on it, and a shelf stacked with kitchen utensils, but no sink. There was also an old blue couch and a carpet upon which we pilgrims sat.

Hasiba had studied at the Intermediate Institute of Textile Industries after leaving high school. Because of this she was known among her friends as one of the "educated proletariat" and belonged to the Communist Labor League in Syria.

We dreamers visited that room regularly to show our loyalty to those poorer classes and to drink tea, smoke, share books, and discuss songs, movies, literature, and art. We talked about what was going on in the world and expressed our disillusion, but despite our great interest in politics, we had little political understanding.

I was having a coffee when a young girl entered the room, a storm of beauty in those drab surroundings. She was holding an old copy of *The Holy War*. I knew the book and its ironic title. It was actually about class struggle. I stood up and introduced myself as Ahmad Ibrahim, a false name I used at the time, as I was wanted by the security forces.

"I'm Widad," she said, shaking my hand confidently. I looked at the book in her other hand.

"Is this particular war holy?" I asked.

"No, Saint Ahmad, this war is thoroughly sinful," she teased.

"So why's it called holy, then?" I asked.

"You tell me, Saint Ahmad. Go on . . ."

"I'm not a saint, and I'm the one asking the question, Mademoiselle Widad," I said with a smile. "I need somebody to tell me what's holy about this war. I don't even know the meaning of the word holy."

Because she pronounced the letter R like a Parisian, I told her we needed a teacher from la ville lumière, a teacher with her fashion sense and way of talking. She smiled and told me she'd like to get rid of her speech defect but hadn't managed to so far.

We continued our meaningless conversation about the word "holy." I observed that it would be a good topic for Arabic composition homework in an elementary school. She joked about her holy schoolteacher and his thick glasses.

Meanwhile, in the discussion going on around us, Hasiba was cursing the imperialism and capitalism that forced us to use violence to fight for our rights. "'Violence is the midwife of history,'" she quoted.

"Do you think comrades Engels or Marx loved violence?" I interrupted. Hasiba gave me a hard stare. "And what is the meaning of holiness in your Marxist lexicon?" I went on, holding up Widad's book.

Looking back, I can say that we knew little about Marxism then, and we ought to have considered Marx as a thinker rather than a prophet. However, at the time, I had read and adopted Marxist ideas wholeheartedly.

After Widad left, I told Hasiba that Widad's eyes were more important to me than *The Communist Manifesto* of our comrades Marx and Engels.

"You're a petit bourgeois," Hasiba fired back.

Widad and I met many more times at these gatherings in Hasiba's room, and finally she confessed that Hasiba had told her how I'd compared her eyes to *The Communist Manifesto*. Trying to continue in the same romantic vein, I whispered that she made springs of pure water flow through my blood.

"Are they holy springs?" she asked, sarcastically. Noticing I was hurt by her teasing, she put a hand on my shoulder. "If you say you love me in a straightforward way, I'll confess my love for you too," she said, leaving me speechless. "Why don't we get together for a beer at Abu Shafiq's," she added.

"Is . . . is tomorrow at ten good for you?" I stammered.

The next morning, as the storm of beauty walked calmly toward my table at the famous Abu Shafiq restaurant in Damascus, I wanted to open my heart to Widad and keep her safe inside it. I told her that my name was not Ahmad and that I was a wanted man. She asked me about my mother and then told me about her father, who came from the countryside near Aleppo.

"He's a barbarian. If he knew about our meetings, he would arrange for me to meet my Maker at once."

Widad and I agreed it was impossible for us to go to the house where I was hiding out. There were four wanted people living there, so the fewer who knew its location the better. But there were times we could stay at friends' homes when they traveled. The first time we were alone together, the whole experience felt like a dream. My heart was on my lips when I kissed her, and on the tips of my fingers when I removed her clothes. As I buried my face between her breasts, I truly forgot who and where I was.

"Today I discovered the meaning of the word holy," I said, after we'd made love.

"And what else did you discover?" she asked.

"Holiness is to feel you are embracing your dream when you hold your beloved in your arms."

"Are you reciting poetry?"

"No, I'm living it. The poetry we live is more important than the poems we read or write."

"Go on . . ."

"I feel as if the angels have escaped their scriptures to bless this moment, and that this room is as vast as the universe."

"I can't talk like you," she said. "All I know is that I love you and I enjoy being together on this bed with you."

CHAPTER 4

FROM SYRIA'S NEXT GREAT WRITER
TO DOG FOOD

"People generally like tragic stories," Lory Kaufman said to me, half-joking as usual.

"Yes, but a lot of powerful messages can wear comic masks," I answered.

"Lory, what are you trying to say?"

"Don't you want to write about your experiences in prison? There must be a lot of stories there."

Lory's question made me look at my past as if I were observing another person. Windows and doors opened and through them I began to see the youth I used to be. Perhaps I could be his spokesman. It was as if I'd left him behind me, frozen in the kind of time that you see on the face of an old statue, the vanishing initials carved in a tree by long-dead lovers, or the unwise decision of a youth's tattoo, now fading on wrinkled skin. I know that other person in whose name I speak occupies a big space in the "I" who is writing now. I told Lory that. He smiled as usual.

"Then that's how it should be . . . when you write it," he said with a wink. And then he excused himself. His wife, Myungja, was calling him.

Lory and I were among a group of people gathered to celebrate the first wedding anniversary of Tarek and Pamela, both of whom had been in the group that met my family when we first landed at Toronto International Airport. As I mingled with the guests, I repeated "Nice to meet you" many times and answered questions like, "When did you come to Kingston?" "You must have been shocked by the cold weather," and other similarly polite and friendly words. Most of these people seemed to me relaxed and well disposed toward the world, as if they were not ruled by "the system" — I was still trying to understand this new system that I'd become a part of. "There's no need to rush," a Canadian friend had advised me, although to me the rhythms of life here seemed so feverish. I took out my phone and typed this observation about how the content of time changes depending on one's circumstances. In Syria, life isn't so fast, but our minds and fears never stop moving. In Canada, the fears may be fewer, but people never stop moving. So I am asking myself as I type, "Why is everybody telling me not to rush?"

Just then, Lory returned. Unsmiling now, he said, "Do you mind me asking about the times they used to pour hot and cold water all over you?"

"I felt lucky when they did that," I replied, smiling.

His eyes widened in astonishment. "Lucky? Did you say lucky? What do you mean, man?"

I laughed. "As you know, when the choice is between two evils, we choose the lesser. Some people think losing a finger is better than losing a hand, and losing a hand is better than losing your head. I didn't generally have the luxury of choosing the method of torture. I had alternating cold and hot water poured over me in the winter of 1980 during my first incarceration, and again in the winter of 1992 when I was detained briefly for the second time. It's much easier to bear than having your bones broken, being hung by your wrists from the ceiling, or enduring the German chair, where your spine is bent backwards until you're temporarily paralyzed."

Lory frowned. He was listening intently, but his whole being seemed to be focused on the events rather than my philosophy about the lesser evil. For some reason, he asked me for more details, and when I gave those, he shook his head, clearly upset. I told him about being detained that second time, in February 1992. I was lying on the floor, blindfolded and shivering with cold in the interrogation room.

"Are you shivering with fear or cold?" the torturer Abu Fahd asked. For the most part, prisoners didn't know jailers' real names, so we gave them ones that suited their personalities — in this case, Father of a Leopard. That's to say, a man possessing the qualities of a leopard.

"Your lips are blue. I'll warm you up," he said, and went away, returning in a minute to pour more freezing water over me. Lying there, blind, I gasped and my whole body clenched, causing me to vomit. He flew into a rage and began beating me with a whip of braided electric cables. The shift supervisor, who only referred to himself as Issam, came in while I was screaming.

"Who's the idiot who brought that idiot here?" he asked.

"Look," replied Abu Fahd. "The filthy bastard's vomited everywhere."

"I told you to bring the bitch who's in cell nine, not this piece of shit. Now clean the room!" Issam ordered, and left.

Abu Fahd loosened the handcuffs and told me to take my blindfold off. Then he delegated Issam's order to me: "Clean this place with your tongue, bastard. Do it! Now!"

I couldn't respond to his obscene order, despite continuous lashes of the whip. Luckily for me, they were in a hurry, and this spared me from providing Abu Fahd with further enjoyment. I used a mop to clean up. When I came out of the room, Joseph saw me. He was the nurse who often helped torture the detainees. He swore at me for being so dirty and, evidently disgusted by my appearance, told me to go to the toilets and wash myself. In the toilets there was a rubber tube connected to a water tap to rinse one's privates, but no soap. I asked Joseph for a piece of soap. He swore at me again, telling me to wait facing the wall. Soon he returned with a bar of good soap.

"I couldn't find any of the army soap that you're supposed to use," he said. "Take this. It's mine."

Joseph used an excellent brand of soap, full of olive oil. To smell it was a pleasure, a luxury found nowhere else in the prison, and I was holding it in my hand. The last time I'd had the chance to use soap, they gave me stuff that smelled like petrol. Someone had stolen the laurel soap prisoners were meant to use and sold it in the market. Joseph's smelled luxurious, its wonderful scent cutting through the damp, mold, and urine stink of the washroom. And although I was still shivering, I had no choice but to bathe in cold water. I got rid of the blood and vomit clinging to my body and had the joy of using my freed hands to rub the foaming soap all over me. The scent and the absolute luxury of bathing with it caused me to try to dance with delight, even though it hurt where the whip had struck me. I also took the opportunity to wash my one set of clothing. I wrung it out as well as I could and put it back on damp. Unfortunately, towels and clean clothes were far away in the house where they'd arrested me.

JAMAL SAEED

One way of torturing is to pour cold or hot water on the naked body of a prisoner.

JAMAL SAEED

"Get out of the toilets, Two," Joseph shouted. Two was the number of my cell and my name until I left that space. I came out and handed the soap gratefully to Joseph.

He struck me across the shoulders with the whip he always held. "Keep it," he ordered.

That little piece of soap represented great riches that lasted for less than a day. The following morning, as I came out of the toilets, Abu Fahd saw me holding the soap and ordered me to open my hand. He struck me hard on the palm and the soap flew into the distance. When I turned to try to find it, he pelted me with multiple stinging blows, shouting, "I bet you were weaned on luxurious soap, son of a bitch."

I ran toward my cell, and it was only when the heavy metal door clanged shut behind me that I felt safe. As I stood there, watching the welts where I was struck begin to rise, I decided that, if I survived, one day I would tell people how this kind of prison makes a sanctuary of a cell and death something to aspire to.

After I avoided being caught when the intelligence services raided my family's home in Kfarieh, I became adept in the world of disguise, living more than thirty months under an assumed identity. I was finally captured on a bus in 1980, arrested, and spent four brutal months in two military investigation prisons before being sent to al-Qala'a Civil Prison, where I enjoyed some rights. Then, in 1981, I was brought before the Supreme State Security Court, the SSSC. This was a special court that the regime used when a civil court wouldn't convict someone they wanted to punish. But even after this exceptional court sent a report to the intelligence services saying there was no evidence to convict me, instead of allowing me to go free, the intelligence service decided just to stop the legal process and send me directly to Tadmur military prison, known as one of the worst prisons in the world. There, any talk of rights, even the right to breathe fresh air, was considered a kind of nonsense.

The different branches of the intelligence services were now to decide the course of my life during the eleven plus years that I spent in various prisons, and after I was released too. Even then, I was required to get authorization documents from various branches of the intelligence services: to justify why I was late signing up for military service, to obtain permission to finish my studies, to apply for a passport or any government job.

In November 1991, for instance, at the Ministry of Culture, Mrs. Najah al-Attar (now vice president of Syria), tried to get me a job in the Department of Composition, Translating, and Publishing. This was after her friend, the novelist Mr. Hanna Mina, vouched for me and praised my writing. She even took it upon herself to ask the required authorization from the intelligence services to employ me. They refused. "The Minister can do nothing further," Professor Hanna told me. I give Hanna the title of professor; even though his academic achievements were modest, he was one of the most famous Arab novelists in the second half of the twentieth century.

The following year, on March 13, 1992, I went back to the Ministry of Culture to inquire about a manuscript of short stories I had submitted, *Majnunat al-Shumus* (in English, *The Suns' Crazy Girl*). Still suffering from a fear of entering government offices, as I walked into the building I noticed an ominous poster on the wall, one I'd previously seen inside the military intelligence interrogation branch. It read: *"There is no life in this country except for progress and socialism."* — *Hafez al-Assad*.

I was received by a slim woman who moved as if she was constantly in a hurry but looked kind and friendly. When she found out I'd come to ask about my manuscript, she said, "Welcome, Mr. Jamal. I'm Nada Abu Samra. Mr. Antun asked me a couple of times if there was a way to get in touch with you. It's good you've come."

She led me to Antun Maqdisi's spacious office. Maqdisi had graduated from Montpellier University in France before my mother was born, and I'd read every article of his that I could get my hands on. For me, and many others, he was a major Syrian intellectual. I was simply awestruck by the idea of meeting him. When we entered, he was absorbed in reading an article in *Le Monde Diplomatique*. A thin man who couldn't have weighed much more than a hundred pounds, he wore spectacles with thick lenses and was also holding a magnifying glass. He put this down gently on the newspaper and looked inquiringly at Nada.

"Mr. Jamal Saeed," she said.

The man, who must have been around eighty years old, stood up and held out his hand. "Hello and welcome," he said. "We didn't know how to contact you. You didn't leave us an address or a phone number."

"I don't have a phone," I said awkwardly. "I live in al-Nahda." This was one of the shanty towns on the outskirts of Damascus.

He walked heavily around his desk and sat on a chair beside me. The pullover he was wearing reminded me of a famous photo of Jacques Prévert.

"What would you like to drink?" he asked. "We have coffee, tea, and herbal teas in the Ministry's buffet." He ordered a coffee for me and a tisane for himself, and asked Nada to fetch my manuscript. When they arrived, he praised my stories and referred to some specific passages. "I've picked out a few that I advise you to delay publishing," he said. "Do keep them. A day will come when you can publish them without paying a price. Publishing them now might expose you to trouble that you could do without. Or, you may choose to publish them outside of Syria, under a pseudonym." He talked in an open, friendly fashion, but underlying his words was a note of fatherly concern and human warmth. He spoke with complete humility, and I was embarrassed by his extreme courtesy. It was as if he were talking to an equal. At the end of the interview, I agreed that his department would publish the stories he had chosen, and as he walked me out of his office, Antun advised me not to stop writing.

"You'll be to Syria what Maupassant was to France," he said.

This commendation, coming from him, embarrassed me as much as it pleased me. I left the meeting on the verge of tears. About eighteen hours after my meeting with Antun Maqdisi, I was in another government office. Blindfolded, barefoot, and with my hands tied, I stood in front of Brigadier General Mustafa al-Tajir, whose face I couldn't see, but whose voice called me son of a whore and promised to feed me to the dogs.

CHAPTER 5

THE FIRST ARREST (1980)

Gesturing with his Kalashnikov, a soldier ordered the crowded public minibus I was riding in to stop. The driver pulled over and turned off a radio playing a song in praise of "the Leader of the March." A round face covered with adolescent pimples appeared at the door and looked over the passengers. "You, the one in the brown coat. Collect your things and get out here."

The only passenger wearing a brown coat, I obeyed, wondering if this was random or if someone had informed on me. One of the soldiers told me to get in their car, a white Peugeot Estate. I refused.

"Who are you?" I asked.

"Get moving, idiot," said a blond soldier, another with a spotty face.

Their leader smiled. "You'll be our guest," he said, "and you'll find out exactly who we are soon enough."

I wanted people to see that my arrest was arbitrary, so I began asking whether there was an arrest warrant from the public prosecutor's office. A soldier told the bus driver to be on his way. None of the passengers could shield me, but I sought their protection all the same. I wanted to read what was in their minds from the expressions on their faces, to catch a glimpse of support from at least one of them. I believe I saw a glint of sympathy in the eyes of one young woman wearing a turquoise jersey. From the preparation manual clutched to her chest, I assumed she was a schoolteacher. But she turned away. After the bus had driven off, I was at my abductors' mercy.

"Do you have an arrest warrant from any official body?" I asked the leader again.

"I'll give you as many warrants as you want," he said, smiling. Then he laughed out loud. "We've got enough for your whole family, Jamal. In fact, for everyone in your village. Kfarieh, isn't it?"

At a look from him, two soldiers twisted my arms behind my back, bound them, and put a blindfold over my eyes. And then, for the first time in my life, I was beaten, right there in the streets. It felt like all four of them were having a go at punching me, kicking me, and swearing at me. I then felt myself being picked up and thrown unceremoniously into the back seat of their car. Suddenly, I felt a strong hand on my neck, and I was roughly pushed forward, my back and neck bent so acutely that I was suddenly gasping for breath. The Peugeot shot off, its driver now heaping curses on the mothers of the other drivers on the road, his hand permanently on the horn. I pictured how they'd make way for him once they'd seen the white Estate, well known at the time as the car regularly used by any number of intelligence services.

I didn't know that those who'd arrested me were from the military intelligence. In Syria, there are different sorts of intelligence services with different names, all of them authorized to arrest people like me. Elements from the department of political security arrested my comrade Muhammad Aboud, who was tortured to death. A man from his village told me that he was his mother's only child. I helped distribute a statement condemning the regime for murdering Muhammad, a believer in peaceful protest.

The driver complained about traffic and said he needed twenty minutes to get from the roadblock where they'd picked me up to the interrogation center. When I tried to arch my neck to relieve the pressure on it and was welcomed by a punch in the face, it occurred to me that I hadn't had a chance to say goodbye to the sky. I remember the sky on that day, December 29, 1980. It was very clear and blue. The sun was high, but for all its beauty, the weather was extremely cold. I dismissed my notion of saying goodbye to the sky and began to think again about the story I was to tell during my first interrogation, how it must remain consistent and not change under torture. Such a transgression could bring down the secret police on my friends. I remembered details of the pamphlet I'd read with the title *How to Face the Interrogator*, and how we'd regarded those who'd given way under torture as cowardly, or, conversely, how we'd almost made saints of those who'd resisted, especially those who'd died. All the same, I felt a great scream of "I don't want to die" echoing within me. The Peugeot finally stopped. Blindfolded, I was dragged into a building and pushed against a wall.

"Just face the wall and don't move," a soldier warned. "Don't say a word. Don't breathe. Stand there and shut up."

Other soldiers amused themselves by hitting my blindfolded head as they passed through the corridor. With every blow, my forehead hit the wall. I calculated time by the beats of my heart, which resembled a stubborn animal caught in a trap. After some hours, a soldier pulled me stumbling down a hall and told me to sit. I don't know why I assumed he'd invited me to sit on a chair. I stretched out my hand, feeling for it.

"Where's the chair?" I asked.

He guffawed loudly. "Abu Ghadab," he called to a colleague. "Please, by your mother's life, come over here. This gentleman wants a chair. He hasn't learned how to sit on the ground."

"Don't you know how to sit on the ground, you shit?" another voice shouted in my ear. Presumably this was Abu Ghadab, or the Father of Anger. True to his nickname, his meaty hand struck my temple. This time my whole body bounced against the wall. No sooner had I steadied myself than a blow from a heavy stick pounded the back of my knees. As they buckled, I found myself sitting on a cold, damp floor.

After a while I felt the need to urinate. "I want to go to the toilet," I said. I didn't know if anyone was there, so repeated more loudly, "I want to go to the toilet." A boot kicked me in the ribs.

"Shut up, bastard," growled a voice. "Do it in your pants."

After a while, the same voice ordered me to stand up, my handcuffs were loosened, and I was led me to a toilet only a few feet away. When the door was closed behind me, I was surprised to be left alone. Lifting the blindfold from my eyes, I felt I'd escaped from the cruel grip of a physical as well as a spiritual darkness, even if it was only for a few seconds.

Exiting the bathroom like a mouse entering a den of cats, I was ordered to replace my own blindfold. I tied it so that I could see a bit of the floor, and then the guard adjusted and tightened the handcuffs. "Congratulations on those lovely bracelets," he said.

The cuffs only got tighter as my wrists and hands swelled, in particular the right one. I could make out a dirty black shoe on the ground and addressed its owner, "The cuffs are hurting me."

"No, surely not," Dirty Black Shoes replied. "They're designed for your comfort." And then he tightened them further. "Does that feel better?"

"No," I said in a strained voice, "they're crushing my wrists."

"Poor wrists," he mocked, and then he kicked me.

The sound of screaming started up nearby, accompanied by the sounds of a vicious beating, angrily shouted questions, and orders for the victim to stop his "fucking screaming." His torturers insulted him, his sister, his mother, and his wife. The man's voice became like the long drawn-out howls of a dying wolf. What were they doing? I could no longer hear the sounds of beating, but the man's muted voice indicated he was still being tortured. He sounded strangulated, a mix of whinnying, sobbing, and howling. They must have stuffed something into his mouth.

"Where did you meet Julaq, son of a bitch?" an interrogator shouted. "Either tell me where he is right now, or the only bit that will be left of you will be smaller than my prick!"

The name of the wanted man, Julaq, sounded Turcoman. I sat on the floor for at least another hour listening to what was going on in the nearby room. The voice of the man being tortured was painted all the colors of pain. It was clear he was suffering unbearably. I was suffering just listening to him. And when his voice disappeared, the silence coming from the next room was even more painful.

"Okay, I want nothing more from you, you bastard," the interrogator shouted finally. "I just want to make you die a thousand times. In the end, you'll long for death and not find it."

And then I heard a door open and a new voice start shouting.

"You idiots! He's a treasure. Get the doctor. Tell him we need him alive at any price."

Subsequently, I learned the word "treasure" meant that the man being tortured was a storehouse of information, and that the officer scolding the interrogators and torturers needed this information. The victim would remain a treasure until he'd given up whatever information he had, after which he would become an empty vessel. The treasure given up would be transferred onto documents and into orders for new arrests to be made, while the empty vessel could be tossed aside, with impunity.

I suffered because I was powerless to do anything to help and also because I expected a similar fate in the near future. Was I about to take his place? Might I fall silent just as he had done? Would the high-ranking officer reprimand my torturers because I was no use to him dead?

In all my reading of advice on facing interrogation, there was never anything to say that a man whose face and name I didn't know would be in a nearby room, that I'd never forget his voice as long as I lived, and that I'd always wonder who he was and whether the doctor managed to save him.

CHAPTER 6

MY PENELOPE WOVE NOTHING

In 1991, after being held without charge or conviction, I was released along with eighty-one others into the streets of Damascus. The granting of freedom was a political stunt during one of Hafez al-Assad's sham elections. They released us at roughly fifteen-minute intervals, deliberately making us wait in order to demonstrate their control over us one last time. As my feet touched the pavement after more than ten years in prison, I felt as if I were floating. Remembering the appointment I had missed many years ago, I became consumed by a desire to go back to the room where Layla, a girl I was interested in, and other friends had waited for me on New Year's Eve, 1980. It was about a thirty-minute walk to the apartment in Baramka, and when I reached it, I longed to relax and sip Turkish coffee in the room where I'd experienced so much before I was twenty. But I didn't even knock on the door, suddenly realizing it would be a foolish mistake to begin my new life by trying to recreate the past.

Having resisted one temptation, I was soon plagued by another. This enticement was even more powerful than the first. It suddenly struck me that Widad and I were now in the same city. Soon I found myself searching for this girl who lived in my memory more than any other I'd known and whom I'd fantasized about in prison.

For years Widad would appear floating in the space of different cells I inhabited. I thought of her as a modern version of Penelope, Odysseus's devoted wife in Homer's epic. Besieged by suitors because her husband was presumed dead, Penelope promised she would choose one of them after she finished weaving a death shroud for her father-in-law, Laertes. But every night she unraveled it, never having any intention of being untrue to her beloved. Widad didn't weave a shroud. She made a scarf of glory, like a victor's olive wreath, which I watched her present to me repeatedly, wrapping it lovingly around my neck, and embracing me in her warm arms. And then in the dark I'd laugh. Glory? What am I talking about?

An hour more of walking found me in Widad's old neighborhood, but, like so much else in Damascus, everything and everyone had changed. Silently, I prayed for a miracle, hoping desperately to see her among the women walking past me on the sidewalk, or on the other side of the street, or emerging from a doorway. But while wandering about for several more hours, the miracle didn't happen. I gave up and trudged over to Uncle Khalifah's house, a two-hour walk on the other side of Damascus.

Over the next few weeks I wandered the streets of Damascus revisiting my old haunts. On one of these ramblings, I bumped into Widad's sister by chance. Perhaps it wasn't exactly by chance. I knew Susan was working at the National Film Institute, so I hung around there when people were leaving to go home at the end of the day. That was when Susan told me that Widad had married only four months earlier. She begged me not to try to meet her.

"You'll confuse her. Seeing you again might ruin her life," she said.

Walking back to my uncle's in a daze, I was overwhelmed with contradictory feelings. As sad as I was that she hadn't waited for me, I was genuinely pleased Widad had a life, that she hadn't cloistered herself away. I repeated, "C'est la vie," imagining my teacher trying to correct my bad pronunciation of French vowels.

Three years later I was at a book fair in Damascus, representing al-Tali'a al-Jadidah Publishing House. I looked up and found a very slim woman smiling at me.

"Ariftani? Do you know me?" she asked.

Of course, I knew everything about her, especially those green eyes and the way she pronounced the letter "R."

"Yes, I know you . . . You are the dream."

I knew I had to restrain myself from hugging and kissing her in public, and from telling her how she'd dominated my thoughts all those years in prison. But I simply couldn't control the tears that fell as we shook hands.

We agreed to meet at the Abu Shafiq restaurant where we'd had a beer some fifteen years earlier. I tried to look as elegant as possible, borrowing a light blue shirt and even some aftershave. I reached Abu Shafiq's fifteen minutes early, my heart pounding like a teenager's. My first disappointment was that there was a sign on the door saying they'd stopped serving alcohol.

Abu Shafiq is one of the oldest restaurants in the west of Damascus. It was one of my favorite places for meeting. It is clean and calm with a lovely view.

When Widad arrived and I could finally hug her, it turned out to be my second disappointment. She seemed cooler, more formal than when we'd met the previous day. We sat and stared at each other for several long seconds until the waiter approached and I ordered coffee.

"It seems there are more and more girls wearing hijab since I went away," I began, trying to make conversation. "It looks as if it's a way of opposing the regime after Rifaat al-Assad's militias stopped women in the streets, shouting they shouldn't cover their heads. And when women objected, the militia ignored the protests and just yanked their head coverings off. Even though most people hate the conservative clerics, choosing to wear hijab is their way of standing up to the regime. But that seems like nonsense to me because it's in their own best long-term interest to . . ."

"Please," she interrupted me, "let's not discuss politics." I nodded and smiled.

Before I uttered another word, she asked me to look at a cloud in the southern part of the Damascus sky. The cloud looked like a flying dress. "Do you remember when you wrote a poem to me?"

"I wrote many poems to you and because of you. Which one do you mean?"

"I mean the one where you weave the clouds to make a tunic for me and decorate it with your heartbeat that echoes love, love, love . . ."

"Yes, I still remember it."

"So do I. You seem fresh, as if prison hasn't affected your appearance."

"I was put in a freezer."

Finally, she laughed, so I began to say the things I had prepared.

"Widad, I confess that you are the most beautiful creature I have ever met. You were with me the whole time in prison. And when I found out you were married, I didn't think for a moment to blame you for falling in love with someone else. It's incredible you waited for me as long as you did."

And then the fantasies that had sustained me through that time in prison were demolished in an instant. Widad began to tell me how she had actually spent the decade and a half since we last met.

"Please understand," she began, "I'm not offering you a confession or asking for forgiveness. I'm speaking as a friend." Ah, the word "friend." "After waiting two years for you, I was finally able to see the world the way it is. And when one of your friends showed an interest in me . . . I began a relationship with him. But I soon realized he wasn't the man for me. I slept with others, but I could never really love any of them. For me, love has become one of those illusions we used to believe in, and I no longer intend to be a woman who trusts false concepts." She paused to see if I was taking all this information in, before continuing. "So, after many relationships, when I finally realized marriage was a necessary social insurance, I married a businessman who wanted me for a wife. He is my husband, but not my man. I'm not telling you all this because I still love you, Jamal. You are just a close friend now."

I stared at her blankly. "Who was my friend that was in love with you?" I finally managed to blurt out.

"I might tell you later."

I looked down at my coffee, trying to find more words there. "I didn't think you had to be like Penelope, but. . ."

She straightened up in her chair. "Who's this Penelope you're comparing me to?" she asked, frowning.

"A character in Homer's *Odyssey*," I explained. "She tricked her suitors by promising to choose between them after she'd finished weaving a shroud. But every night she would undo her . . ." Widad became serious, almost angry, lines appearing on her once smooth forehead.

"Jamal, I'm really not interested in this Penelope of yours. I like to walk through city streets rather than make my way through the passages of books. Didn't you once tell me that being a bird flying in the sky is better than being a bird in a great work of art?"

"Yes, but books, poems, songs, movies, all great works of art, they help society to move forward, to develop concepts and theories. They help us think laterally, outside the box."

She nodded, like a mother when her child says something foolish. "Jamal, you may be smart and educated, but you still have so many illusions," she said. "It's as if we're speaking different languages." Her green eyes, which had always seemed translucent and hopeful, were stony.

"Then what are you interested in?" I asked.

"In a word, money," she answered. Yes, our lives had taken different paths. She was no longer that girl who seemed like a poem or a song. Neither was she my Penelope, waiting for her Odysseus despite the extreme pressures of the world. Although I had returned from my own odyssey, my storm of beauty had, unlike the mythical Penelope, gotten on with her life. Widad had not woven me a scarf of glory, or even a shroud for the dignity of the emotions we had lived.

CHAPTER 7

THE BERLIN WALL, SADDAM HUSSEIN, AND THE WOODEN PENIS

As a child, when my father took me with him to the river near our village, I was amazed by the clear, greenish-blue water. You could see the pebbles at the bottom, all smoothed by century upon century of water flowing over them.

This piece of the Kfarieh river was the place where children learned how to swim, generation after generation.

"When was this river born?" I asked my father.

He laughed. "Rivers aren't born."

"How did it get here?" I asked, and he pointed at the sky.

When we got home, I asked my grandfather, "Jaddi, when did the sky get pregnant and give birth to our river?"

My grandfather laughed and said a lot of things, like skies don't get pregnant, this wasn't our river but Allah's river, and the forest was Allah's too. I began sorting the things around me into those that individuals owned and those that nobody owned, or that only Allah owned. So this path was Allah's, as well as that forest and the pine trees, but He always lent his things to us. I was confused when I told my grandfather how I'd divided things, and he replied, "Everything belongs to Allah."

"Even this green shirt I'm wearing?" I asked in astonishment.

"Yes, even your shirt," he nodded, laughing.

After a few more years of pondering, I told my grandfather that the path to the river had been made by the feet coming and going along it, and that it had needed thousands of footsteps for it to exist in its present form.

The path to the river in Kfarieh.

"So, I helped give birth to it," I explained.

"I see." He laughed. "But who made your feet?"

"My mother and father, I suppose."

He laughed again. "You'll know better when you grow up," he said.

I was fascinated by my grandfather's idea that this river and forest went back to ancient times, when Allah created the world in six days. My young mind pictured how He rested on the seventh day in a spot I knew near the river, one suitable for a great being like him, but I was disappointed when Jaddi told me that Allah rested in one of his seven heavens. As I became older, the books I read made nonsense of the nice tale I'd woven, not only about how the river came into being on the first day of creation, but how the Creator had made all things beautiful.

The dirt path leading to the river, made by many people's feet over time, followed steep slopes and meandered around rocks and large trees. It was only wide enough for one person, but to me it was the most wonderful path in the world, as familiar to my footsteps as an old friend. During my stay in prison, I longed desperately to walk along it with one woman in particular: Widad, whose impulsive laughter made the air sweet around her. I discussed in a rational way with my friends in prison how I didn't want to be a burden on her, physically or spiritually, and how she shouldn't let cobwebs grow between her legs for the sake of being faithful to me. She should not allow herself to be a prisoner too. All the same, I was waiting for her in spite of myself, even when she couldn't come to visit. And I thought of her when we prisoners talked or joked or listened to songs about love, sex, or women.

"If I return to life, I'll see her," I said to Usama al-Misri.

"You haven't left life yet," Usama laughed.

"Life here is more like death," I replied. The absence of women is a big part of hell for men. When there are no women around, the emptiness becomes harder to bear. Their absence makes them appear in the dreams created by our desires, desires that are suppressed, resurfacing only to be suppressed again.

I was a country boy, and near that river most of my dreams were formed. When I was a child, my father would recite the Quran every Ramadan. I would wait for him to get to the part that says, "Gardens beneath which rivers run." I didn't picture the gardens in my head, but the rivers, to me all rivers, were small and pure like ours.

It was beside that river I dreamed of love, of walking with Widad on its banks, of how our clothes became a bed under the broad blue dome of the sky. Once when that actually happened with a girl who wasn't Widad, she said with her eyes half closed, "See how big our house is?"

During my time in prison, I would picture women swimming in the river, or undressing as they prepared to go swimming, or gathering fire-wood on the riverbank. Sometimes I'd imagine them asking for my help because an insect had got into their clothes, so I would search for the butter-fly or the ant wherever I pleased. My fingers would wander over the curves of the woman's body, and then we would both forget the insect that had somehow escaped, at which point I imagined the body being as warm and moist as I wanted it to be, only to realize that this was a lonely man's sad way of making love. Yes, the place where my childhood self believed Allah had rested became my imprisoned adult's favorite place to relax and have imaginary sex.

When I was a child, I used to see cattle and poultry copulating in the open air, and I loved the little calves and chicks that resulted from their activities. Then I came to learn, like many others, how sex was an arena for shame and abuse, despite the fact that it happened many times, every day.

In our village, as in most places on earth, the penis figured prominently in insults, used both abusively and triumphantly. It figured in much of the swearing that took place in prison, too, whether directed by the guards at the prisoners or exchanged between the prisoners themselves.

One day, in Sednaya Prison, the insult took on a physical form. On the day the Berlin Wall was being dismantled, the Baathist followers of Saddam Hussein in Wing B sent a penis carved out of wood to us communists in Wing C. Although many of the imprisoned communists were happy at the fall of the symbolic wall, we didn't appreciate the gloating of Saddam's supporters. My cellmate, Adeeb, who had a quick sense of humor, sniffed the wooden prick and said to the man who delivered it, "Tell them it's not appropriate to offer second-hand gifts."

"And tell them we've got a lot of real live pricks here, too, if they'd like to try one," said another communist enthusiastically. "They're much more powerful than this wooden thing."

Usama, the calm one among us, and leader of the communists' wing, smiled and hid the wooden penis in one of the cloth bags that some prisoners had learned to make. After less than a year, Saddam was forced to withdraw from Kuwait, and Iraq suffered terrible losses. Usama retrieved the wooden sculpture and wrapped it in a piece of cloth, finishing it off with a bow. He sent it back to the Baathists, accompanied by a short note saying, "We're returning your present, and to tell you the truth, we've never used it."

CHAPTER 8

RUFAIDA (1996)

A day after I was released for the third time, I went with my mother and father to weed and water our vegetable garden near the house.

My father asked, "Didn't you tell me those stories you wrote wouldn't cause you any trouble?" I detected blame in his voice and expression.

"My arrest coincided with the publication of my stories, and they asked me about it, but it was not the reason for my arrest," I told him in a broken voice.

"When will they stop hurting you?" he asked, suppressing his anger.

"I wish I knew," I whispered.

We were all silent. I looked at my father's face, and then looked away. My father seemed to fall prey to sudden depression.

During our silence, I remembered the face of the interrogator as he shoved my book in my face:

"What is this shit? When will you stop poisoning society with your dirty ideas?"

"The Syrian Ministry of Culture published it."

"I'm going shit on you and on our stupid Ministry of Culture."

My mother broke the silence. She intervened to change the mood that had descended following my father's questions. With a smile, she asked, "When are we going to celebrate your wedding?"

"After I finish my studies and find enough work to buy milk and diapers for the little babies," I said, trying to feign joy at the thought.

I didn't tell my mother I wasn't thinking about marriage at all. My belief in love extends far beyond marriage. Marriage is a custom that no one has asked me to approve or reject. I didn't want to have children who would be exposed to the terror spread by the intelligence thugs traveling in Peugeots. Children, especially girls, need protection, which I may not be able to provide. I will be a lover, not a husband.

Mother, don't you see the pain I'm causing my father? I thought to myself.

Months later, I found a job in a publishing house in Damascus. I worked in al-Tali'a Publishing House for around fourteen years. And during the first years there, I rented a flat nearby, in the Rukn al-Din quarter of Damascus. The building was only two stories high, and its owner, Mrs. Sahar Hamad, lived on the upper floor with her truck-driver son. Because he was away for days at a time, Mrs. Hamad would combat her boredom by inviting me for coffee in her apartment or checking on the state of mine, especially the kitchen and my supply of food. Food was not a big issue when I was living alone. It was easy to cut up bread into a dish and pour milk over it for a meal. I would sometimes go to a restaurant for hummus and salad. And if I was in a good mood, I would spend some time in the kitchen, frying potato or zucchini with egg in olive oil.

We were drinking coffee when my landlady told me that she spied on me to see if I was eating properly. "I am a mother, you know," she said, "and I'm worried about how my son eats while he is traveling." She sighed.

"You remind me of my mother," I said.

She looked at me as if she were drinking in my words as I described how my mom spent four hours cooking yabrak (a mix of rice and lamb rolled in vine leaves), and how happy she seemed watching us enjoy her cooking, eating her yabrak greedily in ten minutes.

A few days later, Mrs. Hamad visited my room with a plate of yabrak. "Compared with your mother's, of course, hers is better," she said, "but this is not bad."

My landlady watched me while I ate her food.

"Mmm," I said, my mouth full, nodding to express my admiration. "Very good."

"It makes me so happy to watch you eating my food," she told me, and I could see in her far-away smile thoughts of her son.

After that, several times a month, my landlady favored me with various meals — shishbarak, tiny lamb dumplings in yogurt sauce, and mahshi, hollowed out zucchini and eggplants stuffed with rice and lamb and then baked, to name just a couple of her dishes.

One day, when we were drinking Turkish coffee together in her apartment, Mrs. Hamad told me how she used to belong to the al-Qubaysiat sisterhood and that its name derived from its founder, Munira al-Qubaysi, whom she'd met several times. I knew the organization only as one for young Muslim women who were indoctrinated by the use of very strict rules.

"Thank God I escaped their clutches," my new friend said between sips of coffee. "I had to wear a navy overcoat and white hijab, like all the novices. The color of hijab indicated a sister's status. The darker the hijab, the greater their authority over us. I joined because I thought I wanted to learn the holy Quran, but it wasn't long before I realized the ones in charge interpreted it to suit themselves. Oh, how they interfered with everything in our lives. Miss, as we called the head teacher, began to stress how important it was for us to neglect our bodies, to actually despise them as if they were a hindrance. Then she started to forbid makeup, and even the removal of facial hair." At this, Mrs. Hamad raised two very thin eyebrows, both neatly plucked in high arches over her immaculate eye makeup. The brows lowered. "And I was disgusted, absolutely disgusted, when the novices began competing with one another to drink the water left in Miss's glass." She stuck out her tongue and pretended to gag. "That was the end of them for me," she continued. "When I said I was leaving, Miss harangued me about how those who left the order were breaking God's covenant. But I really didn't care what she thought of me then, and I care even less now."

"Maybe that's why we get along so well," I said with a laugh, and we clinked cups.

One morning in the spring of 1996, Marwan Saqqal, the owner of the publishing house where I worked, asked me in his soothing Aleppo accent to check the qualifications of a young woman who was due to arrive shortly. She was a graduate from Damascus University's English department, and a colleague of his friend, Obada Bouzo.

The woman came in, chaperoned by Obada, and as they passed my desk on their way to Marwan's office, I was surprised to see how she was dressed. She wore a long navy coat and beige hijab, with no trace of makeup and unplucked eyebrows, just like Mrs. Hamad had described the Qubaysiat girls. The boss summoned me to his office and introduced me as director of production and her as Radeefa.

"You mean Rufaida, Mr. Marwan," she corrected.

Marwan, well known for his kindness and tact, was embarrassed. He apologized and then covered his mistake by making a joke. "We'll just have to give you a new name, then."

I took a step toward Rufaida, my hands at my sides. "I guess you don't shake men's hands," I said.

"That's right," she said, smiling politely, and laid a hand on her heart.

After she followed me to the typesetting room and keyed in some text I gave her, I was able to go back and tell the boss that her work was fast and more or less error-free.

"Let her start work tomorrow, then," he said. So, with the minimum of formality, Rufaida joined my production team as a typesetter.

As Rufaida left, I could see my colleague Hala Fatoum, our layout designer, eyeing her. A fellow communist, she had spent some years in Duma women's prison; in contrast with Rufaida's highly conservative dress, she sported a low-cut T-shirt that had printed on its front the graphic of a single swallow soaring upwards, the underground's symbol for freedom.

"Where did this Qubaysiya come from?" Hala asked me.

I laughed wryly. "Wherever they usually come from, I guess."

On her first day, Rufaida brought a prayer rug with her. When she prayed at noon, I closed the door of the office and warned everybody off. Rufaida was the only one who prayed at work. In fact, she was the only one of us who followed any religious observances.

I was usually the first to arrive at work, as I lived so close, and I prepared coffee for all seven other employees. Most days Rufaida arrived before the others, so we drank a morning coffee together.

One day she surprised me. "Why don't you pray?" she asked.

I smiled evasively, as many times in prison religious inmates would start with such a question when they wanted to convert me. "God doesn't need to hear the same words from the same person every day," I replied. "It would be boring for both of us. And as I understand it, God knows, and knew a very long time before I was born, exactly what kind of person I would be, regardless of whether I pray or not."

She was listening carefully, and I was waiting for her to attack me for being a heretic, but instead she smiled and dropped the subject. Some mornings later she asked, "Do you believe in God?" but this time I could tell it was out of honest curiosity.

Not wanting to answer yes or no, I replied, "The God who deserves to have me believing in him is a bit different from the God most people talk about. Or the one who is featured in certain books."

"I don't understand."

"Well," and I took in a deep breath, "I don't think God, who is greater than anyone can possibly imagine, would punish insignificant human beings like us. How could He have the heart to burn such tiny creatures in whatever hell some imagine He created? And then would He really renew our skin so He could enjoy burning us over and over again — for all eternity? No. Godliness and sadism can't exist in one character. God isn't, mustn't be, that cruel. No sane mother or father is capable of harming their children or being angry with them for long, and we are supposedly God's children. And God must be sane, and powerful and kind. He doesn't get angry, but acts calmly, affectionately, lovingly. He gives to us unconditionally and pities the weak. And," I paused, worried that I might have gone too far, "we humans are extremely weak. We are deserving of His pity, not of His hellfire."

She was listening intently to me, her eyebrows knit tightly together. Had they been plucked? I wondered. But I didn't ask.

After about a month of unending theological and philosophical discussion about the deity, Rufaida made a surprising admission. It literally froze my coffee cup in midair, just before it touched my lips. "Jamal, I love your God." I put the cup down with a clatter, and unable to reply, I simply stared at her, a deer in the headlights. "But," she finally asked, breaking the awkward silence, "how are we to worship Him?"

I collected myself and picked up my cup again, drained it, and put it down very carefully this time. "Speaking for myself," I began, my voice breaking like a teenager's, "God wants me as a free man, I think, not a slave. I hope to get close to Him by doing good for others."

Finally, during one of our early morning coffee sessions, I confessed to Rufaida that I wasn't at all religious. She laughed in a way that told me she already knew. Emboldened, I continued with what I had planned to say if my confession went well, to finally show this woman what my intentions were. My voice softened as I told her how her fingers were like those of the beautiful women in my friend Hamoud Shantout's luminous paintings. She blushed and her eyes shone when I added how I imagined those same fingers skipping along the keys of a piano.

"It's like watching moonlight dancing over the waters of a gently moving river," I added. Rufaida blinked in surprise, and I pressed on. "And your eyes. No doubt your mother and many others must have told you how beautiful your eyes are." She tried to hide her smile.

The next morning, I gave her my collection of short stories, *Majnunat al-Shumus*.

The following day, Rufaida greeted me with a handshake.

CHAPTER 9

THE BANK OF LITTLE STONES
(MARCH 1992)

I was struck by the abundance of little stones in my first meal of lentil soup in cell number nine of the Palestine Branch, Branch 235 of the military intelligence services. This was an isolation cell, the floor about three feet wide by six feet long, covered entirely by a mattress. Well, calling it a mattress is most probably an optimist's way of looking at things. The top layer was nothing but an old blanket sewn to an underlayer of canvas. And it took a while to get used to the feeble light that made its way through a small hole in the lowered ceiling of each individual cell, a faint glow that originated from just a few bulbs somewhere on the main ceiling, three feet above the cells.

Now, lentil soup was the most common meal we prisoners were fed there, and all lentils sold in Syria come straight from the field, uncleaned and unwashed, and therefore full of small stones. At home mother took the time to pick out all the pebbles before washing and preparing the lentils with love. But the prison cooks weren't as diligent as my mother, and the guard delivering the food was anything but loving. After all, he had to drag the heavy aluminum pot of soup screeching along the floor before banging on each door with the same ladle he used to dole out its contents. The first time I heard the screeching and banging get closer, I was filled with concern. What was that awful racket and what did it mean? And when the screeching stopped directly in front of my cell door, when the banging echoed off it and the lock clicked and it creaked open, I was caught just sitting there, dumbly squinting up at the guard.

"Where's your fucking bowl?" he demanded.

"I don't think I have a bowl," I said.

He looked around my small cell until his gaze fell upon an old plastic container, one which had originally held store-bought sweets.

"Move it!" he shouted, and I grabbed what I now understood was the totality of my dinnerware. After he ladled out two small scoops of the thin meal and banged the door shut, I almost cracked a tooth on the first mouthful. That's when I learned how our cooks were so lazy. From then on, I took care to pick out or spit out the stones before chewing.

When I finished that first bowl of thin soup, to pass the time I counted the stones. There were ninety-eight of them. I needed one more to make up the ninety-nine names of God. I returned the stones to the plastic container and washed them during a bathroom visit, one of the three allowed per day. I didn't have a clear goal of what I would do with the stones and couldn't know then how they would be an escape from watching my days being discarded within the walls of this cramped room.

There is plenty of time in a cell, and events repeat themselves: eating the meager meals, going to the toilet, listening for the sound of the key in the lock or the screeching pots of soup. To fight the monotony my jailers obviously intended I should suffer, I added counting the stones to my daily tasks. Every time there was soup to eat, I washed and added more to my collection. Later I included doing a mental calculation to find out if the rate of stones in the food was rising or falling. All these tasks took no more than an hour and a half on any of these lost days, and often I made the work last longer than need be.

I began to write names and small phrases with my stones. They were like magic spells softening the heavy impact of time, which crawled by during my first weeks and months of solitary confinement. Writing helped me to summon up people, happy memories, and better places. I tried to write short poems with my stones. I remember a kind of haiku I wrote for Widad:

A violet opened her petals
I wish I could melt
as a warm dewy morning upon her lips

The mulberry tree's shadow is the place for family to have meals, play cards or chess, or just meditate.

After that I ventured to create scenes very dear to me: the mulberry tree in front of our house, a sparrow alighting on one of its branches while another flew away. The stones helped me to expand time beyond the confines of my cell. I used them to give concrete form to things I loved, reliving them in my memory; scenes, words, poems, I shaped them all out of stones.

The almost-daily lentil soup was transformed into a mine for extracting little stones, and it became important to turn them from a punishment, and something to grumble about, into a distracting pleasure. I used to make calculations in my capacity as manager of the Bank of Little Stones, as well as the producer, consumer, creditor, and debtor of this rock-based currency. Sometimes I would become owner and client of a business dealing in stones, selling and buying both time and stones, all the while paying the invisible price with the days of my youth.

I distributed the stones in various places to hide them, some in my trouser pockets, which I desperately wished had zips to keep my treasure safe, but mostly they were hidden under the thin mattress.

My wealth eventually grew in excess of ten thousand stones, accumulated during the long months in cell number nine. My bank had five branches, and my mind was kept active trying to remember the number of stones in each, under the corners of the mattress and in my pockets. The stones were all of equal value, despite differences in color and size. A small poem cost 396 stones, regardless of how large they were. Widad's name cost thirty-six stones, but if the letter alif was tall, it might cost as much as sixty. That letter could be made to be majestic, and it reminded me of the cypress trees reaching for the sky in front of my first love Barbara's house. I created a mosaic of those cypress trees, and again it made me think of the tree in front of my own home. I became obsessed with that mulberry tree and made up an even bigger version than before, using my whole stock of stones. It required all the time between lunch and dinner to create, and as the image began to take shape, I could actually see in my mind's eye Jaddi and the two friends who visited him every day. I could see them sitting in the shade of the tree, and clearly heard the old men sipping their tea.

But suddenly the sound of a guard's footsteps brought me back to reality, and I quickly erased the picture that had taken hours to create. I scraped my forearm along the mattress and pushed the stones under it, stuffing them all into a single branch of my bank. I had just enough time to smooth down the rocky bulge as the door opened. I didn't want the guard to question me about my wealth and risk losing my bounty. I used to tell myself jokingly that I was the richest man in all the prison cells of the world. After the ritual evening meal and a final visit to the toilets, I returned to my cell and sat up the whole night reconstructing the tree, this time adding the three old men I'd often seen drinking tea below it.

Yes, in order not to lose my mind, I needed those stones and the ephemeral scenes I created. They helped me escape from the reality I was living.

On another occasion, I asked myself, What if these stones were gold? Gold wouldn't be any better for creating my scenes, and then it occurred to me that I needed clay rather than gold for what I intended next. But I didn't have any clay, and so instead I began breaking off portions of my daily bread ration and making them into chess pieces. The ash from my cigarette helped in forming the black pieces. After a month I had a complete set. For a while, I made the chessboard out of my stones, but when I finally managed to scrounge a piece of soap, I was able to draw the board with it, saving me the trouble of using stones each time I wanted a game. I played against myself, defeated myself, and carried on a conversation between my winning and losing selves, as well as a spectator who'd chime in with his two piastres of advice. The players would often debate when it was the right time to move a particular piece.

An extract from one of the dialogues where I was winner, loser, and spectator:

"If only I'd moved the knight to g5, the whole course of the game would have changed."

"Why didn't you move it, then?"

"A temporary lapse in concentration. So, understand that you didn't win thanks to your skill but because I didn't move the knight to g5 at the right time."

"Victory is often the result of the opponent's stupidity," the victor side of the argument admonished. "One must bide one's time and pounce when the time is right. Timing and patience are everything."

"And truly, what difference would it make?" my spectator side chided. "Whoever wins or loses, the sun will continue to rise and set, outside this cell, of course."

As the winner, the loser, and the spectator, I was experiencing the joy of victory and the bitterness of defeat at the same time, and then ridiculing everything. But the stones and chess were activities that helped me lose my mind in order to save it.

After months in a cell, time seems like a boring game that the feeble light plays on the rough cement walls and the zircon-coated metal door. And time and timing occupied a big part of my thinking. I began to better appreciate how, in the outside world, one's philosophy of time and timing is a decisive factor in activities, not only in achieving a glorious victory or suffering a bitter defeat, but also in simple actions like taking the time to drink coffee in an enjoyable way.

At first I thought these insights were useless in my struggle to survive in jail, but then I realized the exact opposite was true. Time was being used as a weapon to defeat me. I must stick my tongue out at time, as it was doing to me. With the stones and the chess pieces, I began to play with time instead of becoming a plaything in its hands.

CHAPTER 10

HOWL

The shores of the Mediterranean are more suited to howling than the shores of Lake Ontario. Standing beside the Mediterranean, you can howl like a wounded animal without your shrieks being impeded by any obstacles. Here, by Lake Ontario near Kingston, they will come up against the islands facing the shore that break the line where water meets sky. In the Mediterranean, the horizon looks like an infinite space that grows even bigger when you scream and groan and swear. This allows your pain and memories to be cast as far away as possible.

I walk alone near Rockwood Asylum, the abandoned mental hospital overlooking the lake, in an attempt to relieve myself of my defeats. Barb Danielewski, a new friend, once told me that people believe the hospital is haunted. Near this haunted building I see an elderly woman walking her dog. Her expression suggests that she has reached a stage of loneliness where there is no point in looking anything other than indifferent. The black dog that she pulls along, and who alternately pulls her, appears to be the guardian of her loneliness. She doesn't smile like most of the elderly I've met in Kingston. Usually, at bus stops, the smiles of the elderly can be a sign for a conversation to start. This normally begins with the weather, and if the conversation continues, your interlocutor may ask you where you're originally from, how long you've been in Canada, why you chose Canada, your opinion on life in Kingston, and what it is you do now. I've often answered these and other questions with the same funny or stupid jokes. You get used to exchanging expressions of thanks, praise, and astonishment with the people you talk to, mostly out of politeness on both sides, and sometimes sincerity.

When I see I'm alone by the lake, this is when I unburden my soul of the groaning and howling that still clings to it. It is an exorcism that must be performed regularly to keep me free of the malaise that continually builds up like a barnacled crust on my consciousness. The past is changing into voices made by strange beings, like the voices they attribute to the ghosts of the asylum. I touch my chest where the imprisoned voices live. I'm not a ghost, but the past that inhabits me is full of ghosts that poke their heads out more often than I'd like.

I met Hisham for the first time in Sednaya Prison in 1987. I knew he'd been a judo champion in Syria, but he was so much more. When he talked to me about my astrological sign, Pisces, I liked his way of mixing levity and seriousness in a conversation that celebrated nonsense. In a similar vein, I regaled him with one of Ibn Arabi's poems from his collection *The Interpreter of Desires*. I told him how it reveals the relationship between mysticism and love and how purity is violated by experience. I went on to relate one of the many footnotes Ibn Arabi used to embellish his poems. In this one, Ibn Arabi has God asking Man, "Who am I?" The human being is so innocent that he repeats the question back to the deity, "Who am I?"

After subjecting the man to many harsh trials, making him live in a sea of hunger for four thousand years, God asks him again, "Who am I?"

The man answers, "You are my Lord."

"As you see, Hisham, this is the response of a citizen who, after becoming an extension and echo for Allah Himself, turns into a slave."

Hisham laughed in agreement and then launched into a comparison between the different gods that crowd our history and lead us to accept such incredible ideas.

Years later, Hisham made a film when he was released from prison. It was produced in Norway and shown in Western Europe. In the film there is a prisoner behind a door. The prisoner is released, but the door stays with him wherever he goes. The actor actually walks around carrying a door frame. I relate to this. Although I left my door behind me, and I enjoy the luxury of having the light on or off, of taking long walks in a street that doesn't end in a steel door preventing me taking another step, although I choose my own food and the notebook where I record anything I want, I still make comparisons, perhaps more than I ought to, between the two worlds and times: behind the doors and beyond the doors. Never, never can I completely escape from the time I knew behind the doors.

In the hours following my first arrest, my heart fluttered like a bird caught in a trap. Uppermost in my thoughts was how I mustn't give up information regarding some upcoming meetings to my interrogators. Layla was about to arrive from Aleppo, and we were going to meet in the room I shared with my fellow fugitives. My relationship with Layla wasn't on a firm footing yet. Although she was extremely nice, I was going through a complicated spiritual crisis. I was still feeling the effects of recently splitting up with Widad, and at the same time, I'd begun to blame myself for the fact that my future was in the hands of mischievous gods. Layla didn't deserve to suffer the consequences of the choices I'd made. She was possibly attracted to me because I was fighting the regime. Perhaps she saw it as a kind of heroism. We would have spent New Year's Eve 1980 together with some friends. And then, the next day, I had been due to meet Fatih Jamous, a member of the Communist Labor League leadership and a comrade who was at the top of the intelligence services' most-wanted list. I knew that I must not confess to either of these meetings.

The handcuffs were still bothering me. The cries of a man being tortured nearby echoed inside me, drowning out the torturer's taunts. All I knew of the man was his voice, but, as the blindfold wasn't completely covering my eyes, I could see the shoes of the soldiers around me. I began making up nicknames for the soldiers to distinguish them one from the other: Dirty Black Shoes, who tightened the handcuffs; Brown Shoes, who liked tapping hard on my head with his bent index finger; Neat Black Shoes, who responded to my request and brought a key to loosen the cuffs. When he loosened them and I tried to move my hand, I felt how much it had been affected. I couldn't see how swollen it was, and soon it began to feel like fire ants were seething under my skin. Dirty Black Shoes approached me and began beating me on the hand with an electric cable, the exposed copper wires at the end adding an extra dimension of pain. Through the little gap in my blindfold I started to see drops of my blood falling on the ground. As he hit me, he kept repeating, "Move your hand, you animal!"

Suddenly the beating stopped and Dirty Black Shoes moved away. Brown Shoes came into view, and I felt him put a key in the cuffs behind my back. With a click, one of my hands was free and then the other. Immediately, as the blood flow returned, the pain intensified even more. I heard a new voice.

"Take him to the recording office."

I was then hustled upstairs to a room on the second or third floor. There, a quiet voice asked me to remove my blindfold. Hands still trembling, I did so, finding myself in front of a metal desk among a cluster of filing cabinets. The man behind the desk appeared calm and impassive, an exemplary employee, clean shaven, wearing a neat shirt and looking like a schoolteacher who was bored of repeating the same sentences for thirty years. With an expression that gave nothing away, he asked me, "Who beat you on the hand?"

"I don't know."

He nodded his head, took a cigarette from a red packet, and then held the packet out to me. "Do you smoke?"

"Yes."

He handed me a lighter and asked Brown Shoes to bring three tea glasses. Brown Shoes left briefly, and the interrogator and I stood smoking and eyeing each other. He wasn't in any hurry. Returning with the glasses, Brown Shoes put them on the desk. Still studying me, the interrogator retrieved an old metal teapot from a hotplate on a filing cabinet and calmly poured tea. He then asked me to sit at a small table facing his desk, on which were an ashtray and an empty water glass. As I sat, my torturer, Brown Shoes, gently put the glass of tea in front of me and backed away.

The interrogator began asking me personal details and jotting them down on a form. When he'd finished his questions, he calmly put the sheet of paper in a folder and asked Brown Shoes to take me to the amanat room, or deposit room. At the time, I didn't know what that meant. What type of deposit was the man talking about? Are they depositing me there? And who was this Brown Shoes? What was his rank? How were they going to treat me in this room?

The deposit room turned out to be the place where they took away everything that was in your pockets and also your shoelaces and watch. A soldier asked me if I was wearing a tie when he could see that I wasn't. I was slow to answer and almost laughed aloud, when the conscript standing behind me hit me and shouted, "Answer, animal." So I said I was not.

I left the room not knowing that I still had a small coin in my pocket.

I'm still alone beside Lake Ontario, confronted suddenly by a scene that I lived through but never saw: I'm naked and lying bent forward into a V, my back and lower legs crammed into an old car tire. My feet are tied together and raised above my head, stretched taut, so I can't move them. A frayed cable emits a swishing sound as it cuts through the air before landing on the soles of my feet, again and again and again. After a while, I feel that my head is splitting open, the thud of the whip on my feet somehow moving through my body to become a chisel brutally breaking my brain apart. I begin to scream. Somebody puts a piece of dirty cloth in my mouth, stuffing it in with the toe of his shoe. Now that there's no place for my screams to escape, the trapped pressure makes my body feel like it's going to explode. My body soon becomes no more than a garment for a smothered scream, which is overtaken by another scream the moment the previous one escapes.

"Stop!" a harsh voice orders. "We want to interrogate the other animal. It's time to give this animal a chance to account for himself."

There are two animals in the room: "the other animal" is the person who is about to be tortured in my place, and "this animal" is me. They extract me from the tire and order me to run so my feet don't swell up. My eyes are still blindfolded, and my hands bound. I run inside the room and crash into the wall. One of the soldiers laughs and strikes me on the back with the cable.

"Are you blind?" he scolds. "Can't you see the wall?" He orders me to run in the other direction. I run, trying to take small steps, almost running on the spot. He hits me again, hard.

"Move!"

"Awwwwwwwwww!" I scream across the great lake.

Does this emptiness I'm yelling into understand what it means to trip over the bloodied body of a man, so the sound of his shriek echoes through the room, mixing with my own? And does the emptiness comprehend how the victims' cries mix with the laughing of the guards and their orders for you to keep running while they beat the other?

I shout all of this into the empty air above the lake. I don't want to hear the screaming again, I want to discard it and be done with it for good.

"Awwwwwwwwwwwww!"

I don't want that indifferent old woman walking her black dog to see me. I don't want anyone to see me. If somebody hears me, will they think I'm a ghost from Rockwood Asylum? If the well-mannered Suzanne, my wife's Canadian friend, happened to meet me when I was screaming, would I tell her that when I crashed into the wall for maybe the sixth time, one of the soldiers ordered me to punch the wall in retaliation for what it was doing to me? But of course I couldn't because my hands were chained behind my back, swollen and teeming with ants. The torturer was laughing loudly when he hit me for not obeying him. "Now you're going to fuck that wall, son of a whore," he shouted. "Let's see you do that! Fuck that wall!"

Then he began hitting me hard across the back.

"Waaaaaaaaa. Awwwwwwww."

These sounds tell the lake how I responded to the orders. If I told you what happened, Madam, you would think me lacking in manners. Perhaps this is the kind of event best not spoken of. There are plenty of such events in which the guards wanted to break the prisoners' spirits. Do you have the word "break" in this sense in your language? It really means something like "invade and violate." I remember Rateb Shabow, a gentle youth who spent sixteen years and three days in prison, including three years, six months, and three days in Tadmur. Rateb told us that one of the guards at Tadmur used to amuse himself by inventing new ways to break prisoners' spirits, aside from the normal beatings and torture. This guard would stand on the cement roof of the building and spy down into our cell through the ventilation hole, a three-foot opening where the interior rebar was left exposed to work as prison bars. At night, Rateb further explained, one of the prisoners was assigned to stay awake as a night watchman, and so this guard, who was obsessed with sex, took delight in tormenting whoever was awake.

"Hey you fucker. What color is your mother's cunt?" he shouted down to a prisoner.

"Whichever color you wish, sir."

"Answer, idiot. Red?"

"Red, sir."

Another time this same guard asked a man in his fifties, "What color is your wife's cunt?"

I howl, Madam, on behalf of that man who was no longer able to meet the eyes of the other prisoners. I howl on behalf of the many others who were humiliated and insulted. I discover after a while that I'd been talking to the woman with the dog a long time after she'd left. But I also want to tell her why I am relieving myself of the voices that are eating me up inside by launching them over the lake. I look at myself: a late-middle-aged man on his own, carrying inside him the howling of thousands of other people roughly seven thousand miles away, a man talking to an old woman who neither sees nor hears him, and whom he neither sees nor hears. Veils of darkness begin to descend over the lake.

It was much harder in the dark when the electricity failed in the interrogation branch in Damascus. Not only did the lights go out, but the extractor fans bringing in fresh air and taking out the stale air went abruptly silent. *Did we really live with that constant roar?* But soon after that, because the cells were mostly below ground, our lungs began to feel constricted because of a lack of oxygen.

"Mother! I want my mother!" screamed Usama, a different Usama, a sixteen-year-old Lebanese boy who then lost consciousness. He fell on top of the bodies strewn over the cell floor and several of the prisoners woke up screaming. For a few moments there was total darkness until the guards lit their cigarette lighters. Cell number seven was around twenty-six feet long and no more than seventeen wide. In that space eighty-five noses were in search of air. Abu Amr, the prisoner they appointed head of the cell, started to bang on the steel door and the guards began swearing at us. The door opened suddenly.

"Who's the son of a bitch banging on the door?" a guard yelled.

"The guy's about to die," shouted Abu Amr.

"I can't bring him back to life! I'm not God Almighty!" the guard shouted back.

They left the door of the cell open, and the refreshing cool air began to get through to the bodies crammed helter-skelter on the floor. Do you know what I wished for then, Madam? That we could go back to the time before fire was discovered — a time when there were no jail cells or extractor fans or electricity — and roam around the steppes with the other creatures. They took Usama, the Lebanese boy, away. I don't have any other name for him. Usama didn't return while I was there. I don't know if he ever returned.

CHAPTER 11

WE DIDN'T MEAN TO GET MARRIED

When I saw Rufaida for the first time, it never occurred to me for a moment that the day would come when I would go home and be consumed by thoughts of her. I began to see how the hijab that covered her hair didn't restrict her mind, and as soon as I got home, all I could think about was being back in her captivating presence in the office next day.

Rufaida and me in our house in Assad al-Din quarter in Damascus during a celebration for our wedding.

It doesn't snow much in Damascus, but when it does the city rejoices. At least, it did back in 1996. People would pelt each other with snowballs, exchange smiles and laughter, and remember for a short while how they all belonged to the same city. It was on one of these mornings that Rufaida said snow always made her want to eat zaatar heated up on the stove with olive oil. Before I knew it, I was out the door and on my way to the nearby mini-market. There, I scooped up every type of dried spice zaatar mix they had, a large bag of muraqqad, and a big bottle of olive oil.

I rushed back into the office, laden with packages. Hala was standing at the door with a suspicious smile on her face.

"What's with the face?"

"You seem enamored with the Qubaysiya."

"You have an overactive imagination," I commented, going to the kitchen.

"Really? What if somebody's heart is excessively active?" She laughed.

Rufaida seemed so happy and grateful as she opened the bags and saw the pita, the different packages of colorfully mixed zaatar spices, and the oil, that it made me wonder if love just meant giving her all the olive oil and zaatar I could find.

That's when Hala came in, gave me another look, sighed, and then helped

Hala noticed early that I was interested in Rufaida. Hala was one of the few friends who attended our wedding.

Rufaida prepare the zaatar for baking in our lunchroom oven. Rufaida and Hala soon became good friends.

Some months later, at the end of May, while we were looking over the balcony of the typesetting room, Rufaida noticed a single ripe fruit on the top branch of the loquat tree. The tree was about thirteen feet tall, and its fruit was right at our eye level.

"My father says the high up fruits that people can't reach are the sweetest," I said. "They're God's gift to the birds."

"It does look so delicious," Rufaida said.

And once again, like the idiot suitor I was, I hopped over the railing.

"No, no. Come back," Rufaida cried. "If you fall, you'll break every bone in your body." But this only emboldened me. Gripping the railing with one hand, I leaned out as far as I could over the empty space. "Please, please don't fall, Jamal," Rufaida begged. Cunningly, patiently, I was able to grasp a few leaves, then some branches, and finally the limb where the fruit was growing. Ignoring the iron railing cutting into my palm, I leaned out just a little farther. "Jamal!" And finally the fruit was mine.

Hopping back over the railing like the heroic poet Qays, who was crazy for Layla in the ancient story, I offered Rufaida the tiny loquat fruit on my open palm. Her expression was a silent ululation of joy. I then wondered if love meant taking risks to pick a loquat fruit and feeling happy to see the wordless song of joy in her eyes. At midday, I received half a loquat and a long kiss.

Rufaida continued to wear the long coat and hijab in public and at work, but when she started to visit me at my place, she'd hang them on the back of my door. Once, on my birthday, I invited friends to lunch in my room. Most of them had been in prison too. Of course, Rufaida brought an excessive number of presents: flowers, food, perfume, a shirt, and candles.

That afternoon, my old prison mate Ghassan Mardini, who's now an architect, saw Rufaida without her hijab and holding her first-ever glass of wine. "Now she looks like a modern, educated city girl," he mused appreciatively. But when five o'clock arrived and Rufi hurriedly put her overcoat and hijab back on — her mother expected her home on time — Ghassan couldn't help but tease her. "Hey, the Qubaysiya is back."

When Rufaida and I finally declared our love to one another, we agreed to live our lives on our own terms and never formally get married. Marriage was a convention, and nobody had asked our opinion about it. But love, love was our own choice. What's more, we seemed like a good match in another way. Rufaida had confided she couldn't have children because of some growths on her reproductive organs. This suited my decision to remain childless, and so we were content just to have found each other.

We opted for an urfi marriage, a Muslim tradition where couples verbally declare a life-long devotion to each other in front of witnesses. For Rufaida, and for many other young people caught between religion and modernity, this type of marriage sanctified the shared intimacies of marriage, away from the sin of adultery. But her family didn't know about her marriage, and she was still living at home.

But truly, I did feel the responsibilities of a husband. When the growths that plagued her began to cause discomfort, I didn't hesitate to provide the money for a medical procedure.

Some months later, as we sat down to our morning coffee ritual, Rufaida told me she had bad news. "Jamal — I'm pregnant," she whispered.

"I think this is excellent news," I replied without hesitation. "It means the surgery was more successful than we expected."

"Yes, but what about the pregnancy?" she asked.

"What do you want to do?"

"An abortion?" she questioned, a topic that was beginning to be openly discussed by educated Syrians during those years. The next day, we were in the office of a specialist in women's health, an old friend of mine. After the examination, while Rufi was dressing, my friend took me aside and warned that an abortion might cause infertility again, this time permanent. When I told Rufaida, she asked, trying to hide her fear, or perhaps her embarrassment, "What shall we do?"

"We'll marry as soon as possible," I replied. "A real wedding," and Rufaida wrapped her arms around me and cried.

Rufaida then told her three sisters about the urfi wedding, the pregnancy, our plan to get married, and how she knew their mother would not readily agree to it. So, she gave them a message to relay: "If you don't approve, then I'll go away with him, and what will be, will be."

Rufaida and me and a real wedding.

The sisters united to put pressure on their mother. I knew from briefly meeting the matriarch in the past what her inclination would be. I was both a member of a different sect and a former communist detainee, each by itself a sufficient reason for disqualification. But the two combined?

Crying, but under unrelenting pressure from her daughters, my future mother-in-law agreed. Apparently, the sisters had bolstered their argument by declaring that I was a modern man and their sister Rufaida would be allowed to live her life as a free and modern woman, unlike the great majority of women in their society. But modern or not, there were still acceptable conventions, and Rufaida told me it was time to go ask for her hand. The next day, I was at her parents' house, and luckily her mother hadn't changed her mind. But she did raise a finger at me.

"I have one more condition. You must let my daughter keep her own religion."

"This is not a problem," I replied, a hand to my heart. "Rufaida and her Lord know better than I." Maintaining this respectful pose, I asked if the marriage could take place quickly, repeating a white lie Rufaida had invented. "I've been offered a job in the Gulf and would like for us to travel there together."

In order to keep building myself up in my future in-laws' eyes, and to speed the process along before Rufi's pregnancy became obvious, I announced I was taking the additional measure of bringing a lawyer to sign the marriage contract at their home. This would do away with the need for them to go sign the necessary papers at the courthouse and would be seen in the community as a grand gesture by a future son-in-law. A few days later, Ghassan drove me and the lawyer to Rufi's parents' home in his Peugeot. That's when I learned my friend wasn't entitled to act as a witness because he was Christian. I thought I knew a lot about what are called Personal Status Laws, but I didn't know this one. Luckily, such a ceremony is a reason for a family gathering, and Rufaida's brothers-in-law were there to sign their names.

When I told my own family about the wedding, none of them asked me anything about the bride. My mother was very happy for me and said she trusted I would pick a wonderful partner.

CHAPTER 12

MY FIRST INTERROGATION SESSION

I t was three in the morning on December 30, 1980. Sergeant Ghazi Jarrad, indifferent to the dried blood on my shirt and face, got up from his chair.

"If we didn't have to entertain you, I could be sleeping peacefully in my bed," he said offhandedly. Ghazi Jarrad was the head of the information department for the military interrogation branch in Latakia.

I had been led into his office a minute earlier and had my blindfold pulled off. Jarrad was sitting at his desk, reading a report from an open file. He looked up and motioned for my cuffs to be removed too.

"Saeed. Tell me about the secret political meeting at Wadi al-Ghar."

Wadi al-Ghar is a nature reserve. I thought he must be referring to an event that actually took place, an evening near the Wadi, but it was just some friends going for a casual walk. There was no political conference in the woods, as the informer who reported the incident had alleged. The informer was probably Faraj Nadeemeh, a local fool who somehow got a job with the intelligence. He had taken great pleasure in harassing me in high school.

Jarrad stood nose-to-nose with me and asked me again for the names of people who attended what he was now calling "the Wadi al-Ghar Conference." While I wasn't covering for anyone, because there was no conference, I didn't dare give them my friends' names. They would be the next to be arrested. And when I insisted for a third and fourth time that I hadn't been to any conference, he motioned for a guard to slap me, harder each time.

"Sir, I didn't take part in any conference," I said, my jaw now sore, "and to the best of my knowledge, no conference ever took place there." This graduated me up to a punch.

"It wasn't a conference, fine," Jarrad said. "It was a normal meeting in the open. Who was at the meeting?"

"I didn't attend any meeting there." This time a punch to the face and one to the stomach.

He continued to insist on knowing the participants and repeated the date several times, as if the fact that the date was written on the document confirmed its authenticity.

"No, no meeting, sir," I groaned.

Jarrad came very close to my ear and whispered, "You're sure you want to do this?" I looked up at him, confused. He motioned to his men again, and suddenly my arms were twisted behind my back, the cuffs and blindfold roughly put back on, and I was pushed to the floor. This is when the kicking, punching, and whipping started. The pain tore at my body and I began to scream. They gagged me with what tasted like a well-used rag, and the beating went on for at least half an hour. All coherent thought was now banished. There was only pain. I became aware that another man had entered the room and begun talking, but my pain was such I couldn't understand what was being said.

"Brigadier General, that's wonderful news," I finally heard Jarrad say. "We'll smash them, sir."

After the brigadier general left, Jarrad ordered a soldier to stand me up.

"Hey, who said you could get rid of that gag?" Jarrad cried. The soldier responded to this question by punching me on the side of my head. "We don't have time to deal with him now," Jarrad continued. "We'll shit on him later. Hand him over to Abu Taysir," he ordered, using the prisoners' nickname for the guard, the Father of Facilitation.

The soldier grabbed my arm, flogging me vindictively as he pulled me stumbling along an echoing hallway and down a set of steps.

"Watch yourself, fucker. I don't want to fall with you." We continued down another hallway, and I was shoved roughly through a doorway and jerked to a halt. Loud snoring reverberated on the walls of this new room. "Sit on your ass and keep your mouth shut, animal." I leaned against the wall and slid down to the floor, listening to the guard walk away. I was alone with the heavy snoring until it stopped abruptly a few minutes later.

"Who are you?" a hoarse voice asked. The question confused me, and I didn't say anything. Then the same voice, loud and forceful this time, shouted, "Abu al-Layl, come here."

I heard a door opening. "Yes, sir?"

"Who is this shit?"

Abu al-Layl, Father of the Night, kicked me. "Who are you, you piece of shit?" he asked.

"Jamal Saeed."

"Fuck's sake. So, it can talk," Abu Taysir said. "Take off his blindfold and loosen his cuffs. His hands are blue." If I'd been obliged to draw the face of the snoring man, without seeing him, I would have drawn a face very like that of Abu Taysir. He had a big head, dark complexion, blue circles around the eyes, and a frightening gray mustache. "Why did they bring you here, Jamal?"

"I don't know."

He exhaled in an exaggerated fashion. "You don't know. Okay, who sent you to me?"

"I don't know."

"You don't know that either. What do you know?"

"My being here is an injustice."

Abu Taysir laughed loudly. "Abu al-Layl, why are you treating him unjustly? Take him to a chalet so he can relax."

"We don't have any vacant chalets, sir."

"Hmmm. Put him in chalet four then. Don't leave him in the corridor. We don't want him meeting that new prisoner, that Hussein bastard."

I didn't know who Hussein was, but as Abu al-Layl pulled me from his boss's office of snores toward my waiting chalet, I was burning with curiosity to meet him.

CHAPTER 13

CELL NUMBER FOUR

At dawn on December 30, 1980, Abu al-Layl opened the door to the cellblock where the euphemistically named chalet number four was located. It was a dimly lit hallway, about twenty feet long and four feet wide. Lining the walls were some dozen shorter-than-normal doors constructed close together, giving a hint to the size of the cells behind them. There were also five bedraggled men, obviously inmates, lying on the floor watching us enter. As Abu al-Layl opened the door to cell four, I noticed its Yale lock was Italian-made, and when he took off my handcuffs, I noticed they were stamped *Made in Spain*. Abu al-Layl then kicked me into the cell and I fell on top of another human. He gave a cry of pain, but, even before I apologized, he said in a voice full of exhaustion, "I know you didn't mean to hurt me."

"Shut up, fucker," Abu al-Layl said. "If you two even whisper to each other, I'll smash your ribs. You, the new one. From now on your name is Chalet Four B."

He locked our door, and a moment later we heard the door to the cellblock close. Knowing the guard was now out of earshot, my cellmate introduced himself.

"I'm Zaher Antar," he said in a strained voice.

"I'm Jamal Saeed."

I learned that he was accused of being a member of the Muslim Brotherhood. His legs were swollen, and they gave off a rotten smell. A blanket meant for us to share smelled of decay and old urine. It wouldn't keep a dog warm.

"It really smells in here," I said.

"Smells aren't the worst they've got," he answered. "If you don't learn to ignore something as trivial as a smell, you'll soon be finished."

Zaher was in a much worse state than I was, for I hadn't yet been subjected to a complete session of torture and interrogation. I figured the blood on my shirt was from my nose and noticed the blood from the wounds on my feet was drying. But there must have been more wrong with me than I could see, judging from the sympathy aroused in Zaher. Even a passing soldier asked me a bit later, "Who's the idiot that did that to you?"

I tried to make sure my cellmate could rest as much as possible. The cell wasn't big enough for one person, let alone two. It was around thirty-six inches wide and I could tell it was seventy-five inches high and not more than sixty-five inches long because I could almost stand up straight but had to bend my legs when I lay down. And this I did even more than required, pulling my knees up tight so as not to touch Zaher's torn and swollen legs.

As we sat there staring at each other at first, I tried to remove the jagged bits of cement sticking to the cell floor with the coin I discovered in my coat pocket.

"Do we have to repair their prisons for them?" Zaher scolded.

"The fact is, they're not hurt by these sharp bits," I replied. "We and those who stay in these cells after us are the ones who'll suffer."

"We should leave them as evidence."

"There's plenty of evidence of their atrocities. In the meantime, let's not add to our own troubles."

A few minutes later, when he asked me to join him in prayer, he found out I wasn't religious. It was as if a button was pushed, and he didn't make any effort to hide his annoyance. So I didn't hide the fact that I was against political parties that only accepted members from a specific sect. He started to sit up to continue the argument, but winced with pain and, suddenly out of breath and shivering, fell back. It was very cold in the cell.

"Here, let's stop fighting," I said, and I took off my coat, which I somehow still had with me. When I put it over him, he finally relaxed, and a look of gratitude came into his eyes. He fell fast asleep, and when he woke up some hours later, he smiled and said it was the first time he'd felt warm since entering prison. But now I was tired, hardly able to keep my eyes open, and so we agreed to take turns sleeping.

Locked in this tiny closet together, we began to make each other's acquaintance in a more friendly way. The boundaries soon became clear, and a respect developed because of the suffering imposed on us by our common foe.

"Abu Taysir chose us to be a burden to each other," I said smiling.

"They have enough power to force people with nothing in common to share things." He chuckled, the effort to laugh still clearly painful.

Zaher was very optimistic that victory was close at hand, believing his Allah would intervene shortly to help His righteous servants. When I asked him who the righteous servants were, he said without batting an eyelid, "Us," meaning the Muslim Brotherhood. When I smiled, he smiled, too, adding, "I know you have a different view."

Sometimes, when the interrogators needed information quickly from a prisoner, they would take him out before breakfast. They did this to Zaher on my second morning in our cell, December 31. I kept part of the breakfast for him, which amounted to half a spoon of yogurt slopped on a samoun bread roll. I divided the small bun into three portions, eating the smallest for breakfast, along with the yogurt. At lunch all twelve cell doors in our wing were opened, and everybody joined those sitting in the hall. We took turns drinking from a common bowl full of a cold, salty liquid with a few lentils in it. I ate a second part of our samoun then.

At noon on that day, Zaher returned to the cell covered in blood. His skin was torn in many places where the whip had ripped it open. His face was swollen, and he'd lost a tooth. He was panting as quietly as he could, and I was overcome by a feeling that he was going to die in front of me. I begged him not to.

"Don't die, man. Who knows, one day we might walk in the streets of this city arguing with one another, and then end up having a coffee together. I'll say to you, 'If you lot win, you'll act just like the regime,' and you'll say the same to me. Would we really act like them if we were in power? Come on, let's agree that we mustn't do that. Please don't die. We might learn how to disagree without killing each other! Please, I don't want either of us to die. More particularly, I don't want you to die in front of me. Your death will expose how powerless I am!"

The man looked as if he was already dead. I banged on the door.

"What's the matter?" asked a prisoner lying in the corridor beside the cells.

"Zaher's dying," I answered in a distressed voice.

Zaher gestured vaguely. I wasn't sure if this meant "Leave me alone" or "The life we're living isn't worth preserving."

Our cell door opened abruptly.

"What's wrong, assholes?" growled Abu Ghadab. The longer you talked with the Father of Anger, the greater his insults became.

"The man's in a critical condition," said Mayyas al-Sufi, a civil engineering student who was lying in the corridor between the cells.

Abu Ghadab didn't understand. "Say something I can understand, fucker," he shouted. "And fuck the university that taught you how to talk nonsense."

"The man might die," Mayyas pleaded.

"Which particular piece of shit are you talking about?"

Mayyas indicated our cell. Abu Ghadab saw me pressed tight up against the wall beside Zaher. He told me to get out, and I, along with the other prisoners in the hall, watched as the Father of Anger ordered Zaher to wake up. We all winced as the guard poked one of his open wounds with a length of stiff cable. Zaher let out a deep groan.

"He sounds like a pig," Abu Ghadab said. "Okay, I'll get him a doctor. But if he's faking, I'll kill him."

Zaher was away for several hours. Despite my worry for him, I took advantage of the extra space. Wrapping both my coat and rotten blanket around me, I quickly fell into a deep sleep, making up for the deprivations of my first two days of prison life. When I woke, I began waiting for news of Zaher. It was like waiting for news of myself. In the meantime, I listened to the whispering from the corridor. The prisoners out there were ones from whom the interrogators had extracted all the information they could and who therefore didn't need to be kept isolated. And because there weren't enough cells, they let them stay in the hall. Compared to those of us stuck behind the steel doors, they were living a life of luxury. They could stretch out their legs while sleeping, without leaning up against a wall. I admit I was filled with envy.

You, Madam, do you lack space to stretch out your legs or your arms? What you lack is someone other than your dog, not to safeguard your loneliness but to rescue you from it, to listen to the love stories dead and buried in your blood. There was a time when your face thrilled with different emotions, but now you are as lifeless as a desert. How hideous this loneliness is. It has robbed you even of grief.

Listen, try to listen. Zaher returned a few hours after supper, having left shortly after lunch. They gave us three meals a day, but even if you combined them, they weren't enough to feed a cat. Maybe you had a cat before your black dog. At least then you'd know how little food a cat needs.

Supper that night was half a hard-boiled egg and a small potato. A revived Zaher came back to find that I had saved his quarter of the egg and the whole potato. He smiled gratefully as he put them both on the remaining third of a piece of roll and slowly ate.

Shortly afterwards, a male nurse arrived and asked for the asshole who'd been with the doctor. He gave Zaher a pill and said, "If I forget, you have to remind me every six hours to come and give you a pill."

"But we don't have a watch," I said to the nurse. He slapped me hard and told me to repeat after him: "I will not interfere in what does not concern me."

At midnight we heard ships' sirens, fireworks, and gunshots announcing the beginning of the new Christian year.

"Happy New Year," I said to Zaher.

He smiled pityingly at me. "Celebrating the New Year is a heresy we are forbidden to adopt."

Layla has arrived from Aleppo and is now waiting for me with our friends in Damascus. If I had told Zaher that we were going to drink and dance, that I would have kissed Layla and was profoundly sad I'd missed the evening, he could have pitied me, or possibly even hated me. He had assured me that moral depravity was what had brought the nation to its current woeful state. When I asked him to tell me how this immorality was manifested in the life of the nation, he gave me the example of "the abomination" being sold on the high street. He meant alcohol.

"I think since its creation, and even before the creation of the Syrian state as we know it today, Syria has always had alcohol." I told him about the archaeological discoveries that confirm that beer and wine have been produced in this region for thousands of years. Zaher's angry reaction made me abandon the idea of discussing the issue any further. In an attempt to make the atmosphere friendlier, I talked about less weighty sorrows: "Think how many cups of tea and coffee and cozy domestic gatherings we'll miss out on," I said.

"Do you care only about your stomach?" he said disapprovingly, even aggressively. "And what do you know? You've only been in prison for two days."

I then realized that respecting a truce in such close quarters meant not trying to resolve your differences but ignoring them. And he was right about my being in jail for such a short time. I really had no idea of what was going on yet, and so I kept silent. After a while, Zaher began to cry silently. I patted him on the shoulder.

"Trust in Allah," I said.

"And delight in Him," he answered, wiping away the tears with the back of his hand.

That night, I learned how Zaher lived with his old, sick mother, and there was nobody in the house but the two of them. He told me the elderly woman needed him to be there, and ended our conversation by addressing his absent mother: "You have Allah, Hajjeh. He will never abandon one of His servants."

I remembered my mother talking about the divine providence that extends even to a worm in the heart of a rock, and my uncle retorting, "So glory be to Allah as He lets the hunter shoot a bird caring for her chicks. Then they all die of hunger."

I didn't say to the man, who believed he was sacrificing everything he possessed in order to raise the banner of his god, that Allah, as we know from the Quran, is able to do whatever He wants. He doesn't need anyone to raise banners for Him. But I held my tongue, feeling sad for a mother who didn't have her son to bring her to the doctor or remind her when to take her medicine. I made do with asking whether she had other relatives, and he merely answered that he wasn't sure they would take care of her.

We need a throng of good angels now that the sons of heaven have ceased to appear on Earth, I thought to myself, but this I kept to myself too.

By now my friends would be wondering why I hadn't turned up. Had news of my arrest reached them? I longed for their company. Then I suddenly felt incredibly hungry. I laughed, because today I was craving food that I'd recoil from outside the prison. Zaher asked why I was laughing.

"I've discovered life is much better outside of prison," I answered.

"An important discovery," he agreed, and gave the first genuine smile I'd seen from him. He had a very nice smile.

We talked in whispers about food and went to sleep hungry. Next morning, we were each given a very small portion of cheese and half a spoon of apricot jam. I remarked to Zaher that the cheese wasn't enough to fill the gaps between our teeth.

"You need to take a mouthful of water and swill the cheese around your mouth before you swallow it," he advised with a smirk.

"So, where's the water?" We weren't allowed anything to drink in the cells.

The truce now properly in place allowed Zaher and me to get on more amicably — well, as amicably as any two people could while living together in less than ten square feet. Thus accommodated, we fell into a regular routine. In the morning, guards unlocked the cells and prisoners received their first insult of the day, accompanied by a lashing as they went off to the toilet. Our regular guard, Abu al-Layl, would repeat the same sentence to every prisoner as he was whipping them: "Make sure everything's finished in one second, asshole." That "everything" consisted of emptying the bladder and the bowels, and washing penis and anus, hands and face. "I don't have time for you lot," Abu al-Layl would shout every day, over and over again.

When he was absent for a day, Zaher said to me, "We haven't heard Abu al-Layl's voice today."

"So, today he really doesn't have time for us," I answered, wryly.

When we went back to the cells after the toilet break, the rounds of interrogation and real torture began.

The torturer we called Abu Taysir, the Father of Facilitation, would say to each prisoner, "We're very busy. Don't you torture us and force us to torture you more than we want to." And then he would pontificate, "I advise you not to hold anything back or be slow to answer, for this will oblige us to torture you more. Answer our questions truthfully, and this reduces the pain for all of us."

The situation, as Abu Taysir saw it, was that it was our obligation to produce evidence of our guilt and information leading to the arrest of our friends.

Years later, I learned Zaher and I were also inmates of Tadmur at the same time, although we never met there. After Tadmur, and nine years after we shared the tiny chalet, we met once in Sednaya Prison. The devastating years Zaher spent in Tadmur had shattered his hopes of divine intervention. Now he was profoundly convinced his suffering was Allah's way to test him personally. His eyes were dull and resigned. Their provocative gleam had died, and he no longer wanted any sort of real discussion.

Before I left chalet number four, thirty-two cramped days after I'd first been pushed on top of him, I took the coin I still had in my pocket and carved three images into the wall: a bird spreading its wings, a key, and a little sun. Reminding me of these engravings brought the only smile I saw from Zaher during our single meeting in Sednaya.

"They kept me company after you'd gone," he said.

CHAPTER 14

BIRDS AND JINN

At the age of six, I regularly hid in a clump of bushes near my grandmother's house. This is where, holding on to what my mother called my "little dove," I would spray various shapes with my pee. Zig-zags, circles, stick figure people, even letters and numbers. I was "answering the call of nature," as North Americans say, or what Syrians refer to as "seeing to one's needs."

At the time, the only toilet in the whole village was inside Barbara's family's house — built by the French at the end of the 1920s. The house was part of the asphalt quarry's property, so we got to know about the toilet only after the business was nationalized. Until the 1980s and '90s, when toilets became commonplace in almost everybody's home, finishing one's business in the open air entailed wiping yourself with a smooth, palm-sized stone that would then be washed by the rain and purified by the sun. The few intellectuals in the village used newspaper.

"Wiping your bottom, that's all these newspapers are good for," said my maternal uncle, Jabr. He was one of the early members of the Baath party, having joined soon after its founding. But he quickly distanced himself from the organization when Hafez al-Assad came to power and membership became more of a way for its leaders to promote their own interests over those of Syria. Ironically, within a decade, the Baath government's security services had arrested two of Jabr's children, Barakat and Rateb, and three nephews, Muneer, Bahjat, and me. I digress, but life in such a world as Syria is full of seesawing digressions, distractions, surprises, and disappointments.

Once, I had almost finished peeing when a little bird alighted not three feet from me. He stared at me. "Peep," he chirped, and it was as if he was inviting me to grab hold of him. Quickly pulling up my trousers, and not caring if I dribbled on them, I was instantly obsessed by a desire to feel those soft feathers and tap the tiny oat-husk beak. It would be so grand to play with this new pet, to feed it, to take it home and show it off to my siblings and cousins. Hand outstretched, I approached the little creature — but the bird darted away and landed a few feet farther off. I took another step forward, and the bird moved again — and then again many more times. Like a coquettish girl who dodges a suitor's improper kiss, but then turns back with a bright, beckoning smile, the bird seemed to be enticing me to continue the pursuit. Totally infatuated, I felt that nothing mattered to me except possessing him. The chase continued, and soon I found myself descending into a wood. And as the light became dimmer, it seemed the bird allowed me to get closer, but never close enough.

"Come, perch on my hand, little friend," I begged, and swore by Allah's great white beard that I loved it and would never do it harm. But the bird would not respond to my entreaties. Farther and farther into the woods we went, when, and finally, the bird vanished, swallowed up in the pine forest.

I realized the game was over. It was like waking up from a dream. Now, looking around, I found myself under the black veil of branches with the realization that night was coming. This was when the gas lamps in the village down below began to flicker on. They were like pale orange eyes, staring mockingly at me. "You are lost," they seemed to say, and the shrubs and tree branches were transformed into mysterious clawed creatures who were closing in on me. These must be the jinn, the mysterious spirit beings I'd heard the older folk talk about. I felt a chill breeze blow over me.

"Why have you come here?" the jinn hissed in chorus. "What do you want?" This caused a tingling in my scalp, which immediately turned into a full-on shudder rippling throughout my body. "What do you want?" the voices echoed.

"I want . . . I want to go home," I whispered weakly. Lower lip trembling, I tried to run toward the lights of the village. That's when a sharp pain bit into my foot. I screamed like I had never screamed before. "*Yabbooou!* Father, save me!" and then I closed my eyes and promised Allah that, if He delivered me from this evil, I'd do what my grandfather told me was the right way to get Allah's attention. "I'll sacrifice a bull to you!" I cried out.

"Jamaaaal," shouted a voice from the dark. "Don't be frightened. Where are you?"

Was my prayer being answered so quickly? Was it the jinn tricking me? No, the voice was familiar.

"I'm on a path, but I don't know where I am," I shouted, and the pain in my foot began to throb.

"The whole village is looking for you," the voice continued, now sounding closer.

"I don't know where I am," I repeated.

I was apparently in a place called Ashshahrour in Arabic, or the Blackbird. Every piece of land in our village has a name.

My paternal uncle, Ali, and my maternal cousin, Barakat, kept talking with me until they found me, their presence creating an instant refuge for me. Barakat, who was about five years older than me, calmly extracted the thorn that had pierced all the way through my shoe and into my foot.

"Why did you come here?" my uncle asked angrily. "What do you want?"

"Please don't hit me," I begged.

He didn't hit me, but he brought his face very close to mine. "You're lucky we found you before the dab'aa. You'd make a tasty meal for the hyena's wife."

The next day at my uncle's I interrupted Barakat, my idol, who always had his nose in a book. I leaned familiarly against the big stuffed chair he was lazing in, my mouth close to his ear. "I was more afraid of the jinn than the dab'aa," I said seriously. My cousin lifted his head from his reading and stared at me, smiling. In an equally familiar gesture, he then covered my face with his large hand and pushed me back from his space. But that didn't stop me. "Does the dab'aa have a husband and children, like the cow?" I asked.

"Yes, her husband is called dab'a," Barakat said. And then he went back to reading.

"Why doesn't he eat people who've lost their way, and she does?"

Finally, exasperated that I didn't understand that Uncle Ali had just happened by chance to use the feminine word, Barakat looked at me as if I were an idiot. "Listen, none of that matters. There wasn't a dab'aa or a dab'a last night, or any jinn. Especially jinn. They don't exist anywhere. Just don't wander away from the house anymore." And he returned to reading.

"What do you mean there aren't any jinn?" I asked indignantly. "I heard their voices."

"Were their voices beautiful?" laughed Barakat.

"They were like the voices of snakes."

"When have you heard snakes talking?" he asked, with a serious expression. The question took me by surprise. Indeed, I had never heard any snake utter a single word.

"Aren't they the ones making the sounds in the spaces between the rocks where they hide?"

"I don't know. Maybe you're hearing the sound of the air."

I laughed as if Barakat were telling a great joke. For me, the Arabic words for "air" and "wind" were not related. Whereas wind did make a noise outdoors, the air was just for breathing; it was silent. To say the air makes a sound is ridiculous. Barakat had the good grace to laugh along with me. But when I added, seriously, "Trees tremble because they are afraid of the sound of storms," Barakat laughed, and then became absorbed in his book again.

"Don't you like Hafiz al-Assad?" the torturer at the interrogation branch asked. It was after a vicious round of torture, and he brought his face very close to mine. "What do you want?" he growled into my ear.

"I want . . . I want to go home," I said in the voice of a lost child.

I never did fulfill my promise to sacrifice a bull. After all, it wasn't easy for a boy to acquire such an animal, and, honestly, I had forgotten about the pledge by the time I got home. And as hard as it was to be a lost child, it was much easier than being a lost soul in the interrogation branch. Here, I knew precisely where I was, and getting back home from here wasn't as easy as praying for my uncle and cousin to rescue me, even if I'd vowed to sacrifice a thousand bulls.

But my family did try to see me. I was in a building known to most of the inhabitants of Latakia, but it was impossible for them to get access to a place that was more brutal than any demon jinni's kingdom.

The people in my village call the little bird that led me into the forest by a name appropriate to its behavior. They make the word feminine and call it "the Shepherd's Distraction." Grandmother said that the bird had once seduced Grandfather away from his cows, which, left unattended, trampled her vegetable garden.

In my life there have been many projects resembling the pursuit of that bird: plans that are the product of dreams and desires, seemingly within reach but soon to vanish, leaving me prey to terror and disappointment.

But not all birds, in my experience, are harbingers of disaster and dark nights, even in prison. I still remember "the dawn of the bird." I gave it this name to distinguish it from all the other dawns. Not only mornings, but all times in prison resemble an identical, indifferent blank page. On this particular day, I was awakened, like many of my cellmates, by a strange sound. There was a frantic flapping above me, echoing off the walls as something circled overhead.

As I pushed myself up on one elbow, quite stiff from sleeping on the thin mattress, I forced open my sleepy eyes. There in the middle of the cell, with sixty other souls bearing witness, stood Salman Ismail, a quiet and gentle person. Perhaps the most gentle among us. He stood there holding a large T-shaped sponge-mop high over his head. He seemed to be offering it as a perch to a sparrow that was frantically flying in circles around the cell. The little bird must have left the freedom of the open sky and come in through the ventilation hole in the ceiling. Confused and frightened, the bird obviously couldn't find its way back out.

Amazingly, the bird alighted on the miserable tree. Salman then lowered the mop and caught the bird as skillfully as a wild cat would. He smoothed the feathers on its head and neck, whispered something in its ear and kissed it. He then held the bird over his head and pointed to the opening in the roof. When he released the bird, there was a collective gasp, surprising Salman, who realized only then that all his cellmates had been watching. But the bird had somehow understood its benefactor's directions and flew right back up into the sky. "Goodbye," Salman said softly, and he sat down on his thin mattress and closed his eyes.

"That was amazing," someone said.

"Such a kindness will be seen by Allah," another said.

"Yes, you did a good thing," added another.

Salman opened his eyes. He looked sad. "But I forgot something."

Malik Assad, a longtime cellmate, came and put a hand on Salman's shoulder. "What did you forget, my friend?" he asked.

Salman looked at Malik and then up to the ceiling. "I forgot to tie a message to the bird's leg."

"What message would that be?" Malik asked.

"Just four words," he said softly, and everyone in the cell, to a man, held his breath and leaned forward to hear. "Don't forget the detainees."

After the cell went back to its indifferent monotony, I sat next to Salman and tried to make light of the situation. "What good would four words roaming over the rooftops do? Nobody could read them," I teased. "And the note might have been a nuisance to the poor bird."

Salman turned and looked at me, more defiant than I had ever seen him. "Can you predict the future?" he said, with both fire and hope in his eyes. "Somebody might have read them." And then he stared down at his mattress, jaw set and hard.

I put a hand on his shoulder. "I'm sorry for what I said, my friend," I said, and he made a small, gracious bow of the head. I added, "Will you tell me what you whispered to the sparrow?"

He looked at me. "I asked it to visit my daughter, Samar. To tell her that I love her and miss her." Then he turned his face away to hide his quivering lips.

A few days later, Salman had a fit of hysterical weeping. He was convinced that Samar had died. We all tried to calm him down and tell him it wasn't true, saying that there was no way for him to know such a thing.

"I know, I just know," was all he could wail.

We all stood by Salman. Some thought that it was a father's premonition, but others disagreed. According to them, Salman was a father overcome with longing for the warmth of family life, and this longing expressed itself in a violent bout of tears. Like all of us, the man needed to cry, so he pictured that his daughter had died to allow himself some emotional release.

This was not the end of the bird stories in cell number one in Tadmur Prison.

Yasir Makhluf was another interesting prisoner. He openly opposed the regime, even though his mother and father were related to the wife of President Hafez al-Assad. Yasir spent fifteen years in prison because of this unyielding stance. But his familial association with the president did have its perks. Yasir's mother was able to visit him in Tadmur years before visits were officially permitted.

Umm Yasir was like a mother to us all, bringing enormous amounts of food on every visit, enough for all the prisoners in the cell for a couple of days. We didn't have a fridge to keep the food, so we had to devour everything that day. We were as happy as children, or indeed as any starving creatures when they have a chance to eat their fill.

But food was not the only thing we were hungry for. As nobody else could receive visitors, we lived vicariously through Yasir. This meant we cross-examined him relentlessly about life in the outside world until we felt as if we'd had visitors too. It was during one particular debriefing, when all our questions were exhausted, that Yasir recounted the strange conversation he'd had with his mother.

"I sent you a sparrow," she told him. "Did it arrive?"

"What?" he said, astonished. "A small bird came into our cellblock a few days ago."

As Yasir continued, the whole population of cell one again held its collective breath. When he related the story of Salman's sparrow, his mother didn't seem surprised in the least. She just took it for granted that this must have been the very bird she caught in her house and ordered to visit Tadmur two hundred miles away.

"My only regret," she concluded, "was I forgot to tie a message to the bird's leg."

Seventeen years after that bird's visit, Yasir and I lived together in the Rukn al-Din district of Damascus. There, we had a fridge where we stored not only the food we bought, but also what our mothers still sent us. And we shared some of this food with the birds in our front yard.

Nineteen years after the Dawn of the Bird incident, I was in Al Mouwasat Hospital in Damascus, sitting by the bed of my dying sister, Khadija. Every day her friends visited and there was much happy chatter. On the day my sister died, many of these friends returned to pay their respects, many of them ex-prisoners and their families. One of them, a young woman, came and stood in front of me, smiling and speaking in a soft voice that was somehow familiar.

"I'm Samar Ismail, the daughter of Salman Ismail," she said. As memories flooded back into my mind, my eyes filled. Here was the daughter whose father cried inconsolably because of a premonition of her death, but she was now a young woman full of life. The memory of his emotional release seemed to give me leave to weep for Khadija.

Thirty-five years after the Dawn of the Bird, a sparrow alighted on the balcony of the flat where my family first lived when we immigrated to Canada. Seeing the little creature caused me to think of Salman. I wanted so badly to tell him that I was living in a faraway place. It seemed as if he was in front of me, laughing and saying something like, "We are the faraway ones."

The following day, Malik Assad, who had immigrated to Sweden, told me through social media that our friend and cellmate Salman had passed away. After exchanging fond memories of him, we said our goodbyes, and I sat silently alone. I tried to remember if I knew where Samar was living.

I jumped up and looked onto the balcony, at the nearby trees, and even out onto the street. There was not one single bird around that I could ask to carry my heartfelt condolences to Salman's wonderful daughter.

CHAPTER 15

SHOW ME YOURS,
AND I'LL SHOW YOU MINE

I first saw a Barbie doll in a Damascus toyshop during the time I was living underground, hiding from the regime. My friend Jamil Hatmal bought the toy as a birthday present for a relative, and when he showed it to me, it made me think of an old childhood playmate.

"Barbara looked just like that doll," I told Jamil.

"Who's Barbara?"

"My first love — when I was about six."

I started to tell Jamil how the villa that Barbara lived in was a place of fantasy for me. It was built by the French owners of the asphalt company decades earlier for the local manager to live in, Barbara's father having been manager at the time. Jamil just wanted to hear the details about my first love, not her house. But to me, Barbara's magic was an extension of the house's elegant mystery. It was impossible to separate the two. My mother used to say that the inhabitants of the house on the land next to us lived a life of bliss because their roof didn't leak. In winter we had to put bowls and pots on the floor to catch the drips that came through our mud-thatch roof when it rained.

I remember the first time facing Barbara across the barbed wire fence between our properties.

"Has your cow had a calf?" I asked.

"We don't have a cow."

"We have two cows. One's black, the other's red."

"Red like my dress?"

"No, your dress is redder and prettier."

"Can you come and play?"

I answered by lying down on the ground and crawling under the barbed wire, tearing my shirt and scratching my back. When I lifted up my shirt and peered around to see what damage I had done to myself, Barbara was so sympathetic. She came close and looked at the wound, touching my skin softly and saying how much it must hurt. Bravely, like a man, I insisted it didn't hurt, and she continued to insist the opposite. It was our first and only disagreement. Finally, she accepted that it was my wound and I was the one who must know how much it hurt.

Barbara was neat and clean and fair-skinned.

"How old are you?" she asked me.

I stuck out my lower lip and turned my palms upwards. I had no idea what she was talking about.

"I'm six years old," she said. "When's your birthday?"

"What's a birthday?"

"The day you were born."

"I don't know. I'll ask my mother."

They grew beans in the field next to the villa, and because the plants were shorter than us, we crawled over to the wheat field, which would keep us hidden from the house. When I needed to pee, I went off to the edge of the land. Barbara followed and watched as I dropped my pants.

"Why don't you wear knickers?" she asked.

"I don't know."

"I wear beautiful ones," she said, and lifted up her dress.

"All your clothes are beautiful. My shirt's Canadian."

"What does Canadian mean?"

"I don't know. That's what my mother told me."

After a while, Barbara asked me if I could build a house. I assured her that I could and began collecting small stones, and then I did my best to arrange them in an orderly rectangle, big enough for the two of us.

"Where's the kerosene stove, so we can make coffee?" she asked.

I fetched a fairly big stone and placed it in the center of the house. Barbara pretended to light it, and then tore a leaf off a dahlia plant and put it on the stone as the coffee pot. After that she picked two bindweed flowers, one of which she gave to me.

"This is your cup," she said, and pretended to pour the coffee from the leaf.

She sipped her coffee and said it was delicious. I imitated her and sipped mine, too, but bindweed flowers are delicate and our cups quickly withered. She looked at me and asked me if I was going to pee again.

"I don't have any pee left."

"Will you show me your thing again, if I show you mine?" and Barbara lifted her skirt and removed her knickers.

Without replying, I pulled down my trousers, and before she touched me, my thing grew. She laughed. I touched her and said, "Yours is like a big bean flower."

We heard her grandmother calling: "Barbara, where are you?" and quickly dressed.

"I'm here, playing with the boy."

Barbara didn't know my name. Her grandmother arrived and looked at me angrily. She had a face like the evil witches in the stories my granny told.

"Why are you here? How did you get in here?" she shouted. "What do you want?"

Without saying a word, I stomped angrily back toward the fence with Barbara following. As I dropped down to crawl back to my family's property, she raised the barbed wire so I didn't tear my Canadian shirt again.

"Who tore the back of your shirt?" my mother asked when she saw me.

When I told her it was the barbed wire fence between us and the neighbors, she was not pleased. My grandfather laughed and told me the story of the handsome prophet Yusuf, whom the wife of one of Pharaoh's officials tried to seduce. He explained how in the Quran's chapter about the incident, a sign that it was *she* who was harassing *him* was that his shirt was "torn from the back." I asked my grandfather what "seduce" and "harass" meant. He assured me that I'd find out when I was older.

Later, outside, I looked reproachfully up at the sky as my mother did sometimes. "Why did You create this barbed wire that tears shirts, makes backs bleed, and mothers angry?"

"You mustn't go there again," my mother said when, later that evening, I told her everything about playing with Barbara. Well, not everything.

"Why do you call my shirt Canadian?" I asked her.

"Because it came from Canada," my mother said, and then laughed.

"Where's Canada?"

"Far away. I don't know."

I felt frustrated that my mother didn't know everything. She was making fun of our poverty when she said my shirt was Canadian because high-class people wore store-bought clothes. It's true, the fabric of my shirt did come from Canada. However, it didn't enter Syria as a shirt. The cloth arrived as part of a sack containing the flour donated by the World Food Programme. My aunt Jamila said women used to compete with one another, transforming the flour sacks into underwear and other clothing. They preferred the Canadian sacks because they were whiter and the material was thicker and more solid than other flour sacks. She praised my mother's skill in converting the discarded materials into clothes with her Singer sewing machine, and she and my mother exchanged compliments about the various stratagems each devised against poverty. They laughed as they chatted about things that could have made them sad.

We didn't know that Syria had a long history of exporting fine fabrics all over the world, that somehow these never reached our village. We couldn't have afforded them in any case.

Meeting Barbara became quite easy. When she spied me hiding by the fence, she'd sneak over and raise the wire and in I'd go. She seemed to like how I quickly learned that when she turned her back to me, I should undo her zipper. When someone called for Barbara from the villa, especially her grandmother, I'd slide back under the wire and go home. Along the fence, we played bride and bridegroom, and I made Barbara bangles and a necklace of white daisies. Near the high-growing wheat, where the outline of our play-house still lay, we played the game of the soldier returning from battle. This is when I brought her back jewelry and trinkets from shops near the frontline. And under the shade of a huge apricot tree, we played doctor and patient, reversing roles from time to time. I never recovered so fast in any clinic, nor enjoyed the healing process so much as at the hands of Doctor Barbara.

Barbara and I were under the tree, touching each other's things, when we heard an angry voice: "Barbara, what are you doing?" We started like two young gazelles being attacked by a predator, and I truly felt we were. We looked up and there was her grandmother glaring at us. Grabbing me by the ear, she shouted, "I'll roast you alive, you little bastard!" I freed myself from the old woman's grip and went crying to my mother. When I told her what happened, she was livid.

"You've shamed us in front of everyone. Do you know what it could mean if her father decides to take revenge? He might sack your grandfather from the asphalt company."

Barbara's grandmother complained to my mother about my "disgusting" behavior. My mother promised she would take a hot iron to me, a painful punishment that some members of the older generation still believed in, but she never carried out her promise.

A few days later, when she'd calmed down, I asked her why the people in our village were quite happy for the bulls and cows to play bride and bridegroom in front of us, but if we played the same game, they grabbed us by the ear and said it was shameful. She said that cows have calves and give us milk when they play that game.

"Fine. Barbara and I will play bull and cow, and I'll ask her to give birth to a small calf."

My mother tried to hide her laughter, but all the same, still threatened to beat the living daylights out of me if I ever went near Barbara again. So, Barbara and I changed our meeting place and became more careful, which made the anticipation of our playtimes more exciting.

After a while, although I didn't understand the real reason at the time, Barbara was allowed to visit our house, and even her mother, the mistress of the village's mansion, came for coffee with my mother. I suppose it was odd, but back then I didn't question it. After all, I could now openly see my favorite friend, and instead of my mother threatening punishment, I caught her looking between me and Barbara and smiling.

Fadwa was also my neighbor; she had wild hair, dusty clothes, and epileptic fits, so her mother kept a close eye on her. If she went out of sight of their front door, we used to hear her mother calling frantically, "Fadwaaaa, where are you? Fadwaaa, come home!"

And then Fadwa found out I was spending time with Barbara.

"Barbara isn't our neighbor, but we're hers," Fadwa said to me.

"What?"

"She doesn't play with us or even look at us."

"She looks at me."

"No, no, no. Listen. We're neighbors. She's not. Do you understand?"

"No."

"Because you're stupid. Neighbors should play with you and give you apricots off their trees."

"You've never given me a single apricot."

"You don't understand anything. Do we have an apricot tree like the one in Barbara's garden? Idiot!"

"Why do you call me that?"

"Because you're a bastard."

"You're a bitch."

"Fuck you."

This time Fadwa's mother appeared before the hitting started. She grabbed the screaming girl's hand and dragged her away kicking and swearing.

CHAPTER 16

GEOGRAPHY AND GALILEO
DESTROYED MY PIETY

I stood in front of the mirror with Akram, Nadir, and Bahjat, my maternal cousins and childhood friends, laughing as we admired the coffee dreg mustaches decorating our upper lips. It was a work day, and our parents were either out in the fields or at their jobs at the asphalt company. So, dreaming of being older, as many little boys do, we dug our fingers into the Turkish coffee pot and smeared our upper lips with wet coffee dregs. The oldest of us was eight and the youngest six.

My aunt, Umm Bahjat, appeared out of nowhere and, embarrassed to let her see our impatient efforts to become adults, we quickly wiped our mustaches on our sleeves. She pretended to be angry, telling us we shouldn't use our shirtsleeves to wipe our noses, or our mustaches. But she couldn't suppress a laugh that burst out of her and filled her one-room home like an invisible songbird.

"You'll grow up and have your own mustaches, inshallah," she promised.

I had often looked in the mirror and dreamed of possessing a real mustache, and when I didn't see a single hair sprouting, I'd raise my eyes to the sky and urge God to grant me upper lip hair. The mustache I admired the most in the world was my grandfather's. I didn't know how to say that his bright-white mustache was such a fitting symbol for him, a man who was a mixture of kindness, humility, dignity, and wisdom, but I was somehow aware of all of that without being able to put it into words. Indeed, in my mind's eye, I had often imagined my own upper lip full with the same bristly white sign of manhood.

When I was nine, and God hadn't granted me my own mustache yet, the rites of religion seemed like an alternative way into the world of adults. I therefore resolved to join my father and grandfather at Ramadan and fast like them, winning their sympathy and admiration for sticking to it that first year. We relied on our Japanese-made National Panasonic radio to tell us when to eat the early-dawn Suhoor, which is the day's last meal before daybreak, and then later when it was time in the evening for Futoor, the literal translation being "breakfast." Also, just after Suhoor, I would wait with anticipation for the radio to announce, "Now we are going over to an outside broadcast brought to you from the great Umayyad Mosque in Damascus," and I'd listen to praises of the Prophet sung by the most famous religious singer in Damascus, Tawfiq al-Munjid.

As I pursued the devout life, it seemed that the more I learned about God and religion, the more questions I had. My grandfather explained what he could to me, but his answers were evasive when it came to his Alawite doctrine. I only understood years later that part of this sect's principles was not to indoctrinate children until they could make their own decisions. All the same, Jaddi was the one source I had to consult about many important things: weighty subjects such as existence itself, God, religion, and why the electric light in the asphalt company was so much brighter than the gaslight in our houses. Also, "Why don't you need a match to light that lamp?" My questions extended to the mystery of the radio. I was surprised when I first saw inside it and there were no miniature people. I was searching for the power that ruled over existence, inventions, and mysteries, with God Himself being the greatest unknown.

And then in the third year of primary school, when I was nine, my quest to be a man found another path for information about religion: the printed words within our school's fifth grade religious textbook, *al-Tarbia al-Islamia*, or *Islamic Education*. I was only in third grade, but I could easily read and understand the ideas within it. The words on those pages seemed so certain about what they espoused, both for the real world and religion. I came to accept the text as more reliable and interesting than what I thought of as my grandfather's simplistic explanations. But Jaddi didn't appear to resent this.

When I told him what I had learned from the religious book that day, he would smile and not contradict their teachings. I think he was prouder of the fact that I had learned to read so well at an early age. And then when our teacher, Mr. Hashim Badr, taught us about ritual ablution and prayer, I felt that I had finally found what I had been looking for — concrete practices and rituals. I learned the rituals so well that the knowledge gave me a certain feeling of superiority over my peers. And by accepting that prayer was the holy gateway, I was now experiencing the joy of faith. It was the process through which I could become part of the harmony of elements that made up the world, all arranged by a creator who had brought everything into existence from nothing.

Emboldened, I began to ask about the interpretations of Quranic verses, believing that I now possessed the true knowledge to unlock their mysteries. And if I could do that, I would surely own the universe. I had great confidence in the existence of two times and two spaces. The first time and space was the world that we lived in, one that could cease to exist at any moment. The second was the coming realm of eternal existence, the one where we would be divided into the pious sitting in paradise and the wretched sinners whose torment would be renewed over and over again in hell.

But even with this newfound assurance, I was still aware of good people who suffered, and was left with the question, "You who know everything and ordain people's fates, why do You decree misery for one person and bliss for another?" The teacher called me Sheikh Jamal because I had so many questions about God, the Day of Reckoning, and life after death.

When I told my grandfather that I was going to become a Muslim, he said, "You already are a Muslim. Your father's a Muslim and your mother's a Muslim."

"But we're Alawites."

"Alawites are Muslims," my grandfather said with a frown.

"But you don't do your ablutions or pray like it says in the book of Islamic education. You even pray while you're walking, and sometimes you mutter things I can't understand."

"But God hears and understands me," he said with a smile. When I continued to look serious, he bowed his head and went silent. Then he looked up, and, in an attempt to remove the veil he thought was clouding my mind, he said, "Ritual ablution is an attempt to clean the body. However, I don't think the body can ever be completely cleansed. Even if you washed with all the water in the world, there would still be some dirt deep in your entrails. The important thing is that your soul is clean when you turn to God."

"But you don't face in the direction of the Kaaba in Mecca, and you don't pray five times a day."

"I talk to my Lord all the time, and He knows that if I forget Him for a while, it's because He has willed it. And who told you that God only exists if you're facing the Kaaba? God is present everywhere, north, south, east, and west."

"You don't bow down, and you don't prostrate yourself."

"Humility isn't shown by bowing or prostrating, but by what you revere in your soul. God knows how real your love for Him is, whether you're sitting or standing, or whatever position you happen to be in when you're thinking of Him."

My grandfather used to talk as if God were his personal friend, teacher, and inspiration, the One who knew everything. I admired my grandfather's love for his Lord and his trust in Him. The things Jaddi said never failed to have an effect on me. But the magic of the printed word in my textbooks delivered a surer view of the facts. And I was seduced by the rituals: the Niyya, when you declare your intention is pure before prayer; the ritual ablution; the requirement to face the south; the bowing and the prostration, turning your head to the right and the left to greet the angels or your fellow worshippers.

My grandfather didn't object to my praying the way they told us to, and one of his acquaintances even recommended he buy me a book of prayer that followed the Ja'fari doctrine. This described a sixth-century Shia school of religious thought, and with it I applied myself enthusiastically to learn more about prayer.

Back then, we were still fetching water from the spring. Water pipes still hadn't been extended to reach our houses. One summer's day, when I had to perform the ritual ablution before the late afternoon prayer, the only water in the house was the drinking water in a large earthenware amphora. I ended up spilling a lot of it, and when my mother returned hot and thirsty from the fields, she discovered a map of some unknown country staining the floor.

"Is your Lord happy you're adding to my troubles?" she said angrily. "After a hard day's work, now I have to go to the spring and fetch more water."

"I'll get it, Ummi," I said guiltily, picking up the amphora. But she just grabbed it from me and hoisted it onto her shoulder.

"I wouldn't want to lose this too. You might break it while you're saying the du'a at the end of your prayer," she said, and she set off for the spring.

My mother didn't really mind me praying. She just wanted to have an easier life.

In my fifth year of primary school, when I was eleven, our new teacher was Mr. Nazeer Qadira. He was to teach us every subject in the curriculum. In one class he explained surah ash-shams, the chapter of the Quran that describes how the world is flat. He showed us other verses, describing God laying out the world, how He put hills and mountains on it and mysteriously raised the sky without any pillars to support it. In my mind, I imagined God constructing a blue roof over the world. And then Mr. Qadira began our first geography lesson. For some reason I was scared of this new subject, perhaps because the word seemed strange. *Geography*. As far as I could see, it contained no Arabic root. In this class, Mr. Qadira described how the Earth is a planet in a solar system, part of a single galaxy in a vast universe of billions of galaxies. And instead of there being a sky built without pillars, he talked of an atmosphere surrounding Earth. This is what made the sky look blue.

"Wait, wait, wait, wait!" I interrupted.

My outburst caused everybody to laugh, students and teacher alike, and so I looked down in embarrassment. But then Mr. Qadira gently asked me to stand and say what I had to say.

"If the Earth is a ball that turns around and around, why don't we fall off, or get dizzy?"

Again, the other students laughed, the loudest of them being Sawsan. She was a girl who always made fun of me and called me Warty. This was because I had warts on the backs of both hands.

"Can *you* tell us why we don't fall off the Earth?" the teacher asked her. Now it was her turn to stare at the ground, and for me to gloat and smile. "Do any of you know?" Mr. Qadira asked again.

The whole class was silent. And then Mr. Qadira went to the metal cabinet where we kept the sports equipment. Taking out a basketball, he told us to follow him into the schoolyard.

"Who can bring me an ant?" he asked, and within a minute at least five of us brought him a number of the tiny creatures. "Put them on the ball, like it's the Earth," he said, and, with them aboard, he began to rotate it. "If the Earth were the size of this ball," he said, "people would be much smaller than one of these ants. Has any of them fallen off the ball?"

"No, sir," we answered with one voice.

"Very good. So why don't we fall off planet Earth?"

"Because the ant doesn't fall off the ball," Sawsan answered.

"Because we'd be smaller than an ant if the Earth was the size of this ball," said Murad, wiping his nose on the sleeve of his shirt.

Mr. Qadira chuckled kindly and told us a bit about the law of gravity and that we would come to know more about it when we studied physics in the future. Then, with all of us students standing in a circle around him, he carried on with his lesson about the planet Earth, other planets, and the stars. I listened to what he said, and as he talked, I began to be filled with a mixture of sorrow and disappointment. And then these feelings turned into anger. Suddenly, I felt compelled to defend my faith against this thing called geography.

"But sir, you told us in the class on religion that God made the Earth flat."

"Jamal, don't interrupt me again. It's rude. Come to the staff room after school. I'll explain then."

I joined Mr. Qadira in the staff room after school, and, again, he was very kind.

"Jamal, it's good for you to know what's in both religious books and geography books," he said, and he explained the difference between facts and accepted beliefs. "Just because earthquakes don't happen because the bull holding up the Earth becomes tired and shifts it from horn to horn, does it really do us any harm to know some people believe this?"

"But in Islam . . . I read . . ."

Mr. Qadira put a hand on my shoulder and smiled. "Come, it's late. Let's walk home together. We'll talk."

As we walked and talked, I could feel my world crumbling. And by the time I was home, I was plagued with doubts.

"Jamal, eat," my mother said.

"It's time to eat, not think," my father admonished.

Questions multiplied over the next few weeks, and I became more and more tormented. Had all my faith, the thing that would turn me into a man, merely been an illusion? And how could the religious edifice I'd constructed be rocked by the information in a small geography textbook? As for the other book, how could God say something ambiguous or wrong?

I went to my maternal uncle, Abu Nadim. He wore a stylish modern hat instead of a keffiyeh, and he dressed in a suit and tie. He was my only uncle who bought magazines and newspapers. And he wasn't so religious. Somehow, I knew I could trust him. Perhaps he could explain things in a way that would restore my faith. But he only reinforced my doubts. He gave me a magazine that contained a very long and extensive article about the scholars Copernicus and Galileo. They proved the world was a sphere that revolved both on its axis and around the sun. That had landed them in trouble with their Church leaders and they were condemned as heretics. Abu Nadim told me to take the article home and read it, encouraging me to ask questions with absolutely no inhibitions.

"Think any way you like, nephew," he said, "but avoid having discussions with idiots."

My uncle Abu Nadim
was modern in his
mind and appearance.
His clothes and head
cover were different.

CHAPTER 17

THE RADIO WAR OF 1967

S hortly before the 1967 war with Israel, family and neighbors began gathering at our home to listen to news updates on my grandfather's radio. And in the same way that I wanted to become an adult by growing a mustache and becoming religious, I made it a point to join in enthusiastically when they listened to the news. But to tell the truth, I really didn't understand what was being described at first, and so my mind wandered. On one particular evening, my uncle Abu Nadim had commented several times, "The specter of war is hovering over our heads." What exactly did that mean? I had no clue. Looking up to see what was hovering there, all I saw were little moths flitting about the kerosene lamp on a mantel.

"Are those the specters of war Abu Nadim is talking about?" I asked my mother. She looked at me, then at the moths, and made a *tst* sound through her teeth, effectively dismissing my stupidity.

Still bored and wanting my presence acknowledged, I looked to my father. Abi seemed very intent and worried about what the person in the radio was saying. Now, the first thing that came to mind when I looked at him in those days was how many of my schoolmates whose fathers worked at the quarry frequently had money in their fists. I never did. I suppose this is why I blurted out, "Why don't you work in the asphalt quarry like other fathers?" I thought my question reasonable, and so my father's fierce reaction was totally unexpected. In an uncharacteristically loud voice, which everybody in the room could hear, he answered: "I don't want to take orders from anyone.

I want to remain master of my own fate. Go to work because I love my job, and come home when I wish." And then he angrily batted away one of the flying specters whose wings brushed his face. He apparently felt it necessary to further justify his life choices, and to others beside me. "Agriculture is the most honorable of occupations," he bellowed. "The peasant eats from the sweat of his brow, and others also eat from the sweat of his brow." And then, even louder, he repeated a sentence I already knew by heart. "People can do without asphalt or plastic, but they can't live without food!"

My father was probably responding to those relatives who criticized him for insisting on working on the farm and therefore not having cash from a regular paycheck. They said it like he was being lazy. But I knew he spent more time in his fields than the workers spent at the quarry, including the time they spent on their own little vegetable plots. But because money was a necessity for some things, on top of his farm work, Abi was obliged to trade in cereals, timber, or olive oil for cash. But for all the criticism leveled at him by friends and family, our house was never short of food, or alcoholic beverages, something that being Alawite allows. And it was some of those same people who criticized him the most who came regularly to drink his Al Rayan arak, Syria's national drink, and eat my mother's meze, a Syrian type of tapas, during the harsh mountain winters.

As for the other side of keeping a family alive, which meant cleaning, preparing the food the farm provided, and generally commanding a small army of kids, my mother was in charge. Besides making shirts from flour sacks, this included recycling worn garments. As an example, my father's trousers with holes at the knees were cut down to make trousers for me, and frayed shirt collars were reversed and became like new. For our pajamas, Ummi would buy end-of-bolt fabrics and sew them herself. This meant my father, brothers, sisters, mother, and I all ended up wearing the same patterns. I remember the mornings when all of us sat around the breakfast table in identical pajamas festooned with small orange and blue flowers. Ummi wasn't especially pleased about the way we were dressed, nor was she convinced by my father's philosophy of life, especially on the topic of money. This was most evident when the representative from the Singer agency arrived from the city to collect the monthly installment for her sewing machine. She was then often obliged to borrow money from Aunt Jamila. But my father didn't seem concerned. Or at least he didn't act like it. In his view, life on a farm didn't come to a standstill just because we were behind with an installment or had to borrow a liter of kerosene.

During the prewar radio gatherings, our guests sat on the floor of our two-room house, resting their backs against the straw bales distributed along the inside walls. My mother made tea for them, asking me to count how many people there were.

"Four keffiyehs, a scarf, a hat, and three uncovered heads," I reported.

Indulging me, as my mother set out the glasses on her wicker tray, she'd group them, saying, "These glasses are for the keffiyehs, this one for the scarf, this for the hat, and these are for the bare heads," and she'd smile.

With the possibility of war being talked about for some months, the news became so dominant in our lives that we began calling the room we gathered in "the radio room." If a statement from Ahmed Saeed, director of the famous Cairo radio station known as the Voice of the Arabs, was being broadcast, or if a speech by Egypt's president, Abdel Nasser, came on, all the men paused their conversations, which were mostly about their ancestors and their children, their harvests, livestock, and the blends of tobacco they smoked. The women stopped their own discussions on cooking, their hard lives, pregnancy, and childbearing. I participated in the solemn silences, as it seemed to be required.

With their eyes wide open and leaning forward as they listened, the men in the radio room drank in the Egyptian announcer's confident voice and polished performance. I asked my mother why the women didn't crane their necks to listen to Ahmed Saeed's statements like the men.

"Because we're not so stupid," she replied.

I stretched my neck and then relaxed it to see if it made any difference to the sound quality.

When Ahmed Saeed's words poured out of the radio with promises of how Nasser would bestow an Arab paradise upon us, joy spread over the listeners' faces, their eyes glowing at the impact of Saeed's stirring use of language.

"The announcer and I have the very same names," my grandfather crowed proudly.

Ahmed Saeed also talked about the Arab nation, describing it as torn and fractured by colonialism. As I was a child with a wild imagination, and

I suppose because the Arabic word for nation is feminine and colonialism is masculine, the image of a female being threatened by a mythical beast called Colonialism popped into my head. I also took from the words coming out of the radio that colonialism meant modern weapons and soldiers who were cowardly and cruel. Meanwhile, Abdel Nasser seemed to me like one of the traditional Arab folk heroes I grew up hearing about. There was Diab bin Ghanem, who could kill one hundred men with a single swipe of his sword, or the famous Antar, a Black man who performed Herculean tasks to win the hand of his white cousin. And al-Zir Salim: he captured a lion as a gift for his sister-in-law — when she in fact sent him on the quest intending that the lion kill him. And when the radio talked of missiles made in Egypt with names like the Challenger, the Victor, and al-Nasser, (named after our illustrious leader), in my mind, I pictured Nasser as a mythical superhero, a mighty blacksmith at his forge, sleeves rolled up, manufacturing both swords and rockets.

When the announcer finished talking, the men in our house praised his sharp intelligence and deep knowledge, and then went back to singing the praises of the different blends of tobacco they'd recently discovered. They passed around their tobacco tins and rolling papers and began a collective smoke. They did it with so much enthusiasm that it wasn't long before a solid cloud hung in the air above them. I was surprised by the thickness of the haze the people had made out of their cigarettes, when my father asked: "If the colonialist soldiers are cowards, how did they manage to gain control of most of the world?"

"They have modern weapons," answered my uncle Abu Nadim, "the crutch of cowards."

"The brave need weapons too," my father responded. "As you yourself said a couple of days ago, a war isn't a round of arm wrestling."

Abu Hawla, our own local storyteller, with his mustaches curled like an Ottoman sultan's, cleared his throat before recounting one of his recent flights of fancy.

"Nasser is currently engaged in manufacturing a smart bullet," he began, and then he gave his mustache a twirl. "You fire it in the air, and it automatically searches for those sons of bitches who oppress us . . . and then relieves us of them."

The statement was so foolish that not one of the usually quick tongues in the crowd could find words to shout out a terse criticism. The uncharacteristic silence was finally broken by my uncle Jabr.

"Jamal, how about you?" he asked me. "You're still no taller than a fuzzy baby chick. Why are you listening to the radio?"

"To understand," I said with as much conviction as Abu Hawla.

"So, what have you come to understand?"

"We have to hate colonialism."

"Why?"

"Because it's the seven-headed serpent . . . and it's going to bite the nation."

"Who is the nation?"

"The old woman who . . . no . . . no. I mean she's the big mother."

"Where does she live?"

"In the Voice of the Arabs at Ahmed Saeed's house. And Abdel Nasser brings her food every day."

Everybody laughed and my uncle gave me half a Syrian pound for a reward, a sum I usually received only on feast days.

A few days later, on the morning of June 5, my grandfather turned on the radio. And when he heard the news, he turned it up loud. People ran in from the fields and crouched around the receiver. The war had begun. Jaddi even sent me to buy new batteries. "We don't want to miss out on the joy of victory because of flat batteries," he said.

Statements from the military spokesman came thick and fast. The men in the room cheered like football fans after their team scores. The news reports described repeatedly how our Arab armies were advancing, how the Israeli enemy planes were being shot down, and how our air defense systems were forcing them to flee. I didn't understand how planes could flee, because in my mind, fleeing was connected to legs and running fast.

During the first three days, the war seemed more like a radio play than something real. When the military man made a grand statement, our assembled family and neighbors greeted it with jubilation and cheers, and I joined in.

But on the third night, all the people of the village found themselves pouring out of their homes to see a very strange sight. The sky in the west was aglow. It looked as if lights were shining on the nearby hill where the domed tomb of the venerated Sheikh Hakim stood. According to my paternal grand-mother, he was "one of the brave and pious saints of God." But there were no brave saints in the village that night.

"The war has reached us," declared the distraught village mayor. His oldest son, Nasr, served in the navy out of Latakia. "He's dead, he's dead, my son is dead," he wailed.

As we watched another flare lighting up the sky, Abu Salah began to sob too. His son, Salah, was a soldier stationed in the same area. And as another brilliant light streaked through the heavens, he shouted that they were the scattered remains of his boy.

My paternal uncle Ibrahim brought out a big Polish rifle from when he was a trainee in the People's Army, and my father grabbed it and began marching determinedly toward the saintly sheikh's tomb. Instantly terrified, I flung my arms around his legs and was dragged along crying.

"The gun belongs to Uncle Ibrahim!" I howled. "Give it back to him, Abi, give it back!"

And then there was Adnan, a young blond farmer in the village. He had attended a single civil defense class, and so he knew what he was talking about. He started ordering the crowd to extinguish all the lights and paint the windows of their home blue, repeating firmly, "This is no joke! This is no joke. This is a war, and war requires vigilance."

"Where are we going to get blue paint at this time of night?" a sarcastic voice in the crowd asked.

Abu Siddiq, an older, quiet peasant, insisted the women and children should take shelter in the caves and grottoes, and immediately Jamil Ismail, who had just predicted the Israelis would be occupying the village in a few minutes, herded his family up the mountain to a nearby cave.

It was only half an hour later that the radio told us Israeli aircraft had actually attacked Latakia, which was about twenty-five miles away. "But our air defenses forced them to flee," the announcer added. Ustadh Yunis, a well-dressed man who worked as an office clerk at the quarry, explained that the bright lights we had seen weren't anywhere nearby, but in Latakia. They were huge military flares fired by our artillery to light up the sky and expose the enemy aircraft. This allowed our Syrian anti-aircraft guns to shoot them down.

The following day, we went back to listening to the military spokesman's proclamations and patriotic songs. One song's lyrics proclaimed, "Whoever is flying a Mirage jet will flee from the ones flying MiGs." Of course, this was supposed to describe the Israelis being chased away by the Eagles of the Arabs, our heroic Arab pilots. It was written by a popular radio singer, the woman rumored to be the president's lover, Jamila Nassour, known as Karawan. The whole country knew the words to her song's refrain: "It costs me five piastres to wipe out the invaders at my country's borders." Five piastres was the price of a bullet in those days.

After listening to the fiery statements of Ahmed Saeed, my uncle Abu Nadim regularly repeated the story of how the British House of Commons refused to allow the famous announcer to visit Britain with Nasser in 1965. Smiling broadly, Abu Nadim would recall how Nasser rejected the demand of the House of Commons, and this had obliged the British prime minister, Harold Wilson, to deliver a speech accepting the broadcaster's visit. "A man in a thousand," was how my uncle described Ahmed Saeed.

On the sixth morning of the war, the military spokesman's tone seemed to change. I really didn't understand right away but watched my grandfather furiously switch the radio from station to station. And then I understood what every station on the dial was confirming. The Arab armies had been defeated. For the first time in my life, I saw a tear glistening on Jaddi's cheek. This is when I began to understand that war is not a match between two rival sports teams.

The reactions of those who'd shared the radio war with us changed too.

Ahmad Abbas came over and told us how he had smashed his own radio, all the while cursing the "motherfucking inventor" of the "treacherous instrument." My grandfather contented himself with contemptuously addressing his radio as a "lie machine."

Abu Hawla mockingly reminded my uncle Abu Nadim how he had just a few days earlier praised Ahmed Saeed. "The Egyptian announcer deceived us. You said he was worth a thousand men. He's not worth a fart. And that Abdel Nasser, he's a fafush, a big loser."

Not long after this, Ahmed Saeed resigned as director of the Voice of the Arabs. Some say he was fired as the fall guy for Nasser. My grandfather stopped reminding people that he had the same names as the Egyptian. And Jaddi was no longer addicted to listening to the news. But when he did listen, he would shout at the voice in the box, "How do we know you're not lying?"

CHAPTER 18

HAIFA AND THE
BREAKER OF SHACKLES

After the defeat of the Arab armies, the Baathists in Syria adopted the slogan, "Erasing the Effects of the Aggression," which was code for nationalizing foreign-owned businesses. France was especially targeted, as the Israelis had flown the French Mirage fighter jet, a major factor in the Arab countries' defeat. Among the measures taken was the dismissal of Barbara's father from his post as manager in the asphalt company. This resulted in Barbara and her family having to leave the elegant French-style villa.

Standing by the fence as silent as a mountain goat on a rocky precipice, I watched men carrying furniture to a large truck. After they shut its tailgate and secured a big blue tarp over the furniture, they were ready to leave. I then watched the family climb into their white Volkswagen Beetle, or, as we call it more aptly in Syria, the Tortoise. Barbara, wearing a red dress similar to the one she wore when I first saw her, sat on her mother's lap. And as the little white car followed the truck, I had the overwhelming feeling that I must do something. I must recover what was being torn away from me. I ran behind the two vehicles as fast as my legs would carry me. But the VW, apparently not as slow as its Syrian name suggests, soon descended on the road before disappearing into the woods. I kept running until I was close to the place where the Shepherd's Distraction had left me by myself, and there I sat on the ground and wept bitterly. Looking up at the sky, I once again begged the Lord to have mercy on me. I was only asking for a small kindness: that Barbara would come back, and I'd have a reason to pass under the barbed wire fence again. I visited the magic house a few days later, but it looked very desolate despite its splendor and charm.

Barbara never came back. However, her absence opened my eyes to the existence of other zippers in the world. It wasn't long before I discovered another nice neighbor, Haifa, and soon found that she, too, liked playing in the fields and in the shade of trees. One day she led me to what was called Jalfa Cave, which was carpeted in soft reddish-brown earth. That little cavern became a home where we played the game of the returning traveler. This required me to go on a voyage and come home again within a few minutes, bringing Haifa souvenirs of my journey. I would present her with wildflowers, leaves, or choice stones, for which she would express her surprise and gratitude. After arranging the stones and other treasures, we talked about my exhausting journey and how I'd overcome evil spirits and wild animals, and then we began touching each other. I remember Haifa smelt like grass and herbs.

One day, while engrossed in our childish games, we looked up and found ourselves being spied on by four boys who were out on the land guarding their families' cattle. Haifa hurriedly put her clothes back on, and, provoked by the boys' laughter, I shouted, "This is our cave. Leave us alone!" but they just kept laughing.

The next day, our story was on the lips of the whole village, including those of Fadwa, the crazy tomboy. When she saw me, she yelled, "Haifa? You bastard!" and picked up a stone and hurled it at me.

My father ignored the matter, even when he heard my mother shouting that what I had done was shameful and wrong. She looked at me angrily as I wrung my hands in embarrassment. From that day, a question remained stuck in my throat: what was shameful and wrong about what we'd done? I didn't dare ask at the time because my mother's eyes were brimming with reproach.

When more than a quarter of a century had passed since the scandal of Jalfa Cave, and after it had faded into oblivion along with much else, I had cause to remember Haifa and Barbara. As production manager of a publishing house, I was reviewing a poetry manuscript submitted by a young poet who chose the subversive pseudonym of "Shackle Breaker." The manuscript raised questions about the lack of sexual rights for women in Syria. I paused at a text in which she described how her thighs had been branded with hot metal skewers. This was because her mother caught her playing doctor with the neighbor's son in their apartment building's stairwell. When we met, I asked her about it, saying I had escaped a similar punishment.

"My mother led me into the kitchen," Shackle Breaker recounted. "She tied my hands behind my back with her hijab and bound my legs with the cloth belt of her long coat. Then she heated a metal skewer on the kerosene stove and, when it glowed, held it right in front of me. 'Think carefully about this,' my mother said. After the torture ended, and I'd stopped screaming, she brought out a salve and bandages.

"'Why are you treating the burns that you caused?' I asked tearfully.

"'Because I'm a mother,' she answered. 'I burned you because I care about you, and now I'm healing you because I care about you.'"

CHAPTER 19

A SMALL BLACK RADIO

"Jasim Alwan has died."

The snow seems to be floating aimlessly between the sky and earth of Kingston, while Rufaida protests about the chaos of my papers making our dining table an unfit place to eat. The man's death doesn't change that. His death is merely passing news on my laptop's screen.

"We're all going to die one day, Colonel . . ." I say it as if I'm addressing the dead man from six thousand miles away. "Whereas, snow and tidy tables, as well as tables strewn with papers, magazines, pens, and nothingness will live on in the world. No, nothingness can't be untidy. Nothingness is merely a concept. But if nothingness can be conceived, I guess nothingness does exist, so perhaps it can be untidy." I stop and stare like I've just listened to the ramblings of a pedantic idiot. What's the man's death got to do with this early morning philosophical nonsense?

According to the Gregorian calendar, we're at the beginning of 2018. I still see *Happy New Year* signs on some windows, doors, and shop fronts. The announcement of the old army officer's death has reminded me that he was alive. "How would he have been able to die if he hadn't been alive?" My philosophical foolishness continues, but it does conjure up memories. How did this man fit into my life? I never met him, but I did come to possess a little black box that once was his.

My paternal uncle Salman was a driver in the police force, and at the beginning of every summer, he used to visit us with his family. In the summer of 1971, I was twelve years old. I had just finished primary school and was responsible for selling the fruit and vegetables we produced on our land at the market all the way in Latakia. The market was closed on Fridays, so I'd spend the day with my family, and it was on one of these Fridays that Uncle Salman's family was visiting. I was on the floor with my younger cousin Haidar, teaching him to count from one to ten, when Uncle Salman began to speak in his usual affable manner.

"Today Jamal has not left us to go to the market," he said. I looked up to see him smiling at me playing with his boy. "Jamal is a blessing wherever he is, a rose that gives off its perfume without asking anything in return." I was embarrassed by this praise, even though I knew he was generous with his compliments to everyone. Uncle Salman loved eloquence and tried to surprise us with verses he had memorized. It was as if he'd just arrived minutes before from the ancient market of Ukaz, where poetry contests were held for over a thousand years. "Where will our rose study next year?" he asked me.

"In the school in Wata al-Khan."

"You will walk for an hour to get there and an hour to come home in a winter whose rain will chill you to the bone in seconds."

"A fate I accept."

My uncle clasped me to his chest, as if I had just somehow proved myself a genius. Perhaps it was my use of the word "fate" that pleased him. "But it's not an inevitable fate," he said mysteriously.

He then took me by the hand and led me to my grandfather and father, who were relaxing outside. In no time at all, a miniature family council assembled under the mulberry tree. I stood watching the men of my family talking about me. My uncle proposed I go to preparatory school, seventh to ninth grade, in the town where he lived, Annaza. The school there was only a few minutes away from his home, and he said the teaching staff were definitely better than those at the Wata al-Khan school. And yes, there was a good bed, bedding, and a heater in what would be my room. It took no more than ten minutes for my father and Jaddi to agree to my uncle's suggestion.

"Anyone with children and grandchildren like mine should be proud," Jaddi proclaimed, and then they carried on chatting about other things.

A few weeks later I was in the town of Annaza, thinking that not one of them had asked me whether I wanted to be there or not. I missed my mother, siblings, and childhood friends. But I suppose being weaned off village life was a good thing, or perhaps not, given that it started the adventure of what became my life.

I had just put glue on the back of a picture of Abdel Nasser and stuck it on the cover of my history book when Uncle Salman came into my new bedroom. He was accompanied by a tall, broad-shouldered man who sported a white beard and thick glasses. They made him look quite dignified.

I was listening to Fayrouz, my favorite singer, but when they came in I turned off the black radio my uncle had given me. "Jamal, this is Mr. Abu Suhayl, the oldest communist in Annaza." My uncle said this with a laugh.

"Pleased to meet you, Jamal," Abu Suhayl said courteously, and then he too laughed. "I was a Marxist before Noah's flood."

"But your Marx hadn't been born yet," my uncle teased.

"Communism *is* the dawn of humankind," replied Abu Suhayl.

"And what do you mean by that?" my uncle asked playfully.

"Back then, the Earth was for everybody. Nobody owned anything. Sound familiar?"

"Come on," Uncle chided. "Humankind began with the eating of an apple."

"Oh, well, if you want to bring religion into the conversation, please don't forget to mention Cain's killing of his brother."

"That was God's will."

"So, He wanted us to be descended from a killer?"

"Isn't that better than your stories claiming we're descended from apes?"

Their conversation was like a game of ping-pong, and I looked back and forth as the short sentences, accompanied by affectionate guffaws, ricocheted between the two. Abu Suhayl then glanced at what I had been doing on my table.

"Isn't that Abdel Nasser?" he asked, referring to the picture I'd glued to my schoolbook.

"Yes, this is the Arab nation's lost leader," I said, radiating confidence about my hero.

"And where did you get that photo of the Arab nation's lost leader?" he asked with a glint of sarcasm.

"From the police magazine."

"The best place for it." Then he laughed and began reciting the famous speech of Khalid ibn al-Walid, a military leader from when Islam was conquering the Middle East in the seventh century. "By God, there is not an inch of my body that does not bear the lash of the whip or the kick of the boot of this lost leader of the nation."

Was this man implying what I thought he was? I looked at this older friend of my uncle, someone to whom I obviously had to show respect. "But. . . but Nasser wouldn't harm an ant." I said it almost like a question.

That's when Abu Suhayl tapped me on the shoulder to get my full attention. And then, looking directly into my eyes, he continued to recite: "The days will tell you what you didn't know before. The one you refused to provide for will bring you news."

"That's by Tarafa ibn al-Abd," I exclaimed, flaunting my knowledge.

"Did they teach Tarafa's poetry at school?"

"No, I read it in a book of the Mu'allaqaat. My maternal uncle gave it to me."

"Well, if you like reading, I'm going to give you some books."

"Sure. But did you meet Abdel Nasser? Are you saying he beat you?"

"No, I didn't have the pleasure of meeting the lieutenant colonel," he said, again sarcastically. "But I met his jailers and torturers. They flogged me because I was one of the heretics who wouldn't accept the abolition of parliament and the dissolution of political parties. And I had the effrontery to object to the destruction of Syria."

"You're being unfair to Nasser," I protested.

Abu Suhayl laughed uproariously. "Unfair? Maybe. I guess it was unfair of me to tire out his torturers and leave them dripping with sweat."

My uncle and his friend went into the main room, leaving me standing in confusion. This man had provoked me. After the war, I'd heard Abu Hawla and others calling Nasser a big loser, but many people in our village were still his supporters. They preserved his heroic image by putting the blame on his corrupt entourage. My cousin Anan convinced me that certain Syrian high officials had failed to carry out the battle plan drawn up by Nasser. "A military genius," he said. "And what's more," the teenage Anan added, "some traitors gave secret intelligence to Moshe Dayan, the Israeli defense minister . . . in person!"

The snow is still floating aimlessly between the sky and earth of Kingston. And as I recall these memories, I don't know if my cousin was inventing these excuses or passing on what he'd heard from other Nasserites.

But now as an adult, when I think back to the time after Nasser resigned the presidency because of his military defeat, it comes to me: that's when we started hearing patriotic songs being played on Jaddi's radio again. One of the songs described Nasser as the Arabs' only remaining hope and demanded his return. Not long after this, we heard a newly appointed radio announcer describe how millions of Egyptians had taken to the streets calling for his reinstatement. So, in the end Nasser "humbly" returned to office.

And then, as fate would dictate, it wasn't too many months later that the people in the village once again gathered around the radio, this time to hear the report of Nasser's death. They listened, not believing. It was as if Nasser could never die. A few weeks later, the radio was again the most important source of news in our village, reporting on the successful coup led by the Syrian defense minister, Hafez al-Assad.

Abu Suhayl didn't stay long with my uncle that first day I met him. He said goodbye to me kindly, promising to give me a wonderful novel to read. Resting one hand on my shoulder and gesturing out into the street with the other, he said, "In this town everyone knows where I live. You can ask anybody. I'll be waiting for your visit."

After he'd gone, I asked my uncle about parliament and communism. Suddenly, the friendly banter about such matters disappeared. He must have reserved that exclusively for his friend.

"Jamal, it is better for us to avoid taking an interest in politics. You must focus on your studies. You could be a highly regarded member of society one day." He paused, and then went on, "We are neutral. We don't like or dislike any politician. We adapt to every situation. The hand we can't bite, we kiss. And then we pray it will break on its own. Nasserites, communists, Baathists . . . not one of them will give you a single Syrian piastre when you need it. They'll even take whatever's in your pocket. Please, you must keep away from politics."

To demonstrate how it always turns out badly for those involved in political activity, he told me how, as a young policeman, he'd taken part in a raid on the house where a very prominent Nasserite army officer was hiding. This was when I first heard the name of Colonel Jasim Alwan.

"Why did you arrest him?"

"We received orders to arrest him, so we arrested him," he said indifferently. "We didn't ask why." After a pause, he continued, "A special court presided over by Salah al-Dalli sentenced him to death. He tried to be president of the country, but he almost ended up at the end of the hangman's rope. If Presidents Nasser, Ben Bella, and Aref hadn't intervened . . ." he made a slicing motion across his throat. "They all phoned and convinced President Amin al-Hafiz to stop his execution. After all, al-Hafiz and Alwan were old friends from military college. He was spared, but many of his coconspirators were executed as a warning to others. We looted the contents of the house," he said, "including the little black transistor radio. The head of the patrol gave it to me as a souvenir."

By the end of my uncle's story, he seemed satisfied that his cautionary tale of Jasim Alwan was enough to convince me that politics was not a road to travel.

When I lay in my bed that night, I clicked on the little black radio on my nightstand. I wanted to listen to music. But as my fingers touched the radio's knob, the image of Alwan turning that very same dial popped into my mind. And in that imaginary scene, I saw and heard Alwan listening to the same contradictory information that I had heard coming from Jaddi's radio in 1967. I wanted to know more.

While I am making coffee at home in the new world, I find myself addressing the dead man: "I heard your name for the first time from my uncle. I liked you, I guess just because you were a loyal Nasserite, and Nasser was loyal to you. He saved you from the hangman's noose, allowed you to live comfortably in Egypt. He gave you the title of Minister and had you remain active in politics. And so, the little black radio became a spiritual and historical touchstone. From it, to me, to your hand touching the knob and your hand grasping Nasser's; it was a direct link to the man who my younger self believed died before he could prove the extraordinary heroism latent in him."

I wanted to know more, and if Uncle Salman wouldn't talk to me about it, maybe Abu Suhayl would. He seemed to have a breadth of knowledge about the time, and, although I didn't like the way he mocked Nasser, something in me couldn't resist the desire to visit him, even against my uncle's wishes.

Abu Suhayl received me in his elegant room, and we sat together beneath pictures of the communist icons he introduced me to. I noticed that they all had beards, not just mustaches — Marx, Engels, Lenin, Guevara — so I got the idea that all communists had to have beards.

"Hey, you're starting to get a mustache, becoming a young man. The greatest stage of life," Abu Suhayl observed with fatherly smile. "Have a seat, please."

The man listened patiently to an impassioned speech I had prepared in my head, a jumble of ideas about Arab unity; the tripartite aggression of France, the UK, and Israel against Egypt; Nasser's heroism in the nationalization of the Suez Canal; the building of the High Dam; and finally the treachery of his corrupt entourage. But calmly and with immense patience, Abu Suhayl helped me understand the role of the United States and the Soviet Union in Nasser's victory in 1956, and the dangers of political repression. He explained, too, that what I'd read about the sinking of the French battleship *Jean Bart* by the Egyptian navy was just propaganda.

"Propaganda?" I asked. "What's that?" And he explained.

"So, Jamal, don't be a victim of propaganda," he concluded, and as I nodded in agreement, I thought about the two radios and the words that had come out of them.

Over the course of many clandestine meetings, Abu Suhayl freed me from my blind, sentimental belief in Nasser's vision of a united Arab nation, a belief that, like most of the population, I had picked up from the radio. He told me about the repression suffered by those who spoke out during the period of Syria's union with Egypt, and how secular political opponents such as Farajallah el-Helou in Syria and Shuhdi Atiya al-Shafi in Egypt were tortured to death. Nasser's agents in Syria actually dissolved Farajallah's body in acid to cover up his murder. Abu Suhayl also showed me how our Middle East leaders had features in common with Hitler, Mussolini, Franco, and the Colonels' regime in Greece.

But he never failed to praise Soviet heroism and Stalin's greatness, and it seemed as if he would have liked me to replace Nasser's photo with Stalin's. However, the critical thinking he was teaching me had an odd effect, which he couldn't have intended. It made me realize I must not accept any leader at face value, and so I smiled and nodded when Abu Suhayl praised the Russian leader. Still, I came to love the time I spent in that room and most of the education I received there. And I especially enjoyed the smiles of the Komsomol girls from the *Novosti* news publications pinned to my mentor's wall. Later I began to study Stalin on my own, and saw how he really was a tyrant, too.

Some weeks after my first visit with Abu Suhayl, my uncle saw me tearing the photo of Nasser off my schoolbook. "That's good," he said. "We don't take sides. We just look out for ourselves."

The winds are still playing with the snow that floats aimlessly in the sky over Kingston. I tidy the papers and other things lying on the dining table, only to spread them around again, as if the table is just a detail in the broader scheme of things that I am struggling to understand, like Solomon in the Book of Ecclesiastes.

CHAPTER 20

THE ROAD TO DAMASCUS

Three years after meeting Abu Suhayl, I was in tenth grade at high school, living back in my home village of Kfarieh, where I helped establish a Marxist discussion group. We thought that understanding Marxism would help us bring freedom to our country and the world and rid us of dictators.

Our diverse group included my cousin Barakat, who was studying in the Faculty of Agriculture at Tishreen University in Latakia; Jihad Annabeh, who worked in the engine factory; Bahjat Shabow, who was still in ninth grade at school; and Wadha Hamisha, the headmistress of the primary school in Wata al-Khan. I firmly believed that the five of us were preparing ourselves to take part in changing the world by reading a few books. I liked *The Communist Manifesto* because it didn't take long to read and was easy to understand, not to mention the fact that I was fascinated by the irony in it. When our group discussed Engels's unfinished book, *Dialectics of Nature*, I felt that great thinkers were helping us see things we didn't notice, even though those things were right under our noses. The many Marxist groups, of which ours was just one, were a growing phenomenon in Syria, and from them arose the organization called the Communist Labor League. At the time, I thought we were starting to arrange the world so it would be full of justice, love, and freedom.

Forty years after the League was established, and then taken apart piece by piece by the regime, I was asked about it by Ray Argyle. He's the person who chaired the committee that brought us to our new life.

"During my long stay in prison," I explained to him, "I got to know most members of the League. After all, most of us had been arrested and spent years together in various jails. And I had plenty of time to think about events, mull them over, turn them upside down and inside out. Among us were dreamers, knights in shining armor, puritans, Don Quixotes, and a fair number of prophets and minor saints, if you looked for them. But it would be hard to find a pragmatist among us. That would be just one person who could define what our mission should be and come up with a plan of how to integrate Marx's lofty philosophies into a practical working government structure, or how to make it happen.

"We didn't understand the magnitude of the power imbalance between our naïve citizenry and the international powers intervening in our country. Many of us were just focused on the injustices happening and the idea of the future time we thought we were creating. Like lovers and Sufis, we were blinded to reality by our individual passions and delusions. We bore the superior attitude of those who think they know all the answers. We were assured that it reflected the beauty of our souls like the river reflecting the image of Narcissus."

"You're quite the poet," Ray teased when I finished what had been, in retrospect, my overblown monologue.

Our Marxist group had been in place for two years when I finished my baccalaureate exams back in my rural high school. But I did not do well enough to fulfill Jaddi's aspirations for me to become a doctor. I had been too busy with "the cause" to be at the top of the class, as I usually was. But this fall from grace didn't keep me awake at night, for my dream of changing the world absorbed me far more than trigonometry and the sine of an angle. So, after graduation, my grandfather invited me to sit next to him on the wooden seat in front of the house.

"I want my first grandson to be the doctor who treats me in my old age," he said smiling, and then he asked me if I wanted to retake the baccalaureate at a private school in Damascus.

I agreed without hesitation, but probably for different reasons than those of my beloved Jaddi. I thought moving to Damascus would spare me being bothered by the intelligence agents in our village. We were out in the open with our Marxist meetings, and, to provoke me, someone from intelligence had done a poor job of writing graffiti on the wall of our house: *al-Asad is a lion and traitors are vermin that must be exterminated!*

On the afternoon of the very day that I agreed to move to Damascus, a local bully, Faraj Nadeemeh, emboldened by the fact that he now "secretly" worked for military intelligence, walked up to me and stared me hard in the eye.

"We must smash the skulls of traitors and renegades," he declared.

"Are there any in our village?" I asked, pretending not to know what he was getting at.

"You might find one of them inside your shirt."

"How do they have the power to get inside people's shirts?" I asked. "I suppose this means we have to button up our clothes more tightly."

"You'll live in your paternal Uncle Mahmud's house," Jaddi had said just a few hours earlier. "Your parents are happy with this arrangement." So, even though, once again, I wasn't consulted, Damascus was looking pretty good to me.

Another reason I was excited to go to Damascus was to see in the flesh the city that had inspired so many songs and poems, especially those by Egyptian and Lebanese writers. For them, Damascus was splendor personified, the gateway to history, the source of light, the destination of God's messengers and prophets, the mistress of all the cities on Earth. I would see Mount Qasioun from where I imagined the singer Dalal al-Shamali looked over the city and sang how Damascus was "embracing the clouds." And I would gaze upon the Barada River. "Barada, are you and only you the paradise they promised?" al-Akhtal al-Saghir wrote. In those days, I admired the hyperbole of poets celebrating both Damascus and female beauty.

I arrived in Damascus on board a Scania bus on a hot afternoon toward the end of August 1977. When I stepped down from the vehicle, I didn't see anything suggesting the mistress of all cities, but rather a kingdom of noise and crowds. I hadn't imagined Mount Qasioun's slopes would be so bare, and I'd expected it to be much higher. And instead of embracing the clouds in the sky, Damascus seemed to embrace more earthly clouds, made up of diesel and petrol fumes. In time I came to know that the city did not easily give up its beauty and secrets.

After Uncle Mahmud welcomed me with open arms at the bus station, we took a taxi to his house for a welcome dinner attended by all my uncles and their families living in Damascus. The next morning I asked to be taken to the barber, and my uncle took me to see old Abu Lutfi. It was just a short walk, ending with us crossing a bridge over a canal connected to the Barada. The waterway was incredibly polluted, and it reminded me of an old man who had become so decrepit that he was incapable of performing his own ablutions.

"Poems can't have been written to this stream of plastic bags, empty cans, bottles, and who knows what else," I said to my uncle. "Is this the river that poets and musicians compete with one another to celebrate?"

"There's more than one Barada," my uncle replied. "This is the Yazid Canal. It was originally created to distribute clean water to all the people and farms of the area." Then he added, "But now this is the Barada for the poor quarter of the city."

As Abu Lutfi cut my hair, he told me stories where facts were mixed with wishful thinking and old legends.

"When our father Adam arrived in Damascus," he said, "he drank from the waters of the Barada, and his eyes filled with tears. 'Why are you crying?' our mother Eve asked. 'This river reminds me of the River Kawthar in paradise,' he answered."

I asked Abu Lutfi how he knew that Adam drank from the Barada, and he laughed. "It's a well-known story," he said matter-of-factly. And as his scissors danced through my hair, he explained: "Abel came to Damascus with his siblings, our father Adam, and our mother Eve, peace be upon them, and it pleased them to remain here." Then he stopped and looked at me as if he were pouring his words directly into my eyes. "Don't you know the Cave of Blood and the tomb of the prophet Abel on Mount Qasioun? I've seen with my own eyes, the rock still stained with Abel's blood. The tears of the mountain that weeps for him to this day." Abu Lutfi then explained that God made the waters of the Barada taste like the waters of paradise to honor Damascus for welcoming the prophet Muhammad, "peace be upon him." And then the barber was quiet for a bit, and his face took on a serious expression as he added his own contemporary observation: "I've also seen with my own eyes a time when the Barada was taken into people's houses to be used directly. The water was pure and clear as a rooster's eye. But the river can no longer bear the weight of the city. The newcomers do not treat the river as their own."

I left Abu Lutfi's shop with a haircut befitting a serious student. I didn't believe his tales, but he was an entertaining storyteller.

Later, when my class traveled out of Damascus on a school outing, we visited the famous "source of the River Barada," and this was when I finally saw the river that poets eulogized, clear and clean, flowing between lush green banks.

My experience at the private school was very different from what I had experienced at public schools. First of all, the students were all boys and mostly from wealthy families. While they bought their lunches in the cafeteria, my aunt packed me lunches of mana'ish and kibbeh, which, because she was from my village, tasted just like home. I walked to school; the other students were driven. And all of them were religious. So, during salat al-Asr, the afternoon prayer, while the whole school was down on their hands and knees praying in the schoolyard, I, along with my friend Adnan and a Christian student, sat chatting on a large boulder at the end of the yard. And, of course, within a month of school opening, I once again became involved with the local Marxist group.

As I took twelfth grade for the second time, I somehow found it significant to be walking in the street called Straight where the apostle Paul had walked. He entered Damascus as Saul, coming to arrest Christians and persecute them, but on the road to Damascus, God sent a vision to blind him. Then, in the city of Sham, when Jesus's apostle Ananias laid hands on him, Saul apparently saw not only the light of Damascus, but also the light of the Messiah. This is when Saul became Paul and a Christian preacher.

I learned the history of Paul from Father Ilyas Zahlawi, a member of my new group. He wanted to become involved in liberation theology, the Marxist-inspired movement that had begun in Latin America in the 1960s. Father Ilyas accepted the fact that I wasn't religious, and I accepted the fact that he was a believer. Once, I teased him by saying, "I personally followed in Paul's footsteps through the Bab Kisan gate, the place where he escaped ahead of the Jews persecuting him for proselytizing for Jesus. But I think the air and dust must have changed many times since then." It was a pompous teen's way of telling an older person that times had changed and they were out of date.

"The air and the dust may fly wherever the wind blows them, but the streets and the gate haven't changed," he replied calmly. "Just like my faith, they are still there."

On another occasion I said, "Let's suppose that Jesus sacrificed himself for us and paid the ransom for original sin to those in heaven who demanded it. But he didn't rid the world of suffering. In fact, he didn't even save Archdeacon Stephen from being stoned to death while Saul was guarding the crowd's clothes."

Father Ilyas smiled his tolerant smile and said something about heavenly plans and divine will. And maybe I said something about Jesus crying out for help in Aramaic: "Eloi, Eloi, lama sabachthani" (My God, my God, why have you forsaken me?). I can see now how incredibly rude I was as a teenager, and how tolerant my older friend was. But I guess the point is, even if we couldn't totally agree, at least we made an effort to understand each other.

During my time at school, I also visited the Umayyad Mosque, the Great Mosque of Damascus that I'd heard mentioned on my grandfather's radio as a child. I stayed for a long time, contemplating its mosaics, its pillars, the tomb of John the Baptist, and the window ledge where they say the head of Muhammad's grandson, Hussein, was placed after he was martyred in 680.

It was only a few months later, while hiding from the regime, that I was sitting in the theater office of the famous Syrian playwright Saadallah Wannous discussing the history of the Umayyad Mosque. "This holy place is famous for commemorating two severed heads. The prophet's grandson al-Imam al-Hussein and John the Baptist," I said.

"Many were beheaded on behalf of those in power in this city," Saadallah answered seriously. "The Umayyad Mosque is the temple of victors. The place was constructed as a temple for the Syrian deity Hadad, and when the Romans took over, it became the Temple of Jupiter. Then it was converted into a Christian cathedral, and after the Muslims captured it, a mosque."

While I didn't neglect my high school studies completely, I must admit that all of my extracurricular cultural explorations, along with my Marxist activities, did eat into my redo of twelfth grade. So, as a result, once again I didn't have the grades to be accepted into medical school. But my grades were good enough to get me into oil engineering, which my young Marxist self thought was even better. I could see myself working shoulder-to-shoulder with the proletariat, together rebuilding Syria into a workers' utopia.

So, life was good. I even got myself a summer job in the city, allowing me to save some money before starting my first year at Damascus University. I was sanding and painting walls in new buildings, ironically, for a division of the army that was constructing barracks for soldiers and public housing for the poor. And then one day I was to meet a comrade, Youssef Abdelke. He too was a member of the first cell I joined in Damascus. Youssef is now a famous international artist, very disciplined and hardworking even in his youth. So, when he didn't show for our meeting, I knew that could mean only one thing.

CHAPTER 21

FIRST STEPS UNDERGROUND

Comrade Fahd (Youssef Abdelke) didn't show for our appointment because he'd been arrested. I learned subsequently that the homes of Bahjat Shabow, Barakat Shabow, and Jihad Annabeh, all members of the group we'd founded together, were also raided. But in the same way that teenagers know that someday everyone must die but somehow also believe it won't happen to them, I continued going to my summer job. Continued, that is, until one hot August afternoon when my mortality came into sharp focus. With dust caked on my body from a day of sweaty labor, I was only a few streets away from Uncle Mahmud's house, where I looked forward to bathing away the day's accumulated dirt. That's when I saw Anwar, a friend of my father's who lived in Kfarieh. He was standing on a street corner waving at me, and then he started running, his arms opened wide for an embrace.

"I'm covered in dust, Ammo," I warned, greeting him affectionately as Uncle, but he grabbed hold of me. Dust flew as he kissed me on both cheeks, and I laughed happily until he pulled away. The expression on his face suggested disturbing news. "What's happened?" I asked. He blurted out the words as if he were keen to be free of them.

"A patrol from the military intelligence raided your family's house at dawn today. They came to arrest you."

I immediately gave him the key to Uncle Mahmud's, kissed him good-bye, and walked off at speed. I felt as if the street had become part of a nightmare; I expected an intelligence patrol to appear at any moment and drag me away. And so began my thirty-month journey in hiding. But where to go?

For the next hour I moved through the streets like a sleepwalker, eventually finding myself at Adnan's door. My friendship with him had developed, as we were the only two Muslims at school who didn't participate in the afternoon prayers. Adnan had also showed some interest in current affairs, and this, along with our shared secularism, prompted me to try to work him into my political circle. I'd shown him our publications and discussed them with him, but he wasn't very interested in rearranging the world. He had more realistic goals for himself.

"Military intelligence raided my family's home this morning," I said.

"What a bitch to be politically active in a country like ours," he cursed. "What are you going to do?"

"Right now, I'm going wash the dust off," I said.

He followed me to the sink I knew well and brought me a dry towel.

"Someone must have informed," he commented, while I was drying my hair.

"Impossible. We all use code names. We don't even know who the others really are." I was Comrade Abbas, Youssef was Comrade Fahd, and I really didn't know the others' true names. "And if somebody had informed on me in Damascus, why would they raid my house in the village?"

"Okay. Well, what about your university course? Do you want me to help you register in the Institute of Petrochemical Engineering in Homs?"

"No. You shouldn't go to Homs," I exclaimed. "They might be waiting there. If there's no risk, you can enroll me in any branch of Damascus University."

Adnan nodded. "That makes more sense. I know you're not really interested in petrochemical engineering. You just want to be an engineer to work with your silly proletariat. You ought to study arts and literature. That's really your strength. How about English and Arabic literature?"

"It doesn't matter," I said in frustration. And then I looked at him with a smile. "What matters at this moment is whether there's any food in the house. I'm starving."

Now Adnan smiled broadly too. "There are leftovers from lunch. Ummi cooked mujaddara." His mother had become a second mother to me, and I loved her cooking almost as much as my own mother's. Especially mujaddara, a concoction of bulgur, lentils, olive oil, and onions.

"But like all pragmatic revolutionaries," he teased, "you must eat only to fill your stomach. Not to enjoy it."

A minute later I was wolfing down the home cooking. "I enjoy it so much," I admitted.

While I was chewing, the name Salma somehow flashed into my head, and I remembered what Comrade Sameer had said to me last year. He had grown up in the village of Bishraghi, close to Jableh. "If you need any medical help in Damascus, you can rely on a friend of mine, Salma. She's a nurse from my village who works in the main hospital in Damascus. Tell her Sameer sent you." Then he added in a whisper, "She's also the girlfriend of my Uncle Deeb, who's in hiding."

As I left Adnan's house to go to the hospital, where I hoped Salma still worked, I still didn't know where I would live.

"Come back if you don't find anywhere to sleep," Adnan called. There were no extra beds in Adnan's house, just a thin mattress his mother had made from fabric scraps. And seven people already slept in the two rooms. Despite that, I knew Adnan's invitation was sincere. I nodded.

At the hospital I told the receiving nurse that I had severe stomach pains. When she asked me for ID, I said I'd forgotten it, but knew all the information by heart. I told her my name was Ahmad Ibrahim and, after being admitted to hospital, asked if she had a colleague named Salma.

"Salma? I know four Salmas."

"She's from the Jableh area."

"Dark and slim?"

"Yes," I replied. Even if she'd said she was blond and plump, I'd have said yes.

"I think I saw her today."

The doctor diagnosed me with dysentery, based solely on my made-up answers to his questions. After he made out a prescription and left, I asked the nurse how I could find Salma.

"Wait here for a minute."

When Salma arrived, the first nurse stayed and listened. "Hello. I'm Ahmad Ibrahim," I said. "Our mutual friend Sameer Ibraheem sends his greetings. Do you know Sameer?" I asked.

"Yes, he's from the same village as me," she replied, looking somewhat apprehensive.

"I'm a new student in this city, and Sameer said you might be able to tell me about renting a place and give me some tips on how to get by." Although Salma was nodding her head, I could see suspicion in her eyes.

"Yes, of course," she said, and smiled. Satisfied the younger nurse was safe, the other nurse left, and, after checking around us, I turned back to Salma.

"Salma, I'm not sick. I need your help. The mukhabarat raided our house in Kfarieh today and I'm the only one left from my cell in Damascus who hasn't been arrested."

Salma hesitated only briefly. "Meet me at six thirty at the Kafarsousah bus stop. Do you know it?"

"Yes."

I left at once, and to keep off the streets until the appointed time, I wandered around Jalaa Park. I didn't have a wristwatch and so repeatedly stopped people to ask them the time. I got to the bus stop just at six thirty, but Salma wasn't there. *Maybe she's watching me, to see if I'm an agent*, I thought with mounting anxiety. But she showed up just as the bus arrived, and we climbed on board together. Salma took me to Hasiba Abd al-Rahman's house.

When I first saw Hasiba, she was sitting with another teenager, Zayn. Both looked about eighteen, and when I entered, they hid a copy of *The Red Banner*. I pretended not to notice and again introduced myself as Ahmad Ibrahim, a student in the Faculty of Fine Arts. At a sign from Salma, Hasiba and she went out into the courtyard to talk, leaving me with Zayn. She was a beautiful girl, clear skin, in a tight, low-cut T-shirt, and her black eyes gazed into mine. We sat silently, staring at each other, and I dared not look away from her eyes lest my eyes travel downward. Thankfully, Hasiba and Salma returned to begin questioning me.

After some minutes of interrogation, Hasiba glanced at the others and then back at me.

"We have to help Ahmad," she said.

Hasiba would say to me later, "I trusted you when I met you for the first time. There was something sincere in your eyes, and I could tell you were anxious. But the security of the organization shouldn't be built on reading people's eyes, as you know. All the same, I decided to take a risk and it turned out you deserved our trust."

Zayn stood up. "Come with me," she said. "Salma and I will sort out where you're going to sleep tonight."

I went along with the young women to an old house near Shamdin Square in the historic Kurdish quarter. We entered through a gate into a walled courtyard and then into an old two-bedroom house.

"Don't you need to clean yourself up?" Zayn asked.

"I'd like that," I answered.

She pointed to a small room off the courtyard. I peeked through a curtain across a doorway, where I expected a bathroom, but there was just a room with a cold-water spigot and a plastic hose tied to it, and a drain hole in the floor.

"I'll only be a few minutes," I said, but before I could turn away, Zayn touched my arm.

"You'll find a piece of soap on the small shelf. Take off your shirt. I'll wash it for you."

Salma raised her eyebrows. After I took off my shirt, she teased her friend. "Remember, shirts get dirtier under the arms and around the collar."

Zayn gave her a look. "And should they be scrubbed from right to left or left to right?" she asked sarcastically.

With a grin, Salma sat down on an old wooden chair and occupied herself by searching for something in her handbag.

That night, Deeb Ibraheem came to the house. He was a member of the "central committee," something grand and mysterious, in my mind. So, when he walked in, I felt I was meeting the soul of the coming revolution. This initial impression deepened when he told me how he had been living underground for a year. We sat alone, and he fired questions at me to confirm my identity.

"The intelligence services raided my family's house," I said finally. "What do you suggest I do?" He seemed to chew on this question a good while.

"My personal opinion . . . I don't know. The truth is we have to get used to being interrogated. On the other hand, I don't wish you to come to the slightest harm, and what we know so far indicates that the intelligence services are extremely barbaric. You must stay here till tomorrow evening and not leave this house, so we can seek the opinion of comrades on the action committee, our higher command. We're proud that we've abolished the post of secretary general or first secretary and replaced the individual with collective leadership."

I was astonished by how indecisive this member of the central committee was being.

"We have many things to be proud of," I said. "But we must decide what we need to do now."

"You're right. We will see. Don't worry."

Looking back, nobody really expected the brutality that was coming down on our heads. And while we had thought our pure words could change the world, now that a time of action was being forced upon us, the committee had few means to react or protect its members.

Deeb went into the bedroom with his girlfriend. He closed the door with a click. He'd probably decided this was his best course of action in the situation.

I stayed with Zayn in the open air in front of another room that was locked. Neither of us needed to make any great effort to win over the other, but we tried to impress all the same. We admired what each other said in turn about poetry, love, villages, cities, the beauty of the full moon over our heads, the colors of our clothes, and of course, the future of the political struggle in our country. We would do away with poverty, ignorance, and all forms of despotism. I spoke with foolish confidence, with the chasteness of a saint, the soul of a lover, and the natural instincts of a youth searching for someone to share love with. Words came easily, while I was trying to stop my eyes from fixing on that amazing area between her breasts.

While everybody was away from the house the next day, I washed the rest of my clothes and hung them in the courtyard. And while I waited for the August sun to dry them, I wrapped myself in a white sheet. This is when Zayn came back from university with a falafel sandwich and awwameh, a small fried doughnut sweet, to share. She laughed at me in my sheet.

"Peace be upon you, Hajj," she said. "You look like a pilgrim in Mecca."

What I really wanted to tell her was I'd prefer for her to be my own personal Kaaba, the sacred building in Mecca that Muslims gather around to show their absolute devotion. But just at that moment, there was a knock at the gate and in walked a young man wearing a military uniform. I hated his military uniform, but I hated that he'd arrived at that very moment even more. He introduced himself to me as Mirhij, said he was doing his compulsory military service, and after a short chat I guessed he was one of our comrades.

The next day, Deeb came with news. "The action committee has decided that you should go into hiding," he said.

"Okay," I said. Wasn't I already in hiding? "How. . ." I began.

"But you'll have to sort out your own food and accommodation," he continued. "The recent round of arrests was extremely costly, and the organization has no money left. You'll have to work out how you will live."

"But with the mukhabarat after me, it will be hard to find paying work. I'll need false ID."

"I think our comrades can provide that. In any case, at five tomorrow evening you're to go to the back gate of the Hospice Sulaymaniyah. You'll meet a comrade from the Damascus leadership. He'll be able to answer all of your questions. He's a short, dark young man with a goatee. He'll be carrying a small black case and smoking a brown pipe. You will ask him, 'Can you tell me the way to Bab Touma?' and he will answer, 'Please, come with me. I'm going to the bus stop. I'll show you.' He will help you get settled in the broader organization."

Before I left the house the next day, Deeb put his hand on my shoulder again. "You must forget the way to this house. It may be discovered by the mukhabarat and become a trap," was all he said. This was his way of saying I had to find a new roof to sleep under.

Of course, Zayn and I agreed to meet later, and, to my surprise, she gave me the gift of a black-faced Seiko watch with silver numbers. "You're going to need it," she said affectionately, "to know when it's time to meet your friends, including—"

"You, of course," I said, pulling her close, and we shared our first kiss.

It was eight months before I received a very dubious fake ID.

Deeb's description of my contact at the Hospice Sulaymaniyah was quite accurate. I could spot him from across the square, walking around lazily, puffing on his pipe, and gazing into the windows of the arts and crafts stores behind the museum. As I approached, our eyes met and he turned his back on me.

"Excuse me. Can you tell me the way to Bab Touma?" I asked when I was close.

He turned and puffed on his pipe a number of times, considering. Three or four years older than me, he was wearing a Lenin-style mariner's cap, large spectacles with thick frames, and a blue-striped dress shirt hanging over gray pants. And he did indeed have a goatee. But such a curious mustache. It was obvious he couldn't grow hair on his smooth upper lip, so he let the hair on either side of his mouth droop all the way down to his chin. He appeared colorful and oddly eccentric.

"Come with me. I'm going to the bus stop," he said, giving an almost correct response to the question.

"You didn't say please."

"What? What did you say?" he asked in surprise.

"I was told you'd say please in your answer."

He looked at me and, instead of getting angry, laughed. "Zareef," he said, meaning I was witty. "Okay, then, *please*. Now let's go." As we walked, he looked over at me, as if sizing me up, and then he chuckled again. "By the way, I'm Comrade Milad."

"I'm Comrade Abbas," I said, and we continued walking.

"So, I understand you were just about to start university, and you've an interest in literature."

"And now I'm here, in the class of living underground."

"Aren't we all. It's important for me to choose committee work that suits you. But first, if you want to survive, there are things you must know."

"I'm all ears," I said, staring at his glasses. There was something odd about them.

"Intelligence will probably have a picture of you by now. You should change your appearance as much as possible. Grow a mustache," he said. He looked behind us and added, peering over his lenses, "And when you're on the street, always keep your eyes open and don't do anything to stand out."

"Okay, comrade," I said, once again distracted by his colorful clothing and facial hair. "I'll try not to stand out, and, on the orders of the leadership, I'll grow a mustache to hide behind. Say, do you have some fake spectacles you could lend me, like the ones you're wearing?"

"How do you know they're not real?"

"I guessed," I said with a smirk. It was obvious, as the lenses didn't magnify his eyes.

"Don't make fun of these things. They might be what save you from prison. Here, take these. Go on. I've got another pair. Good, they suit you," he said.

"Hey, I'm already seeing things through the eyes of the leadership."

"You really are zareef," he chuckled. "And were you making fun of the way I dress?"

"No, no, comrade. I'm just jealous."

He didn't look like he believed me. We kept on walking. "Another important thing," he went on. "Every day, all the hotels provide the names of their guests to the different branches of the secret services, political, military, and state security. It's like they're all competing. And to catch any one of us is like a great prize to them."

At this I didn't joke. "A government informer in my village threatened me by saying the security forces think of us as cigarette butts to be crushed under their heels."

"Sadistic bastards," he said.

"And don't worry about me being caught at a hotel. I haven't any money for that," I said, holding out my empty palms and shrugging.

"Any other questions?" he asked.

"Where can I live?"

Now he held out his palms and shrugged. "Sorry. We'll be in touch. But Comrade Abbas . . ."

"Yes, comrade?"

"I think you and I will get along," he said, smiling. "A sense of humor can help get you through the worst." And then I was initiated into the important protocol followed by underground groups before the age of cell phones and the internet. Every five days, group members would meet with a specific colleague at a time and place designated at the previous meeting.

This was to ensure that neither member had been arrested. If one didn't show, the other alerted the other members to regime activity. And with that arranged, Comrade Milad disappeared anonymously into the crowds of Damascus, along with his inconspicuous facial hair, mariner's cap, and dress shirt.

CHAPTER 22

LOOKING FOR A CEILING
TO SLEEP UNDER

S o, here I am. My nervous humor has subsided and once again I begin to walk with no destination in mind. Soon I'm on King Faisal Street, shoulder to shoulder with hundreds of people, but I've never been so alone. With my index finger and thumb, I stroke my upper lip to feel the stubble where my mustache is going to be allowed to sprout. I no longer need coffee dregs to draw one. But while I must leave my facial hair to appear in its own good time, I have more immediate concerns, like where I'm going to live and how I'm going to feed myself.

Some hours later, I find myself once again at Adnan's house, taking him up on his offer. Mazen opened the door to me, and he didn't seem his usual cheerful self. Instead of inviting me in, he asked me to wait while he got his older brother. Adnan was different from before, his face tense with a smile that looked as if it was pasted on. I followed him into the house like someone expecting a mine to explode. Adnan, still attempting graciousness, bid me sit in a chair in the main room.

"What's happened?" I whispered.

"I'm really sorry. I was so upset by what's happening to you that I told my family . . . that you are wanted by the security services . . . for political reasons. My father went crazy."

Just then Adnan's father, a tall, imposing man, stormed into the room and loomed over me.

"Dad . . ." Adnan began, but his father put a hand up for silence.

"Listen, you," he shouted at me. "You can go to hell if you want, but you're not going to take us with you. This is the last time I want to see you anywhere near my house!"

I stood up to head for the door, but Adnan blocked my way.

"Dad, please," he pleaded.

"Your friend must understand that we all have our own ways of getting through life," his father boomed, "and his way is not our way."

Adnan's mother came into the room, holding a dishcloth in her wet hands. She was staring at me with the worried eyes of a mother.

"Abu Adnan, please . . ." she said to her husband.

"Go back to washing your dishes!" he ordered.

Again, I tried to leave, but Adnan wrapped his arms around me and pulled me close. "Wait for me at the bus stop," he whispered.

Meanwhile, Adnan's mother was still watching me, her eyes full of concern.

"Go back to washing your dishes," her husband shouted in an even louder voice.

I felt as if I was suffocating and rushed out of the door, across the courtyard, and into the street.

As I walked hurriedly toward the bus stop, Adnan caught up with me. I was embarrassed for him to see tears streaming down my face. Adnan's house wasn't paradise, but I felt more upset than our father Adam when he was kicked out of Eden. Adnan put a hand on my shoulder. He seemed as upset as I was.

"I'm sorry, I'm sorry," he kept saying. "Where will you go?"

I waved a hand in the air. "I don't know," I sobbed. "I'll find a place."

"Let's . . . let's go to Mahran's."

I had visited Mahran with Adnan once before. A metal staircase led up to the second-floor apartment over a commercial business. The apartment was a single room with a closet-sized chamber for a toilet, along with a tiny sink and counter. It was a place designed for renting to poor migrants from the countryside. The thing that had caught my eye that first visit, though, was a buzuq, a small stringed instrument, hanging on the wall.

"The buzuq is the symbol of a Kurdish identity," I'd said. Mahran's eyes lit up at the fact that I knew something about his culture. We talked about the injustices done to the Kurds, and when I said I didn't understand why Kurds, who'd lived in Syria for more than half a century, were not granted Syrian nationality, he replied like all those confident of their national identity.

"Fifty years? We've been here since the beginning of creation."

Mahran's hospitality had made me feel much better.

A few hours later, when we said goodbye, Mahran announced, "I'm your sacrifice," which is a Kurdish way of saying you like a person so much that you'd give your life for them. So, I was very surprised when I went to visit him a few weeks before going into hiding and he didn't open the door to me.

"I don't think Mahran wants to see me," I told Adnan. "I knocked on his door the other week and, even though I saw him at the peephole, he didn't let me in or even speak to me."

An embarrassed smile spread across Adnan's face. "Um, I was the one who didn't open up the door for you. Mahran gave me a key so I could be alone with my girlfriend. And then I was too embarrassed to tell you afterwards."

Mahran welcomed us effusively.

"It's good to see you again, Jamal. I enjoyed our talk," he said as he welcomed us in, motioning us to take a seat on the floor. I sat, feeling incredibly hot and claustrophobic.

"Open the window . . . please," I gasped.

"Yes, yes, of course. What's going on? What's wrong? Do you need something to eat?"

I shook my head violently and cringed at the thought of food. I was no longer hungry. In fact, the thought of food disgusted me. My mind couldn't stop replaying the scene of a while ago, and I was surprised that it had hurt me so much. I put my hands over my eyes and began to try to heal myself with a silent monologue: I entered Adnan's father's house in the spirit of a knight seeking protection from a friend and was driven out like a beggar with leprosy. I've begun to pay the price of opposing a regime that terrorizes people.

I understood Adnan's father, an army sergeant working as a mechanic at a military garage, only wanted to protect his son. Abu Adnan, like most Syrians, had accepted that opposition to the regime meant destroying their futures for reasons they saw as frivolous and stupid. But why could he not have said to me more calmly, "I'm sorry, but we can't help you pay the price for your opinions."

"Why do you look as if you carry all the sorrows of the world inside you?" Mahran asked. "Last time, you were joyful and your laughter flowed like the River Tigris."

I opened my eyes and tried to calm down enough to explain myself, and decided the best way to explain was to tell them about our house in the village. And as I began, I imagined there was a third person in my small audience, the man who had just loudly banished me from his home. As I spoke, I alternated between tears and laughter.

"My parents' house has a courtyard surrounded by a stone wall eight feet high. And there's a door-sized entrance in the wall, but when my father built it, he didn't put a gate in it to keep people out. And just inside the courtyard he also built a private room with an unlocked door. The room has a short-legged table upon which my mother always keeps three clean and neatly folded mattresses and blankets. There's also a wood-burning stove and fuel. This room is for any passersby who can't find a place to shelter on a cold or rainy night in the mountains."

"Why no gate in the wall?" Adnan, the city boy, asked.

"This way they don't have to knock before entering. On most winter mornings, my mother provides them with a hot breakfast too."

"You have a good father and mother," Mahran said, and he stood up to get three glasses and a bottle of student-quality arak.

Now Adnan looked like he was about to cry, so this time it was my turn to put a comforting hand on his shoulder. The father's sins shouldn't be visited on the son. During this pause in the conversation, Mahran took down the buzuq from the wall and sang us a song in his mother tongue. It was about the young Kurdish activist Leyla Qasim. She was executed by the Iraqi Baath party in 1974. We only understood "Leyla Qasim" in the lyrics, but the sad melody made her name sublime. Mahran translated some of the words afterwards, and they made me realize that someday they could apply to me.

Leyla has gone from the land of Kurdistan
And left her name to light up its skies

That night I slept on the floor on a folded blanket, although Mahran tried to insist that I sleep on the iron bedstead. The next morning we drank tea on the balcony, and then climbed up to the flat roof. It was a beautiful day.

"Oh, I love sleeping on the roof in summer," I said.

"Well then, I'll give you the extra key for the main door. You can come and go on this roof whenever you want. I'll leave a mattress and cover here, too, like your parents. Please come, even if I'm not home."

I was so happy. My mother used to say, "A roof is a protection. When the roof is put on, the house is complete." And here I am; I have succeeded in finding a roof and no longer feel like a beggar.

I left Mahran that morning feeling very grateful and renewed, and walked briskly toward the Hospice Sulaymaniyah. I was to meet Zayn at two in the afternoon, and I ended up passing time in a remote corner of the gardens of the National Museum across the square. There I ate the lunch I bought from a cafeteria set up at the Hospice Sulaymaniyah for soldiers. Fifty-five piastres, about twenty cents American, bought me a pita sandwich filled with labneh, a cream cheese made from yogurt, along with a cup of tea. This haven for soldiers, ironically, became a regular place for me to buy meals.

And then Zayn appeared for our rendezvous, our first date. To my mind she moved like a gentle breeze, her large laughing black eyes clear and joyful.

"Right on time," I said pointing to her gift, and although it was obvious we wanted to embrace, this would have to wait until we could steal a kiss behind a tree.

Our romantic first date was spent buying me underwear, new shoes, a shirt, and trousers at the secondhand market, as well as a fake-leather duffel bag. It would serve to hold all of my worldly possessions.

"This bag is my home now," I said to Zayn.

"Can it be big enough for both of us?"

I laughed. "You can live in my eyes, and I'll protect you with my eyelashes."

"That's as much as I could hope for, and I don't know what I'm really feeling. But when I'm with you, I feel that I'm flying."

"Zayn, I think I do know what you're feeling, but we don't have a place to do it."

"Jamal, please, be polite," she said with a coy smile.

"Yes, yes, I understand that you have to say this, but if I didn't say what I said, you might think I was impotent."

"Well, whether you're impotent or not, I'm going to count to five and tell you something. One, two . . . I love you, Jamal, I love you, I love you."

I laughed. "And without counting, Zayn, I love you."

Comrade Milad hadn't gotten back to me with my assigned job yet, but I got my first taste of covert operations in Damascus the next night. I helped Zayn distribute the leaflet I saw her hiding the evening we met, the one criticizing the arrests of members of our organization. It was dangerous work. With me taking handbills that I'd tucked under my shirt and dropping them before each door in a chosen neighborhood, Zayn walked behind, making sure we weren't being followed. It took about two miles before we ran out of leaflets, and then Zayn grabbed my hand and we skipped like children to Mahran's. The three of us spent the evening together, and after supper we drank wine and Mahran played his buzuq for us, singing about love in the mountains of Kurdistan. Although we didn't understand the words, it didn't matter.

"The melody is like white birds dancing in a violet sky," Zayn mused.

"You listening to the tune makes it even more beautiful," I added.

"I'll sleep on the roof," Mahran said, getting up.

That night, not for one moment did I think about my past or future.

A few days later, I met Comrade Milad, who assigned my tasks. I needed to be a member of an authentic political cell in Damascus again. I imagined working with Comrade Milad and the others for many years to come and that we'd change the world. Instead, we became prison mates for many years, at both Tadmur and Sednaya Prisons. So, some changes that we didn't aim for, and of course didn't like, took place, such as having to leave our homes. It was only in prison Milad used his real name: Wael Sawah. He is using his real name now, too, as a journalist in San Diego.

Before our arrests, I had volunteered to write the reports on our political cell meetings, and the others agreed because my handwriting was easy to read. Each report had to begin in a formal way, with the phrase, "Comrades . . . Communist Greetings," and end with, "Victory to Communism."

This tradition lost its glamor soon, and I made no attempt to hide my sarcasm for such static clichés, which aroused the rage of some comrades.

My other mission had me working with a Comrade Ghamr. I didn't know at the time that this man with startling blue eyes and a beard reminiscent of the Russian poet Pushkin was Jamil Hatmal, who went on to be an internationally known writer and eventually had to go into self-exile in Paris.

Jamil and I also became good friends and even met a couple of times a week outside of League business. Whether we were sitting in a corner of the Azm Palace or walking from the Umayyad Mosque to the Jewish Quarter, and then to the Chapel of Ananias in the Bab Touma borough, our conversations were always about authors, poets, and artists. Once, when I told Jamil how much I liked the French poet Jacques Prévert, he brought me a collection of Prévert's poems that were translated into Arabic and hadn't been published yet. Even underground, Jamil still had his publishing connections. Most of the books in my duffel bag were from his rich library, and even though they made my bag so much harder to tote around, I would never have considered discarding a single volume.

As for our other work for the League, we were responsible for secretly distributing our organization's newspaper, *The Red Banner*, to the writers and intellectuals of Damascus. It was only four pages, originally, eventually expanding to twelve. My job was to visit these renowned personages at their offices or homes, while Jamil would watch from a distance. This was to observe their reactions and to check whether I was in any danger. Thinking back on it now, it was an incredibly hazardous and stupid thing to do, but what an education. It allowed me, someone with only a high school education at the time, to come into contact with some of the greatest intellectuals of Syria.

Zakariya Tamir, now one of the Arab world's most famous short story writers, was editor of the magazine *al-Ma'rifa* in Damascus. He received me in his office and made fun of communist writers, me included, but he did it in such a way that I couldn't help but laugh. And he donated the largest amount of anyone to support the continuing publication of our newspaper.

At the cultural office of the Syrian Baath newspaper, the poets Bandar Abd al-Hamid, Suhayl Ibrahim, and Adil Mahmud took the envelope containing our newspaper, smiled, and said thank you. It was as if I were just a postman.

But this was better than Mikhail Eid, a writer and translator who chased me away from his front door, threatening to report me to the mukhabarat if I ever brought the paper to him again. Years later, as a publisher myself, I was on some business at the offices of the Arabs Writers Union. There, I listened to Mikhail boasting to another translator how he had supported the secular opposition back in the day. I must admit, I took great delight in embarrassing Mikhail by describing in detail how he had kicked me out of his house.

There were various other reactions to my visits. I was excited to visit the house of the poet Nazih Abu Afash and sit to drink tea with him. As I was very enthusiastic about his newly published collection, I tried to engage him in conversation about it. Though courteous, he wasn't at all forthcoming. It was the same when I asked him his opinion on some of the articles in *The Red Banner*. I thought at the time that great poets must not feel the need to have conversations with mere high school graduates. Jamil informed me later that Abu Afash had contacted him in a panic, telling him how the mukhabarat had sent some young agent to catch him out.

We decided to stop visiting some people, since they felt uncomfortable or in danger, but I felt so honored to continue calling upon others on a regular basis, sometimes even being invited to their homes. I might not have been attending university, but I was receiving rare private lessons, every so often with tea and biscuits.

Dr. Nayef Ballouz taught aesthetics in the Faculty of Philosophy at Damascus University. When I visited him at home for the first time, his German wife opened the door to me, and I was struck by her height and accent when she spoke Arabic. Both she and her husband were very attractive and interesting people. Dr. Ballouz not only raised important questions to broaden my horizons, he also taught me how to interpret the ideas in books in a way that would allow me to apply them to different aspects of life. These are philosophies I still employ almost every day. As for the struggle we were engaged in, one day he ended our conversation with the following somber advice: "Now that I've read a number of your publications, I'd like you to convey some of my observations to your leadership. The most important one is how the League is pursuing tasks it can never achieve. This is a waste of your collective efforts, and I fear your group's sacrifices will most certainly be in vain." After he let that sink in, he added, "There are fires that give off light and warmth, Jamal . . . and then there are fires that only spew smoke."

The dramatist Saadallah Wannous had the greatest influence on me. Meeting me in his office at the Qabbani Theater in Damascus, he took the publications I handed him extremely seriously and debated their content with me, just as if I were an equal. Never in my life have I met a more profound debater. Saadallah convinced me how bad those Marxists are who quote Marx's sayings in the same way that religious people quote their prophets. He helped me break the habit of using condescending, dogmatic language on others or being dazzled by such language in return. After each meeting with him, I felt that he was releasing me from being in the thrall of any icon.

When I brought back to the committee the ideas I'd formed under the influence of Saadallah and Nayef, a few of them welcomed my attempts to search for greater political awareness, but most, still caught up in their dogma, disapproved strongly. I relayed to them the danger of letting long-term strategic goals take the place of those we could realistically achieve in the here and now. Yes, the organization may call for the overthrow of the regime, a goal I saw as ultimately the right one, but at the time we didn't have enough resources or influence to overthrow the mayor of a village consisting of three houses. Their responses included, "This is a step along the road to defeatism," and, the most cutting, "You're talking like an intellectual!" I guess, as I was still only young, I was hesitant and afraid of being wrong, or worse, being shunned by my comrades. After all, I was a wanted man and had nowhere else to go. But as I started to think more objectively, the organization began losing some of its sparkle and magic.

CHAPTER 23

SAINT SISTER THERESA

For the next several months, I took to moving between Mahran's roof and the home of my old high school principal, Mr. Suleiman. I was very surprised to learn he was part of a different Marxist group. And occasionally I resorted to crashing in the room of another friend, Uqba. Uqba had been a fellow student in preparatory school, and I ran into him again in Damascus at the popular Bouz al-Jaddi restaurant. This was a favorite spot for poor students who went to eat inexpensive meals made with what we know as ful in Arabic, or fava beans in the West. Uqba was attending Damascus University, studying electrical engineering, paying his way by working as a security guard at a building site. They provided him with a bare room in the building under construction, which was always full of dust from the work going on around and on top of him. But even under these humble, dusty circumstances, when I lay on his extra mat before falling asleep, I looked around enviously, wishing I, too, could secure a similar job and have a place of my own. Then I wouldn't have to show up at friends' doors or, as I did with Uqba, show up for a visit and then stay over on the pretext that it was too late to go elsewhere, even though both of us knew the truth.

I was getting very weary of being an underground teenager, a fugitive from people who wanted to do me harm, and, worst of all, being constantly broke.

One autumn day in 1978, I met Jamil in front of the Mariamite Cathedral. The afternoon winds were playing with the dust in the streets and distributing it indiscriminately on the passersby. Jamil said we had to go west, then glanced at his wristwatch and said, "I've been informed that a young woman will be waiting for you in front of Nawfara Café in forty-five minutes."

While we waited for the time to pass, we talked about various things: the sad life of Anna Akhmatova; the notion of time in the poetry of Saniya Salih; and Layla Qasim, who wanted to wear Kurdish national dress when she went to the gallows.

I wonder what made us recall the sufferings of these women at that particular time.

Before he left, Jamil asked if I had cash on me. I had a couple of Syrian pounds and he gave me five more.

"You might have to invite her for an ice cream at Bakdash," he said.

I wasn't expecting for a moment that the young woman I was to meet

These stairs, behind the Umayyad Mosque, end at the courtyard of Nawfara Café. I met Wadha on these stairs. She brought me money from my father when I was hiding.

would be Wadha Hamisha. When I arrived, she was passing the time by looking at the eastern wall of the Umayyad Mosque.

"Wadha! I can't believe it!" I cried.

Wadha spun around and a beautiful smile broke out across her face. She
grabbed my hands like she'd never let go and her eyes filled with tears.

"Is it really you?" she asked. "Everyone's been so worried."

"No, it's not me at all. I'm a substitute." I grinned.

Her laughter reverberated off the mosque's walls. Wadha's high emotions
came from the fact that, out of all the members of our group, she was the only
one not yet in hiding or arrested, although she soon would be.

"You look thinner," she said.

"And yet I've put on weight."

"I don't understand."

"The mustache, the spectacles, the city dust sticking to my hair — and
this fugitive life weighing on me, it's all made me feel heavier."

Wadha's smile faded, and then she fished out a white envelope from her
bag. "From your father," she said, handing it to me.

I opened the envelope and saw money — a lot of it.

"Where did my father get this kind of money?"

"He sold one of the two cows. He's a wonderful man."

"I'm happy and sad at the same time," I said. "Plowing requires two
cows; not to mention they'll be losing gallons of milk per day."

"Keeping you is more important than keeping the cow," she said, smiling.

I looked down at the envelope full of cash. "Wadha, Bakdash ice cream
parlor is nearby. Can I buy you a cone?"

I sorely wanted her to stay, but Wadha didn't have time for ice cream.
When she left after only fifteen minutes, I felt as if I had been robbed. Her
short visit made me see how much I was longing for those I could no longer
be with. And I forgot to ask which cow Dad sold. Ummi liked the black one
because she gave more milk, while my father liked the yellow because she was
good at plowing.

Later that night, and with little thought of the consequences, I took the
hard-earned cash from the envelope and made two piles. One was enough for
a month's living expenses, plus the price of a sweater, socks, a towel, soap,
toothpaste, and more underwear. My bag was growing ever heavier, making

me long even more for a permanent shelf for my toothbrush and shaving things. The rest of the money I gave to Jamil, three times what I kept, for the leadership to share with other comrades whose families didn't have cows to sell. When I told Jamil what my father had done, his eyes filled with tears.

And to repay Mahran for his longstanding hospitality, I splurged and bought a roasted chicken. I hadn't seen him for a week, and so I was looking forward to seeing him smile when he saw my treat. I let myself in with my key and went to relax on the roof until my friend came home. That's when a man in his thirties came out of the apartment.

"Who are you? How did you get in?" he demanded.

"Sorry. I'm here to see Mahran."

"Mahran's gone away, brother, to Qamishli, I think. You're the third person who's come asking for him today."

I took the key out of my pocket and handed it to him, apologizing for disturbing his evening. And then I set off to share the chicken with Uqba.

Two more months went by, and I stretched my one-month budget to two by having only one meal a day. When my money completely ran out, there was an attempt to secure some from the committee for me and for a Comrade Salam, the two youngest members of the organization in hiding. Deeb Ibrahim told me that the committee was out of funds from outside donations, and so he suggested to the committee members that it was time to dig down into their own pockets, although even the executive members were having trouble paying their own bills.

"I suggested we each give the price of a beer to help you two. And could you believe that Comrade Abu Sami crossed his arms and said he wasn't ready to give up his beer?"

"No. I wouldn't have expected that of him." I actually felt quite hurt by this.

"And yet he let you donate three-quarters of the money from the sale of your father's cow. Unbelievable."

"I guess not all communists are the same," I said.

Most of the committee members did sacrifice their beer money, but that didn't give much relief. Zayn brought me dried figs that I added to the contents of my bag and, when she could spare it, gave small sums of money from the university allowance her father gave her.

Where are you, Mahran? I want my roof back. Returning to hunger is more unpleasant than experiencing it for the first time.

I moved between Uqba's room and Principal Suleiman's, and even though neither of them ever complained, I began to feel more guilty and angry.

One day, as Zayn and I were walking along Barada Street, she put a hand to my forehead. "You're warm. And you don't look right."

"I don't feel that good, but what's really annoying me is I'm still homeless. I'm so sick and tired of sleeping on other people's floors."

Zayn thought for a moment. "The house where we met is unoccupied now. The whole quarter is being demolished to make room for a new apartment building. You could stay there for now."

Even before we got close to the house, it was obvious the neighborhood had drastically changed. An unbelievable stench hung over the whole area as the demolition work on the streets had transformed the river beside it into a putrid swamp. Walking up to the door, I could see one of the windows had been smashed, and things were worse inside. The walls, floors, everything was discolored and smelled of mold. The sheets on a bed that had once been a proud white were now yellowed and wrinkled. The table had a cheap blue nylon cover, and the broken clock on it was stuck at two minutes to eleven. But at least this was somewhere that would save me the daily embarrassment of turning up at friends' doors. Zayn looked like she didn't want to leave but said she had to catch a bus to her parents' home near Hama. She put a container of water on the table, kissed me, and, with a last worried look from her beautiful dark eyes, left.

That evening my fever rose, and the mosquitoes from the swamp appeared. I was too tired to leave the house to get away from them, and so I sat on the edge of the bed and just stared at the stains on the wall. The stains began to dance as I sat swatting the stinging insects, and as the sun went down, I began to see rats appearing and disappearing. Eventually, my head began to throb and sweat literally poured out of me. This is when I, too, began disappearing and reappearing.

I feel like a toy in the grip of a nightmare. And I'm so thirsty. I get up and guzzle down all the water Zayn left me. Flopping down on the bed, I haven't the energy to raise my feet onto the mattress. Oblivion.

My eyes pop open and my whole body is itching. I look down and see how the filthy sheet is further stained with squashed mosquitoes and blood. When I realize it is my blood, I know I'm awake. But somehow I am not alarmed. I let my head fall back over the side of the bed and look at the hands of the broken clock. It's upside down, but still stuck at two minutes to eleven. I think of the old saying that a broken clock is right twice a day. I'd like to be right once a day.

"How long ago did the clock stop at two minutes to eleven," I ask nobody. "Why are those hands so lazy they can't make it to the top?" And even I know it's a terrible joke. I turn my head, and a rat is very close to my face. "Waaaah!" I scream, and the rodent runs off. To become food for rats, what a nasty ending. I turn my head, and there's another rat, its eyes looking right into mine. "Waaah!" I scream again and, using the last of my energy, jump to my feet. Looking around in the dim light, I see at least half a dozen rats. "Heeeeelp!" I scream at the top of my lungs, but nobody responds. Nobody. No comrade rushes to my aid. Not one of the millions of Syrians or billions of people on Earth shows up to help me. Not even the secret police, those hunting me, come to claim me. I am alone. I collapse back to the bed.

"Jamal, is that you?" I hear, and feel myself being turned over. I can barely open my eyes. I have no idea how much time has passed but it's still dark. "My God, Jamal. What's happened to you?" I can't answer, but some-how I recognize Mirhij, the comrade doing his military service. His palm feels so cool when he touches my forehead, but I can see him grimace at the blood that comes away on his hand. "You're on fire!" he says, and the next thing I know I am being thrown over his shoulder and carried down the road to a doctor's office.

The physician gave me some free medical samples and told me to drink plenty of fluids.

"I don't have any cash on me," Mirhij lied.

The doctor stood tapping his stethoscope against his palm, staring at us knowingly. "Pay me later," he answered.

Soldiers, like students, are poor, but all the same Mirhij manages to buy some vegetables and a small cooking pot on the way back to the hovel. With the sun just about ready to rise, the rats are back in their warren, Mirhij has gathered fragments of wood debris, and he's lit a fire on the floor. Mixing the ingredients in the pot, he puts it on the fire, and we watch in silence as it comes to a boil and then simmers away. We don't have spoons or bowls, and so we wait for the soup to cool and share it directly from the pot.

"I came last night to pick up some of the League's pamphlets I'd hidden here," he tells me.

"So the pamphlets are the reason I'm alive," I say.

"And they are the reason why the only place you found to sleep was this infested house!" he laughs.

"You're right! All we do is write pamphlets and move them from one place to another," I say seriously.

A while later, the soup and the doctor's samples have me feeling a tiny bit better.

"Listen, Jamal, I have to go back to the barracks and might not be able to come back again this week. You can't stay here, and, in your state, you shouldn't be by yourself."

When Mirhij left, once again I didn't know where to go. Three days until I was due to meet Jamil. Meeting was the only way to communicate and to confirm that the people who came to the appointments had not been arrested. I needed some place to lie low and try to get better, but shyness and a feverish bad mood prevented me from showing up at Suleiman's or Uqba's. I needed a place for a few days.

And then something flashed into my mind. On a high school field trip to an ancient monastery north of the city of Sednaya, I'd learned there were rooms provided for poor travelers and the sick. So, using my drastically dwindling funds, I boarded an early morning bus to Sednaya. After about an hour, I was climbing the long flight of steps to the monastery, lugging my big bag step by step. It wasn't easy, but I finally arrived and found myself talking to a Sister Theresa. I made the sign of the cross and told her I'd come from Beirut and been robbed, which had left me with no money or documents. Also, that I'd slept by the river and been bitten by mosquitoes, giving an excuse for my appearance. The sister interrupted me.

"This is God's house, so I will help you. Maybe you don't want to tell me who you really are, but the way you crossed yourself is very wrong."

"Please forgive me, Sister," I said, and as I told her the truth about my situation, she remained poker faced. She put a hand to my forehead and had me stick out my tongue.

"You need to stay until your strength returns," she said finally. "But I should warn you, the intelligence services come to the monastery from time to time and ask for the names of our visitors."

For the next three days, Sister Theresa took care of me like a mother looking after her child. At night she came and put cool towels on my forehead, and many times, day and night, she had me drink fluids of different colors — green, yellow, brown — telling me the names of the herbs they were infused with and what their properties were. As she sat with me, she asked about my family and whether they knew where I was. And sometimes as I rambled on nostalgically about my parents, the farm, or all my brothers and sisters, I found her staring at me sympathetically. And the food — she fed me very well.

An ancient monastery. It is said that this convent was founded by Byzantine emperor Justinian I in 547 AD. It is run by a group of nuns.

On the morning of the third day, not yet feeling recovered but knowing how important it was to keep my meeting with Jamil, I told Sister Theresa I was ready to return to Damascus.

"Impossible. You're not recovered . . ." she began, holding up a hand to feel my forehead. But I took hold of her wrist and smiled.

"I'll never forget you, Sister. I hope I can return the favor one day."

I noticed her eyes glistening with tears, but she smiled. "I pray you'll be fine. Peace be with you."

Fifteen years later, I was finally able to return to the monastery to keep my promise, only to find that Sister Theresa had died of cancer three years earlier. I lit a lot of candles before I left my home in Syria. Whenever I light a candle anywhere, I remember Sister Theresa and often address her: "We, the living, light candles so that our souls may find rest. But I light a candle for your soul. Theresa, may your memory be eternal!"

On my way back to the bus station, I could feel my temperature rising again, and when I took my seat in the middle of the bus, I quickly fell asleep.

"Wake up!" a voice shouted. "You need to pay." It was the ticket collector. The fare back to Damascus was seventy-five piastres, but my shaking hand could pull out only sixty-five from my trouser pocket. The petty official protested as loudly as if he'd caught a thief.

"This is all I've got," I said weakly, but he carried on rebuking me.

"Why did you get on the bus, then?" he screamed.

"This is all I've got," I repeated, the sweat from my fever and tears mixing. I was a child again, remembering my father handing out single piastres to all the children at Eid al-Fitr, the feast to celebrate the end of Ramadan. To us, each small coin was a worldly treasure.

"I should throw you off . . ."

A hand from behind reached out and took the ticket collector's arm.

"Shame on you for embarrassing this young man," the hand's owner said reproachfully, and he handed the bully twenty-five piastres, insisting that the ticket collector keep the change. I bowed my head, feeling the other passengers' eyes devouring me.

Both the kindness and humiliation continued. As I stood up to get off the bus in Damascus, another man in the seat in front of me pushed a Syrian five-pound note into my shirt pocket. As I looked at him, my tears flowed again, and he gave me a small smile and a nod.

It took almost an hour of trudging with my heavy fake-leather duffel bag to keep my meeting with Jamil. When we saw each other, he scratched his head, and I pushed my spectacles up on my nose. This was the sign that we both believed we weren't being followed. Because of my state, he allowed me out of his sight only because I promised I'd be staying at Principal Suleiman's that night. I walked for a long time with my bag, and, even though I was still not fully recovered and needed looking after, I hesitated as I approached Suleiman's door. I extended my finger toward the bell, but I couldn't manage to press it. Lately, when I rang someone's doorbell, or knocked on their door, the sound of it echoed inside me, because I felt so embarrassed and shy.

Suddenly the door opened, and the principal's elderly father was standing there, a warm smile on his face. But still I started in fear and took a step back.

"Jamal, what's wrong?" he asked.

I was so embarrassed, I wanted to vanish into thin air. I asked hesitantly if Suleiman was at home.

"Yes, please come in. Suleiman, you have a guest," he called, keeping his eyes on mine. Principal, or should I say Comrade, Suleiman greeted me in a friendly way.

"I know I smell," I said. "I mean, I haven't washed since . . . I'm sorry . . . there's nowhere . . . you know . . ."

"Jamal, welcome. There's still hot water in the bathroom. Do you have underclothes?"

"Yes, in the bag. Clothes and a towel."

"Have a bath, and I'll make something to eat for both of us."

In a tub full of hot water, I could feel the weariness and sickness melt away. After dinner, I told Suleiman about my trip to the monastery, the house of mosquitoes and rats, and the clock with its hands stuck at two minutes to eleven.

"It sounds like a nightmare invented by Kafka," my old principal said.

"Lucky you didn't become food for insects and rodents," his father added.

I fell asleep telling them more about Sister Theresa.

"You dozed off talking about the monastery," Suleiman said as he poured me coffee in the morning. "Sister Theresa sounds like an angel of paradise."

I left Suleiman's house, once again not knowing where I was going. I had no League assignments, and so I wandered the streets, shifting the strap of my heavy bag from one shoulder to another. By afternoon, I was sitting in my regular spot at the Hospice Sulaymaniyah. Zayn was still at her parents', and so I sat alone, remembering how this had been a spot where we had shared some wonderful times. And I could finally feel my fever breaking. I took a deep breath. The air felt good.

This was when I saw someone familiar in the distance. It was a young man sitting in the courtyard of the Sultan Selim Mosque, watching people feed the ducks. I realized who it was, and then, like telepathy, he turned. His astonished eyes beamed at me, and then there were two familiar grins.

"Radwan!" I called.

"Jamal!"

He ran to me while I struggled to get up, and we embraced. I hadn't seen Radwan Ibrahim for about a year and a half. We got to know one another at a seminar on the function of literature held at the Cultural Center in Latakia. My provocative questions to the convener attracted his attention, and he invited me to his family's house in the city of Tartus. I enjoyed their hospitality for several days while discussing the state of the country, literature, and art, all with much enthusiasm and a lot less knowledge than we were aware of at the time. We quickly developed a solid relationship. We visited one another and eventually I showed him the League's publications. But I hadn't seen him since I'd left for Damascus to finish high school.

"Jamal, if I'd known I'd see you here, I'd have made for this mosque the moment I arrived in this crazy city." Radwan was doing his military service, and once again, he opened his home to this needy traveler.

"I share a house with five students from Damascus University," he explained. "It has three rooms, a kitchen, and a bathroom. You can use my bed when I'm at the base during the week. And we'll buy you a mattress for when I have time off."

"Oh, Radwan, thank you. But I have to tell you —"

"I've already heard from our friends in Latakia. You're in hiding. That doesn't matter," he said. My face was wet again, but not from fever sweat. Before we reached the house, he'd had a copy of his door key made for me.

"But I have no —

"Don't worry about money."

"But how long can —"

"As long as you need, brother. Stop worrying about it."

Just like that, I had acquired a bed, a roof over my head, and even a door key.

CHAPTER 24

DOOMSDAY
(FEBRUARY 1981)

I watched as the blond patrol chief put our prison transfer documents in the glovebox and then shut it with a click. We were being moved from the Military Intelligence Branch in Latakia, to where, I did not know. I was in the back seat of another Peugeot station wagon, my left wrist cuffed to Hussein Muhammad's right. I glanced furtively at the faces around us. Beside me, next to the right rear door, was an intelligence agent with dark skin and curly black hair. Next to Hussein was another with light brown skin, olive-green eyes, and wavy hair. The driver looked like Charles Aznavour, the Armenian-French singer, with his prominent forehead and jaws, sunken cheeks, and big ears. As the white car set off from Latakia, the patrol chief turned around in the front passenger seat and held up two rubber blindfolds. I had come to hate those things.

"I don't want to blindfold you two, so please don't force me to." Then he added, "All conversation is forbidden. You can talk to me, but only if it's absolutely necessary," and then he faced front again.

"May I know where we're going?" I asked politely.

"You'll know everything soon enough," he said, still facing forward.

The guard next to me jabbed me in my ribs with his elbow, and I let out a yelp.

"Don't ask stupid questions," he said.

The chief turned around, looking angrily at his subordinate. "What's going on?"

"He can't take a joke," my tormentor said innocently.

The chief looked blankly at the guard and then at me. "You'd better get used to this one's jokes."

The journey from Latakia to Damascus took seven hours by car in those days. We had to remain silent and listen to Radio Damascus or the walkie-talkie messages between cars and dispatchers. That made us apprehensive, although we couldn't understand a word. We also listened to our guards gossiping about a colleague they called Abu Raad, joking about how stupid he was.

"Listen to this," the chief said. "One time the lieutenant sent him to buy a box of tissues and he came back with a packet of women's sanitary napkins. 'Don't you know the difference between tissues and sanitary napkins?' the lieutenant asked him. 'When the shop owner gave them to me, he said they were women's tissues, so I thought they must be softer. I was cheated, sir. It's not my fault.'"

"I don't think paved roads have reached his village yet," the driver said in a high voice, quite unlike Aznavour's.

"Abu Raad is also obsessed with gold and gold prices," Green Eyes said. "Every day he goes to the goldsmiths' market and comes back to work either downcast or delighted, depending on whether the price of gold has gone up or down. But he never buys or sells any of it." Everybody laughed.

"But he's fearless during a raid," Curly Hair said, "and doesn't even take cover when bullets are flying all around him. He's a hero then."

"Or even more of a fool," Green Eyes countered, which caused more joviality.

When we reached the city of Homs, the Peugeot was brought to a stop in front of a café.

"Do either of you have cash?" the chief asked us.

"Yes," chorused Hussein and I. With my right hand, I drew a hundred Syrian pounds from my pocket, and Curly Hair grabbed it.

"Is this enough?" he asked the chief.

"Yeah," he laughed, "I'll get cheese sandwiches for everyone." And as he got out of the car, he waved what was almost the last of my money, adding, "According to Abu Raad, this will buy more than twenty grams of twenty-one carat gold. It should be enough for a few sandwiches."

When he returned, the smell of hot cheese filled the car. After eating mostly lentils and boiled potatoes for the last month, the sandwiches were incredibly delicious. But they were so small that I was left wanting more.

As the car sped along, my eyes devoured the sky, clouds, trees, and people's faces. It was as if I were storing up scenes to chew on and enjoy in the drab world of jail cells to come.

My eyes roamed over the faces of the Peugeot's passengers. There was no resemblance between any of the six of us. It was as if we were descended from different races. What love affairs or forced marriages had produced this diverse group? My very limited knowledge of such things didn't allow me to form an accurate view, but in my imagination the chief was like a Roman soldier. The driver looked as if he were born into a family of survivors from the Armenian massacre in Turkey sixty-six years earlier. The agent beside me had lips that suggested he was a descendant of the pharaoh Thutmose, but his eyes were like Tamerlane's. And perhaps one of Hussein's forefathers came from Crete. As for me, I remember Mahran saying, "You could be a Kurd, like me."

And then, as usual, my thoughts went sideways.

Syria is like this Peugeot, bound for an unknown destination with its prisoners and jailers all on board. This country is a destination for refugees and invaders. It clothes itself in the gifts of its rapists and tears off the clothes given to it by its lovers. It suckles some of its children with love and cruelly abandons others in the street.

I entertain myself with these thoughts in order to forget the now familiar Spanish-made bracelet wrapped around my wrist, but my thoughts change once we reach the eastern outskirts of Damascus. I suddenly begin to scan the streets, looking for Widad. That's when the patrol chief gives his two agents the dreaded black blindfolds.

"Put them on these two."

My next crazy idea is to use my nose as a kind of radar to detect Widad's distinct scent, a perfume I would recognize anywhere. But then the chief orders Hussein and me to keep our heads down, I guess wanting to look like he's doing his job when we arrive. I lean forward, and Curly Hair shoves his hand between my shoulders and pushes me down harder, making it difficult to breathe. I gasp for air, taking in the assortment of smells of Damascus, the most prominent of which is diesel, and I realize how desperate my fantasy was.

If you are to survive, Jamal, you must be practical. Don't think about the past; it is behind you. Don't think of the future; it hasn't come yet. Think about what you need to be aware of every single second. To start with, concentrate on breathing.

"We've arrived," the chief finally announces, and my tormentor relaxes his hold on my back. "Thank God for our safe arrival, boys," pronounces the chief.

"May God save you," I say, giving the customary response.

"Who's talking to you, animal?" Curly Hair snarls, elbowing me hard again.

Blind to the world, I feel myself pulled out of the car, led into a building, dragged up one flight of stairs and down another, and then yanked to a stop. I hear the chief talking to an official.

"Sign the receipt, please. We have to return to Latakia at once."

I feel my cuffs being removed and the patrol chief's voice tells us to take off our blindfolds and give them to him. I'm next to Hussein, facing an official behind a metal desk. The fellow's red-rimmed eyes suggest he hasn't slept or is tired of his job. Without a word, the chief, Curly Hair, and Green Eyes leave.

"Names?" and Hussein and I tell him our names.

"Abu Sakhr," he calls, and then sits back, staring at us with his red eyes.

Abu Sakhr arrives, a younger version of his boss behind the desk, and I hope he doesn't fit his name, the Father of Rocks.

"Take this fucker out of the room. I'll need him back shortly."

"Which fucker, sir?"

"Whichever fucker you want."

In a shower of obscenities, including references to my mother's body, Abu Sakhr grabs me by the arm and pulls, shoves, and kicks me into another room.

"Stand facing the wall, fucker!"

When I'm kicked and pulled back into the office, the red-eyed official asks me questions and takes down my personal details, glancing from time to time at a document beside him. Then he tells me to put the contents of my pockets, the black Seiko watch Zayn gave me, my brown belt, and my last seventy Syrian pounds, into a bag. And then I hear a voice from the other room.

"Take this bastard to cell six," the voice says, and I turn to face the sound, presuming they're talking about Hussein and that I'll see him there soon.

The guard slaps me so hard it causes my lower lip to slam into my upper teeth, ripping open the flesh. I taste my own blood.

"Who said you could look sideways, fucker?"

"Take your fucker to cell seven," the red-eyed official says. And as I'm dragged away, I wonder if I'll ever see Hussein again.

The Father of Rocks strong-arms me to the hall and hands me over to a jail guard. This soldier, carrying a whip plaited with electric wires, leads me along, walking as if he is carrying a heavy weight and mumbling a song whose words are incomprehensible. When he opens the gray-painted, blank metal door, hot air wafts out, laden with a blend of disgusting smells. Is it possible that we human beings smell so repulsive? A tall man who looks like George Orwell stands by the door. I have some difficulty understanding what the guard says to him. "A new sheep for you, Chief!" Then he looks at me and says, "Please go in, your honor. Welcome to our ten-star resort." And he shoves me into the cell, laughing idiotically as he slams and relocks the door.

"Shinky has a strange sense of humor," the tall man says, referring to the guard by the slang word for someone who looks disabled and moves oddly and has a blank stare.

"Does he ever use that whip?" I ask.

"Not that I've seen. I think it's just to scare people, because of his infirmity."

It takes some seconds for my eyes to adjust to the dim light, but as the whole of the cell comes into view, what I see is an unbelievable heap of people crammed into a cell that can't be more than seventeen feet wide by twenty-six feet long. The first thing that comes to my mind is that it must be a long-forgotten Goya painting called Doomsday, and after being lost for so long, it has suddenly sprung into life.

Yes, in real life, in front of me, is a pile of humanity; people sleeping, sitting, and standing. They are all wearing light clothes, or are bare-chested, while I am still in my winter things. I'd left my brown winter coat for an old man at the investigation branch in Latakia.

This fast drawing shows how people were crowded in cell number seven.

The tall George Orwell, whose hair is mostly gray, holds out a hand to me.

"I'm your brother, Abu Omar, head of the cell, arrested a year ago."

"Jamal Saeed."

"Hello, welcome. Please sit down," As I sit cross-legged across from Abu Omar, I hear murmurs from the crowd and look to see dozens of eyes studying me.

"What's your name again?" Abu Omar asks kindly. "And where were you born? What's the charge against you?"

"I'm Jamal Saeed, from Kfarieh in the Latakia region. I was accused of belonging to the Communist Labor League."

There is an inhalation of breath throughout the cell, and I see most stares become like daggers. Yes, it's as I feared. I am trapped in a cell with members of the Muslim Brotherhood, haters of all things that are not them, especially communists.

"Jamal Saeed," a voice calls from among the Brothers. I follow it to see a man who looks like the oldest prisoner in the cell. He is sitting, leaning against the wall, not too far from me.

"Yes, brother?" I ask.

He leans forward, his thin face, sunken cheeks, and few discolored, rotten teeth accentuating what he has to say to me.

"Hell needs fuel for its fires, and God creates communists to provide it," he says bluntly.

Abu Omar calmly held up a hand to the old man. "Recite, 'There is no god but Allah,'" he said, a polite way of saying, "Change the subject," but the old man was bolder than that. He leaned forward again, more threateningly this time.

"Is being a communist what you're accused of, or are you really one of those filthy bastards?"

I looked around at all the glaring faces, trying to absorb the hostility confronting me. I only had a second to decide how to respond.

"May I know who you are, sir?" I asked.

"God's poor servant, Abu Naim."

"Pleased to meet you, Uncle Abu Naim."

"You haven't told me if you're one of those people who don't distinguish between the lawful and the forbidden."

I took a deep breath and did my best to reply calmly. "For me, the forbidden is exploitation, as well as man killing his brother man because of a difference of opinion or belief. I also see the forbidden in the torture we're subjected to, and the way we're crammed together in places like this." And then I added, "I glorify freedom, justice, and peace."

Abu Naim did not like my oblique answer, and he began to shout shrilly. "I wouldn't mind being crammed together in the next world with my brothers, but not with a blasphemer like you!" Grumbles of agreement rose from the crowd. "Have you no shame . . ." Abu Naim began again, when a man with dark skin and equally dark, blazing eyes raised a hand that meant "Enough!"

Abu Naim, his face still filled with hate, leaned back against the wall. "As you wish, Doctor."

Abu Omar continued his questioning as if nothing had happened.

"Are you a smoker, brother Jamal?" he asks.

"When I have cigarettes and it doesn't disturb those around me."

Abu Omar nodded. "Ah. Well, if you want to smoke, you must register with our brother Abu Maysara." He pointed to a very thin man with a brown birthmark above his left eyebrow. "It's so close in here, only one person may smoke at a time. Also, because it's very crowded, nobody may sleep on his back. It's better to sleep on your right side, with your heart facing upward, as Dr. Muhammad has instructed us." And he indicated the dark man with blazing eyes. I inclined my head and smiled by way of greeting.

"Doctor," I said.

Dr. Muhammad bowed his head and smiled in return.

"Each of us sleeps for four hours on his side," continued Abu Omar, "and because there's not much room, we sleep lying in alternate directions, so one person's head is next to his neighbor's feet. Many finish their sleep sitting up and we take turns standing for three hours during the day. As for using the toilet and washing, you must register with our brother Abu Ahmad." He indicated a short man who had lost his front teeth. "He organizes the rotation."

"These three- and four-hour shifts . . . ?" I asked. "How will I know what the time is? They took my watch. Is there one in the cell?"

Abu Omar winked, the way people do when it's about something officially banned.

"Of course, in cases of sickness, the schedule I've outlined may be disrupted somewhat," he continued. Pointing to one of the men sleeping, he added, "Our brother Osama has epileptic seizures sometimes, or, say, when brothers come back from interrogation with blood all over them. Then we have to give them some space."

"Of course, as is proper," I agreed.

"Your space will be here," he continued, "next to brother Shahada. Hey, brother Shahada," he called, and a man got to his feet. He had red hair and freckles, a heavily lined forehead and a drooping lower lip that betrayed the displeasure he felt at now having less space because of me, a dirty communist.

"Say hello to brother Jamal."

"I'm pleased to meet you, brother Shahada," I say, "and I apologize for making things more crowded than they already are." He just stared back at me, like he was putting up with a leper.

I stepped next to Shahada, gave a small smile, and sat. He wedged himself in next to me, and we both sat, like all the others whose turn it was to sit, with our knees up and facing forward into the dimness of our collective solitude. I was now a small part of the mass of humanity covering the rough cement floor of a dimly lit cell. Quite soon afterwards, Dr. Muhammad asked Shahada if he could change places with him for a while, so he could greet me properly.

"I'm Muhammad Akif Rustum, pediatrician from the town of al-Haffa."

"Hello, Doctor. Al-Haffa? I'm from Kfarieh. I suppose that makes us neighbors."

"Yes. I'd like to have met you in your beautiful village or in my town. But it is God's will that we meet here."

After we'd chatted for over an hour, with him casually bringing up many subjects — I suppose to make an assessment of me — it was time for the evening prayer. Dr. Muhammad invited me to take part, but I made my excuses. I was the only one who didn't join in. After prayers, he came and sat with me again.

"I appreciate how you didn't want to lie to yourself or to us by not joining in the prayer, but be aware there are eighty-five prisoners in this cell of four hundred and forty-two square feet, and eighty-four are believers." I nodded slowly, my eyes showing I understood the gravity of my situation. He chuckled. "Tell me, why do communists in Syria have so many different positions?"

"I suppose for the same reason as do Muslims or nationalists or any group anywhere."

I could tell he was expecting me not to be able to reply to him so succinctly, and that he at least respected my non-confrontational response.

"You're from Upper Kfarieh?" he asked.

"I think you want to know what sect I'm from."

"How did you guess?" he said with a smile.

"My parents are Alawites, but I'm not religious. When I was a child, I wanted to be a Muslim according to what was set out in my school textbook on Islamic education."

"So, why didn't you do it?"

Instead of relating my inability to reconcile what I'd learned in geography about the roundness of the Earth against Quranic verses, I made a joke of it. "I was afraid of being punished for apostasy if I abandoned Islam." When a professed Muslim leaves the faith as an adult, they can be put to death.

Again, he moved on to another topic, and I was surprised that he actually made himself vulnerable. "You know, Jamal of Kfarieh, I never imagined that I'd find myself crammed in a cell with eighty-four people like this. What about you?"

"No, sir. And it didn't occur to me that I'd share an egg with six other people, like I did in the Military Investigation Branch in Latakia."

"Nobody would believe us if we told them that, would they, my brother?" he said agreeably. "Or most of what we're experiencing." And then he slapped me on the knee playfully and stood up. "It's Shahada's turn to sleep now. I'll move over to my space, so he can reclaim his."

Dr. Muhammad left and Brother Shahada returned, bringing his angry face with him. He sat and muttered some prayers for a while, suddenly breaking off and staring at me. He had something to say.

"If you were told that this cell built itself, would you believe it?" he asked.

"Of course not."

"So how can you believe that the universe was formed without a Creator?"

"Every phenomenon has a cause, for sure. I think —" but before I could continue, he lay down on his side.

"I don't want to argue with you," he said.

"I didn't think we're arguing, brother. We're just..."

"Please don't distract me from praying to my Lord," and he continued his prayers, which were soon followed by snoring.

I look around. Those who are awake are pretending to ignore me. In turn, I ignore the aggressive looks. Again, I am alone in the crowd. In my solitude I remember pictures of famous paintings I've seen in the large art books Jamil Hatmal lent me from his and his father's libraries. The crowded conditions and hostile expressions push me again to think of Goya's paintings, specifically, *Witches' Sabbath*; so many bodies all crammed together, all with sunken, hungry eyes, all looking to devour a young man with features like mine, dressed in a white shirt. And then I imagine Kandinsky standing in a corner of the cell, disgustedly painting things he hadn't expected to encounter — the terrible smells, unreasoning hatred, and the sounds of snoring. How could sounds and smells in the air be put to canvas? How would Kandinsky paint Brother Shahada's mutterings? Chagall also appears. He's roaming above us in the fetid air, collecting the prisoners' dreams, most of which feature delicious meals.

The next day began the routine that I followed until the day I left, and I did everything I could not to disrupt it. When it was time to wake up for prayers, I rose and gave up my place, going to the toilet area to wash or sit quietly beside the cell door with my head down. It was the only time I let my imagination roam freely, my version of praying, I suppose. During meals, I helped distribute the food equitably, and I washed and tended the wounded when they came back after a rough interrogation session. If they let me touch them, I comforted the forlorn. And if they dared talk to me, I spoke with them about their worries and their families. But never, ever did I allow myself to talk religion.

The doctor and I, even though he was highly educated and I only had my high school diploma, spent many hours a day over the next weeks exchanging ideas, for if we couldn't satisfy the hunger in our bellies, at least we could feed our minds.

"I read Dostoevsky and Tolstoy, and I used to like to paint when I was studying medicine," he told me one day.

"Isn't painting forbidden in Islam?" I asked, and he smiled and explained at length what I already knew, that it was forbidden to paint beings with souls — but I listened as if I was hearing it for the first time.

One day, when he caught me noticing people eavesdropping on our debates, he put a hand on my arm. "I am enjoying our conversations, but you must remember, we are eighty-four Muslims here."

"We are eighty-five prisoners," I replied, "and eighty-five hungry men."

He flicked his wrist at the eavesdroppers, to at least make them stop staring. "I respect your patience," he said, "and the way you refuse to be provoked."

A few days later, we were eating our usual breakfast of a third of an unleavened samoun roll, a few grams of labneh, and three olives per person. We also had tea with oil floating on it, almost everyone taking sips from an old army bowl that we passed around. About half of us had a small plastic sweet container, from when someone would buy themselves halawa, from the prison. We could buy this sweet and cigarettes, that's all. When the containers were empty, they became a personal tea or drinking cup.

Just as everybody was preparing to get on with the cell's regular routine, we heard a key turning in the lock. Abu Omar got to his feet, taking his place as sentry and welcoming committee of one. The door opened, and Shinky ambled in with his whip over his shoulder.

"Are all your bastards awake?" he asked. Abu Omar waved his hand over the room and smiled.

Shinky then read out four names and ordered them to pack their things. A number of prisoners began praying for God to protect these brothers, and I found myself saying "amen" at the end of each chorus. Then I realized that there was a variety of opinions as to what was going to happen to those leaving. It became obvious that some thought the four were being released from jail for good, and so on top of the praying, there began a chorus of begging for those who'd be free to give news to the families of those still in jail. Some even asked them to memorize their families' home phone numbers. And then they were gone.

When the door clanged shut again, I could feel there was a slight but discernible change in our accommodation. *Luxury*, I thought. And then Abu Omar asked me and Dr. Muhammad to reorganize the shifts and the space for the prisoners. I had gained, if not trust, at least some recognition. The doctor and I sat down as a committee of two and, with most of the cell crowded around, we began to plan the various aspects of the complicated realignment. I suggested we give the old man Abu Naim a better place. The doctor said we needed to make some "special arrangements," and I understood him to mean new time slots for the debates on religion and politics, and the need to maintain the sessions for memorizing the Quran. There were three in the cell who already knew the Quran by heart. I suggested it would be more efficient if those studying the same courses were next to each other, and there were murmurs of agreement.

"How can we measure out the new spaces?" the doctor asked, and Abu Maysara's hand appeared holding a cigarette.

"This is exactly four inches long . . . and I want it back!"

The doctor then began directing the men to change their positions, eighty-one pawns on an oversized chessboard. I crawled around with the measuring tool, being careful not to spill any tobacco or break it. Before, there were one and a half cigarette lengths between each prisoner's hip, but now there would be one and three-quarters. Of course, there were complaints.

"Abu Amer has a quarter cigarette more than me," complained Abd al-Rahman.

"This is unfair, brothers," Abu Jaber cried. "I'm a large man. I need more space."

I looked to Abu Omar for guidance.

"Ignore him," the head of the cell said. "When he sits, his fat ass will take up more room anyway," at which the whole cell laughed, including Abu Jaber.

Soon everyone was settled.

"I think I can feel the extra space," a Brother said, laughing, and everyone agreed without rancor. There definitely was a new lightness on most faces. People love having more room everywhere. A few Brothers even dared sneak me a little smile, and I overheard old Abu Naim whisper something to his neighbor.

"Communists are more compassionate than some Brothers."

"You're making progress with the common people," said the doctor with a laugh, and that's when the key turned in the lock again. The door opened.

"Here, Chief, you bastard," a guard named Abu al-Nar, the Father of Fire, shouted. "Take these sons of bitches."

In trudged seven more prisoners. The door slammed shut behind them. The lightness in the room evaporated.

"It's Sisyphus and his rock," Doctor Muhammad said to me.

"Sisyphus's rock always weighed the same. Ours just got heavier," I answered.

Among the seven newcomers was a boy of seventeen whom I'd met at the interrogation branch in Latakia.

"Imad," I called, rushing to greet him. But before he could answer, Brother Shahada interrupted.

"Are these communists too?" he asked.

"No!" the seven newcomers and I shouted in unison.

Over the next while, the mood in our small cosmos changed somewhat. A number of the Brothers stopped being overtly hostile to me. They weren't overtly friendly, but all the same, their relaxed body language around me made the hardliners even angrier than they had been. And then, one afternoon, Abd al-Salam, one of the moodiest and least hygienic of the Brothers, pointed a judgmental finger at me.

"You must be killed twice, once because you're an Alawite and once because you're a communist."

"Odd," I said. "I can't say I know who would deserve this double sentence." This must have confused him, for he didn't have any comeback.

"Surely not me," I continued, "for logically it would be difficult to believe in two contrasting ideas like the Alawite doctrine and communism. They are very much at variance with each other." I thought at the time the man was only trying to provoke me, and nothing more, for he took his place on the floor again. I thought I had done well in using my wit to diffuse the situation, until Dr. Muhammad sat down and looked at me seriously.

"I take back what I said about you not being provocative," he said. And then the good doctor took out his beads and began to pray.

The next morning, after more than a month of the same daily routine, I automatically woke just before the dawn prayer. And it's lucky I did.

I was lying on the cement floor when Abd al-Salam and two other men suddenly rushed at me. And then Osama, the epileptic, jumped to his feet and handed Abd al-Salam a bundle of clothes rolled up to form a pillow.

"God is great!" Abd al-Salam shouted, and attacked me, trying to cover my mouth with the makeshift pillow.

I couldn't believe what was happening. I felt like a hunted animal and survival instinct kicked in, giving me unprecedented strength. I used my feet and hands to push against Abd al-Salam and his pillow, and he fell over the other prisoners. I stood up, screaming, "Nooooooo!" Amer rushed toward me, but Dr. Muhammad moved fast and placed himself between my assailants and me. Dr Muhammed shouted, "Noobo, stop, go back to your places, Amer, Abd al-Salam, Abd al-Rahman."

"But . . ." said Abd al-Salam, rising as he spoke. Before he could continue, Dr. Muhammad put his hand on the man's mouth and shouted, "Go to your place!" Osama's face was near my feet and his eyes looked broken. I heard the voice of a jailer close to the door: "Cell number seven, what is this noise, animals?" Then the door was opened and Shinky appeared with three guards carrying whips.

"What is going on?" Shinky asked.

I spoke. "Osama may need a doctor . . ."

"Little Communist," Shinky replied angrily, "are you the head of the cell? Shut up!"

Abu Omar began to explain, "As you know, Osama gets epilepsy sometimes. We try . . ."

Another guard intervened, "Listen, shit. If I hear any whispering, I'll fuck your mothers with this," and he pointed to the whip he was carrying. Then the door slammed shut, and we heard their footsteps moving away.

"Okay, it's over," Doctor Muhammad said. "Get back to your places."

The doctor was still standing in front of me. Several times he repeated, "There is no power or strength save with God." Then he asked Shahada to make the call to dawn prayer. A heavy silence descended. In a low voice Shahada made the call to prayer, the worshippers lined up, and I gave up my place to them as I always did at prayer time.

"Do those heroes want to kill me?" I asked Doctor Muhammad when the prayer was over.

"I'm relying on your forbearance. I think you can understand . . ."

I interrupted him and confronted the whole cell: "Whatever's going on, I'm not going to get a prison guard to stand up for me against a fellow prisoner."

"All of us saw that. I respect you," came a voice from the crowded human mass.

Dr. Muhammad walked up to me and put a hand on my upper arm. "Brothers," he said, "any harm done to this man, I will consider as harm done to me." He moved his hand to his chest, then added, "Jamal will sleep next to me."

I spent the following days sleeping anxiously — as penguins do, with one eye open. After a few weeks, I was moved to another prison, where I slept, as humans do, with both eyes closed.

CHAPTER 25

APPLES
(JUNE 1991)

My parents' house was no longer as crowded as it had been during the two months following my first release from prison in April of 1991. The people of the village had visited me frequently, curious to see what changes in my appearance and mental state had occurred as a result of my being locked away and tortured for so long. But now I was as familiar to them as the rocks and trees around the village.

On the outside, our house hadn't changed much during my years away. But within, the kitchen had been divided to create a bathroom and inside toilet, and we now had running water and electricity, making hot water readily available. No more heating water on a wood stove. And outside, although the ancient mulberry tree looked just like it did when I left, there were strings of little electric lights hanging from its branches.

"That refrigerator means we eat leftovers," grumbled my grandmother. "I liked it better when we cooked fresh food every day."

"Electricity has made women's lives easier," declared my mother. "But I'm still busy enough."

The biggest absence was my grandfather. Death had taken him away from us while I was in Tadmur, and his original brown Japanese radio was gone too. In its place was a television. Most of the inhabitants of the house, and our relatives down the road, followed the nightly Arabic soap opera transmitted on the only channel available at the time, and this prompted a new family tradition. Every night, my grandmother sat sleeping in front of the television until the episode was over, when she would be helped to bed. And then the next day one of her grandchildren would relate the events she had missed. I was glad that the room by the front courtyard was still a place where passing travelers could spend the night, but sad to see the walls of the house in disrepair. I thought that repairing the cracks in the wall might help repair the cracks in my soul, to help lessen my feelings of sorrow and disillusionment. And so I immersed myself in house repairs and then any other work I could find, hoping it would act as a bridge for me to cross back into a normal life.

Informers kept up regular visits to the house. We made clear to them in various ways what they already knew very well: their visits were not wanted. But the informers in our village were sufficiently thick-skinned to ignore our contempt for them. I made up my mind to leave the house when they arrived, but their appearances weren't the only reason to roam around the village with its familiar houses and fields. I also needed to visit my old friends, the river and the nearby woods. I was searching for the child and adolescent I once was, and it seemed to me that something of him could be found hidden along the forest trails, in the trees, behind the never-changing rocks, or in the corners of the caves I used to frequent.

It was my opinion that they didn't need to demolish the French villa where Barbara used to live. It wouldn't have been in the way of the large school they built next to it. But some fool bureaucrat or politician had ordered its demolition anyway. The high wall and the iron bars on the windows of the new school reminded me of the bars and walls in prison. I walked the unpaved streets by old houses that hadn't changed much, and by new villas built by rich city dwellers who wanted a summer house. When the old residents saw me, I guess I was still more interesting than the things on their recently acquired TV sets, for they came out of their homes to offer me Syrian mulberry juice, Turkish coffee, and advice, some of which contained much wisdom and some of which was fairly stupid. Be that as it may, they gave me fruit from their trees, food that they'd cooked with their own hands, and it was all steeped in the love, warmth, and general goodness that I'd lacked for so long.

My grandmother's house had vanished. It had gone back to the earth. Almost nothing of it remained. I'd lived in that house with Sitti between the ages of six and twelve. The place was big enough for us and our cows and our supply of dried vegetables, pickles, grains, dried figs, butter, and jams, and our cows' supply of barley, oats, and hay. Made in the old style, the building had people and their livestock living together. When the cows came back from pasture, they went through the wide door in the middle of the structure and turned left to where their feeding troughs were. We, on the other hand, turned right into the part of the house reserved for humans. In summer, my grandmother and I slept on the roof. I watched the stars and meteorites until sleep overcame me, while our cows slept in front of the house, chewing on their cud and dreaming their cow dreams. But now everything was gone, except the old clay oven that looked to me like an old man who'd been pensioned off. The only time this oven was used was to bake arghifah, a thin salty bread my grandmother used to make, a comfort food we couldn't get at the baker's. In fact, the stove was used for over twenty-five years after the house disappeared, not only by us, but by all the neighbors when they wanted to bake what became known as the village bread.

In the spring, after they flowered, the apple trees bore fruit. They were like breasts announcing themselves under the clothes of teenage girls. I went around our orchard and those of our relatives and began consulting with my father to estimate what these orchards could yield. I had this idea that we might be able to profit by marketing not only our own apples, but also those of the other orchards around us — if their owners were willing to cooperate.

I attended the meetings between my father and the owners of the other orchards, listening as he negotiated to buy their fruit while it was still on the tree. I also witnessed the purely verbal agreements, the only document being a page at the back of my father's notebook. There he recorded the names of the orchards' owners and a number indicating the agreed amount.

One day, Wadha Hamisha came, the school headmistress and comrade who shared with me the dream of changing the world. I wasn't as effusive or in the mood to tell jokes as I'd been before, and she could see that. Sitting down at the long harvest table where my large family used to take meals, she watched silently as I moved like a ghost, preparing coffee. I sat down, and she looked at me as I poured.

"So, what have you got planned, Jamal?"

"I'm preparing to harvest and market apples with my father," I said flatly. She sipped and nodded her head.

"Good. Good. But you look depressed, my friend." I didn't comment. "Don't worry. It's natural. It will pass over time." Again, I didn't comment. "Can you tell me about what happened? Just a little bit?"

I took a sip of coffee and put the cup down on the table in silence. After a few seconds, I began to tell her about daily life in prison, and just a few of the gloomy stories. She sat quietly. After about twenty minutes, I made tea, and when I sat down again, I saw she had a moist tissue in her hand.

"Could you do any writing inside?" she finally asked, and I got up and went to my bedroom. When I returned, I was carrying a shoebox, which I put on the table. She peeked in. "You wrote on these?" The box contained some several hundred sheets of the paper I'd salvaged from unwrapping cigarette packs, all crammed with very tiny writing. There was also a pile of tissue-thin airmail paper, again with words crammed from top to bottom, side to side, and with no margins or spaces between lines. "How, how did you get them out?"

"A guard who wasn't one of the bad ones saw me give them to Khadija and luckily looked the other way."

She then reached into her purse, pulled out her reading glasses and picked up one of the delicate sheets of paper. "Wow," she finally said. "It's really hard to —"

"Maybe this will be easier," I said, and I handed her a lined schoolbook. "Khadija bought me this, too, to transcribe."

"Bless her," said my friend, opening the book. And then I watched her purse her lips and start to read. I felt like a student waiting for a grade. Several minutes later she had finished what I knew was a short story, and she put the book down and looked at me, her eyes wide. "Are you planning to publish?" she finally asked.

"La," I said, meaning no. "I'm just writing for myself."

She continued as kind teacher. "Listen, Jamal. I'm positive the staff working in the Directorate of Writing and Publishing at the Ministry of Culture would be glad to publish your work. I'm sure of it. Most of them are against the government's repression, especially Antun Maqdisi. He's the head of the department."

"I know who he is."

"I'm going to Damascus in a week. If you get something ready by then, I will deliver it for you."

After a long pause, I looked her in the eye. "I'll let you know," I said dully.

When Wadha left, I went to put the box back in my room. And then I stopped and stood thinking for several minutes. I turned, sat back down at the table, spread out all the papers in front of me, and opened the notebook. I began transcribing another story. Meanwhile, unknown to me, a small drama was happening in front of the house at that very moment.

My father was in the courtyard finishing his lunch when a relative, who was also a government informer, walked boldly through the doorway with no gate.

"It's afternoon nap time," my father told him. When the informer carried on walking toward the house, my father placed his ample bulk in his way. "What do you want?" he asked.

"Aren't you going to make me a cup of coffee, Abu Jamal?"

"We don't have any coffee for you, and I have to get back to the fields."

"But you said it's nap time." Silence. "Are you trying to get rid of me?"

"Think what you like."

My father came into the house, and, when I didn't hear the door close, I turned to see him darkening the doorway. He walked up behind me and looked over my shoulder.

"Those words squashed together will be sure to catch that bastard's eye," he said. "You don't want to end up in prison again."

"Mmm," I responded blandly, and went back to transcribing.

"What are you writing?" he asked.

"Short stories I'm going to submit to the Ministry of Culture."

"Could they get you arrested again?"

"No, I don't think so," I said, continuing.

My father, always supportive of me, was dubious. "Keep those things out of sight. Those bastards are counting your every breath."

I finished transferring the stories in four days and gave them to Wadha.

"I'm waiting for them to be turned down with a polite apology," I said with a laugh.

By late summer the apples we agreed to market had ripened in the orchards and now had to be picked, sorted, and arranged in wooden crates. We organized a team of ten workers paid by the day, plus me and seven of my brothers and sisters. I arrived at the designated orchard at five in the morning and picked apples till midday, and then went home and sorted them with my mother, father, and siblings until eight in the evening. And then I slept like a dead man. This routine was repeated for many days, until one pleasant September day I shot out of bed and hurriedly put on my work clothes.

"I slept in," I called to my mother, scrambling for the door.

"Sleep is the little brother of death," she said. "Drink your coffee before you go. Life ends, but work is always there. Enjoy a little."

But I shot off to the field as if I'd been stung.

While he was sorting apples, my father often looked at the red and yellow fruit and remarked, "Gold. No, more precious than gold." He almost kissed the fruit and regularly repeated his usual piece of wisdom. "There is nothing more generous than the earth. It gives you back many times more than you give to it."

"These apples are gifts of God," my grandmother corrected him.

He nodded. "There is no god but Allah. But I've never seen the sky raining apples down on me."

"But it rains water that irrigates the land."

"Have you ever picked apples like these from the forests of Allah?"

My grandmother was not convinced by this, and also didn't understand sorting the apples according to their size: excellent, first, second, and third grades. "They're all apples," she would say. In fact, she thought some of the small apples that had absorbed enough of the Lord's sunshine were more delicious than the larger fruit that hadn't got enough sun.

Each day, I earmarked a crate where I put the fruits that were damaged. Its contents were free to whoever wanted them, the workers or our neighbors. Next to it was another crate for fruit that was so broken it couldn't be offered to anyone. It was cut up and given to our two new cows. One day I picked up an apple with skin as wrinkled as my grandmother's face. I looked at it for a while and then threw it in the cows' crate. But it was too late. The sight of that apple took me back a dozen years. It was the outdoor vegetable market near the apartment Radwan Ibrahim had allowed me share with him and four university students. I was in hiding and penniless, so, without my housemates knowing, I went to the market and joined the very poor who fed on the scraps. Fruits and vegetables discarded after the vendors left. On one of these "shopping" days, I picked up a wrinkled apple and remembered the day I asked my father to turn me into a moving tree.

I continued rummaging around the square and discovered some loose cabbage leaves that had been thrown away because of rips or bruises. But I still deemed them somewhat edible. I also found a potato, half of which was not rotten, some little tomatoes, and a quarter of a cauliflower. When I was alone at home, I took out my treasures and began preparing them. That's when the apartment door opened and in walked Salah, the bespectacled math student with whom I shared a passion for music. He caught me picking and cutting out the rotten bits of food, and then dropping the good bits in a pot of boiling water. After a moment of staring at each other, Salah turned without a word and left. I thought he was trying not to embarrass me, but he soon returned with roast chicken that I knew came from the shop around the corner.

"I'll share this with you, and you share your food with me," Salah suggested.

"What I have isn't food," I said, not wanting to be the object of pity.

"Of course it's food, and healthy food too," he said, and he took a fork and helped himself to some cabbage and a bit of the potato from the pot. Putting them on a plate, he asked, "Do you think we should add a little black pepper, salt, and olive oil?"

After we had shared the chicken and boiled vegetables, and after my stomach and brain felt so much better, we agreed that I would cook for both of us, and he would provide the meat and vegetables as necessary. In this way I learned a different type of cooking, which consisted of putting everything together in one pot and leaving it on a gentle heat until it was done. Most of the time this resulted in a kind of soup that we ate with bread.

Another memory came a few weeks later when I was sitting on a mat outside on our farm, sorting crate after crate of apples. I picked up a yellow apple tinged with red. Ten years before, I'd held and inspected a similar apple while sitting on a cell floor in Tadmur Prison. It was less than a month after I'd arrived, and I still wasn't hardened to the daily monotony. That's when thirty apples arrived in the cell. We were used to having half that amount of fruit, if any. As a comrade walked around with the crate, my eyes were seduced by a yellow apple tinged with deep pink "cheeks," as my father would say, and I delighted when it became mine. Well, ours. Thirty apples distributed among sixty prisoners meant I was to share the chosen beauty with a fellow named

Salim, someone who'd been here much longer than I. Thinking of my father as I rolled the apple in my hands, I smiled and held it tightly. And then I gave it a sharp twist and broke the prison apple cleanly in half, as only an apple man could. I immediately felt like I was back in my father's orchard with him smiling at my skill. I laughed and turned to offer Salim his half, but he was not smiling. In fact, he looked horrified.

"Why did you do that without asking me?" he protested.

"I'm sorry, brother. It's no big deal, is it?" I said still smiling, but he began to shout.

"I was going to save mine for later, and now it's going to turn yellow!"

"I'm sorry," I said, instantly crushed, and I put both halves of the apple beside his blanket. "I made a mistake. But it was out of habit. I'm sorry."

"Stupidity increased in the world after the word sorry was invented. You ought to be more careful."

"I'll try."

"You behave as if you're living alone."

"It's true. What you say is true. I'm stupid, and I'm sorry . . . sorry, sorry, sorry, sorry."

"Yes you should be sor—"

And then I blew up and shouted hysterically, "Enooooough! I've had *enough!*"

The orchard and my father's face vanished from sight. I buried my head under my thin prison blanket and, now in the lower depths of hell, I dissolved into wracking sobs. I could no longer eat my half of the apple, even when a contrite Salim offered it to me. In fact, I couldn't eat anything for the next two days.

There are literally tons of apples in front of me, all waiting to be sorted.

I have to forget. I have to forget.

"Jamal, what are you thinking about?" my mother asked, returning from the house.

"Nothing, Mama," I said.

"That sigh was hot enough to fry an egg. And you look miserable. Something must be rolling around in that head of yours!"

"Believe me, Mama, the only thing rolling around in this head right now are apples."

CHAPTER 26

THE ROAD TO AL-QALA'A
CIVIL PRISON

"What do you think the baker would lose if he actually left this samoun in the oven until it was ready?" Dr. Muhammad asked.

Abu Omar was picking out some of the uncooked dough from the center of his bread. "He'd lose his bad reputation," he chuckled. And then he looked at the goo, shrugged, and popped it in his mouth. The meals here were so small, we were always hungry.

Meanwhile, I was brushing some of the soot from my samoun. "At least today it doesn't smell so much of the oven's diesel fuel," I said with a laugh.

"There is that," Dr. Muhammad agreed, finishing the last of that day's share of six olives.

With my samoun dusted clean of soot, I broke it into three pieces. This way there was some left for the next two meals. Other prisoners, believing the first meal of the day was the most important, ate half of their samoun, or sometimes more, while others rationed theirs differently. I was a "thirds" guy.

Cell seven in the Military Interrogation Center was still reminiscent of the doomsday painting I had invented for Goya, although I must admit I was now accustomed to living in that hell. Yes, I was part of the painting, living in a perpetual state of impending doom. This was because, even if the animosity against me was tamped down for the moment, I never knew when some Muslim Brother might slip past Dr. Muhammad's protection and do me in. But amazingly, I had been able to stow this fear into a neat little compartment somewhere in my head. That is what allowed me to laugh at the black jail-house humor that kept some of us marginally sane.

"You know, young Saeed," the doctor said, leaning back against the wall. "Now that I've known you almost three months, I think you would make an excellent Muslim Brother to work in policy."

Abu Omar's eyebrows shot up at that, and he looked over curiously to see my reaction.

"Well, thank you very much, Doctor," I said. "I take that as a compliment. But during the time we've been together, I've come to think you would make an absolutely superb communist."

The three of us burst into laughter, but when I looked around, there were the usual Muslim Brothers who looked angrier than usual.

The small rectangular door in the larger cell door opened, putting a stop to our levity. It was used by guards to look in on prisoners or shout orders. It was known locally as a shurraqa, basically meaning something to let in air.

"Hey," Shinky called out to us, rapping his key on the door to get our attention. "Prisoner Jamal Saeed. Collect your things."

I guess I must have looked confused, for Abu Omar repeated the guard's order. "Collect your things, brother Jamal," he said with a smile. My heart beat faster as I heard the door unlock. "Go on, collect your things, brother."

"I don't need them," I said getting up. I would leave the entirety of my possessions, my towel, my small plastic sweets box, and a curved piece of plastic that served as a spoon. Another new prisoner would need the towel and not everybody had a plastic box to use as a teacup.

"It seems you've completed your mission, Alawite," one of the Brothers said, meaning he still believed I was a spy.

"No, no, you're going home," another said enthusiastically.

"Or to another prison, or cell," yet another added. "I've been in four prisons and lost track of the cells."

Dr. Muhammad shook my hand vigorously and kissed me on both cheeks. "I'm not going to give you any advice, young man. People like you know what has to be done. Enjoy your freedom."

"Kiss the sea for me," Imad the teenager added, "and don't forget us."

But Abu Omar wasn't so optimistic. "We all hope you'll be released," he said, "and that will make one less person in captivity." Then he repeated the expression he used whenever bidding a prisoner farewell: "Al-kharij mawlud, al-dakhil mafqud" — the one who gets out is reborn, and the one brought in is lost.

The cell door was now wide open, with Shinky waiting for me to finish my goodbyes. Finally done shaking hands and getting the last of the dirty looks, I walked out into the cellblock. I turned to take one last look at the faces I had become so familiar with, but Shinky, despite his ailments, had quickly slammed the door shut. I stood there, thinking about what had just happened. I was now separated from doomsday by only a few seconds and a steel door. And I was standing outside the cell without handcuffs for the first time. Could it be true? And then I noticed the paper in Shinky's hand. On it, printed in large letters, was the word "Release."

"C'mon," Shinky said, and I walked down the hall, able to swing my arms. As we walked up the stairs from the cell level, not only did the light and the air seem to get lighter and brighter, but also my mood. I dared begin to imagine how I would spend my day in Damascus. We stopped at a small office.

"In here," Shinky said to me. "Here he is," he said to someone in the office, and he turned and limped away. A dark-skinned young man, who looked like he could be an athlete, came out holding the same bag that my possessions were put in when I arrived. He handed it to me. I smiled at him as I took out both my belt and watch, put them on, and stuffed the cash into my pocket. Amazingly, it was all there.

"Got all your stuff?" he asked, and I smiled again. "Sign here." And then he put the paperwork on his desk. I turned and began winding the watch. Oddly, it had stopped at one minute to eleven, a minute later than the clock at the house of rats and mosquitoes. I was smiling at the coincidence, wondering for a moment which place had been worse, when I felt someone grab hold of my arms.

"Up against the wall, fucker," the guard shouted, and my face and chest were slammed hard against the wall. *What? Why?* My cheek was now squashed against one of the many photos of President Hafez al-Assad pasted up around the prison. My eye was glaring at his epaulette with the symbols of his rank: crossed swords, two stars, and an eagle. "Stay here, fucker," the guard said, and he walked away. I stood without moving for over a quarter of an hour.

Another body was pushed up against the wall next to me.

"Stay there. Don't talk," another guard said to Hussein. My Hussein. I waited for the guard to leave.

"I saw it with my own eyes," I whispered excitedly. "On a prison document. The word 'release.'" Hussein, looking much thinner and his skin somewhat jaundiced, smiled.

"We'll go to my sister Wafa's first," he said. "She makes great coffee."

"And then we'll have lunch at my uncle Mahmoud's. And after that I hope I can introduce you to Widad."

I felt a hard blow on the back of my head, accompanied by "Shut up, bastard," and my head collided with the president's image so violently that sparks flashed before my eyes. My legs wobbled, and I leaned on Hussein so that I wouldn't fall again.

Perhaps in the universe that Mr. President rules, the word "release" has many meanings, or no meaning at all.

But still, even then, I held on to a modicum of hope. The paperwork said "release." Maybe the guards were just getting their final kicks.

We stood there in silence for some minutes with the guards behind us. The only one talking was a guard relating how he had finally "gone to paradise" with his girlfriend. I smiled. *Liar.* That's when I heard the familiar zip and click of handcuffs being opened, and suddenly my wrists were locked behind my back. They did the same to Hussein.

This is a mistake. The paperwork. The paperwork said release.

Two other guards showed up.

"Okay, they're all yours," the muscular guard said.

Immediately, the new guards grabbed hold of us and began marching us through the corridors.

"I read the word 'release' next to our names on the document," I said in desperation to the guard clutching my arm. He laughed.

"Yes, yes, you're being released — from this winter resort," he said with a sarcastic laugh. "Spring has begun, and we're taking you somewhere nice to spend the summer."

Yet another guard opened a door for us, and the blinding light of the sun blotted everything from my vision. When I was finally able to see things again, there in the courtyard was a ZiL truck, whose heavy metal doors were opened like yet another mouth waiting to be fed. And behind the truck were four

Kalashnikov-carrying guards ready to bring us to wherever we were going. As they turned to view their new charges, one in particular stood out. The surprise must have shown on my face, as it certainly did on the face of my old classmate. His eyes went wide, not only with shock, but also with what appeared to be embarrassment. And as they came to claim us, their weapons slung over their shoulders, each took one of our arms and led us perfunctorily over to the vehicles and roughly half-carried us up the few steps and into the truck's belly. As they did so, the eyes of my old pal were just a few inches from mine. But still, neither of us said a word.

"Sit down there," the leader of the guards said, and Hussein and I sat on one of the side benches, while the guards sat on the other. We sat silently facing each other.

Mustafa? How in the world did you come to this?

In the winter of 1973, I bought a sweater from one of the many bales of clothes at a market stall in Latakia's Ugarit Square. The merchants here specialized in selling secondhand European imports, and this sweater really was a find: pure colors and soft wool.

"It looks big for you," my father said.

"Just a little bit. I'll grow into it," I said. "It's good quality. It will last." My father smiled. "Wise," he said.

When I proudly wore the sweater to school a few days later, Mustafa came up to me. He was three years older but had repeatedly failed to move up, making us classmates in ninth grade. Not much taller than me, he was wiry and strong, but also shy and quiet.

"That's an amazing sweater. I don't like dark colors," Mustafa said, pointing to his own drab pullover. He grabbed the sleeve of my prize with his index finger and thumb, feeling the soft wool. And then his eyes brightened. "Would you sell it?"

"No, I just got it," I said, and his look of disappointment was so profound, it made me sad. The next day I held the sweater out to him. I tried not to respond to the trembling of his lips and look of confusion.

"How . . . how much?" he asked. "I swear, I'll pay any price."

"I'll trade for your sweater."

When I sat down at my desk, I opened my notebook and wrote another of my worldly observations: "Poor people love elegance too."

After school, Mustafa came up to me, proudly wearing his new sweater. "Jamal. Come to my house. Please."

"Okay," I replied.

Walking to his home, I tried to discuss some of the subjects we'd studied at school that day, as I often did with other classmates. But Mustafa just made a face.

"How could any sane person like math or geography?" he asked.

"Okay," I answered.

"Yabo, look what my friend Jamal traded me for my old sweater," Mustafa said to his father when we got to his house. Abu Mustafa was a day laborer, getting work as and when he could. He was a very thin man with huge, bushy eyebrows and an equally bushy mustache. He didn't say a word, but I watched as he, too, felt the soft wool with his yellowed smoker's fingers. Umm Mustafa, also very slim, smiled at her son's happiness and patted him on the shoulder. And then she smiled at me.

I watched Mustafa now, flaunting his Kalashnikov, remembering him when he was a shy youth who preferred to sit at the back of the class, hated math and geography, and complained about his mother's cooking.

Over the weeks that followed, Mustafa, an excellent hunter and fisherman, continually brought my family birds and river fish. When my mother told him his family deserved his catch more than us, he replied that all the fish and birds in the world wouldn't be enough to repay me. Ummi and I watched him walking away, swaggering like I'd never seen before. He must have felt proud to give us these gifts, products of his expertise at hunting and fishing.

"He's in your class?" Ummi asked, somewhat astonished. I nodded. "Can you help him in his studies?"

I shrugged. "He has no interest."

"Well, he might be a simple boy, but he seems kind-hearted."

Mustafa seemed to have grown taller, and his eyes no longer had quite the defeated expression they'd had in our schooldays. I'd lost track of him when he didn't pass ninth grade and didn't return, so I guess he eventually took a job working in the mukhabarat. For here he was, staring at me with a Kalashnikov across his lap. I could sense the other three guards noticed the recognition in our eyes.

The truck had two small windows covered by iron grilles. We weren't blindfolded, and so, as we drove, I stretched my neck around to look out at the people and the buildings. I could feel the soles of my feet itching to stroll those streets. At the same time, I was trying to work out where we were headed. When we got near al-Nasr Street, it seemed we were on our way to al-Qala'a prison.

Suddenly, Mustafa addressed me. "Detainee, don't look out of the window."

Mustafa was the first guard to call me "detainee" instead of addressing me with multiple curses.

"What does it matter if I look out at the road?" I said, staring him straight in the eye.

The other guards looked to see his reaction to such impertinence from a prisoner, and so Mustafa puffed out his chest and, in the tone of an officer commanding his troops, fired back, "Carry out the order, and then protest."

"Go on then, do what the *lieutenant* tells you," another of the guards said with a laugh.

"Is Mustafa a lieutenant?" I asked.

"Aha. I knew it," the guard said. "You know each other."

"Don't call me Mustafa!" my old classmate said in a strangulated voice.

Another guard prodded me with his rifle butt. "Tell us. How do you know *Lieutenant* Mustafa?" he asked, and the others laughed. It was obvious that, once again, Mustafa was the least among them, the butt of their jokes. And for some reason, it annoyed me that they were treating him so.

Go back to your birds and fish, Mustafa. Back to the fields that know you as well as you know them. Get away from this filthy mockery of a job where you can only get a sense of power from making others suffer. You can get food for your soul elsewhere.

"I asked how you know the lieutenant," the other guard repeated.

"We were at school together," I answered.

"I'm not proud of that," Mustafa exclaimed, "because you are a traitor."

"Why do you say that, Mustafa?" I asked.

"If you weren't a traitor, they wouldn't have arrested you."

"I was trying to defend the poor who hate eggplants, geography, and gloomy colors," I said, looking Mustafa in the eye.

For a second I saw confusion in his eyes, as if memories were flooding back to him and he was trying to make sense of the situation. And then he fell back on his training, spewing out a cliché as loudly as if he were standing at attention and answering a drill sergeant.

"All the detainees have betrayed our president and are serving our enemies," he declared, and I saw his eyes flick toward his comrades, to see if they approved of his response.

I took a good look at Mustafa. Because he was in the mukhabarat, he didn't have to wear a uniform. But the way he was dressed was pitiful; an old multicolored flannel jacket with an equally multicolored paisley shirt with frills running down the front, buttoned right up to the neck. And his slacks, bright green polyester. Yes, Mustafa still liked bright colors, and no doubt his clothes were bought at another secondhand stall. He truly had failed in his attempt to imitate the elegant man he so desperately wanted to be.

Shortly before we arrived at the prison, one of the guards, the head of the patrol, asked me why I was smiling.

I looked at him, still smiling. "You can imprison my body, but my soul is free enough to laugh, as you see," I said, widening my grin.

Mustafa reached across the aisle to hit me on the shoulder with the butt of his rifle. "How can you laugh?" he shouted angrily. "Are you glad you're going to be thrown behind bars? Happy to lose your future? Why didn't you think about your family? Your mother? Are you crazy? Crazy?"

My smile faded. Now I understood. Mustafa was angry *for* me because he saw a friend in trouble, and he wasn't in a position to help. In fact, it was his job to humiliate me. He was in an impossible position. I then spoke very quietly.

"Please tell your mother that I loved the eggplant she offered us when I visited your home," I said. "Tell her I wish her a long and healthy life." And then I bowed my head.

"I'm telling you I don't know you," Mustafa shouted, "and you don't know me! Why are you talking to me like this?" And when I looked up again, his lips were trembling, just like when I first held out the sweater for him those many years ago.

"What do you want us to do with this crazy traitor, Lieutenant?" one of the guards asked and laughed. Mustafa didn't reply.

As I got off the truck at the entrance of al-Qala'a prison, Mustafa held his Kalashnikov across my chest. "Even though you don't deserve it," he said, "I'll let your family know where you are." And then from under his fingers holding on to the butt of his weapon, he dropped a small object into the pocket of my shirt. He and the others accompanied us inside al-Qala'a, removing our handcuffs and handing over the transfer papers with their stamps and signatures, goods to a new warehouse. I never saw Mustafa again, but he did make good on his promise, telling my family where I was.

Later, when I reached into my pocket and took out Mustafa's gift, I found it was a common key ring with a picture of a little robin. Its wings were outstretched as if taking off in flight. I wondered whether it was an amulet Mustafa kept to remind himself of the woods and birds he adored. Or was it the final installment for the sweater? I put my index finger through the ring and muttered to myself.

Although I need to unlock doors more than most people do, I don't think I'll be using this key ring any time soon. I don't have any keys, Mustafa.

CHAPTER 27

IN THE CITADEL
(AL-QALA'A CIVIL PRISON, APRIL 1981)

There was a small sign on the door of the room that read, *The Prison Pen*. Hussein and I entered and stood in front of a pleasant-looking but quite overweight policeman. He sat behind an old iron desk and was dressed in a formal beige uniform with a heavy linen shirt, red and gold insignias on the broad collar, and the word "Police" embroidered on its shoulder boards. His matching peaked cap sat on the table next to him, along with neat piles of documents and files. He looked up, smiled, and scratched his neck.

"Welcome, young men," he said. I noticed he was holding a silver Waterman fountain pen.

Does the sign on the door mean they assigned a room for this specific pen and even gave it a policeman to look after it? Ridiculous. Jamal, stop letting your imagination run away with you. This is serious.

The officer took his time reading our transfer pages, his lips slowly moving as he took in the information on one page and then the other.

"Who's Jamal?"

"Me," I answered.

"Good." And then he began asking questions.

Now I'm watching this particular pen fill in the same symbols that make up the information we've been asked at the other prisons: my name, my father's name, my age, my place and date of birth, my height, the color of my eyes, and so on. The policeman used an ink blotter to dry some of what he wrote, and then he looked at me, a wry smile on his face.

"I see you're to stand before the Supreme State Security Court," he said. The SSSC was set up to prosecute activists, politicians, and anyone else opposing the regime. "Do you realize that activists like you two are both smart and foolish?"

"Are you asking me a riddle?" I asked politely.

"You will discover what I mean when you grow up." And then he looked at my document again and shook his head. "You were supposed to be in university, and yet you're here. Why not be a doctor or lawyer? Contribute to Syria." I was about to reply when he continued his fatherly lecture. "You are the same age as my older son, and even share the same name." The policeman, Abu Jamal, smiled and scratched his neck again, appearing to think before he continued. "I will test your intelligence, young man. Explain this verse. Three living things drag the dead, the dead speaks while the living are silent."

"I've actually heard this riddle before," I confessed. "The three living things are the fingers and the dead who speaks is the pen, like the one in your hand."

The overweight policeman smiled. "You could have pretended not to have heard the riddle before, to appear more intelligent."

"Then I wouldn't be honest." He nodded his appreciation, and I continued. "You know, since the invention of ballpoint and felt pens, ink pens like Sheaffer, Mont Blanc, and Tropen are mostly found behind glass, as treasured possessions in people's china cabinets or displayed prominently on their owners' desks."

"I love writing with fountain pens," the policeman said fondly, and he took out a few more of his prized collection from a desk drawer. He seemed proud to show them off, the best being a dark blue Parker with a silver cap. Not high end, but popular because it was flashy.

"Oh, my uncle has the same pen. He's a policeman too."

"Your uncle should have taught you not to get involved in political issues," he said, sounding fatherly.

"Tell me, why is this called The Pen Room?" I asked.

"Because this is the room where the pen writes the information." He answered as if it were self-evident.

I suppressed a scornful laugh and stopped myself from adding that pens also record information in interrogation rooms and newsrooms, and in the bedroom of a teenager who writes about the dresses the neighbor's daughter wears. But here and in the more brutal interrogation rooms around our country, the pen does not move according to the wishes of the policeman, the jailer, or the torturer. It moves according to the wishes of the prison governor and so on, until you reach the source of all movement and — silence.

The policeman glanced at the documents in front of him. "Your turn now, Hussein," he said, and began taking down Hussein's details.

I watched my friend give his answers with a look of total dejection on his face. And when the police clerk had completed his task, he once again scratched his neck and began a lecture on his favorite subject.

"You know, the word 'pen' can mean an important writer. For example, we call Taha Hussein the Great Pen." He paused for a moment, scratched his neck yet again, and continued like a shaykh in front of his followers. "Almighty God was the first to glorify the pen. In the Quran there is a sura called the 'Sura of the Pen.'" Then he held his Parker close to my face. "The pen is even mentioned in the first message the Angel Gabriel revealed to the Prophet Muhammad from the Lord of the Worlds."

The policeman went silent, briefly looking to see the effect of his little lecture. And then, when neither of us responded, he looked at his register, made a few last scribbles, and then closed it with a snap. "The two of you will be in cell two in the Towers. Come." He put on his hat, struggled to his feet and led us out into a small rectangular courtyard. There were more offices, as well as cell doors, and stairs that led to other levels. I had read much of the history of the Citadel, and it was impressive beyond what I had expected. But now, in such a place, with the high walls of massive ancient stone, I didn't feel so much like a student of history as a bird trapped under a vast sky. The policeman pointed toward the door of cell two, our new home. But something looked odd to me, and then I realized the door to the cell was not solid metal. There were bars that let air and light in, something quite different from what we were used to. "Wait by the door, and I'll send someone to open it," the lover of pens said.

Amazingly, we were left without anyone guarding us. Nobody ordered us to turn our faces to the wall. Police and prisoners walked by, ignoring our very existence.

I took a closer look around me. In the middle of the courtyard was a pool with a central fountain spouting water, as you would see in many traditional houses in Damascus. And then my eyes were drawn up the length of the high walls. Making up their height were thousands of huge monolithic stones, some smooth, some textured, but all finely fit together. Each showed the craftsmanship of another age. And there, keeping a close watch over the city for the last thousand years, was the Citadel's iconic tower.

It came to me that before my arrest I'd distributed a statement demanding the release of two comrades who were also here in the Citadel: Jaffan al-Homsi and Husam Alloush. Their names were mentioned many times in our organization's newspaper and leaflets. In fact, Hussein was caught red-handed distributing the flier about them and describing how a certain prisoner had died under torture. That's probably why he was treated so much more severely than I was.

"We must find out where Jaffan and Husam are," I said, feeling no need to check around me or whisper.

"Yes, you're right. For sure."

"Have you met either of them?"

"No. Have you?"

"No."

"Perhaps they're in cell two, in the Towers," Hussein said forlornly, his face full of melancholy.

My poor Hussein. You have enough sadness for the whole of a stricken city. Here we are in the Citadel of Damascus. Many armies have engaged in devastating wars, and many have died to get the key to this place. The Seljuks couldn't keep the key. Around nine hundred years ago, Shams al-Mulk inherited the Citadel from his father, but he couldn't hold on to this "impregnable" dwelling either. Turkmen, Seljuks, Mamluks, Ayyubids, Mongols, and French have all roamed these halls. They came riding on finely caparisoned horses, carrying swords, spears, compound bows, and quivers full of arrows. Some of the invaders used catapults and destroyed the stonework in their struggle to get the key to the Citadel. And after they'd conquered it, they strengthened its fortifications in an attempt to keep themselves from having the same thing done to them. But, Hussein, you and I arrived onboard a Soviet ZiL truck with four guards whose guns were also Soviet. There were no grand horses, and nobody was killed. We entered without having to fight for the key, even though we had no interest in such an ancient obsession. The police just opened the door and pushed us in. Past rulers entered the Citadel of Damascus with high hopes, and it became a place where they felt safe. The nationalist version of the history books sang their praises. Mustafa, one of the poor whom we thought we were defending, considered us traitors. They brainwashed him and robbed him of his village innocence. Hussein, we are going to live where Shams al-Mulk dwelled and where Saladin spent evenings with his friends and the commanders of his army. We are guests of a past hidden in the stones and high walls. We won't be attacked by cavalrymen or have huge stones and fireballs hurled at us from catapults.

We lived in the modern world, or so we thought. The use of this place is now intended to push us modern dreamers back into being eleventh-century subordinates.

Damascus Citadel is now a historical landmark. The castle was used as a civil prison building until the eighties, and I was a prisoner there for seventeen months.

I looked at the circular pool in the middle of the small courtyard. It must have originally been made with the same fine stonework, but somebody had obviously coated it with modern cement and placed a single metal pipe in the middle to generate a fountain of water. This caused an echoing babble to bounce off the surrounding walls. It made me think of my childhood river back home and, somehow, this relaxed me. And then I read the signs on the doors of the rooms surrounding the courtyard: *Prison Governor, Deputy Prison Governor, Association for the Care of Prisoners* . . . and then my eyes went wide. *Library.* And they went even wider as I spied two other signs with arrows pointing down a narrow walkway. One read *Theater* and the other *Kitchen.*

"Hussein, there's a library here," I say enthusiastically. "And a kitchen, and even a theater."

"Everything connected with prison is shit," he said morosely, staring blankly into space, rubbing one shoulder, wincing, and then the other. He was in physical pain. I looked back at the words on the signs. They were written in white paint on black metal, immobile, as if the letters had gotten used to hanging there, their muscles pulled taut and stiff against the cold, black steel. And then I looked at my friend and finally saw what had been staring me in the face.

The theater and the kitchen are extremely important, Hussein. The mouth devours the offerings of the kitchen and the eyes and ears consume what's presented onstage. We human beings spend a lot of time satisfying these orifices, maintaining them and cleaning them and preparing them to be satisfied anew. Have you seen the words "Kitchen" and "Theater," Hussein? They are written in white paint on black metal. They don't move, as if they have got used to hanging there, their muscles pulled taut and hard on the black metal. Did they string you up by your arms, Hussein? Who invented this kind of torture? How did they hang you, Hussein? Did they hang you by the wrists and let your body dangle so your toes almost touched the floor? I haven't been subjected to that, but I saw a man who was. They let me see it on purpose, in order to terrorize me. His groans were indeed terrifying.

"Hussein, did they torture you?" I asked quietly.

"I didn't believe human beings could be so barbaric," he said, avoiding my eyes. "I don't want to talk about horrible things."

"Of course, my friend, of course. But look what they have here. A theater. I wonder what the stage is like and what plays they put on. Isn't it something to look forward to?"

"Maybe it's where they carry out executions."

"Hey, you said you didn't want to talk about such things," I said, forcing a chuckle. But I wasn't just trying to play nurse to a friend. I had to take care of myself. Depression can be infectious, like a fit of yawning or the plague. I pointed toward the ornamental pool in the middle of the courtyard and again tried to distract him. "Did you know that the people of Damascus call these little fountains bahra? Bahra is the feminine form of bahr, the sea. Imagine, this little pool is the female version of the mighty sea."

He finally looked over at me. "Water is becoming increasingly scarce in this country," he said, deadpan. We just stared at each other.

"Wow, you really are determined to stay gloomy," I said, and then we both finally burst out laughing.

That's when three policemen entered the square dragging a struggling prisoner. They ordered him to undress, threw him in the pool, and let him flounder, keeping him from finding his feet by repeatedly shoving him with bamboo canes and slapping his face when he grabbed hold of the fountain's edge. And when they did finally yank him out, they kept him on his knees, handcuffed him, and began beating him with the canes. As he lay there groaning, a short man emerged running from the deputy-governor's door. His sparse mustache failed to hide the deep scar on his upper lip, which was more prominent than the epaulettes denoting his colonel's rank. He motioned that the beating should stop and went up to the prisoner, a man in his thirties, naked except for soaking boxer shorts. The colonel squatted down and put his face very close to the prisoner's.

"Basim Rafi," he said plainly. "If you just tell me where the drugs came from, I won't let them abuse you anymore. Tell me. How can a prisoner get a hold of five kilos of hashish? Five!"

They hauled the prisoner up and dragged him into the colonel's office. It seemed these were familiar goings on here, for leaning against a wall and calmly smoking a cigarette was a tall, elegant man who had calmly watched the whole event. He nodded at me, and I nodded back. I looked over at Hussein. His expression was now even gloomier than before. I took his arm and approached the man.

"Excuse us. Are you a prisoner?" I asked.

"Do I look like the prison governor?" The man laughed. "I'm Abu Ahmad al-Sharqawi, ten years a guest of this hotel."

"Oh, I'm sorry, but honored to meet you. I'm Jamal Saeed. Do you know a prisoner called Jaffan al-Homsi, or one called Husam Alloush?"

"I know them both. They're not here. They're in the Citadel, in the same cell as me, in fact." He smiled.

"Isn't this the Citadel?" I asked.

Like someone giving a geography lesson in primary school, he explained, "The whole prison complex is known as the Citadel, all surrounded by the same wall. But it's divided in two. The place where we're standing is the Towers. What's called the Citadel is about a three-minute walk from here. Jaffan and Husam are lovely fellows," and then he laughed. "Their only flaw is that they're political prisoners. Please, please tell me you two aren't political prisoners."

"I'm afraid we are." I laughed in turn.

"Thank God I'm in here for something unrelated to politics. Brother, most people know when they're getting out, and they might not even have to serve their full term. But political prisoners have no idea when they'll be released. None. They pay a high price for saying something they could have kept to themselves." And then he chuckled. "Communists earn the wrath of both governments and the Almighty — and all for no good reason!"

"What are you in here for, Mr. Abu Ahmad?"

"You're not going to believe it — few do — but I'm innocent. I was falsely accused of the rape and murder of a minor. I swear to you, I'm innocent. Where are they putting you?"

His statement, so casually made, caught me off guard. I couldn't answer.

"Cell number two in the Towers," Hussein answered.

"But they're all Muslim Brotherhood."

"Muslim Brothers!" Hussein replied. "Can we move to your cell, to be with you, Jaffan, and Husam?"

"Move to the Citadel first."

"How?" Hussein asked.

"A sweetener."

"What do you mean?" I asked.

"Pay that fat policeman in the Pen Room."

"How much?"

"Ten Syrian pounds."

"What if he gets angry and refuses? I could get into trouble."

"Refuse?" Sharqawi guffawed. "For ten more pounds, he'd probably drop his pants."

I returned to the Pen Room and put ten pounds on the desk, trying to make the gesture look casual. The policeman looked at me, surprised, and scratched his neck. I smiled and took a deep breath.

"Please, could you transfer us to the Citadel? It may be difficult for us to get along with the Muslim Brothers."

He grabbed up the ten pounds and stuffed it into his pants pocket, shifting in his chair to get his hand past his stomach. "Aren't you from the Muslim Brotherhood?" he asked.

"No, we're communists."

"God forgive you, you should have told me . . . Fine." He opened his black book, wrote something with his Waterman and blotted it carefully, blowing to speed the drying. "We could transfer you to cells five and eleven in the Citadel. What do you think?"

"You know best. Thank you very much."

Sharqawi and a very thin policeman escorted us from the Towers to the Citadel. We went up a flight of stone steps, along a corridor, down more steps, and into a room that looked part barracks, part office. Two young policemen who were sitting smoking cigarettes on a metal bed looked up indifferently and just stared. There was another officer in his forties. He sat behind a cheap metal desk and looked enquiringly at us, too, smoothing his hand along the hair covering a bald patch. Our escort put a sheet of paper on the desk.

"Which one of you is Jamal?" asked Comb-Over.

"Me."

"You'll be in cell number eleven. You're Hussein?"

"Yes."

"You're in cell five. Please, go ahead. Sharqawi will show you to the cells."

We went through another door that led to a large courtyard with cells all around it. For the first time, I took a good look at Sharqawi. His face seemed to possess the innocence of a child. Could he really have done what he was accused of? And why did he have the run of the place?

"What would the two of you think about a cup of coffee?" Sharqawi asked.

"I'd be really grateful," I said, reaching into my pocket, but he put up a hand and gave a host-like smile. "Shukran," I said, thank you, and we walked over to a small outdoor cafeteria selling hot drinks. It looked like the fellow running the place was an inmate.

"How do you like your coffee?"

"Black, no sugar," I said.

"And you, Hussein?"

"The same."

Sharqawi ordered five coffees. And then I realized that nobody had asked me to hand over my watch or confiscated my money. I began to wind the black Seiko, and its second hand began to tick forward.

"What time is it?" I asked Sharqawi.

"Three minutes past eleven," he replied, handing over our coffees. "I'll be back shortly."

I looked at Hussein and raised my eyebrows, as if to say, "Well, isn't this different?" and we sipped happily, eyeing our new surroundings. I was then drawn to look at the beautiful clouds in the sky. I hadn't been able to watch that movie for many months.

Sharqawi returned with two young men, one with a reddish blond beard, the other tall with spectacles and a thick black mustache.

"Do you know these two?" he asked me.

"I haven't had the pleasure."

"Do you want to guess?" he asked, his eyes full of mischief.

I pointed to the youth with spectacles. "This is Jaffan?"

"No, that's Husam. Jaffan's the one with a beard."

"Oh my God. This is incredible," I shouted. "I'm Jamal Saeed and this is Hussein Muhammad."

The four of us embraced warmly. Jaffan and Husam had been transformed from names in a communiqué and the *Red Banner* newspaper into men of flesh and blood. And incredibly, they knew about us too.

"We heard the two of you had been arrested," Husam said, "and that you were being held by the military intelligence in Latakia."

"Yes. And after that we were transferred to the Military Investigation Branch in Damascus. How do you know?"

"Bad news travels fast," Jaffan said.

"Prisoners can have two visits a week," Husam explained. "That's how we keep up to date and get things from our families."

"Wow. This is heaven compared to where we've been," I said. "There we get nothing."

"Here you can get whatever you want," Sharqawi said. "Food, drink, or even drugs. But not a woman. Impossible. Here, the real prisoner is your penis."

There were only three unoccupied chairs in front of the buffet. "Let's go to the school office to relax," Sharqawi suggested.

"School?" I exclaimed. This was getting better.

"Yes. And Sharqawi is school secretary," Jaffan said.

I thought they were joking. "What do you have to be charged with to be made headmaster?" I asked sarcastically, and then felt bad for making a joke at Sharqawi's expense. He had been very welcoming and helpful. "Sorry," I said to him, but he just laughed.

"Actually, the Ministry of Education appoints the headmaster," Jaffan said. "He's not a prisoner. Hey, you know what? If you and Hussein volunteer to teach illiterate prisoners to read and write, we could get you transferred to cell number ten with Husam and me. Most of our cellmates are students and volunteer teachers."

"You can apply for that tomorrow morning," Husam suggested, "but now you must be hungry, like everyone who comes from the investigation branches."

"That's the truth," I said. "We've been starving for months."

Husam went ahead and ordered food from another little stall in the yard, and this time Husam and Jaffan treated.

"The sellers all look like inmates," I observed.

"Yes," Jaffan explained. "They pay high rent to the jailers, but they keep a bit of the money, and it occupies them. Besides a coffee stand and grill, there's a barber, a sundries shop, and we pay for the good showers. Say, it will take about thirty minutes for the food. What about having a shower while you wait?"

"*Yes!*" Hussein and I said at the same time.

"Wait here. I'll go get you some fresh underwear and towels from our cell. Family and friends are always bringing us these things. We have a lot. And would you rather have laurel soap or shampoo? We have plenty of both."

"*Laurel soap!*" Hussein and I shouted in unison again. Made in Aleppo, laurel soap is famously good for everything.

While we waited, once again I gave Hussein a look to say, See, things are getting better.

Returning with towels, fresh underwear, the soap, and even soft new linen pajamas, Jaffan led us to a bathhouse. In front of it was the shop that sold basic items for the prisoners. This place was run by a short, dark-skinned prisoner with a wide tobacco-stained smile.

"Rakan is in charge here," Jaffan said, giving the man a pound bill. "This is Jamal and Hussein. They arrived today."

"Hello, welcome. Your obedient servant, Rakan Afash," he said, waving his hand in a happy blur. Jaffan went off, and Rakan told us we could buy a new loofah and a blade for a safety razor. The razor he rented for when you were in the showers. "They're very good, not only for your face, but down here too." He laughed, pointing his long fingers downward. For lice, I presumed.

There were no doors to the shower cubicles, just curtains. Each stall was no more than ten square feet, with a showerhead and two knobs to control the temperature. I delighted in the hot water, the delicious scent of the soap, and the lather that covered me from head to toe.

When bathing in such a tiny cubicle is a dream come true, you have to question what's been done to your mind in those harsh military prisons.

Emerging from the bathhouse feeling and smelling oh so clean, we found Sharqawi, and Husam waiting with a large stainless-steel tray heaped with food for the five of us. It looked to be several pounds of lamb kebab, grilled onions and tomatoes, salad, and a pile of pita. The smell of it teased me as we walked to the school office where, trying my best not to look greedy, I devoured my portion. It was more food than I'd normally eat in a week at the investigation branch. But curiously, even though I was so full and knew I shouldn't eat more, I wanted to. So I closed my eyes and sighed, allowing the food to settle. And as it did, I could actually feel the constant buzz of hunger that had been gnawing at my brain for months go silent.

"I'll give you gang of four a chance to plot against the government," Sharqawi teased, putting a hand to his heart as he left.

"Listen, you two," Jaffan said when Sharqawi was out of earshot. "We're among convicted prisoners here. Thieves and murderers. They're not the same as us. You must watch what you say. Keep your distance from them.

You'll probably see fights, and knives will appear from nowhere. Always be respectful and serious. Never make fun of anyone or comment out loud on strange behavior. Do you understand?" Hussein and I nodded, and Jaffan went on. "Did Sharqawi tell you he was innocent?"

"Yes. Is it true?" I asked.

"Nobody knows. But he was sentenced to death more than ten years ago, and when he hears someone outside the cell at dawn, he thinks they're coming to drag him off to the gallows. That's when he pulls a blanket over his head and we can all see it shaking. The terror only passes when we reassure him that there's nobody in the yard, and by the time breakfast is delivered, he's back to the way you see him. Executions here take place at dawn."

I looked at Hussein. He was still gloomy and troubled.

"Here we can see the sky, Hussein. Look! Don't you think that cloud looks like Velasquez's painting *Venus in Front of a Mirror?*"

Everyone looked at the cloud.

"The similarity is in the curve between the shoulder and the bottom," remarked Jaffan, "and there's a similarity in the roundness of the bottom too."

Hussein shook his head, as if to say there was no similarity whatsoever.

"Sky, sun, hot coffee, a shower, then a meal of grilled meat and fresh salad. This is bliss, Hussein."

Hussein nodded sarcastically. "Bliss in prison," he declared, as if reading off an advertisement. "The Citadel is the peak of pleasure. Enjoy, brother prisoner."

CHAPTER 28

WILLIAM'S TREASURE

At dawn on my first morning in the Citadel, I heard the familiar beautiful voice of the muezzin calling us to prayer from the Umayyad Mosque right next to my new home.

"Allahu akbar. Allahu akbar," echoed the call. God is great. God is great.

A chorus of five voices repeated the words, and it went on, the muezzin and then the chorus, all through the prescribed adhan, or call to prayer. I sat there on the mattress of my iron bedstead in cell eleven, the sad chorus of amplified voices reverberating off the city and into my cell, and I felt a profound connection to my mind that day.

That connection is very clear, and my grief is pure and delicate. Was it only five months ago that I was walking with Jamil Hatmal in these neighborhoods near the prison? Then, as the call to prayer continues, I can see in my mind's eye how the adhan always seems to startle the pigeons, making them first tremble and then explode up into the sky, the chant of the muezzin orchestrating their aerial dances.

Jamil, my friend, you're still strolling around out there while I'm locked in here. You are still experiencing the colors and smells of the spices in al-Baẓouriyah market, the books on display in al-Miskiya, and the men exhaling smoke along with their worries at Nawfara Café. I can only experience it again in my mind. Most remembered about our walks is watching the women catching men's eyes, even when they are obliged to wear their long, loose jilbab or cover their face with a niqab so only their eyes show. Do you remember, Jamil, the discussion we had in the market,

Souq al-Hamidiyah? You and I agreed that the oppression women suffer doesn't mean that their feminine power is invisible. They have many ways of expressing it; the way they walk, their voices, and the hypnotic movement of the fingers, all effective in spurring men to look upon the women furtively, but take in everything.

In a short time, Jamil, the corrugated roofs of the souq will again be crammed with people; all shapes, sizes, ages, all with their own mysteries. How I thirst for the city that flows so close, within range of my senses, a river of sweet water my dry lips cannot taste.

In the Military Investigation Branch, before I came to the Citadel, Dr. Muhammad told me that the Umayyad Mosque was the only mosque in Damascus, and perhaps in the world, where the call to prayer was interspersed with a call-and-response chorus. My nemesis and floormate, Shahada, interrupted to declare that making music in this way wasn't allowed in the call to prayer, and a long discussion followed as to whether the musical style was based on an Ottoman interpretation of Islamic law and practice or on the tradition and practice of the prophet Muhammad.

"Come now," Dr. Muhammad beseeched the glowering Shahada, "did not the Messenger of God appoint a person with a beautiful voice to give the call to prayer?" And then he told the story of how it came about: "A valued companion of Muhammad, Abdullah bin Zaid, had the call to prayer come to him in a dream. When he told the Prophet about it, Muhammad declared the dream an authentic vision and asked bin Zaid to teach a singer, Bilal al-Habashi, the words of the call exactly as Allah had sent them. And why was Bilal, a black brother from Ethiopia, chosen? Because he had the most melodious voice in all the land." When the doctor finished, I think he was expecting Shahada to acquiesce. But not on that day.

"Performing the sacred call to prayer as a melody is not only abhorrent," Shahada declared in a booming voice, "it is forbidden. It turns the call to prayer into a song performed by . . . by . . . by impudent buffoons!"

Waking up on a bed with clean sheets, and not on a hard floor next to Shahada and eighty-three other stinking men, should have made my heart glad. But no. Perhaps it was the sad music and the city that I was so close to and yet so far from, but I was overcome by a deep melancholy. Hussein was right. Prison was not the place for happiness. And adapting to prison was surrender to slavery.

Two weeks later, I am sitting at a table in the prison square. It's sunny, and I'm drinking coffee, both my own university study books and my teaching assignments in front of me. I'm chatting amiably with Khalil Barayyiz, another prisoner and author. He is also the leader of cell number eleven, where I was first assigned.

"Look at you," Khalil says. "Not here any time at all and already a teacher and a university student."

It's hard to believe all that's transpired since I first met this man. I walked into number eleven wearing my new pajamas, my dirty old clothes rolled up under one arm. A fellow wearing a simple religious-type gown greeted me. He had a strong smile surrounded by scraggly salt-and-pepper hair and beard. He held out his hand and grasped mine firmly.

"I'm Khalil Barayyiz," he said.

"The author of *The Fall of the Golan Heights*?" I asked.

"The very same," he replied, looking a bit surprised, but smiling.

"I'm so very pleased to meet you," I said. "I have so many questions . . ."

"Well, thank you and welcome. But first why don't we get you settled?" And he showed me to an upper bunk bed. "It overlooks the courtyard, and you can use the window as a small closet for your things. And you'll have a good view of the television as well."

"Television?" I said in amazement, and there it was, a fairly new color TV sitting on a table in the middle of the cell.

I wanted to ask more about the book that had led to Barayyiz's kidnapping by the government and his imprisonment in 1970. How to start?

"You were an intelligence officer, weren't you?" I asked.

He corrected me firmly. "I was head of reconnaissance at the front. No longer an officer, in any case. How did you know?"

"Abd al-Ghani Ayyash told me about you and lent me your book."

"I don't know him. You read the book?"

"Of course."

"Oh. So . . . what did you think?"

"It raises important questions about the outcome of the June War. So, as a reconnaissance officer at the frontline in 1967, you saw how Hafez al-Assad, the minister of defense at the time, and other Baathists didn't try even to protect the Golan Heights."

"Exactly," he agreed.

"And then Syrian intelligence had you kidnapped from Lebanon?"

"Yes, I thought the truth was important, but the government . . ." and he flicked his wrist to mean all that doesn't matter now. "But, you liked it? The book?" he asked earnestly.

A prisoner in his sixties laughed out loud. "Barayyiz, that book was the cause of all your troubles and still you're fishing for compliments? You're lucky they didn't . . ." and he sliced his forefinger across his neck.

"Don't talk about politics," the old prisoner said in a grinning stage whisper to me. "The walls have ears. And they might put you in prison." I smiled at his bad joke, and he handed me a set of brand-new sheets. After how I'd been sleeping, they smelled and felt like heaven. "I always have clean sheets, blankets, and pillowcases for the new arrivals," Khalil added. "Try to hang on to them for as long as you can."

And I did, even when, a few days later, both I and Hussein were able to join Jaffan, Husam, and Sharqawi in cell number ten. It hadn't been so difficult.

I volunteered to become a member of the team to erase illiteracy. I would teach English for beginners. Hussein volunteered to teach English to prisoners who already had a background in the language.

At the investigation branch we slept on a concrete floor with no covers or pillows. Eighty-four men in a room less than five hundred square feet. At al-Qala'a, we all slept on bunk beds with five feet between the beds, forty-eight people in over a thousand square feet. Half the people and more than twice the space. Each cell had a large washroom with one basic toilet and a large sink for washing our faces and clothes, if you didn't want to pay for taking it to the laundry. A laundry! In this cell I chose a lower bunk. This way, at night, I could sit on my bed and use the table between the beds to write on.

While the prisoners stayed in the square during the day, the doors to their cells were closed. Our cell was an exception; the door remained open and we could get in or out whenever we wanted. This way we had more time to work with our students. After that, students could then do their homework and study until 6 p.m. But after that, it was impossible for anybody to concentrate. This was when all the television sets in all the cells were turned up very loud, and, in fact, I had to wait until after midnight, when the single channel available stopped broadcasting, to do my own personal writing. But on nice afternoons, I'd sit at a table studying or marking papers in the prison yard, often exchanging ideas with interesting people like Khalil.

Also, I used to meet with the students I was teaching to read and write. Hamid, one of those students, was still on trial for the murder of his step-father. When I saw how calm he was, I couldn't imagine he would commit murder. As a student, Hamid was eccentric. He was enthusiastic during dis-cussion and in his writing. He seemed to be very clever in some lessons, and in others he seemed vacant and unresponsive, as if under the influence of a drug. It caught my attention that regardless of his mood, he would leave the class whenever his friend Salim passed by the window of the classroom. Hamid introduced me to his friend Salim once, and he tried hard to persuade him to join the reading class, but Salim refused.

"I'm not crazy about stuffing my head with books and papers," he said with a laugh. "Life is meant to be enjoyed. I will drink the water that God has rationed for me, and then I'll die. Right, Mr. Jamal?" I shook my head listen-ing to Salim's philosophy, looking at his hair and mustache that resembled that of Ezra Pound as a young man.

"Let's go and have tea," Salim said to Hamid. Then he looked at me and said, "Goodbye, sir."

After they moved away, Jaffan approached me and described the insep-arable duo using an Arabic expression: "Those guys are two asses in one trouser." Then he continued: "What do they want?"

"Hamid wants to persuade Salim to attend my class."

Jaffan nodded.

My eyes moved to the most enigmatic of all the prisoners. We had exchanged smiles and nods several times, but he always looked back down at what he was doing.

He was a tall, quiet man who always wore light beige pajamas and spent his time making gift items. This included threading colored beads onto covers for shisha pipes, little medallions with phrases beaded on them, or small purses and women's handbags.

I first noticed him when I was walking about with Jaffan a few days after arriving. To me he looked like a film star, someone possessing the powerful presence of Omar Sharif or Anthony Quinn.

"Who's the tall prisoner in beige pajamas?" I asked.

"The oldest prisoner in the Citadel, William al-Sharouti," Jaffan said. "He was imprisoned before my mother gave birth to me. A very nice man. He was arrested in 1959, I think, when Nasser was president of Syria and Egypt!"

"That's a long time in here," I said.

"He keeps to himself," Jaffan added. "He's friendly enough, but nobody really knows anything about him. But the rumors and gossip? Everybody in jail lives for rumors and gossip."

"Like what?"

"The main one is that he works day and night with his beads to make huge sums of money to buy his freedom. Some will tell you about a mysterious prisoner who smuggles William's money to a contact on the outside. Others subscribe to the 'William's Treasure' theory, that he's hidden his cache of money somewhere in the prison. But if you ask him anything about any of it, he just shrugs."

It was true about the gossip. Over the first weeks I heard many theories.

"William is one of the Lord's mysteries," declared Sido Suleiman. Sido was the prison barber, sentenced to twelve years for robbery with violence. As his sharp scissors flew about my hair, he went on and on. "Nobody knows where he hides his money. He makes gifts out of beads and the Association for the Care of Prisoners sells them and gives him some of the profits. He's content with the food provided by the prison authorities and never buys anything extra. You'd need a pair of pliers to extract a single penny from him. So, that's why I want to know," he said, pausing his scissors next to my ear, "where is all the money he's been saving for over twenty years? Where?" and then he snapped the scissors shut as an exclamation mark.

Issa al-Khalil, a famous bank robber, was known as the Arab Robin Hood and nicknamed "Abu al-Fuqara'," Father of the Poor. After a heist, he gave most of the money he stole to the needy. He told me his own anecdote about William.

"Once a year at each and every Christmas," Abu al-Fuqara' began, "William puts on a formal suit from the 1950s. Tall, clean-shaven, and bespectacled, he looks like a government minister who has leapt from the pages of an old newspaper. On Christmas morning he attends Mass in the prison theater, and then he brings out a folding chair and sits by the door of his cell, number five, calmly sipping tea. It's the only day of the year he doesn't work with his beads. If you sit with him and ask about the treasure, and believe me I have, he will just ignore you and start talking about the sea in Alexandria. 'There's no sea in the whole world like the sea in Alexandria.' That's all that William will say about it, the sly old dog.''

The "sly old dog" sounded interesting, and so I decided to introduce myself before going to the school. I walked up to him with my arms full of books.

"Good morning, Mr. William," I said.

"Hello, good morning to you, young man," he said, his concentration still focused on the beads he was sewing onto a lady's handbag.

"How are you?" I asked.

"I'm fine," and then he looked up. "How about you?" he asked pleasantly.

I noticed he still spoke with an Egyptian accent, as if he'd just arrived in the prison straight from the streets of Alexandria. His white hair and pale complexion, and the large gentle eyes behind his spectacles, gave him a venerable, dignified air. He also had the type of smile that drew you to him, when he decided to share it. He treated me as if we were already acquainted, shifting his gaze between me and the little beads he was threading, following a pattern on a sheet of graph paper.

"I'm new in the prison. They told me you are the oldest inmate."

"I think that's true," he said indifferently.

"May I ask what you were charged with?" I inquired. "And have you been tried yet?"

"Believe me, young man, I don't have a clue what they're up to," he said, and he went back to his work.

I stood there politely, waiting for him to ask questions about me, to continue the conversation, but he just sat staring through his reading glasses, picking up beads with his long, curved needle and stitching them into his project.

"Well, I'd better be off to class."

"Yes, good," he said. "It's best to keep busy."

CHAPTER 29

HASHISH SMUGGLERS GIVE LECTURES ON ENGLISH LITERATURE

I met Adnan, whose father kicked me out of his house, by chance, near the Mariamite Cathedral. When he told me that he had enrolled me in the English literature department, I didn't take it seriously. But now I admit it's good that he did. Because even though I was in civil prison, it was now my right to present myself for the university exams when the regular students wrote them in May. And so, that became my aim. But passing the first-year courses was going to be a big challenge. The academic semester started in September, and it was already April. I had only a month to prepare. Damascus University's first-year requirement toward a liberal arts degree included drama, prose, poetry, composition, French, translation, English grammar, and national culture, which was just the current regime's Arab-Socialist policy. I could get course notes from Jaffan, as he'd been a student in the same department from the beginning of the year. All studying and preparation for exams was done without access to the university professors and entirely in the prison. The only time I could set foot on the university campus was to write the exams. But Hussein, who already had his degree, agreed to tutor me, and I also had two other prison professors.

There was Mr. Anthony, an old Englishman arrested while smuggling a large quantity of hashish on Syrian territory. He was in love with all things Elizabethan. And then there was Paulo Sciaviti, an Italian in his forties who, in order to make money to finance his farm, had also turned to dealing drugs. He was caught during his first transaction. Paulo told me about his French fiancée, who sent him packets of chocolate and novels by Nikos Kazantzakis, Gabriel García Márquez, and Hermann Hesse, all in English translation. He swore she was one of the few French people who loved the English language, and therefore he did too.

I used to write paragraphs in English and give them to Paulo, who corrected them with a red pen. When I declared in a panic that I was certain to fail with this number of mistakes, he would laugh and pat me on the shoulder.

"Jamal, whether you pass or fail, the sun will always arise the next day."

The day of my first exam, a patrol consisting of four policemen took me to the university in a Toyota Cruiser, which looks like a big Jeep. Sometimes the guards left the cuffs on me until we got to the exam room, and sometimes they took them off while we were walking about. On my first visit, I was without manacles, and so I walked through the halls with two Kalashnikov-carrying officers in front of me and two behind. Students assumed I was the son of a senior government minister under protection, but when they found out I was a political prisoner, many of them expressed their sympathy. Salwa Zakzak had the courage to approach me and said she was ready to ensure I had the books and resources I needed. Salwa is still a short-story writer living in Damascus.

Once, the lead guard wanted to leave the cuffs on me while I wrote my exam.

"Okay," I said, and I started waving my arms in the air, showing off my Spanish bracelets. The jingling garnered a lot of looks from the forty other students in the hall.

"Hey, don't do that," the guard complained.

"Why not? I'm not ashamed."

"Just don't."

"You could take them off," I suggested with a smile, still holding the cuffs high over my head. He removed them.

Besides keeping busy with my studies, I regularly had more than fourteen students who wanted to learn English and twenty who needed rudimentary literacy instruction. At first I had high expectations for all of my charges, but I soon had to accept that all of them would just learn what they were willing or able to at the time. Many of these students came to class high on drugs, so they slept, or were unable to recall things they were taught a day, an hour, or even minutes earlier. Hamid was one of these. He was always pleasant and really wasn't that stupid, but when he wasn't obviously high, he was either sleeping or looking out the window for Salim.

It wasn't uncommon to see blood during loud quarrels and physical fights, and even a few knives or broken glass bottles drawn. Jaffan's advice had been good: I had to be careful in dealing with the convicted prisoners. Being a teacher, I had to interact with many of them, and behaving formally but friendly, and never judgmental, gave me a kind of immunity. It was easy to detect a short temper, misconception, mental disorder, or addiction.

I ended up passing six out of the eight university exams, failing drama and prose. This upset me until I was told I was going to be able to enter second-year studies the next semester, and I was really happy that I'd be able to write make-up exams in September. This meant I wouldn't have to wait another year before I got back on campus. But the implications of that were made clear when a guard was putting handcuffs back on me after the last of my first-year exams.

"You should have taken the opportunity to see your family in the open air," he said. "You could have invited them to see you on campus."

"If only you'd told me that on the first day of the exams."

"Don't worry. You can do it next year."

Next year? I thought. *Will I still be here?*

Every day, from the beginning of the broadcast at 6 p.m. until it ended at midnight, we either enjoyed or had to endure the deafening sound of TV.

News bulletins usually started by emphasizing the importance of what the president was doing that day, often with the phrase, "The President welcomed . . ."

Most prisoners liked the American sitcoms popular at the time. Things like *B.J. and the Bear*, in Arabic called *B.J. and the Monkey*. Kojak, a bald New York City detective, went around solving crimes with a lollipop in his mouth. The show was so popular, a Middle Eastern candy maker created the same type of confection on a stick and called them Kojaks. I didn't watch any of these inane shows, preferring to talk with my fellow prisoners, and we had to sit close to each other to be heard. There were a few good programs, like an Egyptian historical drama series called *The Night Granada Fell*, about how the Spanish Catholics took back the city after seven hundred years of Muslim rule. Besides excellent writing and meticulous research, it starred Egyptian actors Amina Rizk, Tawfik El Deken, and Abdullah Ghaith, who were very dynamic, great performers.

The lighter Middle Eastern fare included clips of comedy from well-known Egyptian and Syrian performers, and there was a program that featured European performers, called *Stars and Lights*. From it I got to know European stars and their music: Mireille Mathieu, Demis Roussos, and Baccara. Baccara's song "Yes Sir, I Can Boogie" had Hussein and me searching in vain for the word "boogie" in that year's edition of the Mawrid dictionary in the prison library.

At the end of each TV night, the program *Tomorrow We Will Meet* included videos of Egyptian dancers such as Soheir Zaki and Nagwa Fouad performing Middle Eastern belly dances. These were beautiful and talented young women, and Fouad actually danced at the Bolshoi in Moscow. She liked to tell people that Kissinger flew all the way to Cairo to watch her dance and proposed marriage to her. These performances were accompanied by the prisoners' sighs and sexual remarks, showing how frustrated and repressed we all were.

Fahd al-Dhiyab always repeated the same sentence whenever he saw the plump, fair-skinned Soheir Zaki on the screen: "I'd swap the rest of my life for three minutes in her arms."

And then Ibrahim Mithqal would follow with his usual invocation, "Brother, three minutes just isn't enough."

The routine of getting up, making food, teaching, studying, building friendships, television time, and then writing in my journal after midnight continued, and in that first year I can honestly say that I took only two partial days off. One was Eid al-Fitr, and the other was Christmas Day, 1981. Looking from my cell door across the courtyard to cell five, I saw William, just as the Arab Robin Hood said he would be. He was dressed in his immaculately tailored suit from the 1950s, sitting on a folding chair, slowly sipping tea. I went over and wished him a merry Christmas, and he graciously motioned me to the seat next to him. We talked. Well, I did most of the talking because, no matter how much I gave up about my life, he just sat there appearing to be immensely interested, but never shared any of the intrigues that had brought him to his life behind bars. The closest he came was when he got a faraway look in his eyes.

"To be young and hopeful," he sighed. "I remember that. More tea?"

The new year of 1982 continued in the same manner. A few students progressed, a few fell away, some just kept attending for their own reasons despite making no progress, and new ones signed up. I began my second year of university studies, under the eyes of my three prison profs, on the subjects of Shakespeare, literary history, more prose, poetry, and the English novel *Moll Flanders* by Daniel Defoe. I still had no court date, and every time I saw William I began wondering if I would replace him as the eccentric old man walking around in my pajamas all day.

But I did start to believe that the short stories I was writing after midnight were actually getting better.

That's not a bad way to word that sentence, I thought to myself, and I smiled. I looked at my Seiko. One in the morning. Time for bed.

"Do you smell something burning?" I heard Jaffan ask.

"*Fire!*" somebody shouted from outside the cell, and everybody in my cell ran to the locked door or looked out their top-bunk windows. Black smoke began pouring out of the windows of cell number five and then, poof, a bright undulating light began to pulsate throughout the whole of the cell.

The prisoners there started pressing their faces against the bars to get air, and the night filled with cries and shouts. And then one shrill, bloodcurdling scream rose above all the rest.

"He's dying! He's dying!"

"Fire! Police! Abu Talal!"

"Fire! Fire! Save them!"

"Let us out!"

The smoke began rolling through the bars of the cell door, and the cries of the men trying to breathe became more desperate.

"Into the bathroom, the bathroom," someone shouted. "We'll be safer in the bathroom."

The commander of the detachment, Abu Talal, and three policemen, hurried to unlock cell five, and its occupants flooded out into the yard, all coughing, rubbing their eyes, and arguing.

"Did you see, did you see?"

"I think he's gone. Finished."

The guards ran into the cell with their inadequate handheld fire extinguishers, and all we could do was watch. About twenty minutes later, with our faces still pressed to the bars, and with all of the prisoners of number five still milling about and arguing, it suddenly became deathly quiet. That's when two policemen came out of the cell carrying a stretcher between them. It had a sheet covering a lump, with small trails of smoke wafting up from the still form.

The next morning all the prisoners were in groups getting details from those who were there.

"I saw it all," a man from number five said. "In the afternoon, Salim was talking pleasantly with that new prisoner Muhannad, and when Hamid joined them, Salim asked him to make tea for their guest. 'What am I? Your servant?' Hamid asked. 'For our guest,' Salim said. 'Please, light the kerosene stove to boil the water.'"

"Was he jealous?" somebody asked.

"Insulted?" another suggested.

"Who knows? They're both fucking crazy, or were. But I saw how during television they shared drugs, and after midnight, we could all hear them argue more angrily than usual. I think they got some bad stuff."

"We were used to them quarrelling," another prisoner from cell five said.

"You're sure it was Hamid?" I asked. "He's so quiet in class."

"He confessed that he poured kerosene on Salim, while Salim was snoring in bed, and then set fire to him. Drugs."

"What's left in the cell?" someone asked.

"The iron bedframes. That's it. Everything else is burned up."

Just then William quietly walked past. We all watched him go to a table and sit by himself, his hands softly clasped in front of him. It was the first time since Christmas that I hadn't seen him with a crafts project. Our group shuffled over to him as one.

"William, are you alright, my friend?" I asked.

He paused and looked up at me and the others, and then took hold of his pajama lapels. "We survived. I, these pajamas, and this pair of shoes."

"How about your suit and other clothes?"

"Just me."

"But your crafts and supplies?" Jaffan asked.

"Just me," William repeated.

"How . . . how about your treasure?" Fahd al-Dhiyab asked.

William laughed, as if Fahd had made a joke. "All burnt up, afandim," he said.

"Can you tell us where you hid it now? Please?" Fahd asked.

William just smiled and got that faraway look in his eye. "Have I ever told you boys how's there's no view of the Mediterranean like that from my home city of Alexandria?"

"Yes, you did, a hundred times," Fahd said, laughing.

William laughed in reply.

CHAPTER 30

LETTERS, SHORT STORIES, AND EXAMS

I send letters to people who live inside me. I don't write them down, but make do with dictating them to myself in my solitude, even in my new country. I address my sister Rosa as I walk by Lake Ontario: *Autumn casts its colors on the trees of Kingston. I wish I could put these colors in your wardrobe.* Then I say to my sister Asmahan as I examine the trees: *Every tree in a forest has its own captivating features, and together they share in creating a festival of colors, all without effort or planning.* Then I talk to my father, who died a year after I arrived in my new home. *Here you don't need to dig up rocks and transfer soil to grow your fruit trees.*

Jamil Hatmal's face emerges from among the many in my head. Jamil returned to Syria from his Parisian exile in a shroud over a quarter of a century ago, and here I am, on my walks in the new world, still composing many letters of the sort that never arrive. But I also wrote him a great number of real letters during my stay in the Citadel.

Prison regulations meant that Jamil didn't have the right to visit me, as he wasn't an immediate relative. But still he came almost every Monday, able to enter with all the other visitors by paying a small bribe, what's known as barteel in Arabic.

"A friend can visit you here, sure," Jaffan explained. "The guards just make sure neither the visitor's nor your name is entered into the log. On visiting days, just make sure that you're walking by the guest fence, in case someone comes to see you. If you're questioned, just claim you're on your way to the library."

Two weeks after I arrived, there he was, standing by the fence.

"Jamiiil!" I shouted as I ran over to the prisoners' side of the visitors' fence. My heart was dancing in my chest. Standing in front of me but behind two iron grilles, Jamil seemed as if he were about to produce Midhat Pasha Street from his pocket and unroll it before me so I could walk along it and see the colors of the spices in al-Bazouriyah market, and smell their fragrance, then lose myself in the alleyways of old Damascus.

The two iron fences were separated by a five-foot walkway, where a policeman walked back and forth between about seventy inmates on one side and the same number of visitors on the other. The iron structure had a fine wire-mesh screen that not even a finger could fit through, but exactly across from each other were small metal doors that the guard could open from the inside. We were all shouting, prisoners and visitors, not only because we were excited or emotional. Out of the cacophony, we each strained to hear the voices of our friends and family.

"Your mother sent you a plate of yabrak."

"Don't get another lawyer, brother. All lawyers are liars."

"Your son can't come today."

And the volume of noise was such that even the content that should have been whispered had to be shouted.

"I'm sorry to say, brother, your wife has been seen with Abdullah without a chaperone."

I can still hear the words Jamil greeted me with. "The streets of Damascus miss your footsteps. The others are well and want you to look after your health." He meant our comrades.

We continue to shout and repeat ourselves, when suddenly the policeman starts dragging his baton along the metal grille to create a loud clanging sound.

"Come on, come on. The visit's over."

How can it be over? Have the thirty minutes gone this quickly? I haven't said half of what I want to say or heard half what I want to hear.

Jamil leaves after giving me a week's supply of newspapers and magazines via a policeman, who passes them through a little door in the fence. We ask if we can shake hands. He laughs and says we can try, so we stretch our hands through the two openings and our fingertips touch.

"Okay, that's enough. The second visiting time has begun." After Jamil is gone, I find myself thinking that encountering Damascus from the Citadel is like love through a cloudy pane of glass.

I began writing letters to Jamil because of the noise at the fence. Real letters of paper and ink. I wrote them on Sundays and the policeman gave them to him the next day, charging me a small fee for his "compassionate" behavior. Seeing that the guards gave my letters to Jamil without reading them, I tried including the poems and short stories I was writing and, to my surprise and delight, only a week later my poem "Ta'aalu, Come" was published in the magazine *Ufuq*, out of Beirut. That was the first piece of mine to be published professionally. I read it through several times, and this was when I, like all writers, realized, *No text can ever be complete. If I wrote it again, I'd delete some things and add others. Any work, however good, can always be better.* To my continuing delight, the following week *Ufuq* published my short story "Ra'ihat al-snawbar, The Smell of Pine Trees." Both were published under my real name, and we decided in the future I should use different pen names. The name we used the most was Sinan Saleh. Sinan was an ancient revolutionary in the time of Saladin, and Saleh was my father's name. But having my work finally published made me happier than the fee the magazine paid me for it, which wasn't a pittance.

In addition to writing articles, short stories, and poems, I began to translate and sell some of the material I found in the magazines and newspapers Mr. Anthony lent me, always attributing original authors or publishers. Because of Jamil, I had a monthly income equivalent to the salaries of three policemen, and, amazingly, he always refused to take an agent's commission. All this stopped after the Israeli raid on Lebanon in June 1982, although I didn't stop writing.

Jamil didn't miss a visit until he himself was imprisoned for a few weeks. He visited me once more after his release and subsequently escaped to Paris in 1982. He returned to Syria in 1994, in his coffin.

I don't know if Jamil kept my letters somewhere in Damascus or if he took them with him when he went to Paris. I do know he published a short story about me, entitled "Abu Saleh." He must have taken some letters with him because this story included paragraphs from one of my letters, along with his comments.

I remember I wrote to him about how I'd come to know the books in the prison library, how rudimentary the place was — more of an accessory than a real library. Because of the Citadel's odd, ancient layout, to get to the library from the prisoners' courtyard meant I had to walk down some twenty steep steps of a roofless stairwell. Looking up to the sky made the feeling of being trapped even more acute. At the bottom of the stairs was a short hallway from which one then had to walk up another seven steps to the small room converted into the inadequate place of stored knowledge. I wrote Jamil that this is where I first met Abu Khaldun, the prisoner whom the administration had appointed librarian, paying him a small monthly salary. A lanky, swarthy fellow, he always looked like he was looking for someone to listen to his chatter.

The walls around the library had taped to them simple verses of folk poetry written on cardboard. Written in clumsy diwani script, a decorative style of Arabic calligraphy, some verses sang the praises of Syria, describing it as a tender, loving mother. Other verses spoke of all mothers as holy, pure, and chaste.

"Who wrote these poems?" I asked Abu Khaldun, thinking they weren't very good.

"In all modesty," he said, putting a hand over his heart, "I amuse myself by writing poetry when I get bored of reading. What do you think?"

"A nice way of entertaining yourself," I said, taking pains not to sound critical. "Anyone reading your description of the mother as holy, pure, and chaste might believe that every mother is the Virgin Mary."

"Yes, all mothers are Mary," he said, smiling proudly.

Jamil, Abu Khaldun's poems on motherhood are part of the rubble of rhymed poetry. In fact, they're part of the rubble of culture, the youthful critic in me declared. *They ignore what women suffer in this part of the world. The women in them appear as luminous beings who pluck children from the good Lord's trees. What's more, they are stripped of their desires and lusts, and even of the vaginas through which prophets, thieves, prisoners, and hangmen all must pass.*

A policeman entered the library holding copies of the *Washington Post* and a *Newsweek* magazine. "These are from your embassy," he said, adding, "What language are they in? I'm supposed to inspect them."

"English. Don't you know English?"

"I can hardly read *Surat al-Kawthar* in Arabic," the policeman said with a laugh, "and it's the shortest sura in the Quran." The section of the Quran called *al-Kawthar* is only ten words long and even small children understand it. The policeman tossed the magazines on the table and disappeared.

"What embassy sends you these?" I asked Abu Khaldun.

"The American Embassy. I'm a US citizen. I have a house in Chicago," he said proudly.

"So, what brought you back to Syria?"

"Who drinks from the water of Damascus always strives to return," he said, quoting a famous saying.

"And how did you end up in here?"

"My second day back, I borrowed a Cadillac from a friend to go watch the Russian Ballet at the Damascus International Festival. On my way, I passed a white Peugeot. I did it in a perfectly legal manner. The Peugeot driver began sounding a siren and flashing his lights, and then he deliberately bumped the back of my friend's car. The bastard broke the taillight! I pulled over hard to the side of the road and the Peugeot came beside me, its passenger window already down.

"'What the fuck is the matter with you assholes?' I shouted at the other car.

"'You'll soon find out who's an asshole!' the man in the passenger seat shouted back. 'We'll send you back up your mother's cunt!'

"'To talk this way,' I screamed back at him, 'your mother must have fed you filth with her milk.' And four men jumped out from the car and came at me like . . . like a herd of bulls. One of them was holding a Kalashnikov, one a baton, the others pistols. So, I had no choice. I grabbed my own gun."

"Didn't you know who those guys were?" I asked in astonishment.

"All I knew was I was being attacked. I brought down the one with the Kalashnikov and the one with the baton too. One of the survivors fired at me, but he missed, and a shot from my gun pierced his forehead. I was protecting myself. I was acting on instinct. Three of them were killed and, as God is my witness, I didn't want to kill anyone. But sometimes it doesn't need more than a bullet in the head for death to take charge of a situation. I was shooting to ward off evil. Afterwards, I was convinced it was God's will that nobody was able to resist."

I nodded as I listened to the story. I felt as if I were watching a movie in which Abu Khaldun was playing the role of a cowboy, driving a Cadillac instead of riding a horse, and thinking his action was all part of a divine plan.

When September 1981 came and I was able to rewrite the exams I had failed, the best part of going back to Damascus University was meeting up with many friends from high school and those whom I'd become acquainted with during my first exams. Most of the police who took me there and back got to know me and became quite tolerant. They allowed me to sit on the grass with other students after the exams, so I could socialize and discuss schoolwork. But as nice as the policemen became, and perhaps because of it, strolling around campus in their company allowed me to get a good understanding of the university's layout. And this in turn encouraged me to come up with a plan — a plan to escape.

After passing my make-up exams, I began to prepare in earnest for the second-year exams in January, and then for the ones in the spring. Mr. Anthony, the small-time drug smuggler and admirer of all things Elizabethan, mentored me on Shakespeare's *Hamlet*, and he truly helped me understand the complexity of Hamlet's character. I did, however, have to live through his interminable speeches about his beloved Elizabeth the First. For some reason, this bothered me. He argued that if she hadn't supported Shakespeare, the bard wouldn't be known today. I guess to me that would be like saying Hafez al-Assad was the one who determined what art was allowed in our country and took credit for it, because that's what he did.

But there was something not quite consistent in Mr. Anthony's argument. A few weeks later, when he was supposed to be helping me with my course on Christopher Marlowe's *Doctor Faustus*, his sagging jowls quivered as he spoke about the mysterious circumstances surrounding the death of the great writer. He enthusiastically denied the theory that Elizabeth I had decided to get rid of him.

"Wait a minute," I interrupted. "You argue that the queen could elevate Shakespeare . . . if that's so, she could also demote Marlowe. She had good reason, given that time in history. He was an early atheist and didn't support any church."

"No," Mr. Anthony insisted. "I think you are projecting. Marlowe's death was the result of a bar brawl." And then he again began praising his Elizabeth I at length. Ah well. I decided to let it go. The truth was, I found it more entertaining to wind up Mr. Anthony and then watch his antics as he went about praising his precious queen from the past.

My dear friend, Jamil. After the library closed today, Abu Khaldun, the prison librarian, came and found me sitting alone in the prison school. I was studying my university subjects.

"Come, walk with me, my friend," he said. "I've memorized some interesting new poems."

New? I thought. And so, we walked around the prison grounds with Abu Khaldun reciting rhymed classical poetry. I took a turn reciting some that I knew, but when I tried adding modern poets, like Adonis, Muhammad al-Maghout, and Ounsi el-Hajj, Abu Khaldun stopped me.

"Modern poetry is something invented purely for those people who are incapable of writing a poem in the rhymed classical style," he said.

Snob, I thought, and then he recited some of his own new poems. I still didn't see much value in his work but kept this to myself. After all, he didn't seem to have many friends and I didn't want to hurt his feelings.

I got my own comeuppance about being a snob from my Italian prison professor, Paulo. When I practiced writing paragraphs in English, he would continually criticize me.

"This is why you didn't pass the prose course last year, you stubborn boy. Where's your thesis at the beginning? Where's your thesis, eh?"

"Art shouldn't have a formula," I countered.

"Art!" He laughed. "You're creating art?" And then he took his finger and pushed the ball of his large nose up in the air. "I didn't realize you were an artiste, and not a university student locked up in a prison," he teased.

"I don't see the problem," I argued. "The reader will understand by the end."

"Nope," he'd argue back. "Thesis, then proof. Thesis, then proof! This is how it's done in English." This went on for weeks, with me loudly standing up for my principles and the sanctity of artistic expression.

Finally, just before my exams, Paulo said to me calmly, "Jamal, we're working so you pass the exam in prose composition. Once you've passed, you can begin your essays any way you like."

CHAPTER 31

MY GREAT ESCAPE

*D**ear Jamil, my second-year exams begin soon. Because of this, my visits to
the prison library have become less frequent. They just don't have the books
I need. I've therefore asked to temporarily cut back on my teaching duties to study
more. But while studying on my bed, I couldn't ignore a piece of gossip that came
in through the open door. It was very disturbing, so I got up and joined the group
just outside cell number ten.*

"I heard it from one of the guards," a prisoner was saying to the others
around him. "Farhan Raziq told the prison governor that Abu Khaldun used
the library for paid sodomy."

"Disgusting," said several.

"And," the gossiper continued, "Farhan said he had two witnesses willing
to testify that Abu Khaldun had offered them cash to sodomize him."

"Did they . . . you know?" asked another.

"Farhan said they refused."

"Farhan just wants the librarian job for himself," another added dismis-
sively, and I could agree with that. The man fancied himself a member of
the literati and boasted to everyone how he knew ten thousand bait by heart,
very short individual lines of classical rhymed poetry. And I even heard him
brag to a bone-thin inmate whom he liked to bully that if they weighed all the
books he'd read, they'd weigh fifty times more than the indigent prisoner.

The gossip continued that, because an accusation of sodomy was so serious, the governor called Abu Khaldun to listen to what Farhan and the two

witnesses were accusing him of in person. And when the first one testified in a confident tone, Abu Khaldun spat in his face and called him both a liar and son of a whore. The prison governor lost his temper and slapped Abu Khaldun hard on the face, causing the accused to scream hysterically at the top of his lungs.

Knowing Abu Khaldun, it wasn't inconceivable that he had lost his temper, whether because of being falsely accused or because the prison governor had slapped him in front of the others.

I went back to reading an analysis of Moll Flanders, and when I looked around the square again, I saw Abu Khaldun buzzing around erratically like a bee whose nest had been wrecked by thugs. I walked up to him and took his hand.

"Abu Khaldun, please tell me, what's wrong?"

He hauled his hand away. "Wrong? What's wrong?" he shouted. Everybody sitting at the coffee tables turned and stared at him. "Is there anything right in this world?" he screeched to the sky. It was as if he were quarrelling with the air he was breathing.

"Abu Khaldun, why are you acting like this? Please, don't be so sad."

"My father taught me that I should be angry, not sad."

"Please, my friend. Don't let your anger make things get worse for you. Tell me, please. Is it about what I heard happened with the governor . . . ?"

That's when he put his hands over his ears, grimacing as if he were in pain. He couldn't bear to hear the rest of my sentence.

"Leave me alone, Jamal, leave me," he said, and he hung his head and strode back toward the library. I let him go, accepting it was just one of those crazy, emotional moments that prisoners go through. I'd check on him in the morning and maybe even let him recite some of his poems to me.

Jamil, my friend, I hadn't visited the prison library for a long time because of my need to focus on my studies. But this morning, because I was worried about Abu Khaldun, I went. If only I hadn't.

The smell reached my nose when I was about halfway down the twenty steps to the library. That's when I looked up and saw a mass of smoke billowing down the seven steps leading back up to the library. I stopped in my tracks, blinking to make sure what I was seeing was real. Through the dark, descending smoke I could see flashes of flame dancing around the form of what looked to be a human-sized marionette. *No, please!* I ran almost to the bottom of the stairs, my impatience preceding me, but a policeman blocked my way. That's when the marionette ran out of the smoke and stood transfixed at the top of the landing to the library, exposing its blackened form. A corona of flames danced around what had been the mediocre poet. I moaned, and the image of the Vietnamese monk Thích Quảng Đức flashed into my mind.

Something mysterious tried to make its way out of my eyes to save Abu Khaldun from the flames. That's when half a dozen policemen with fire extinguishers ran in from another corridor. They blasted clouds of fire retardant up the stairs, enveloping the poor creature. There was a popping sound as the flames were snuffed, and then everyone just stood there in silence, watching. As the smoke subsided, the rigid corpse teetered forward.

"Abu Khaldun, no!" I shouted.

It fell over as if in slow motion, slamming face first on the stone steps with a loud crack. Everybody winced. And then the body became slack and tumbled down the rest of the stairs like a rag doll, falling to the hallway floor only six feet away from me. I stared at the blackened, lifeless heap.

"Get back to where you came from," a policeman shouted in my face. In shock, I turned and plodded in a daze back to the prison yard. I must have been holding my breath because, as I finally refilled my lungs with air, I almost suffocated from the smell of human flesh and smoke wafting up from my clothes. And I couldn't stop my imagination from recreating what Abu Khaldun must have seen, what he must have felt and thought from inside his immolation. I clenched my eyes tight and my attempt to transfer myself into his mind was so strong that I involuntarily screwed up my face. I could hardly breathe.

"What's wrong with you?" I could hear Jaffan's voice ask. I opened my eyes and saw him looking at me anxiously. I burst into tears.

"Abu Khaldun has burned himself to death. Abu Khaldun is dead."

Jamil, after Abu Khaldun's death, the prison governor summoned the two witnesses and one of them confessed he'd testified in exchange for Farhan giving him fifty Syrian pounds. Farhan spent three months in solitary confinement, and his dream of becoming prison librarian never came true. And apparently he never again boasted about the number of poems he knew or books he'd read.

Life went on. Another prisoner was appointed librarian, but the thought of going back to the place horrified me. I continued my teaching and self-study under the direction of my prison tutors, and soon it was time for two January exams. I was again pleased to see others of my age who had similar ambitions, although while they went home to their families, I went back to my cage.

This is when I seriously began to put my plan of escape into action. It would happen between my two September exams. It was very simple and depended on the trust that had grown between me and my minders. After finishing my second exam, I would request that the guards take me up to the university exam office on the fourth floor, and I'd ask them to wait in the hall while I asked about some previous marks. I presumed they would grant this wish, as it appeared there was only one door in and out of the office. But I knew there was a second door that led to a back staircase going to the rear of the building. As soon as I entered the office, I would quickly run down the steps to the olive orchard behind the university, where I'd meet a student friend. He had agreed to bring me clothes of the kind worn by peasants from Kafarsousah. Their traditional clothes included wide trousers that I could wear over my own pants. He'd also bring a keffiyeh to wrap round my head, a pair of spectacles, and even a razor to shave off my mustache. From there we would walk quickly through the orchard and make our way to the main road, where we'd catch a taxi. After that, I'd go back into hiding or find a way out of the country.

I decided to spare my comrades in prison any responsibility and not tell them of my plan, although I felt some remorse. I knew they would be interrogated. And the members of the police patrol who had given me their trust, they would no doubt be punished. But freedom, man! No prisoner must pass up an opportunity to escape, and, if the deaths I'd seen in prison weren't enough, I now knew that the relatively stable situation I was in could change at any instant.

The only time I was tempted to tell somebody about my escape was when I was sitting with Issa al-Khalil, the Robin Hood of Syrian bank robbers. I listened as he offered money to a prisoner so he could be released on bail before his trial. And Issa had to sell his TV to get this cash.

"Take the money and escape," Issa encouraged. "Don't show up for trial. Everybody knows the verdict already."

"But you don't know me," the prisoner said. "I might not pay you back a single piastre."

"I'm not lending it to you." Issa laughed. "I'm buying a prisoner's freedom. That is a huge pleasure for me. If I didn't do it, it would weigh heavily on me for the rest of my days."

I still thought it best to keep my plans to myself.

Months passed, and the simple logistics were put into place. My outside conspirator even volunteered to hide me for a few days at his home before I went into hiding. I thought about somehow going to Lebanon, although that country was at war. I also thought about finding a way to get to Cyprus or Turkey. I decided to figure that out later. In prison it seemed so easy to me, as if it was just a question of moving around on a two-dimensional map.

The lead-up to my great escape went smoothly, and I made sure I continued to appear the diligent student. The final plan was this: I would sit the prose composition exam on September 12, 1982, and afterwards I would have a visit with my mother. When I told the guards of my mother's visit, they were happy I'd finally taken their advice. And then one day after the prose composition exam, during the drama exam, that's when I would make my escape.

"Your coffee is great today," Hussein said to me.

Hussein, Jaffan, Husam, and I were in cell ten. It was about 7:45 in the morning, and we were sitting facing each other on two beds, enjoying our morning beverage before the cell was unlocked.

"So, tomorrow you write your prose exam, and then a few days later you write drama," Jaffan said. "What have you got planned for your studies after that?"

Studies? Nothing. Escape from here? Yes. Worrying about what will happen to you and the guards when you're all interrogated? Very much. I hope you'll forgive me.

There was the sound of the cell door being unlocked.

"They're opening early," Hussein observed. "Good. I really want to get a haircut this morning." He drained his coffee and stood up. "See you later . . ."

"Good. You're all together," Abu Talal, the kind policeman, said.

"Where did you think we'd be?" Hussein asked, a smile on his face. He was finally relaxing.

"The four of you, collect your things and go to the Pen Room."

"What's up?" I asked.

"Do I look like the prison governor? Collect your things. Come on."

Oh my God. Maybe I won't have to escape. They're going to free us.

I stood, ready to exit through the door, when I felt Jaffan's hand on my arm.

"We each have to get a suitcase from storage, and after we pack our own things, be sure to fill it full of extra new clothes, just in case we're transferred to another prison," Jaffan said.

"But we might be released," I said enthusiastically.

He snorted. "Inshallah."

I was the first to enter the Pen Room. There was Abu Jamal, the fat policeman, sitting at his desk, signing some papers with his beloved Waterman. I smiled at him, but he didn't smile back.

"Your trials have been canceled," he said. "I hope you'll all be released soon." I could feel a smile start to form on my face when the sound of footsteps came from behind us. I turned and my budding smile wilted. There were four men holding Kalashnikovs, handcuffs hanging from their belts. I swung my head back to Abu Jamal. Our eyes met for the briefest of moments, and then he looked down, his lips pursed. "May Allah protect you all," he said, and he blotted his signature before handing the paperwork to one of the guards.

I was handcuffed to Hussein, Jaffan to Husam.

The guards had a tight grip on our arms as we walked through the same halls as when we'd arrived.

"Where are we going?" I asked, but the guards just pulled us along silently. I looked at Hussein, and he looked back, his face once again turned to stone.

"Come on," a guard ordered, pulling us forward. We were back in the courtyard where we'd arrived. We were out of al-Qala'a Civil Prison, the Citadel, sixteen months after I had arrived.

No trial. Is that good?

I looked up and there it was, possibly the same ZiL truck in which we'd arrived, its back door yawning open, waiting to once again swallow us up.

CHAPTER 32

HONORING THE GUEST AT TADMUR PRISON

As I tried to protect my head, the tip of the lash hit my black Seiko watch, instantly transforming its crystal face into a collection of cracks and splinters. My watch never worked after this, remaining frozen in time at seven minutes to eleven.

The ZiL took Hussein, Jaffan, Husam, and me from the Citadel back to the Military Investigation Branch in Damascus. And even though this new sojourn into the investigation branch didn't last that long, returning to hell is always harder than entering it the first time. I was met by the same red-eyed mukhabarat agent, and he asked and recorded the same questions and answers as he had nineteen months earlier. Again, he took my watch, brown belt, and cash, putting them in a cloth bag. He signed for my suitcase full of clothes. And then I was put back into the hands of the same dark muscular guard who sadistically slapped me about the face and neck, told me to keep facing the wall, insulted me, and, of course, used me to hone his kicking skills. This time I was in cell eight, with my comrades separated, each in a difference cell. And once again I was a lonely detail in a Goya painting, sitting amid the rubble of people — all suffering from hunger and fear, all existing with our own hideous odors and filth. The cell was populated with new faces, but not that different in essence from those I'd seen before, mostly Muslim Brothers.

Only two days later, on September 13, 1982, they called us four back to the office and gave us our possessions back, including the suitcases. When I asked the red-eyed mukhabarat the time so I could wind my Seiko, he mocked me and asked if I had an important appointment. "Three minutes after six," he said. "Don't be late, make sure to arrive on time. They are waiting for you." He giggled.

A guard in a brown shirt cuffed only one of my wrists. He did the same with other prisoners, leaving the second cuff loose. Brown Shirt asked me if I was waiting to become a minister after a political coup. He was imitating investigators and seemed to dream of being one of them.

Soon, we found ourselves facing the back door of the car.

"You and the Muslim Brothers are in the same trench, the trench of reaction," Brown Shirt said.

"Same prison, same cell, and maybe even in the same Zil, but we're not in the same camp," I said.

"Smart-ass." He laughed, and got into the van where twenty-three young Muslim Brotherhood students sat, handcuffed in a chain. I discovered later that they had been arrested while they were high school students. Brown Shirt ordered them to make room for "these four communists."

They locked the loose ends of our handcuffs to the same long chain all the other prisoners were attached to. As we sat down, the young men had to make room for us and our suitcases, which we put in the middle.

The young Muslim Brothers looked more afraid of what was about to happen than we did. The one sitting opposite me had the eyes of a petrified statue, and the youth to my left looked like a child, his facial hair barely visible.

As the ZiL snorted into life and roared forward, my neighbor whispered, "Do you know where they're taking us?"

"No," I replied. "I hope we're not on the way to Tadmur." His eyes went wide, trying to understand the implications.

"I've said farewell to my brothers in God," he said, "and they all hope I will go to paradise. Would you be so kind as to pray for me, my brother?"

"I hope with all my heart that you'll be safe," I answered.

"I'm asking you to pray to God. I want to be saved by God," he said, trying to smile. "Is it so hard for you to ask something from God, brother?"

"No, not at all." What could it hurt if it gives him comfort? "I hope God will help you and be with you." My unorthodox prayer seemed to help. His smile widened just a little.

Half an hour later we were leaving Damascus by the city's eastern exit, and I was now certain we were on our way to the infamous Tadmur Prison.

During my stay in the Citadel, we learned from newsletters smuggled in, in a false-bottomed suitcase, how our organization had held a conference in Lebanon. There it was resolved we would now call ourselves a political party rather than a league. Less than a year after the conference, most of the comrades who had attended were arrested as soon as they reentered Syria. With this in mind, to pass the time, Hussein, Jaffan, Husam, and I began recalling the names of the detainees we hoped to become reacquainted with and others we knew only by name.

Then came a murmuring from the other twenty-three occupants of the ZiL. We saw that all the young Muslim Brothers had their heads down and were fervently praying. We sat in silence to respect their expression of faith. It sounded like they repeated themselves. And then again. This went on for some minutes until, finally, I touched the arm of the boy next to me. He looked up, somewhat annoyed.

"May I ask what you're praying?"

"The Prayer of Fire. Please, brother, join us," he begged. "It's a prayer for protection. It beseeches God to look upon our situation, and help us endure torture, and allow us to enter His paradise."

"Really?" I asked.

"Yes, and if you repeat it forty-four hundred and forty-four times, you will certainly be protected."

I looked at my comrades, and then back to the boy.

"Please go ahead. Perhaps we'll join you." We didn't. But when he lowered his head and continued, he said the words more clearly for our benefit.

"O God, send perfect prayers and complete peace upon the Prophet through whom all problems are resolved, sorrow is dispelled, needs are fulfilled, wishes are granted, good ends are achieved, and by whose virtue clouds are filled with rain."

They went on repeating the same prayer over and over again, and after a while we comrades continued our conversation. But after an hour of listening to them, I wanted to know more about their ideas. I leaned forward and tapped the arm of the boy sitting opposite me, the one who looked like a petrified statue. He raised his head as if I'd awakened him from a profound dream.

"Which is more powerful, terror or faith?" I questioned.

"Whichever God wills," he replied, as if it was obvious, and he went back to praying.

I look at the faces of these young Muslim Brothers. While I can't agree with their ideas, and they've been manipulated by cynical forces to be used as cannon fodder, still, their piety seems sincere and their fear genuine. They look like trapped prey. They lower their eyelids in submission to God, expressing their humility. In any other situation, I'd say these are good boys. I touch the arm of the boy next to me, and he looks at me with an expression similar to that of the boy across the aisle.

"Does the believer go straight to paradise after he dies?" I asked, "or does he wait in the grave until the Day of Reckoning?"

The question took him by surprise, and he just stared at me dumbly. Suddenly I realized, with no little shame, that this was a very inappropriate time to be challenging someone's beliefs. I smiled and patted his knee.

"It will be alright," I said. "I'm very sorry to interrupt."

They prayed for the rest of the four hours it took us to get to the city of Palmyra, and a few more minutes to get to its east end where Tadmur Prison lay. We heard the back door of the ZiL truck being unlocked, and it swung open. It was now night and our four guards in civilian clothes were standing staring at us. Watching from behind them, illuminated by the prison's security lights, was what appeared to be a sea of military police, all waiting in their crisp beige uniforms and blood-red berets.

"Come out," Brown Shirt called with a smile, and he pointed to the boys at the back to exit first. One by one the young Brothers came forward, their handcuffs were released from our common chain, and then each was pulled out of the vehicle. One of our guards stepped into the doorway, blocking us from seeing what was going on, but after the first three youths disappeared, it became abundantly clear. We began to hear yelling and screaming.

"Shut up, fucker."

"Close your eyes, fucker."

"I'm going to fuck your mother when I finish with you, fucker!"

And then a voice just outside of the ZiL shouted joyously, "Now for the Honoring of the Guest Ceremony," and that was the last laugh of the day.

Soon it became necessary for our guards to come into the truck and drag the rest of the teenagers out.

". . . sorrow is dispelled, needs are fulfilled, wishes are granted . . ." I hear the last Muslim Brother murmur as he's pulled past me and literally tossed out of the truck.

"Are you ready to be an honored guest?" Brown Shirt asks sarcastically as he releases my handcuff. "Go on, go," he says with a laugh, and, as I pick up my suitcase and hold it over my head, two of the other guards grab my arms and throw me into the clutches of Tadmur's military police.

"Head down and close your eyes, fucker," a guard several inches taller and about a hundred pounds heavier than me yells into my face, and then he slaps me so hard I spin around.

"He said close your eyes, you pile of donkey shit!" another policeman shouts as he drives his blackjack into my stomach. I double over.

Insults, slaps, cracks, screams, and pleas for mercy now combine and echo, cacophonous in my ears, a discordant symphony of pain. The guards take turns, moving from one prisoner to another.

"Fucker! Fucker! Fucker!"

"Mama!"

"Mercy!"

"Allah!"

"Take 'em through the gate," an authoritative voice yells, and with punches and kicks they begin herding us through an opening in a high cement wall.

Suddenly, peeking through my eyelashes, I see what looks like an iron bar coming at me. It connects just below the shoulder.

"You've broken my arm!" I scream.

"We'll smash your head in, too, you son of sixty whores!"

Three more guards converge around me, and I try to protect my head from the blows raining down. But suddenly I hear a crack as a truncheon gets through and descends on my skull, followed by the pain. I fall to the ground, grab my head, and feel the instant swelling of a large bump. Hot, sticky blood, my blood, begins to ooze out.

I'm sitting at my table now thinking back. The winds of October 18, 2020, are bringing down more leaves from the maple tree outside my window. My hand goes to my head, seeing if I can still sense that distant pain. How can one person be the son of sixty whores all at the same time? And why do the soldiers repeat the number sixty to make their insults more emphatic? Many military people do it, even the Syrian defense minister called Yasser Arafat a son of sixty thousand dogs and sixty thousand whores. But why should I care about these details now?

I don't know when the suitcase flew out of my hands. And I don't know how I became part of a heap of prisoners huddling together against a wall trying to protect one another. But the military police broke up this mound of quivering humanity, pulling us apart with their clawing hands and blows from their whips and truncheons. I tried to crawl away from the group as it broke up, but a guard with a whip followed me, bringing it down on my back and head over and over again. That's when I lifted my arm to protect my face and his lash broke my black Seiko.

"You, son of a whore, get up!" he orders. "Hands by your sides. And you, fucker, stand behind him."

I stand up as ordered, but I can't keep still. My whole body trembles and my arms involuntarily rise and fall, wanting to protect me. Meanwhile, a young jihadi is pushed against my back and a guard hits us, two in one blow, with a long, heavy pole across the sides of our heads. The crack reverberates in my head, and the teenager drops.

Guards scream as the abuse continues, and we prisoners scream as we receive their kicks and lashes. But screams don't protect. Our voices, like the howling of wounded animals, are our only means to express pain, to complain about injustice, to beg in vain for mercy, or bear witness to nobody but ourselves that we've fallen into the hands of barbarians.

After about forty minutes of arbitrary abuse, the guards make us form a line, one behind the other.

"Take one step forward!" comes the order, followed by the crack of a whip and a howl. "I said take one step, fuckers," and the line begins to trudge forward. This is when our training for life in Tadmur Prison formally begins.

"Close your eyes and keep them closed, fuckers!" This is rule number one at Tadmur.

"Keep your heads down, sister-fuckers! Down!" Rule number two.

Everyone who raises his head slightly or opens his eyes is pulled out of the line, thrown to the ground, and severely beaten.

After about a half hour of shuffling forward and stopping, shuffling forward and stopping, I am pushed hard from the back and feel the atmosphere around me change. Daring to look through my eyelashes, I see I have been pushed into a room. I'm standing before a dark-skinned man with gray sideburns. I blink and dare to open my eyes wider. He doesn't comment on the fact that I am looking straight at him and asks me the same questions I've answered in all the other prisons. Using a Bic stick pen he quickly fills in his forms. He, too, wears a military police uniform and his red beret hangs on a nail on the wall. He reads out his questions one after the other, the last one to find out whether my body bears any distinguishing features.

Cuts and bruises.

"Next," he says, sounding bored, and another prisoner is pushed forward.

I turn around and look to see where to go. That's when a young policeman of average height, and with a blond mustache, rushes over and backhands me hard, his calloused knuckles ripping into my lip.

"Shut your eyes, fucker!" Once more I taste the saltiness of my blood, and then the young policeman grabs me by my upper arm and pulls me back into the yard. "Piece of fucking shit!" He begins beating my face. "Eyes closed. Head down. Fuck, fuck you! Fuck, fuck you!" he screams during each blow. I stagger, but somehow stay erect, suddenly realizing I'm bleeding profusely from my mouth and nose. After about a dozen hits, and miraculously still on my feet, I'm being dragged back in line. I gag as blood is also now running down my throat. And my ears, they are ringing as if storms were raging inside them. Perhaps this, and the many other times I had been slapped, punched, and hit on both sides of my head is why I now need hearing aids.

The line continues to move forward incrementally, three fingers at a time, as we say in Arabic, and I still squint through my eyelashes, desperate to see what is going on. I see a blow coming and wince just before it lands on my temple.

"I knew you were peeking, fucker! Do you want me to find a dog to fuck you?" I really close my eyes this time, shuffling my feet until I bump into the person in front of me. Bam! Another blow to my head.

"My eyes are closed!" I yell, and I receive another blow.

"Don't speak, ass-fucker!"

The atmosphere around me changes again, and the line of twenty-seven living human bodies is now entering a small windowless cell. About 270 square feet, it's nothing but a concrete floor and an open toilet in the corner, all lit by a small bulb, like the kind used for a child's night-light.

Three guards saunter in. The one in the middle holds a whip in his hand and talks while the other two tap their truncheons against their palms. There are stains on their crisp uniforms, hands, and faces, blood appearing black in the low light.

"Against the wall, fuckers," and we comply. "Now, you bastards stay like that all night. Don't move unless you're told to . . ." and he expertly flicks his whip, causing its tip to crack as it rips into a boy's back. The teen screams and cowers against the wall. Everybody stands motionless as the cell's steel door slams shut.

In the profound silence that follows, I open my eyes and look around for my friends. We acknowledge each other and meet in the middle of the room, our eyes widening as we take in each other's condition. One of Hussein's eyes is black and blue. Blood is already crusting on Jaffan's forehead. Husam's right cheek is quite swollen on one side. I go to touch it, but stop.

"Are you alright? Is it broken?"

"Nothing broken, don't worry."

Hussein steps in front of me, first looking at the deep gash on my lip and the crusted blood under my nose. He looks down, his mouth agape.

"What?" I ask, following his eyes. What had been a white shirt is now tie-dyed bright red.

According to Jaffan's watch, it was one o'clock in the morning. Since my Seiko had its face shattered and stopped working before eleven, that meant they'd had fun with us for more than two hours.

"We'd better get some sleep," Jaffan said, always the practical one, and we lay down on the floor.

"Hey, you boys," Hussein called to the cell's other occupants. "The guards are gone. Lie down and sleep." But they just stood where they were. "Suit yourselves."

I lie down and put my shoes under my head as a pillow. I instantly feel the cold of the floor draining the heat out of my bones, but I don't care.

My mother's words came back to me again: "Sleep is the little brother of death." I always thought of this phrase as just one of her many humorous, poetic creations, but what was happening to me today gave it a different meaning than before. Sleep could now be used as a temporary, but pleasant, type of death. One where you might escape to dream about walking down a quiet country road or use your senses to see and smell the blossoms on an apple tree. One could even play with little birds that tempt you to chase them into the woods. But the pain, the pain! The dead don't dream. I don't believe they dream. Death puts the machinery of dreams out of action.

I try to forget about my treasured broken Seiko. I try to forget about everything. I quickly doze off, sleep my refuge from madness. And I, like many prisoners, would come to use this method of escape, this refuge, often over the coming years.

CHAPTER 33

THE WELCOMING CEREMONY

The following morning I'm woken up by the sound of the door unlocking. As one, my friends and I jump to our feet and face the wall. Two policemen enter.

"What the fuck?" says one. All the jihadi boys are still standing, but clumped together, leaning against each other, puppies piled asleep on top of one another, but astonishingly, still standing. A guard flicks his whip, making a loud crack in the air. All the sleeping boys are instantly awake. "From now on, whenever you hear a key in the lock, wake up, stand up *straight* against the wall, and shut the fuck up!"

I hear boots pass by me and close my eyes tight. I hear two prisoners being ordered to go out of the cell to bring in everybody's breakfast. Suddenly, there is the sound of a whip on flesh.

"You opened your eyes, motherfucker."

"How will I find the food?"

"The same way a blind dog finds its food, asshole."

"Time to eat," one of the policemen shouted a minute later, and I heard the sound of the door being locked. I turned and opened my eyes. One jihadi youth is holding a large bowl of tea, the other a bowl of green olives.

"A blind stray has a better life than us," he says. "At least it can smell its food in peace."

Before any of us has attempted to take an olive, the key turns in the lock again, and we obediently turn and stand with our heads bowed, eyes closed, facing the wall. Three policemen walk in and slowly spread out around the room. I hear a thud and a boy screams, there's the clatter and splash of bowls falling, and the boy begins to cry.

"Yesterday was the ceremony to honor you," said a policeman happily, "and today is the ceremony to welcome you. But today — today . . ." he added, and there was real joy in his voice, ". . . we'll make you see stars at noon." There was a silence. "Well, what the fuck are you fuckers waiting for? Get into a fucking line. *Now!*"

Not one of us says we haven't had time to eat. Lesson learned.

We grope our way into a line and make our way outside, the blind leading the blind. Once again, a constant stream of orders begins to rain down on us, accompanied by blows and insults. The whips descending on us from right and left determine our route.

"Faster, fuckers. Pick up your fucking feet. Faster." And the blows continue.

Instinctively, I raise one arm to protect my now sensitive head.

"Put your arm down, whore. I'll cut it off and stuff it up your ass."

"You, you shit. You in the blue shirt. Come here."

Again, daring to look through my eyelashes, I see those wearing blue shirts turn in the direction of the voice.

"I only want this blue-shirted fucker. The rest of you sons of sixty whores into the yard."

I bumped into what I guessed was the entranceway to another yard and heard the screams of what I supposed was the intended man in the blue shirt behind us.

"Mamaaaa! Mamaaaaaa!"

"I'll fuck your mama, you son of a whore!"

This new courtyard was paved with asphalt and surrounded by cells with solid black doors.

"Faces to the wall. To the wall. First bastard on the right, take a step to the right. Don't you know your right from your left, brother of a whore?" The sound of baton on bone.

"Aaaaaah! Aaaaah! Please, sir . . ."

"All of you fuckers. Extend your arms horizontally and stay at arm's length from each other. And you four . . . you know who you are . . . go to the far left of the line. Hurry up, assholes."

We were the four who knew who we were and we ran over to the left.

There came a loud knocking from inside of one of the cell doors close to us.

"Ask that son of sixty whores who's hammering away what the fuck he wants," yelled the voice overseeing the welcome ceremony. "And you four. Remove all your clothes except your underpants." More banging on the door, this time sounding increasingly urgent. "Who the fuck is knocking on that fucking door? Bastards!"

"Cell four, sir," came the muffled voice from inside the cell.

"I swear to God, I'll fuck your mother and your sister, cell four. Why are you bothering me? We've got work to do."

"Sir, we've got someone dying in here."

"When he dies you can let us know, you shit."

We are barefoot and almost naked. I shiver, not because the September breeze in the desert can be cold, but from sheer terror. I've been afraid before, but not like this. Now we're given an order to take down our underpants. We hesitate and whips descend on our backs. We drop our pants.

"Now, perform the usual security movement," comes the next order. We don't understand. A policeman shouts and whips one of us. "Squat, son of a whore! Now stand up! Squat again! Stand up!" We repeat this maneuver twice. "All clear, sir," the guard finally announces. "Nothing fell out of their assholes."

There's another banging from the cell, and the voice of the officer explodes.

"I'm going to fuck your whole family, cell four! What the fuck do you want now? What?"

"He's dead, sir!" comes the voice from inside the cell.

"You two baladiyya," shouts a policeman behind me. "Tell the sergeant to bring the key to cell four. Somebody's snuffed it."

What do they mean by "baladiyya"?

Before I can ponder this, a torture party begins in the middle of the square. They're using car tires. I know this one well. I'm standing to the far left of the line, with Jaffan, Hussein, and Husam. The party begins at the other end of the line, and I don't know if I'm happy to wait or would rather get it over with. This time I do keep my eyes closed. But this doesn't stop the sounds of successive beatings, screams that degenerate into guttural cries, pleas for mercy, and unintelligible prayers, all mixed with unrelenting choruses of curses and insults.

"No, for the sake of God!"

"Mother, mother!"

"Allah, save . . ." followed by the sound of gagging.

The atmosphere in the courtyard grows more oppressive, and I can actually feel the weight of fear and terror hanging in the air.

"The sister-fucker who passed out is coming round," shouts a jailer.

"He can go to hell. Do him again."

Now it's my turn. They cram me into an old car tire, ass first so I'm folded with my legs in the air. Two young men wearing civilian clothes approach, carrying a three-foot-long heavy stick with a noose knotted around one end. They shove my feet inside the loop and pull it tight. Holding on to the stick, they raise my feet high in the air, with my buttocks on the asphalt of the yard and my back propped against one half of the tire. The policeman addresses the two men: "Baladiyya, raise his legs nice and high. The bastard's eyes are open all the time."

The two jailers take turns forcefully striking the soles of my feet. I am so wedged in the tire I can't move. Once more, I long for death. I scream. I turn into a screaming lump of pain, but still the blows keep coming. I feel my body shattering. All I want is death.

One of the guards orders them to stop and then tells me to get up and run on the spot. The jailers begin to beat me across the back. I look behind me. The guard with the blond mustache flies into a rage and he begins hitting me randomly.

"We'll have to gouge your eyes out. Don't you know how to keep them shut, you son of a whore?"

"Stop," I hear a guard's voice echo from the other side of the universe, and before I can catch my breath, he's screaming in my ear. "Get up! Get up, you bastard. Get up and run on the spot!" I feel a boot strike my head. I'm pulled out of the tire. I fall on my hands and knees. I want to collapse, when a boot catches me in the ribs. I hear more insults being hurled at me, but the only sound I understand is "F." I struggle to my feet, which are begging for mercy, as fresh blows fall on my back.

"Run, bastard, run!" I hear. "Run on the spot!" and my eyes pop open involuntarily. My nemesis, the young policeman with the blond mustache, is standing right in front of me. He flies into a rage and lunges at me, hitting me with his fists and baton.

"Don't you know how to keep those fucking eyes shut, you miserable bastard? I'll gouge those eyes out if you don't learn!" I close my eyes, and, although I'm swaying, I begin lifting my feet one after the other in a pathetic, slow run, trudging to nowhere as I listen to the last of my comrades receive their Tadmur welcome.

And then it's over. My ears are ringing, my body is throbbing. My eyes now have the rules of Tadmur beaten into them. They are closed.

As my ears whistle and echo, the officer supervising the welcome ceremony orders us to get dressed and shouts for the four of us to go to cell number one. I open my eyes again and look at the doors. I can't see numbers. There aren't any numbers on the doors.

"Shut your eyes, bastard," shouts the guard, and then he kicks my hip with all his might. I fall to the asphalt, but the fear of getting kicked in the head again forces me to get up. I hear the creaking of a heavy metal door nearby.

"Cell number one ready for inspection, Sergeant," shouts a man from inside the cell.

"Hey, chief, you bastard! Take this garbage! They're just like you! Teach them how the system works here!"

We, the aforementioned garbage, limp into the cell and the door is slammed and locked behind us. I open my eyes and see some sixty prisoners turn their faces away from the wall and look at us. I immediately recognize Faiq Huwaija, Wael Sawah, Fatih Jamous, Halim Roumia, Ali Burazi, Jihad Annabeh, and Samir Abbas. The look in their eyes tell us that they want to truly welcome us, but warm embraces don't go with the cuts and bruises left by whips, sticks, and military boots. And then something extraordinary happens. We laugh, and they laugh. It's like their eyes wipe our wounds clean, and we all talk at once. Ahmad Aboud, chief of the cell, is a large bull of a man, an ex–military warrant officer with extraordinary leadership skills, a love for his men, and an iron will to both protect them and to keep order. He is known as the Bulldozer.

The Bulldozer came over and, without touching us, examined each of us from head to toe. "Good, good," he kept saying. "You're whole. You'll survive." And then he called out to the others, "Fellows. Do you know these four as comrades?" He couldn't have spies infiltrate the cell. When he was satisfied we were all well known, he smiled. "Welcome," he said, and then he clapped his two large hands loudly. "From here we can begin." And everybody cheered. Except me. It occurred to me to sabotage his enthusiasm and say, "Begin what, exactly?" but I didn't want to be rude. The torture certainly comes at a price, I thought to myself.

We milled about, greeting those we knew and putting faces to names we'd heard. And then we all sat down on the floor and the other three arrivals gave an update of what we knew was happening in the outside world. But as Hussein, Jaffan, and Husam took turns telling the latest news, something was really bothering me. I couldn't hold it in.

"Who were those guys in dirty civilian clothes helping the jailers?" I interrupted. "And why are they called baladiyya?" Some in the cell were clearly surprised, obviously thinking that learning the outside news was more important than my question.

"Those are military prisoners, not political prisoners," Fatih Jamous answered quietly. "Mostly army deserters. They call them baladiyya, municipality, because they do municipal jobs, collecting garbage, cleaning, distributing food —"

"And helping jailers torture the prisoners," I interrupted.

"If the occasion demands," Fatih Jamous agreed with a smile.

"After all," the Bulldozer added, "the guards end up so tired from the honoring and welcoming ceremonies, they need help."

"Poor guards," a voice called from the back of the room, and the whole cell laughed, including me.

A key turned in the lock. We all became instantly silent, stood up, and turned our faces to the wall.

"Ready for inspection, Sergeant," the Bulldozer shouted as the door opened.

The sergeant ordered the lunch to be brought in and two comrades, their eyes closed, hurried to collect it. When the door was locked again, I turned and looked at the so-called lunch. I hadn't eaten in almost twenty-four hours.

Can a human really eat this?

CHAPTER 34

DEBATES IN HELL

The key turned in the lock of cell number one in Tadmur Prison. We stood up and faced the wall, bowed our heads, and closed our eyes. The sound of the key always aroused fear and anticipation. The door opened. The cell chief barked a military command: "Atten—shun!" Then, "Cell ready for inspection, Sergeant."

At first, this military style of command took me by surprise, but I grew used to it, just as I grew accustomed to living in the heart of the terror that accompanied us during the whole of our stay in Tadmur.

"Send some of your bastards to get this fodder," shouted a guard outside. "Move it, fuckers!"

For breakfast we were usually provided with a varying number of olives. Sometimes the day's offering was just enough labneh or jam for each of us to spread a spoonful over a single pita. There was always tea with a film of oil floating on top. For lunch, the baladiyya left two large plastic washbowls of food just outside the door and, later at sunset, one bowl, usually soup. Each time, one or two prisoners had to go out and fetch them, and this is when they would be routinely subjected to various kinds of abuse. The level of abuse all depended on the guards and their moods that day. Some of the guards came up with unbelievable ideas, so we shared our fear of likely torture by taking it in turns to go out of the cell. We divided ourselves into groups, taking turns to bring in the food, accepting whatever punishment was meted out, preparing the meal so it was edible, and cleaning up afterwards.

One unique bit of torture perpetrated on a prisoner was devised by a guard we ended up naming Abu Clipper. It was he who was inspired to set fire to Faiq Huwaija's hair with his brand-new Clipper cigarette lighter.

"Who said you could raise your hand, asshole?" we heard Abu Clipper shout outside the cell. "Stop trying to protect your hair, damn it. You're getting in my damn way, stupid fucking . . ." and then he'd hit him.

"Please, please, sir."

"This is a new Clipper lighter I bought today, son of a whore. Show some respect."

"My hair's on fire!" Faiq screamed.

"Even if your whole body's on fire, don't fucking move," Abu Clipper screamed louder. "Keep still as a statue. Damn it! The more you move, the more butane I waste. Stand the fuck still!"

The whole cell could smell Faiq's hair burning, and as I stood motionless against the wall with my eyes closed, my blood boiled as I pictured the scene going on outside. And it boiled even hotter as I realized how powerless I was. I fantasized about what would happen if the sixty of us turned as one and attacked this bastard of a guard. So what if we died? The life we were living here was no life at all.

Finally Abu Clipper shouted, "Take the food in, you bastard. What are you waiting for, smelling up the yard with your fucking hair? Damn it, man, you stink."

As soon as the food was in and the door locked, we turned around to see a vision no surrealist could have invented. Faiq was standing there with his bangs singed. His hair was shrunken, his curls melted into his scalp. Everybody just stared dumbfounded as Faiq turned his palms upward in a gesture of incomprehension. And then . . . he laughed — and each and every one of us joined him. Soon the laughter turned into cross-chatter, which then took the form of a debate, a debate that was serious, funny, painful, and hopeful. It was one of the many debates we had in cell one. It was how we spent so much of our time.

"There's no justice in torture."

"For the sake of equality, we'll demand that we all have our hair set alight."

"Equality? And did you say justice? Both are no more than abstract concepts."

"But Marx showed how it could be possible."

"If only Dr. Marx could spend a few days with us here . . . perhaps he'd rethink his theory when his beard is set alight."

"It's a question of luck, don't you see? It seems Faiq is under the influence of the planet Saturn, and that's why he has bad luck. He is very unlucky."

"And the rest of us are lucky?"

"So, you're saying Saturn is the reason Faiq's turn to bring in the food came on the day Abu Clipper bought a lighter and needed to play with it?"

"It's a complicated subject. Perhaps Faiq's hair attracts fire."

A chorus of laughter erupted. "Akhrus! Shut up!"

There was the one suppertime when Ahmad Rizq, a medical student, went to bring in the lentil soup. This day, very unusually, it had arrived extremely hot.

"Ouch!" we heard him exclaim from our places by the wall.

"Why did you move your hand away from the bowl, son of a whore?" the sergeant yelled.

"I'm sorry, Sergeant. It's hot," Ahmad said.

"Not as hot as your mother's fucking cunt," came the rejoinder. "Put your hand in the soup."

"What?"

"You heard me!"

"But it's —"

The sound of a lash, punches, and kicks. Probably three men were beating Ahmad.

"Carry out the order," shouted the sergeant. "Put them in. Put your hands in the fucking soup right now!" And then came Ahmad's shrill scream as his hands plunged into the burning liquid. This was followed by the staccato of more whip blows. I gritted my teeth in anger, not able to unclench them until I heard Ahmad back in our cell, panting in pain. As the door slammed shut, we turned, someone grabbed the bowl, and Ahmad rushed to the tap to run cold water over his wounds.

We are just prey, waiting to be hunted down.

"It's nothing, comrades," Ahmad managed to say. "A simple burn." He laughed and then winced. The rest of the evening was spent in silence.

"What makes us laugh when we come back from a round of torture?" Salman Ismail asked me the next morning. But I didn't have time to answer. That's when we heard the guard we called the Rooster shouting the way he always did when approaching a cell.

Musab al-Nabhan, another medical student in our cell, gave him this name because of the way he strutted around the yard, always shouting his whole time on duty, reminiscent of the overdressed officers who grabbed power in the 1970s. The Rooster was the one to always call us out in groups of ten to · have our hair and beards shaved. We weren't allowed the tools to do it ourselves, and it really just ended up being another form of torture.

Emerging barefoot on the hot asphalt, I turned to face the wall. The Rooster hit me hard on my back with a whip.

"Turn to the wall more quickly, asshole!" he screamed, and just as I lowered my head and closed my eyes, I saw him tuck his whip under his arm. It reminded me of that preening egomaniac who ruled Libya, Muammar al-Gaddafi. And then I felt someone grab a handful of my hair at the back of my head and start the military assault of forcing hair clippers over my face and neck. Because they were hand clippers, not electric, they pushed, clipped, and pulled. Pushed, clipped, and pulled, partly cutting, partly ripping. As my head was shoved around, it continually bounced off the wall.

"This bastard has a tough beard," the Rooster screamed in my ear. "It needs softening," and there was the sound and feel of spit landing on my face. "Natural shaving soap to moisturize the chins of you sons of whores." And then I felt my mustache being assaulted in the same manner. "And these mustaches. Mustaches are for men, not you fuckers. They're all going to vanish today." It went on, the cutting and pulling of hair, the scraping and cutting of skin, and suddenly my turn was over, capped off with a sharp slap on my face.

"Na'eeman," the barber said, the customary salutation after a shave. It was like saying "bless you" for your refreshing change of appearance.

But it wasn't over.

"Stand on one leg," the Rooster ordered. "I'm going to hit you, and if you don't fall over, you can go back in the cell. But if you do fall, we continue your salon treatment." He hit me across the back of the neck several times, and I didn't fall over, so he began kicking me savagely on the knees and hip. "Fall, you bastard, fall! Why don't you fall?" he screamed, and when I finally collapsed on the ground, he gave a self-satisfied chuckle. "I've yet to see one who doesn't fall." Then he added, "Okay, na'eeman, bastard," and he placed his whip on the top of my head, signaling for the barber to shear the top of my head some more. When this indignity came to an end, I was yanked to my feet and the Rooster slapped my face again, "Na'eeman, bridegroom," he said. I was pushed back against the wall, and, by the sound of his voice, the Rooster had already turned to the next man needing to be coiffed.

"Na'eeman," I whispered to myself, totally exhausted. But our tormentor still had a lot of energy to spare. He obviously loved his job. He turned to my cellmate Nasir.

"And now for you, you fucker with the mustache of a whore's pussy. It's your turn," he said, and laughed. Nasir sported a huge handlebar mustache like the philosopher Nietzsche. "I'll enjoy plucking this crop of hair," the Rooster crowed, and he actually began to pull out Nasir's mustache before he set the barber on him.

As our group of ten returned to the cell and ten others took our place, we looked in amazement at each other's bloody faces and scalps, replete with cuts, scrapes, and tufts of hair sticking out every which way. It was like we had been transformed into bizarre cartoon characters. Those less bloodied let the more disfigured wash up in the sink first. This had to be a group decision, as we didn't have a mirror. Someone finally came up with the idea of placing a basin filled with water in the area known as the kitchen. There the light and shadows were such that it allowed the water in the basin to reflect a reasonable image of our blood-streaked faces.

Narcissus used to contemplate his beauty in a river, and here we are staring at our bloodied wounds in a washbowl.

When the episode was over and everyone had returned to the cell, when the door was shut and we could hear the Rooster's crowing fade into the distance, we looked at each other and laughed loudly at our collective grotesqueness.

"Comrades," the Bulldozer called. "Laugh, but do it in silence. You'll only give the guards another reason to return and abuse you."

"How do we laugh silently, comrade?" Jaffan asked.

"The same way we cry silently," the Bulldozer answered.

Here we miss the touch of tenderness to release the weeping that stays inside us.
Tears fall inwards like little salty moons.

And so began another spontaneous debate. "Friends," I said, "Salman asked me earlier why we laugh when we return from torture."

"We're consoling ourselves, making fun of our misery," somebody offered.

"Yes, as the well-known saying goes," added another, "the worst calamity is the misfortune that makes you laugh."

Some interpreted our laughter as the result of a temporary sense of security; others suggested it was an attempt to restore some kind of equilibrium, or that we laughed because we derived strength from merely rejoining the group.

"I'm not going to bother too much to find out the reason, but when laughter comes, I won't resist it," added someone with beautiful simplicity.

We were still listening to each other's theories on the therapeutic value of laughter when the key turned in the lock. Yet again, we got to our feet and turned to the wall.

"Take the fodder in, you animals."

The Bulldozer volunteered to fetch our lunch this day. The police made do with only swearing at him, and once the door was locked, we turned to see our cell chief unscathed.

"See, his star is rising. He is free from the effect of Saturn."

"Akhrus!" A chorus of laughter erupted.

"Two pieces of good news today," the Bulldozer announced. "The rice is just overcooked a bit."

"Allah be praised," came a voice.

"What's the other good news?"

"There are fewer flies than usual in the sauce."

The whole history of Tadmur seemed to be steeped in flies.

There was one bowl of rice and a second of tomato purée and potatoes. I looked at what they'd sent. It was true. There were fewer dead flies floating in the sauce today.

It was Hussein's and my turn to prepare the lunch. His first job was to retrieve the boiled potatoes and wash them off in the sink. Mine was to take care of the insect-laced sauce. As I carefully carried the bowl over to the toilet, I shook my head in amazement.

"Why do they waste tomato purée? Why don't they cover the food to protect it from the insects?" I asked aloud.

"If they're happy to waste lives, why not tomato sauce?" Jaffan suggested.

I flushed the mess away.

"And the flies have to eat," came a call from somewhere in the cell.

"They're very considerate of flies."

"But they're dead."

"A last meal."

"Couldn't they at least wash the potatoes?" Hussein asked, peeling off the dirt encrusted skins and cutting out the rotten bits. To do this he used a bit of hard plastic as a knife.

"And then you would have nothing to do," someone suggested.

"See, they are considerate of prisoners."

Potatoes peeled and cleaned, they were put back into the newly washed bowl, and garlic, salt, and tahini were added. These were items bought collectively by the cell. And then we mashed the ingredients together using the back of a heavy plastic dish. Our lunch entrée now complete, we then plated equal portions of the mash on ten largish plates right beside the overcooked rice. Each plate was shared by six people. The plates were round, so one of the six would use the long handle of a wooden spoon to separate the food into triangular portions — and lunch was served. The groups of six huddled around their plates, each person using his own wooden spoon to scoop up his portion of mash and rice. In reality, our limited resources meant that all meals ended up similar, dominated by the taste of garlic and tahini, and I hate garlic.

One suppertime they gave us the surprise of six cans of fava beans. Now, a person who wasn't even that hungry could finish a whole can of the legumes by himself, but we were sixty hungry people. So, to be fair, we poured equal portions of the beans into ten halawa sweet containers and each group of six had one portion to share equally. It was like a special treat.

In my early years in Tadmur, the writing on the tahini jars and cigarette packets was almost all we had to read. There were the contents, address of the factory, and various trademarks. They were like rare first editions to men starved of reading material. So, when the fava beans appeared, I couldn't help myself. Slowly and carefully, I removed the label from one of the cans and strategically dropped it on the floor. The can looked so naked I almost put the paper back. Had the guard noticed the wrapper gone, he might have amused himself by torturing me for a while. Not that he needed a pretext.

If he notices it missing, I'll say it fell off while the cans were being emptied. All the guard cares about is the number of cans. If six cans come in, six must go out.

I took the chance.

What did I want from that piece of paper? Nothing except the pleasure of dealing with the printed word, the pleasure of reading, reading anything, and the pleasure of contemplating the design of the label around a can of beans. After the guards took the cans and food bowls, and when the cell door was locked, I hurried and recovered the paper by the sink.

"Listen, everybody," I called excitedly. "Listen." I read the list of contents out loud, and when I got to calcium chloride, a discussion about preservatives started up.

Pushing his spectacles up the bridge of his nose, the lawyer Samir al-Latif praised them. "Preservatives have saved millions of tons of foodstuffs from going bad."

But Salman Ismail shook his head, saying they were poisons that increased the likelihood of incurable diseases, deprived people of fresh food, and even affected the flavor of the food. Samir nodded in agreement and was about to say something, but Salman went on, "In this cell we wish we were like beans in a can. The chemicals preserve them. What preserves us? Nothing."

"Salman, we were talking about the pros and cons of preserving *food*," the Bulldozer said. "You have strayed from the topic."

"The topic has strayed away from me," Salman retorted glumly. "But going back to food," he said, becoming dreamy, "I think dried foods are healthier and more natural than canned food."

Now the group began discussing different kinds of dried foods and how almost every roof in Syria once had food spread across it, drying in the sun. Our Bedouin comrade, Fawaz Kadru, told us how they dried yogurt to preserve it in the Syrian desert.

"It's women who have traditionally been the ones to prepare jams and dried fruit — and pickles too," I added.

"All you think about is women," said tall, kindly Adnan Bahluli with a laugh. "You manage to insert them into any conversation."

"Of course. Why not?"

"If only they imprisoned you with women."

"Then I certainly wouldn't pray to be released so quickly. In any case, what I was *trying* to get at was how a new generation of women has begun to move away from traditional food preservation. It's because many have entered the labor market and because of the increasing availability of food in cans, which of course contain preservatives."

"So, what's your point? You're bothered that women no longer dry figs and apricots?"

"No, he's bothered that his fig and apricots have dried up in here." This garnered an especially good laugh.

"But you know . . ." I added, changing the subject, "my father used to say femininity is a bottomless well."

"Yes, bottomless. Unknowable?" a voice came from the crowd, and there was a collective sigh.

"So as a boy you heeded your father's words and went in search of bottomless wells?" another joked. "I've heard the gossip."

"Again, why not?" I asked. "And my fig is working just fine."

"Yes, we've heard you in the night."

"And sometimes during the day."

A few days later we had an especially long debate about our cell's finances. They had begun to dwindle precariously. In Tadmur, they didn't take our money away. Every couple of weeks, a guard would come around and we'd write up a list and pay him to bring things from a storehouse. A few spices, types of food, plates, halawa sweets, wooden spoons, some medicines, things like that. As good communists, we pooled our money, and a committee decided what things and how many we should purchase. This turned out to be a very efficient and effective practice. It really stretched the money for the good of the whole group. However, after a year and a half, with no visitation rights, there was no way to receive money from our families. Our resources were becoming seriously depleted.

This was when Fatih Jamous proposed a plan to stretch our failing funds, a plan that received almost unanimous approval: medicine first, then food, then whatever other necessities were allowed, clothes, wooden spoons, plates, plastic cups, and lastly, tobacco for the smokers. I took part in a lengthy discussion about the number of cigarettes a smoker was entitled to per day. This particular discussion took up much more time than any issue discussed in the corridors of the United Nations, in seminars on Marx's economics, or Freud's theories of libido. Those hostile to smoking mobilized convincing arguments.

Our comrade Abu Al-Harith, a philosophy teacher, said, "We need food more than the cigarettes that we consume and that consume our health. We have to preserve our health, not destroy it."

"What you say seems logical," said Samir the lawyer, who always pushed his spectacles up on his nose when he talked, "but it doesn't take into account the actual need to smoke. I consider smokers as sick people and nicotine as necessary medication for them." Clearly a smoker.

Abu al-Harith made precise calculations to demonstrate the benefits of reducing each smoker's allowance by one cigarette per month and putting the money saved toward food. "And therefore," he proclaimed, like a preacher in a pulpit, "I would invite comrades to vote against increasing our purchase of the tobacco that spoils the health of all of us by polluting the air in the cell. In fact," he said, drawing his oration to a close, "I ask you to vote for decreasing the amount spent on tobacco and increasing the amount dedicated to improving our diet. And I suggest that we buy some olive oil."

"Yes, I miss olive oil," added someone.

"It's a frivolous luxury," objected another.

"Is it really possible to decrease the number of cigarettes to less than three per smoker?" chimed in Rustum, sounding like this was inconceivable.

"I suggest we lower the tobacco budget by buying the same number of cigarettes but procuring cheaper varieties for those who want them . . ."

Suddenly, we heard the sound of pounding feet in the yard and the key turning in our lock. Many more feet than usual, and they seemed to be marching in time. We fell silent, and stood up, and faced the wall. The door opened and now I heard a large number of military boots rushing into our cell. I tensed. It was only two years earlier that whole cells of prisoners in this factory of death were machine gunned into oblivion. Was it our turn? And then came the voice of the Bulldozer.

"The cell is ready for inspection, Sergeant."

"Men ready for inspection, Lieutenant Colonel," the sergeant called, following protocol.

"About turn," came an unknown voice. None of us prisoners dared move. "I'm telling you prisoners to turn around."

"Cell one, about turn — now," the Bulldozer barked. We turned.

"Open your eyes," came the unknown voice.

We opened our eyes. Facing us were about twenty policemen, all standing at ease. None was carrying a weapon. I saw the faces of many of the guards who had gleefully abused us, but now they didn't look so omnipotent. They looked like calm, obedient lambs. And standing in front of them was a short fair-skinned man with light green eyes and a face like an inflated balloon. He strutted over the concrete floor with the arrogance of a peacock, looking at each prisoner in turn. It was as if he were estimating our weight and abilities. Then he looked at the sergeant who had overseen the brutality since I arrived.

"Warrant Officer Muhammad."

"Yes sir."

"Cell one is under my command."

"Understood, sir." Then the lieutenant colonel turned and exited the cell. "Atten—shun . . . About face . . ." called the sergeant, and the policemen followed their new commander.

"Inspection complete, chief," the Bulldozer called to the sergeant, and, watching the scene carefully, I swear I saw a small smile come over the Bulldozer's lips. The sergeant stared at our leader for a second, turned, and left.

The cell door slammed shut.

What the hell does "the cell is under my command" mean?

CHAPTER 35

PRIVILEGES GRANTED BY
THE GOVERNOR

When the prison governor's first visit to our cell was over, everyone began to talk at once. In my part of the cell, Jaffan heaved a sigh of relief. "When the military police stormed the cell," he said, "I thought there was going to be a massacre."

"A massacre? Just like that, man? How you love to exaggerate!"

"What d'you mean 'exaggerate,' man? Aren't we in the era of massacres?"

"Yes, I remember the Muslim Brothers killed eighty officer-cadets in '79. An old man cleaning up after said the smell of blood was so heavy in the air, he had a vision. A prophecy that the same scent would soon spread across the whole of Syria."

"And here in Tadmur, hundreds of unarmed Muslim Brothers paid the price for an assassination attempt on Hafez al-Assad. They just opened the cells and . . ."

"That's what I thought was happening to us."

"I was in Aleppo when al-Assad killed dozens in the Masharqa and Bustan al-Qasr quarters. And he did it during the festival of Eid al-Fitr."

That made me remember how, at the Citadel, nobody could help but hear and feel the tremendous car bomb the Brothers detonated in al-Azbakiah, the center of Damascus. It killed dozens.

"And don't forget Hama," a voice added.

"Hama," came a collective groan. This had been the worst atrocity up until then. In al-Qala'a prison, news reached us of daily massacres in the city of Hama throughout February 1982. The city of Hama, on the banks of the Orontes River in west-central Syria, was besieged by its own government for twenty-seven days. This was because the city was a stronghold for hundreds of fighters of the Muslim Brothers, who rose up against the regime. Al-Assad's men not only bombed and attacked Hama mercilessly, they also stopped food and medical supplies from getting in. The regime didn't care that most of the residents were innocent civilians, and even now nobody outside of the government knows the real death toll. One thousand, two thousand, eight thousand, twenty-eight thousand, forty thousand? They're all guesses or propaganda. But even though it was suppressed, the news of what happened traversed the whole of Syria, causing an upsurge of sympathy from the public. As we were powerless to act, we were filled with a profound numbness, causing the air we breathed on every street, in every home, and even in the jails, to become a thick, stifling pall. It made me feel like I'd walked in thousands of funeral processions for people I didn't know and whose bodies lay moldering in unknown graves, or no graves at all.

As the animated debates continued, I went over to the Bulldozer and tapped him on the shoulder.

"Ahmad, what does it mean to be under the command of the prison governor?" He looked as if he were trying to fathom the depth of my ignorance.

"Didn't you go to military education classes in secondary school?"

"I went, but . . ."

"It means only the prison governor has the right to give us orders." When he read the continuing ignorance on my face, he rolled his eyes. "They won't be able to torture you when you bring in the food."

"Oh. Are you sure?"

"I'm not sure of anything. I'm just explaining the meaning of the military phrase."

The key turned in the lock. We did what we usually did: stood up, bowed our heads, and faced the wall.

"Atten—shun!" shouted the Bulldozer. "Cell ready for inspection, Warrant Officer."

"About turn," the warrant officer ordered. We turned. "Open your eyes and raise your heads." As we raised our heads, we saw the warrant officer was actually smiling. "On orders from the prison governor, Lieutenant Colonel Ghanem," he announced, "prisoners of cell number one are now exempted from closing their eyes and facing the wall when the door opens. And during your time in the yard, you can walk freely." There was a shocked, unbelieving silence. "We know that you have not carried out acts of terrorism, but," and he raised a finger in the air, "you are guilty nevertheless." Of course we are guilty. Guilty of wanting to be free. "Now, with discipline you will be able to preserve the privileges granted to you by the governor, so be grateful." Then he turned to the Bulldozer. "Chief."

"Yes, Warrant Officer."

"Despite this leniency, you must continue to line your men up five by five at the noon roll call. We don't want any problems. Understood?"

"Yes, Warrant Officer."

"Any questions?" the head guard barked.

"Can we smoke in the yard during the exercise period?" Salman Ismail asked.

"What kind of question is that?" This was the face-saving response the warrant officer always gave when he had to ask his superiors how to answer a question. As he made for the door, he turned again. "Oh, and Fatih Jamous, you're wanted in the governor's office." We all stood silently, looking at the sergeant and each other while Fatih hurried to change his clothes.

After Fatih left, the Bulldozer explained that Fatih was the prison governor's cousin and a childhood friend, and that our comrades Munir Hasoun and Adnan Zahra were from his village too. Perhaps this might explain why we were being offered these privileges. And while Fatih was away for more than an hour, we aired our various opinions on the message the sergeant had delivered.

"Privileges. Did he say privileges?" someone mused. "A goat can open its eyes without being granted a privilege. Cats can stay awake when they want and sleep when they want. And we have to go to sleep at seven p.m. or act as if we're asleep even if we're awake."

"Yes, but we've been doing it so long, it's almost like we've denied ourselves the right to open our eyes. So now that someone says we can open them, it's like we really think it is a privilege."

"We're deprived of so many of our rights . . ."

"What are you trying to say? It's our right to be free? What's the point if we can't achieve it?"

"Excuse me, excuse me. Claiming back some of our rights won't do us any harm."

"But will it do us any good?"

"When the Lord wanted to make a poor man happy, He made the man's donkey disappear and when the man found his donkey, he forgot his misery and almost flew for joy. And here we are, rejoicing because we're given the right to open our eyes, forgetting that we're prisoners."

"I don't understand."

If I get out of Tadmur one day, I'll say that I opened my eyes and raised my head, not because I fought for this right, for to fight here is fatal. But violating tyrannical rules is beautiful, however it comes to pass.

We were still debating back and forth when the lock clicked, and as the door creaked open, I saw him again, the barbaric sergeant with the blond mustache. The drum in my chest began to beat automatically, an unseen percussionist going berserk. And then a wide-eyed Fatih walked in, and everybody just stood staring at him. Blondie seemed disappointed that we weren't all scurrying for the wall, but he followed his new orders and didn't react ferociously as usual. He just left. The drum in my chest began to quiet, and I relaxed, and we stared in amazement at Fatih. His arms were piled high with newspapers and pamphlets, more words than anyone had seen since getting here. The cell hungrily converged on the governor's cousin to see what he had brought us. There were pamphlets issued by the Baath Party's educational office and the newspapers well known as government propaganda organs. Normally we wouldn't be caught dead with this stuff, but we were so starved of the written word that the newspaper broadsheets were pulled apart, and people devoured and traded the sections in an orgy of literary consumption.

"Who's got the section with page seven? I've finished six."

We read everything, recognizing that within the news articles there would always be a central theme. The headlines seemed to compete with each other to see which could bestow more greatness on Hafez al-Assad: "Inspired leader," "Builder of the new Syria," "Leader of the Arab nation," "Leader of the march of the party and the people," "War hero," "Pioneer of world peace." We also read poems; short stories; book reviews; movie reviews; birth, wedding, and death announcements; and advertisements for everything from shampoo and chewing gum to fizzy water. Those reading the entertainment section argued about the beauty of movie stars, and a nice photo of rising star Sophie Marceau especially caught my eye. We gazed at black-and-white photos of Marilyn Monroe, Brigitte Bardot, Elizabeth Taylor, and Katharine Hepburn.

"It's not fair to ignore Claudia Cardinale," Musab remarked.

"So is it fair to ignore our own stars, like Muna Wassef, Naglaa Fathi, or Soad Hosny?" And then came the sound of a key in the lock again. That lock was getting a good workout that day. It was comical to again see everybody having to stop themselves from running to the wall, including me. But we did stand to attention, all eyes on the door.

"Cell ready . . . Sergeant," and as the door opened, it was obvious that the guard also found it odd to have us staring at him.

"Time to breathe, Chief," he finally said. Time to breathe meant exercise time in the sun.

As we filed past the sergeant like sheep, I could see most of us were ready to form a line and put a hand on the shoulder of the person in front of him, to walk once more with our eyes closed. But the Bulldozer came and pushed our arms down and wagged his large finger.

"At ease. Walk as you will."

So, philosophical theorists be damned. Having penalties and abuses removed is better than continuing with them, as opening your eyes is better than being forced to close them. And moving freely during "breathing time" is better than plodding like a blinkered mule, a beast circling a well to pump water, no longer stubborn, and literally in blind obedience to its master. One doesn't need theorizing or sophistry for any of this, whatever your ideology.

It was like a miracle. I felt like a man who'd been locked in a cave and was looking at the sky after years. There above me was a blue cloudless desert. It was obvious that most of us felt the same because we just gazed up at the sky and began wandering around aimlessly.

"Look," someone called, pointing up.

An aircraft was flying so high it looked smaller than a goose. Behind it two parallel lines of exhaust trailed noiselessly. They met, mingled, and faded away as the aircraft moved off into the distance. I looked back at the massive yard of the prison that housed anywhere between four and twelve thousand prisoners, depending on who you talked to and whether they calculated how many souls it was built for or how many had been crammed in.

"Yasir, do you think this yard is big enough for a plane to land in?"

He looked up and squinted. "Not big enough for that one. It would need an international runway. A small Cessna or Piper maybe. Or a helicopter."

"They would do," I said, still looking up dreamily.

"Hey, maybe we can open our eyes and walk about, but a plane ride out of here? Don't get carried away."

I laughed and, for the first time, studied the interconnected roofs running for several hundred feet over the line of cells. I had been too preoccupied with being abused all the other times outside, but now I saw our prison in detail. A sparrow hopped around blithely on the low cinderblock wall that ran along the edge of the flat roof. It seemed unconcerned about the guard stationed a few feet away. With his Kalashnikov at hand, the guard fixed his gaze down on our group and then directly at me. His long, frowning face appeared to wonder how we got to be walking about so freely with our eyes open and our heads up. This had to be a gross violation of the natural order his knitted eyebrows seemed to cry. He began to raise his weapon when a dark-skinned guard, one known for his proficiency with a whip, appeared beside me. He held a palm up to his colleague on the roof.

"Who are these assholes?" the guard on the roof called.

"They're under the command of . . ." and the man beside me jerked his thumb upwards.

The guard with the Kalashnikov made a face and carried on over the roofs.

CHAPTER 36

FIRST-CLASS PRISONERS

We were no longer forced to go to sleep at 7 p.m. "I heard that out of all the prison cells, we and the Democratic Baathists are the only ones to live under the new rules."

At the time nobody really knew the exact number of cells at Tadmur. The gossip was there were thirty-eight similar to ours, crammed with some sixty to one hundred and ninety-five prisoners. There were also smaller isolation cells, like the one I was originally stuffed into with Zaher at the investigation branch. And then there were apparently nineteen punishment cells that were used for solitary confinement. Over the years, I ended up keeping in touch with many other Tadmur alumni from all of the groups, but I've never known one who was in those underground cells. Make what you will of that.

"I guess we're first-class prisoners now," Salman pronounced.

"It must be because we were non-violent," added Musab al-Nabhan.

"That's just the excuse the governor uses," Jaffan corrected. "It's really because Fatih is his cousin."

And we took advantage of our new status, one of the perks being that we could stay up late. One of the first things we did was arrange regular evening seminars. Anyone could talk about any subject he wanted to. The topics ranged from lectures on our villages and cities; the comparison of customs of nomads, city dwellers, and peasants; types of regional cooking and food preservation; and even our love affairs.

When someone mused how it would be good to be able to write again, Musab devised a way to accomplish the task the very next day. He collected the foil-lined cigarette packs and carefully opened them up, gingerly pulling apart the glued edges. He then soaked them to remove the foil inner layer and flattened the wet paper to dry on the cement wall. This resulted in several dozen pieces of paper about five by six inches. While waiting for the first sheets of paper to dry, he rolled the foil he'd separated into a ball and scraped it along the outer shiny paper of the larger wrapping that the individual cigarette packages came in.

"It leaves a line," Musab shouted. "It leaves a line. It's a pen! A pen!" He was as elated as Archimedes making his ancient discoveries.

Musab then hurriedly compressed and sculpted the ball of foil until it was like the tip of a pencil and fashioned a barrel for it by rolling some paper into a narrow tube. Slipping the tip into one of its hollow ends, he continued by wrapping string at the one end to bind the tip to the barrel, winding it down the shaft to give it strength. I watched as he tested it again, and a broad smile came to both of our lips. By the next day, he'd also discovered that the writing was darker if the paper was rubbed over the heads of people with oily hair. And so began our renewed pleasure of writing.

I took to soaking different fruit and vegetable peels — pomegranate, apples, and onions — to concoct a kind of ink and watercolor medium. Using a matchstick as my first brush, I created simple paintings. They were mostly birds and women. Some birds by themselves, some women by themselves. One was a woman holding two smiling birds where her breasts should be, with many other birds flying into infinity behind them.

The invention of the pen enabled us to write poems and stories or to take notes on each other's lectures. As time went by, we added evenings devoted to stories and poetry, the study of philosophy and different religions, history, sociology, and anthropology, all either professional specialties or areas of past studies by our fellow inmates when they were eager students.

After about five months of being first-class prisoners, our lives changed. Our families were allowed to visit us. Each inmate was allowed one visit every three months. So that not a month went by without at least two visits, we coordinated with each other as to when we'd get to see our families. With those visits came supplies of food, clothing, books, magazines, newspapers, stationery, and cash. All of this was shared by everyone. Equally important was knowing the news of our families and the outside world. These updates were also shared among us and discussed in the evenings.

Among the purchases with our new supply of money were cigarettes in bulk. Ten packets of smokes came wrapped in a large beige-colored sheet of paper, about sixteen by twelve inches. The Bulldozer, having seen my creative obsessions, presented me with the paper and watched as I lovingly flattened the creases with the palm of my hand. Inspiration didn't take long. Within seconds I folded it in two, making what would become a newspaper of four pages. And then, using the ink and tools I had created myself, I quietly began to fill in the blank spaces.

First I drew a cartoon inspired by a lengthy discussion we had one evening. It was on the concept of a central ring at every stage of a political struggle. The cartoon featured a woman wearing panties made up of a set of interconnected rings, like chainmail, and a bald politician looking at the rings, perplexed about which was the central one. I also wrote a short poem about the seven days of creation. On the sixth day, the servant says to his master, "What I don't understand is how this foolish world allowed me to get on so well before you arrived." And then, on the seventh day, the master disappears and the servant rests.

Seeing what I was up to, Musab wrote a satirical piece on the dangers of peeing into the wind, while Jihad contributed a short feature about the patience and gentleness of the donkey. By the next day, this experimental issue number zero was ready and only in need of a title. Fatih suggested we called the newspaper *The Seagull*, as that bird was a symbol of reaching land after a hard sea journey.

This experiment evolved, and when we were able to have our visitors bring real reams of paper, we eventually produced thirteen issues of our newspaper, some of which had between eighty to a hundred six-by-eight pages. I became the editor and production manager, a harbinger of my publishing future, and it broke my heart that once everyone in the cell had read them, we felt they should be destroyed. Each time *The Seagull* was soaked in water until it dissolved and then flushed down the toilet, I felt the anguish of Sisyphus as he watched his rock roll back down the hill.

Another way we exploited being first-class prisoners and overcame the boredom and depression emanating from the concrete and metal all around us was to perform a play without a stage. We chose a play originally by Peter Weiss, *How Mister Mockinpott was Cured of his Sufferings*. Saadallah Wannous, the famous playwright to whom I had delivered *The Red Banner* some years earlier, had adapted it for Arabic-speaking audiences. He had renamed it *Hanzala's Journey from Slumber to Consciousness*. Many of us had seen it at the Qabbani theater in Damascus. Not having the script, we simply improvised. I got to play the lead role of Hanzal. Afterward we held a discussion about our production, at the end of which, along with all the members of the cast, I smoked a cigarette with great enjoyment. It was such a triumph, even the anti-smoking Abu al-Harith was lenient that evening.

"You all deserve a reward, Jamal," he said, adding, "I just wish it could have been a harmless one."

On the anniversary of Hafez al-Assad's coup against his Baathist comrades, Lieutenant Colonel Ghanim, Fatih's cousin, visited our cell and read a speech. It was entitled, "The blessed corrective movement, led by the leader of the march of liberation and correction, the heroic fighter Hafez al-Assad." We all stood silently, trying not to look too disinterested. After all, this was the man who had made our lives so much easier. And then the governor ordered us into the yard for exercise period. Loudspeakers were broadcasting songs in praise of Hafez al-Assad. The doors of almost all the other cells were open; although those cells' occupants had been granted the right to open their eyes for the day's celebration, they couldn't come out. This meant that as many as could took turns crowding at each doorway. There, with their clothes in tatters, they looked like ghosts with their sunken cheeks and eyes, watching us as we sauntered by with our improved appearances, courtesy of the food and clothing brought by our visitors. It was the only time in my five years at Tadmur that I had a glimpse of any prisoner not from my cell. I made a quick hand signal to a group from one of the cells, meaning "Who are you?" and one of them pointed upwards with his index finger, the recognized sign that they were of the Muslim Brotherhood. Another signaled to ask who we were, and I bent my index finger in the shape of a sickle. He then pinched his hollow cheek, and I felt deep sorrow for them.

During the music and festivities, the guards ordered the Muslim Brothers to applaud excerpts from al-Assad's speeches broadcast over the prison radio and to shout, "Our soul, our blood, we'll sacrifice for you, Hafez." And even though most of them did parrot this empty vow to avoid punishment, when the celebration ended, the guards nonetheless dragged a good number of the Brothers from their cells, and we watched as they beat them with gusto, just as they had previously done to us.

The impoverished state of the Muslim Brotherhood prisoners led us to discuss ways we might help them. Visits from our families had been going on for more than half a year, so we had a pretty good stockpile of extra clothing, and food, just like we'd had at the Citadel. However, when we put forward the idea of sharing our excess with the Muslim Brothers, the Warrant Officer Nazih told us not to ask about that again.

"They've got everything they need," he declared.

In 1983 and 1984, once every week, a black comedy of military field trials was held for the Muslim Brothers under the windows of our cell. At about 9:30 in the morning our whole cell would settle down and listen to the tables and chairs being set up, followed by the officers greeting each other and giving orders to subordinates. This was followed by the sound of the guards bringing a long lineup of Muslim Brothers, accompanied by beatings, which stopped on the dot of ten. That's when one of the three presiding officers would call the name of the first prisoner.

"Abid al-Zahar." A man is brought forward. "Are you Abid al-Zahar?" the officer asks.

"Yes sir."

"Don't you have any moral, patriotic, or religious boundaries, you murderer?" the judge yells.

"Sir, I swear to God, I've never killed anyone . . ."

"How can we believe a criminal like you? We have documents that say otherwise. Get out of my face." And that is the end of Abid's trial.

From the gossip we heard, another officer recorded the verdict without the accused learning his fate. There were only two possibilities: acquittal or execution.

"Hasan al-Banna Salama," shouted the judge angrily, and another man was rousted in front of him.

"Your name's an accusation in itself." This was because he was named for the founder of the Muslim Brothers. "And your father was an akhwanji" (slang for Muslim Brother), "so what else could his son be?"

"But sir, I had no part in my naming," pleaded the prisoner. This caused an outburst of laughter from the guards.

"Is your father still alive?"

"No sir."

"When did he bite the dust?"

"In Nasser's time."

We pictured the judge recording a verdict, then asking for the next prisoner. And so it went on. Once, we counted eighty Muslim Brothers being tried in an hour and twenty-eight minutes, with nobody knowing what their fate would be.

Several years later, when I had occasion to talk to a Muslim Brother who had been at Tadmur at the same time, he told me that death sentences were carried out in yard number six within days. A man would be called out of his cell with no ceremony. However, the cellmates would pray and say their goodbyes because they knew that most likely they'd never see this Brother again. As for those acquitted, most times the innocent weren't released for years. A story went around, although I don't know how true it was, that the lieutenant colonel visited the special cell where the acquitted prisoners were kept. In a generous mood that day, he asked the prisoners to present their demands.

"Sir," one prisoner dared to inquire, "we've been acquitted. When will we go home?"

The prison governor chuckled. "Relax, don't worry. You'll have to be released in the end, even if you're here for a hundred years."

Being first-class prisoners also had an effect on our cleanliness. Before our elevation in status, once a week we formed a human train that shuffled its way to the showers. With our eyes closed, heads bowed, and a hand on the shoulder of the man in front of us, we were steered along by a guard with the tip of his whip in the mouth of the prisoner at the head of the line.

"Have a pleasant bath," guards would taunt us, as they beat us along the way, the lead guard pulling and pushing the whip left and right, our line snaking in waves around the yard.

The shower room was a moldy place featuring cubicles of cracked tiles and slippery floors, which were a problem when a guard was watching and you had to keep your eyes shut. The guards further amused themselves by turning off the hot water in the winter and the cold in summer. Because there were so many of us, they often ordered us out before we'd rinsed the soap off our bodies.

But this situation didn't continue under the new governor. Not because he forbade the abuse, but because he closed down the showers, meaning that all prisoners in all the cells had to wash with the cold-water hose next to the toilet. Again, our new privileged status allowed us a better solution, and we were the lucky ones.

Our general council, the name we gave to our group as a whole, agreed on a plan where each cell member could bathe with hot water once during the week. Using the funds from our continued family visits, we procured a bucket and a heating element. We then made a bathing rotation, where each day eight or nine of us could take turns heating up a single bucket's worth of fresh hot water to give ourselves a sponge bath. Ali al-Na'im, one of our larger cellmates, made a good-humored protest.

"A bucket might be enough for Musab al-Nabhan. He could swim in it. But it won't even wet my belly."

Six months after becoming first-class prisoners, our "privileges" also extended to us being allowed to have a mirror and shaving tools in the cell. We were given one double-sided safety razor and thirty blades. One side of a blade per prisoner. The Bulldozer was the first to use these boons. Crowding around him, we watched him take a towel from being heated in the bucket and wrap it around his face to soften his beard.

"Just like at the barber shop," somebody said, and I swear most of us giggled with vicarious pleasure.

The Bulldozer then slung the towel over his shoulders, soaped up his face, and raised the safety razor dramatically before proceeding. It was as if he were performing a miracle for all to see. Nobody said a word as the fresh blade glided through several weeks' whiskers. When he was done, he took the damp towel, wiped off the excess soap, sat up straight, and smiled broadly.

"Na'eeman," Samir said. This time it wasn't said as a sarcastic taunt, like when the Rooster abused it. It was meant as a sincere traditional blessing, one small example of our beautiful Arab culture.

"Na'eeman," Salman repeated, laughing.

And then the salutation rained down from all sides, with even the most sedate of comrades joining in with repeated joyous shouts. "Na'eeman" was shouted from every mouth again and again, accompanied by raucous laughter. It was a rare moment of collective harmony and joy. That day became a milestone, and it was possible to classify all events according to whether they came before or after Na'eeman Day.

CHAPTER 37

SILVA'S SON BECAME A RIVER GIFT

"Jamal — Saeed. Visitors for you," shouted the sergeant. I must have looked surprised, or more accurately, stunned, for I just stood there. "Hurry up."

So excited to meet them. Finally.

The visit was always a surprise in Tadmur Prison. The prison's administration did not inform any prisoner that his family had been given permission to visit, and we couldn't correspond with the outside world. As I rushed to get ready, my cellmates worked to find better clothes for me to wear, or at least ones that fit.

Walking through the yard with the sergeant, he warned me the visit was not for exchanging information about what was happening here or in the outside world at large. It was to reassure my family about me and me about them, nothing more. There was a sudden crack of gunfire nearby. I began to tremble. Was the announcement of a visit just a pretext, a trick to get me to go with the guard? The drum in my chest, quiet for some months now, began to frantically beat. Had I somehow offended a guard or the governor? Had someone accused me of something during torture? I mean, who were those bullets for? I slowed down for a moment, but having no choice, meekly fell in behind my escort. I put a hand to my cheek. My face felt cold. The blood had already drained from it. The sergeant led me toward a door and turned the handle. I walked through into a small room, my head down, my heart pounding in my ears. I looked up .·. . relief. There were my father, mother, and four of my siblings. Unlike at the Citadel, here we were permitted face-to-face visits, and so the first thing I did was fall into my mother's arms. It had been more than two years. I just stood there, breathing in her familiar scent. She held me tight, kissed my ear, and whispered.

"Don't be afraid, Jamal. They're firing in the air to celebrate the president's recovery. He just got out of hospital."

I pulled back and looked at her. She had aged a bit, more worry lines and grayer. "How did you know I was . . . ?" She gave the same look I'd seen often when she seemed to be reading my mind.

I'm a mother. Of course, I know everything about you.

"You are the light of my eyes," my mother said. "How are you?"

"As you see, I am well. But seeing all of you, even better now."

It took several minutes for us to greet each other with long hugs and wan smiles. And then we sat to talk, the sergeant sitting watch by the door. My mother, always a rock of strength and dignity, sat holding my hand. Abi, my father, was the hardest-working person I've ever known. But he was also the quietest without a few sips of his beloved arak. He just sat there, older and grayer, too, sinking further into his sadness by the minute. My younger twin brothers, Ahmad and Yousef, must have grown a foot or more since I last saw them. Hair was starting to sprout from their faces. Mother told me they were doing just as well as I did in high school.

"Better than me?" I asked them.

"Of course," they said in unison.

My eldest sister, Asmahan, was a woman now. She was going to Tishreen University in Latakia to study math and physics. Khadija, three years younger, was blossoming into womanhood too. She would go to Tishreen to study biology. I was astonished. Not that they had the talent to study those subjects, but that I had missed all that time watching them achieve their goals.

Personal achievements were fine to talk about in our meeting. Health was acceptable, the weather too. And then Ummi, my mother, inadvertently crossed the information exchange line.

"We're all well, thank God, but it's not easy to get hold of everyday necessities. Your brother queued for six hours outside the store to try to get hold of ghee, but came home empty-handed. No, don't worry. Everything's fine, but it's not easy to find what you want. Money isn't the problem . . .

but, you know, you can't eat money!" The sergeant looked annoyed and cleared his throat, so my mother took the hint and repeated words she'd heard on the radio. "Our country's under siege. Outside forces want to bring us to our knees." The sergeant smiled, and she added, "They are the cause of our misery." Mother made *them* responsible, but it wasn't clear who *they* were. I understood her innuendo, but I felt sad. It was because of me that she had to engage in this Orwellian talk and that I couldn't protect her from it.

"What about Mahmud?" I asked.

"Your little brother is well too. He's taller than me now," mother continued. "He came with us." I looked confused. "They wouldn't let him in without an ID card, but he can't get one because he's not yet fourteen." She laughed. "And we don't intend to cut off his legs so they'll let him in without an ID." The sergeant looked annoyed again. Not having a sense of humor was part of the job, I guess. Ummi saw this and added hastily, "He'll be fourteen before the next visit and he'll get ID." The sergeant smiled. "There's nothing like time for solving even the most difficult problems," she added. But apparently the sergeant projected his own meaning onto this, perhaps interpreting it to mean that in time the regime would pass, rather than that in time my brother would be older.

"Visiting time is over," he announced abruptly. Everyone rose to their feet.

"The next visit will be at the end of the summer," Abi said, finally completing a full sentence. "What would you like us to bring you?"

I told him I wanted grapes from the vine that climbed the poplar trees and an apple from our orchard. Both would be in harvest then. I knew my father's trees were a source of pride for him and was glad to see him smile when I mentioned them.

My family left. I forgot to ask my father: "When you sent me money with Wadha, which cow did you sell? The black or the yellow?"

In 1984, the prison governor was transferred. The reason was said to be his loyalty to Rifaat al-Assad, the president's brother, who had led a failed coup. The governor's deputy, Barakat al-Ish, took over from him and, luckily, our privileges remained the same. By that time there were about seventy prisoners in our so-called communist cell, so the new governor had to break us up into two cells. Some of us moved to a smaller cell known as the dispensary, and others moved to the newly created cell that had been used as prisoners' showers. I was lucky enough to remain in what actually had been a health clinic, as it boasted its own concrete courtyard. The courtyard had an outside barred door to the prison yard, so we were allowed to sit in the sun during the day.

After they allowed our family to visit us, we used to distribute what we got from those visits equally. Within a short time, the families of the prisoners coordinated with each other to determine what each family would bring the prisoners and when. Our families brought enough pajamas, towels, underwear, cooked or preserved foods, vegetables, and fruits, in addition to coffee, tea, and yerba mate, and of course they didn't forget the metal straws for drinking yerba mate.

For the last three harvest seasons my father had been bringing us crates of white grapes and apples after every harvest. At the end of August 1987 we received an especially huge quantity of his grapes, sixty kilos, as well as apples, pears, and figs. And coincidentally that year, another cellmate's visitors brought a similar load of red grapes. What to do with all of these grapes?

The General Council, made up of all the inhabitants of the cell, met to discuss whether we should make wine. A minority was of the opinion that making wine must be against the prison rules and if we were caught, we would risk losing all our privileges. Another argument was that the best wine was made from grapes harvested after Eid al-Salib, the Feast of the Cross, on September 27. However, the majority decided we shouldn't wait and should keep half the grapes for eating and use the rest for wine. For fermentation vessels we used three twenty-liter jerry cans that had been used for extra water storage. All the preparations went well, and after two weeks, the juice was happily bubbling away. This was when the disciplinary officer showed up. He read every single prisoner's name off a list and told us to pack our things and get ready to leave the cell.

"I'll be back in an hour," he said. "Be ready."

"Where are we going?"

"You'll know soon enough."

Everybody presumed we were moving to another cell, so we'd have to act fast and dispose of all our illegal items. There was a knife we made out of half a pair of scissors that someone found lying out in the yard. We ground it sharp only to cut food, but if the guards found it, it would be classed as a weapon. Musab destroyed any papers that might cause us problems. There were critiques we'd written commenting on magazine articles on politics, minutes from meetings showing we operated as an organization within the prison, that we had a general council, a leadership structure and a committee for managing the resources received from visitors. And as our money was normally held by the resource committee, we distributed some cash to everybody in case questions came up during an inspection. It fell to me to get rid of the wine.

"No use crying over spilt wine, or our wasted time," I muttered as I poured the now frothing juice down the toilet. As I waited for each jerry can to empty, I thought about all of my father's wasted effort, the loving attention to the grapes as they grew, the harvesting, doing without the profit from selling them, and the bother of transporting the many fruit crates to the prison.

"Didn't we say just eat them as grapes?" Abu Luai said as he watched the last of the wine being flushed away. I didn't defend myself by saying we had so many grapes they'd have gone bad before we could eat them all. I held my tongue. I knew that Abu Luai was just expressing his fears. We were all afraid, and each of us had to respect the other's right to overcome anxieties in their own way.

I then began packing my clothes and other possessions. This included almond husks and olive pits that I'd carved into English capital letters and flowers. These were to be sent to my sisters as presents. I also dared to include my greatest treasure, the notebook I'd carefully and slowly created out of the paper from cigarette packages. This notebook contained the last draft of the novel I'd been working on for almost five years. I began writing it after a fellow prisoner, Mustafa Khalifa, told me a curious true story that dated back to the First World War.

"Some boys were swimming in the Euphrates near the town of Jarabulus, right on the Syrian-Turkish border," Mustafa began. "There they spotted a small, odd-looking boat. Perhaps it was a child's toy. But curiously, it appeared to have a rooster tied to it, like a ship with a colorful flag. The best swimmer among the boys swam over to the boat and found it wasn't a toy, but a basket. The basket was made of walnut wood, and when the boy got close to the basket, the rooster fluttered its wings. The boy looked into the basket, and to his great surprise he found a baby staring back at him. He swam back to the river bank, pulling the strange cradle behind him, and boasted that the child was the river's gift to him. The story of 'the river's gift' became the talk of the region, causing an Arab feudal landowner, whose wife could not bear children, to show up at the boy's home.

"'I'm here to buy the baby from you,' the imposing lord declared. 'How much?'

"The usually brash boy, now afraid, asked the lord for one gold lira, but the feudal lord was generous that day. More generous than he'd ever been in his life. He gave the teenager seven times his asking price.

"This was because the feudal lord was madly in love with his wife," continued Mustafa, "and did not want to upset her by marrying another woman to produce an heir. Now, what's curious about this is that most men, especially wealthy men, would insist on having an heir from their own loins. But not this lord."

"That is very curious," I said, but there was something else bothering me. "Mustafa, where did the basket come from? And why a rooster?"

"Ah, I was getting to that. I think it came from upriver, across the border in Turkey. The mother must have put her baby in the basket and placed it into the river to save him from being murdered in the Armenian genocide. And perhaps she included the rooster to attract the attention of people on the riverbank when it crossed the border from Turkey to Syria. The rooster would make it more likely for her little one to be rescued, especially if it crowed."

"I see," I replied. I began to imagine the horrible conditions the mother was facing.

"Someone should write this story," Mustafa said.

"Indeed, someone should," I replied. I began to picture the face of an Armenian woman who walked along the Euphrates River asking about her son. She used the Turkish and Armenian languages with the Arabs, Kurds, Assyrians, and Syriacs she met, who all spoke different languages.

After watching her baby float away, her eyes and heart following him, she found herself hurrying to the south, the direction in which the river was running. She watched from behind some trees as her husband and fifty other villagers, all bound together and with heavy rocks tied to them, were pushed into the Euphrates.

She continued her way to the south, but she was soon surrounded by a group of sneering soldiers. She wasn't murdered. The soldier who grabbed her claimed her as his slave, and for twenty years, he used the woman as a servant — for cooking and cleaning, and for other things. The soldier was not always cruel. Some days, he was tolerable, but never a day passed when the woman did not think of her son. Thoughts of him were especially painful when she saw a boy about the same age as her son would have been.

When the Turkish soldier retired, he took to drink. He became even crueler, except when he was passed out, drunk. Finally, not afraid of him anymore, the woman killed the soldier in his sleep and went off on a quest to find her boy, now a young man. She met a Kurdish smuggler who helped her with no expectation of any favor in return. He was always kind and pleasant, never pressing himself on her, even though to the outside world he was a smuggler and a thief. He even gave alms to the poor from the proceeds of his profession. And he was the first person in twenty years who asked her a very simple question.

"What is your name?"

For a moment, she had to think. "Silva. My name is Silva."

"Silva," he repeated with a slow and appreciative smile.

Because of all this, the woman fell in love with the smuggler. And then, while traveling through the Taurus Mountains, the smuggler stole a sheep, which he slaughtered and grilled, all so Silva and he could share a feast. It was a romantic setting in which, with a full moon shining down on them, the smuggler fed Silva by hand. It made her feel like they were the first and only two people on Earth. As the moon began to wane, the man stood and took Silva by the hand. She willingly allowed herself to be led to a cave and there, for the first time in her life, she made love for love's sake.

The Kurdish smuggler joined Silva on the quest. When they got back to the Euphrates and crossed over to the Syrian side of the border, the story of the basket with the rooster was still well known, and villagers told her who had adopted her son and where to find him.

I decided as I wrote the novel that the story of the baby in a basket would be similar to the story of Musa as the Quran tells it. Also, that the child's biological family had named their baby Harut. The feudal family who adopted him would consist of a Kurdish mother and an Arab father, and they decide to call the child Muhammad. He would have Syrian, Assyrian, Chaldean, Circassian, and Turkman friends, all shepherds, peasants, and tradesmen. And his family's wealth would allow him to study at the American University of Beirut, where he would become acquainted with more of the components of the mosaic that makes up the Arab East.

When I finished working on the fifth, and what I thought was the final, draft of the novel, it seemed to me like a set of windows opened on the cruelty and kindness, love and hatred, killing and coexistence of all the religions, sects, and nationalities that abound in the Levant and Mesopotamia.

After I had written the last sentence, I lay on my blankets and smiled up at the ceiling. "It is good," I whispered to myself, echoing God's pronouncement at the end of His sixth day of creation.

CHAPTER 38

JUST WRITE IT AGAIN

Before the officer returned, the blond sergeant came to check on us. He wasn't as aggressive as he was when I first arrived. Five years older and a little fatter, his youthful zeal was pretty well spent. That's probably why we never saw a guard over thirty, except for officers. Blondie confirmed that we were not changing cells but being moved to another prison entirely. Also, we were going to leave very soon.

Now, like ants in imminent danger, we rushed to organize things. Many of us had sewn bags for our possessions made out of worn-out clothing. Those without such luxuries took a long-sleeved shirt, buttoned it up, stuffed in their things, knotted the ends, and then tied together the arms as the strap for a shoulder bag.

My bag was made out of the completely worn-out blue jeans I originally bought from the money my father got from selling his precious cow. This made the fabric all the more precious to me. When I made the bag, I didn't think I'd ever use it. It was just a way to amuse myself for a few days, and I couldn't bring myself to discard a symbol of my father's love. I looked at the suitcases and bundles we'd all prepared for our departure. They appeared makeshift and impromptu, a visual metaphor for the life we were living, and reminding me of a Jack Kerouac quote: "Our battered suitcases were piled on the sidewalk again; we had longer ways to go. But no matter, the road is life."

We then hurriedly added our names to the walls as victims of this cell and read for the last time what other prisoners had written before us. The clearest of this graffiti were two lines of poetry high up on the wall, a quote from the ninth-century poet al-Shafi'i:

We blame our time though we are to blame. We are all that is wrong with our time.
Wolves don't eat the flesh of wolves, yet we eat each other in plain sight.

If we had been a detail in French photographer Yann Arthus-Bertrand's project to document Earth's features from the sky, we would have appeared like creatures wandering aimlessly, and his hypothetical camera could never have captured our characteristics. I don't know whether our outward appearance gave any indication of what was going on inside of us.

"The prison we're going to can't be any worse than this," I commented to Musab.

"It doesn't take much intelligence to know that," he said with a laugh. "A worse prison than this doesn't exist yet."

Yan Arthus-Bertrand is a French photographer and movie producer. He visited Syria in 2009 and took many photos from the sky, and made a photograph exhibition on Tishreen Park in Damascus, where I met and interviewed him.

The officer returned and told us to get into groups, each consisting of five detainees, and then we were led by the officer and eight military policemen out through the prison gate to the waiting vehicles. Today we'd travel in a convoy of three Russian ZiL trucks and two armed jeeps. Once again, we had Spanish handcuffs put on one wrist; as we climbed up into the transport, the other cuff was clamped around a common chain. And as they had grouped us alphabetically, Jaffan was chained right next to me.

"Listen up, prisoners," a young voice shouted. As one we looked to the door. There stood a short, stocky police officer who looked like a young bull calf. "We don't want any problems en route," he declared, and then he tried to look serious. As men who had all been beaten within less than an inch of our lives, we just stared back at him unconcerned. And then he slammed the door shut.

I lifted up my arms, showing the Spanish bracelets. "We're locked in a box with these on. What problems is that silly little bull man talking about?"

The convoy set off, and I was able to stand and look out the barred window. Robbed of the outside world for so long, I wanted to see the Temple of Baal or any of the ruins of Palmyra. But all I could see was the desert and a man in a keffiyeh riding a motorbike. Disappointed, I sat down. It was a bumpy ride to the new prison, and so we all bounced and swayed with the vehicle for the majority of the trip.

About four hours after leaving Tadmur, we finally stepped out of the back of the ZiL truck like men stumbling onto solid ground after a long voyage at sea. We were standing in front of the big black door of a huge modern building. It looked the opposite of all the military prisons I'd been in, brand-new, not ancient. Our truck was the first to disembark, and we walked in single file into the building. As we did so, a military policeman ordered me to empty the contents of my bag onto the floor.

"Where did you get this wonderful bag?" he asked with a laugh.

"From the Yves Saint Laurent shop in Tadmur," I replied.

"Yes, the height of elegance and good taste there." He continued to laugh as he unearthed my notebook from among the clothes. He glanced at it for a second, unaware that it was a novel I'd slaved over for five years, and tossed it into the corner amid a pile of other previously confiscated items.

"Please, sir. My notebook. May I have it back?"

"No personal papers, pens, or pencils allowed," he said indifferently.

I guess I was too used to being a first-class prisoner, for I continued talking. "Please, sir," I begged, and in the pain my eyes seemed to get through to him, at least for a moment.

"Sergeant, this detainee wants his notebook," the guard shouted.

"It's forbidden," the sergeant shouted back from down the line. And then I noticed they were confiscating all the notebooks, papers, and pens that had come in the first truck. I hung my head and moved along.

"Okay, truck one, move down the hall — now. Next truck," a corporal yelled. "Truck one, wait against the wall for your turn at the Prison Pen room. Now," he shouted again. "And be quiet!" As we passengers of the first truck leaned against the wall by the Prison Pen door, the corporal who had just yelled at us came and politely asked if I had tobacco. I did have a couple of cigarettes and offered him one. He gave me a match to light my cigarette, and I looked around at the freshly painted walls and ceilings and smooth, unscuffed floors.

Soon it was my turn to enter the room, where a warrant officer with a big head and thick lips sat. He was breathing heavily and wheezed as he asked questions. I put out my cigarette, even though it was only half finished, and he gave me a slight nod of appreciation. He must have been asthmatic. We continued the questions, him asking the same, the same, the same, the same questions, and I answered the same as I had over the years. I watched as he filled out the forms as carefully with his plain ballpoint pen as the fat policeman at the Citadel had done with his Waterman.

"That's it for you, Jamal. Thank you. Make your way out and call in the next man."

After a while, Warrant Officer Nazih showed up. We'd known him before at Tadmur.

"Sergeant. Take them to Floor One, Wing A, Corridor Left, cell ten."

"Yes, sir. Prisoners, follow me."

I was profoundly sad they had confiscated my novel, and as I trudged down a hallway with my group, my sadness turned to grief. It was as if I had just lost a piece of my soul. And I hadn't been able to defend it.

"Why?" I murmured. I felt like a bereaved mother whose son had been killed in front of her. Jaffan patted my shoulder. I tried to suppress my grief.

Keeping myself busy by figuring out my new surroundings could be a way of addressing this sorrow. We stopped at a door leading to one of the wings of the prison. The upper half of the door consisted of iron bars; it was shiny black while the cell doors were gray. As the door of the wing was opened, we walked into a long corridor, two hundred feet long, seven feet wide, and ten feet high.

Along the length of the outside wall, above a row of cast-iron heating radiators, there was a string of more than fifty small windows, their lower ledges about seven feet in height, so the prisoners could see only the sky and discover again what they knew well: the sky is the home of clouds and flying birds.

Just inside the doorway to the cellblock, there were piles of bedding stacked up against the wall.

"Every one of you will take an insulator, a mattress, a pillow, and three blankets into the cell," the warrant officer said. A mattress and a pillow in a military prison! What pampering! "Pick a cell chief to deal with the prison staff in case of need," the warrant officer added.

I noticed the cell doors here were different too. All my cells in previous military prisons had been constructed of solid concrete walls and a solid steel door with a small rectangular door that a guard could open to shout through, the shurraqa. But here, while the cell door had a similar shurraqa, the top and bottom of each wall and door had a row of steel bars about one foot high. This was significant, as they let in both fresh air and light from the corridor. I counted the doors, ten identical ones. When we got to the last one, the guard unlocked it.

"Twenty of you have to get into cell number ten," the guard ordered.

We chose Ahmad Najm as our cell chief. He was the best suited among us to put up with the daily interaction with guards.

It was clear from the look of the place that we were its first inhabitants. Our new place was about seventeen feet wide and thirty-three feet deep, with a washroom at the end of the cell. We placed our mattresses along the lengths of the two facing walls, and this gave each of us room to sleep lying on his back with his legs completely stretched out. It also allowed us to have a three-foot-wide walkway down the center of the room. As for the washroom, its soft-tile floor was easy to clean, and in addition to a sink, we had a shower here too. But that wasn't all; we actually had a urinal. This fixture caused a serious debate. We had to decide whether we should use the urinal as a storage shelf for our few plates or keep it for its intended purpose. Those who thought the urinal should be used for storage won the day; they had four votes more than their opponents. The walls and the ceiling were painted light gray, and the floor was smooth linoleum. This made it super easy to keep clean. In the middle of the ceiling was a lamp with a white, frosted-glass cover, which emitted a soft faint light, both during the day and all night long.

The next morning, after breakfast, all the cell doors were opened, and prisoners from different cells were allowed to mingle in the hallway until five that evening. The authorities had also put all of us communists in one wing. I found out too that the prisoners from the other trucks hadn't had their notebooks confiscated. This gave me hope that mine could be retrieved. But then I became concerned. If I used the precedent that the others hadn't been denied their papers, perhaps instead of me getting mine back, all the others would have theirs taken away. But everybody who had read my novel encouraged me to ask, and even insisted that I at least try.

"It must not be lost," was the consensus, and so I requested a meeting with the prison governor, Lieutenant Colonel Barakat al-Ish, who had moved from Tadmur with us.

"What do you want to meet His Excellency for?" Warrant Officer Nazih asked.

"My notebook was confiscated yesterday, and I need it back."

"You don't need to meet the prison governor for that, number ten. I'll get you a new notebook to make up for the blank pages in your old one."

"No, you don't understand, sir. There were no empty pages left in my notebook."

"So, why do you want it then?" he laughed. "Used things go in the trash."

"The trash? No, no, it mustn't. There are things in the notebook I must preserve."

"Like what?"

"A novel."

"A novel? Really? Who wrote it?"

"I did."

"You? You wrote it? From your head?"

"Yes."

He laughed again. "So why are you so worried?" I looked at him questioningly. "Come on, man! Think about it. You wrote it, okay. Just write it again." And then he put his hand on my shoulder. "You're going to have enough time in here to write it over and over and over again."

CHAPTER 39

HUNGER STRIKE AFTER
IHSAN'S DEATH

A s I lay comfortably on my new mattress in Sednaya Prison, I thought about how the monastery where I had enjoyed the care of Sister Theresa was only five miles away. It seemed such a long time ago.

There were only twenty people in our cell, instead of sixty or more. Some cells even had less, for a while. We were among the first prisoners to arrive at this new facility, but over the next weeks, it opened its gates to truckloads of passengers from the various interrogation branches as well as al-Mezze and Tadmur military prisons. Sednaya Prison is also known as the Mercedes. This is because the building consists of three long concrete cellblocks, or wings, that connect at the center. This causes the structure to resemble the logo of the famous German car brand. And because Lieutenant Colonel Barakat al-Ish now allowed all prisoners to circulate in the corridors outside their cells, and most of the guards were more talkative, it didn't take long for inmates to understand the layout of the whole prison. Knowledge of our surroundings was something completely new to us. No prisoner at Tadmur had any inkling of the layout of that hellhole.

Each wing at Sednaya had three floors of cellblocks, and each cellblock had two corridors, designated Left and Right. Both corridors had barred entry doors from the central administration block, followed by a two hundred–foot hallway with some fifty windows on the outside wall and cell doors along the inside. After the tenth cell, there was a short hallway connecting the Left and Right hallways. All this gives cells designations of Floor 1, 2, and 3;

Block A, B, and C; Corridor Left and Right; and cells numbered one to ten. Along with nineteen other prisoners, my first cell here was 1-A-Right-10.

There was also a curious design element in the building that, after getting settled, we exploited to make contact with inmates in other parts of the prison. Between the back walls of the cells, there was a four-foot gap, running from the top of the building to the bottom. I presume it was to allow air to flow out of the barred bathroom window high up on the wall of each cell, but the gap also allowed us to communicate with the cell behind us. This was how we learned that the occupants of Left-10 were from the faction who called themselves the Democratic Baath Party, one of the two Baathist factions that lost the power struggle against al-Assad's so-called Socialist Baath Party. They were anything but socialist. These "democrats" were different from the Saddam Hussein Baathists, who were just mercenaries, housed in Wing B. The Hussein Baathists were the jokers who sent us the wooden penis.

In the early days at Sednaya, the short corridor at the end of the hall was guarded, not allowing us and the other cells in the left corridor to mingle. This is why we resorted to talking through the barred bathroom windows. But then, inexplicably, the rules changed, and we were free to walk both sides of the corridors during the day.

We learned that this faction of Baathists was beginning to regard our communist factions with some admiration. They were becoming aware of Marxist doctrine and were debating whether to adopt Marx and Lenin as their new icons. This was odd on several levels. First, most of us were young enough to be their sons. And while they clearly thought that we were, as the old Arabic saying goes, their "worthy successors," most of us didn't see them as our "excellent forbears."

"We pass the baton to you with confidence," declared Abu Abdullah, one of the Baathist leaders.

"I'm afraid that as you get to know us," I replied, "we'll be different from what you imagine."

And I remember one senior parroting an old quote of Lenin's: "Marx's doctrine is omnipotent because it is true."

We just laughed in his face, and he looked so hurt that we tried, in vain, to explain: "Economics, sociology, and philosophy didn't end with

Dr. Marx. They must develop and change with the world. Marx knew this better than his apostles."

But he and most of the other middle-aged Baathists didn't understand. They continued proudly and passionately to recite excerpts from the great Marxist-Leninists, offering them as tokens of their solidarity, or at least their profound fellow feelings. I now knew how my parents felt when I spouted half-understood political rhetoric. But it was even more profound than that. There were those among us who were seriously reconsidering Leninism, and others who were awaiting new results from Gorbachev's perestroika and glasnost, which had helped expose the shameful oppression of those living under the socialist system and contributed to the development of liberal tendencies among the communists. Most of us had managed to escape from regarding Marxism as a religion, and some even thought that developing Marxist and other philosophical concepts was vital for our times. The main question from my perspective was: Would these political earthquakes truly lead to social justice, ensuring decisions were made by votes, not guns?

Yes, some of us had graduated from regarding Marxism as a religion but still thought that developing and combining Marxist and other economic concepts was important. In short, Marx had to be looked at as a thinker, not a deity. But we who had come to this conclusion were in the minority. And now to meet these older, newly converted Marxists who were so far behind in their political development. I must admit that, after only a month and a half of enduring their enthusiasm, several of us stopped going to visit them.

The new prison had a large outside exercise area. It was pleasant, but we got to enjoy it only once. When the group from our cell returned indoors, we found that all the cheap loudspeakers installed high on the walls of the corridor were blaring out songs celebrating the seventeenth anniversary of Hafez al-Assad's coup. Our tall, dark-skinned cellmate Ihsan Izzo couldn't stand the crackling noise coming from the ceiling, or the message, and so he climbed up on the heating registers and turned off the speakers he could reach.

He was seen doing this by a stocky little sergeant who had been given the nickname "Radar." This was because he was always looking around, as if searching for something he'd lost, and his ears were so big his constant turning made him look like a revolving radar antenna. Radar decided to punish Ihsan on the spot, grabbing his arm and screaming that he was transferring him to a solitary confinement cell in the basement. When Radar returned to our block, the Bulldozer, who had become the head of all the cells in our wing, told Radar it was vital that Ihsan have his high blood pressure pills. The Bulldozer knew all of his boys' situations as well as their own mothers. But Radar refused over and over again, ignoring the Bulldozer's repeated pleas. When the sergeant later brought the lunches and stood staring at us through the black bars of the wing's door, we all begged him again, but he stubbornly refused.

"We'll decide whether he needs these pills," he said arrogantly.

Fatih Jamous stepped right up to the wing's door and stared fearlessly into Radar's frowning face, made darker and more ominous for being pressed into the rectangular opening. "You'll be the one responsible if anything happens to our friend," Fatih warned.

Radar sneered at Fatih, and then at all of us. His contempt was palpable. "I think the best thing would be to send you all back to Tadmur," he growled and departed.

That night Governor Barakat al-Ish visited our cell. He told us that Ihsan's condition had deteriorated and that he'd been moved to a military hospital. I stared at al-Ish in shock, suddenly realizing how this was the first time any of us had seen him not wearing his lieutenant colonel's uniform. He had come to us in a civilian suit. A black civilian suit. For some reason, its fabric reminded me of mourning ribbons.

So, Ihsan has died and they're giving us the news in stages.

Now all I could see in front of me was Ihsan's smiling face, but with his eyes forever closed. I wasn't the only one who thought this. When the governor left our wing, everybody discussed their fears, although we clung to feeble threads of hope. Three days later, when Abu Hussein received a visit from the outside, we learned that Ihsan's body had been handed over to his family.

There was only one way we could protest, and so, on November 19, 1987, the whole wing went on a hunger strike.

When the fruit arrived, as usual just before lunch, the Bulldozer, our wing chief now, told the duty sergeant we were on hunger strike to protest the actions of his colleague that led to the death of our comrade. The sergeant made us get back into our cells and locked the doors. On his orders, the baladiyya threw apples into the cell between the bars supporting the wall, and we angrily tossed them back, a spontaneous expression of our rage and impotence, impotence in the face of death and the concrete blocks and iron surrounding us. After about an hour, the prison governor, al-Ish, came in his military uniform, with many soldiers. His solution was to distribute us among different cells in the three wings and three floors of the prison. Breaking us up would stop the communication and coordination of further dissension. Out of the 180 larger cells in Sednaya, I think only about a third were being used at the time, so they were able to make sure that all of us were completely separated from our comrades. I was among the group that transferred to Floor 2, Wing B, Corridor Right, cell nine. As soon as we'd arranged the bedding and blankets that we'd brought with us, we sat down in silence. As we were the only occupied cell on that wing, it was eerily quiet for a few minutes, but our colleague Jasim broke the silence and began reproaching himself and the rest of us.

"We should have carried on banging on the doors until they took him his medication," Jasim complained emotionally. "We should have fought with the prison administration to save his life, not protest about his death after."

"What's the use of bringing this up now?" someone asked.

"Yes, why torture yourself?" another added. "It never occurred to any of us that Ihsan would die so easily. He looked as strong as a horse."

"It didn't occur to us because we're thoughtless," Jasim snapped back.

"Okay, we're thoughtless," said another. "So why didn't you suggest banging on the cell doors until it was too late?"

"I agree. I'm more to blame than all of you because I thought of it and didn't do it. And I didn't do it because I'm a coward."

Suddenly the cell was boiling with emotion and argument, our voices echoing in the empty corridors. This is when Bassam Salim began to sob hysterically, and so we brought our commotion to an end. We sat sullenly, a few of us consoling those who had become over-emotional. But a couple of hours later Hani Salat rekindled the debate.

"What did we do when our comrade Abu Artin stood in the middle of the cell in Tadmur, screaming 'I'm going to die, I'm going to die' over and over and over again?" Hani asked. "Did we go on strike? No. We consoled him and just kept our heads down."

"That was in Tadmur," someone answered. "But here, maybe we can make a difference."

"Do you really believe that? Do you?" Hani said, looking about. He was daring someone to answer. I was about to open my mouth when he said in disgust, "Our hunger strike will just be dogs going hungry, and nobody will hear about it."

"I'd rather you didn't call us dogs," someone complained.

"You object to being compared to a dog. Dogs have a better life than us. And even if people do hear about this on the outside, do you think anyone will open their mouths? They'd end up in here with us."

"Well, I don't go on hunger strike just so people will hear about it," another chimed in.

"Yes, yes. I understand that going on hunger strike in prison is a form of rebellion. Heroic hunger," he said sarcastically.

"Hunger isn't the goal, and most of us have had much worse experiences."

"Yes, we have been through worse. And sure, some of you feel guilty and see this as a type of atonement. A purification . . ."

"Nonsense. We haven't done anything wrong. We have nothing to atone for."

"Yes, we have," Jasim cried. "I can't stand the idea of poor Ihsan suffering without his medication, but. . ." he sputtered.

"But what?" another challenged.

"Don't harass him," somebody shouted.

"I'm not. I'm just talking logic," came the reply, just as loud, which caused another storm of voices to echo throughout the cell and hallway.

"*Enough!*" I shouted at the top of my voice. "Stop this absurd discussion. Please."

There was complete silence. It was perhaps the only time in my life I had shouted so loudly. A guard opened the shurraqa and asked what the noise was.

"Noise? What noise?" Ahmad Najm, our new cell chief, asked innocently. The guard gave us all a dirty look and closed the door. I now found myself apologizing to everyone, acknowledging that many discussions in prison can become absurd and that we were all on edge.

The baladiyya continued to bring us meals at the normal times and took them away, untouched, when they brought the next meal. After three days we ended the hunger strike. Some prisoners weren't well, and not eating would just harm them more. We sent the governor a message that we were ending the strike, our only request being that all of our comrades be put together along one corridor again. His reply was no reply. It seemed that he wanted us to ask over and over again before he complied. As for Radar, whose stubbornness had caused Ihsan's death, we never saw him again. Speculation was that the governor probably transferred him to another assignment, not only because he had caused an unnecessary fatality, but because the governor had to protect his own position. Tadmur was out in the desert, so there was little accountability to anyone. But Sednaya was in a city, and word got out.

Around two months after our strike ended, the prison governor agreed that we communists could again all be in one wing, which became Floor 2, Wing C in the Left Corridor. Being together again made daily life less difficult. About a month later, and for the next two years, groups of between fifteen and thirty of our comrades, who had been arrested in a severe crackdown, started arriving in our prison. They were put with us on Floor 2, Wing C, and when all the cells were full, they were put on the third and first floors. To communicate with them, we used the bathroom window, this time by means of a rope made from strips of old clothes with a pull-string bag attached to carry our notes. To let someone know a message was coming, we would tap out Morse code on the bathroom pipes. Our pull-string bag enabled us to send pens and papers, so that we could find out prisoners' names, and which cells they were in. They sent details of what they'd endured in the investigation branches, including information about their confessions. It was crucial to communicate this information urgently, not only for the benefit of those already in jail, but because most forced confessions were about people who were still free, so we had to smuggle this information out to them as soon as possible.

It was around this time in my incarceration that I realized just how many hundreds of us from our organization were in jail. This showed that our Communist Labor Party had joined the other political parties who had already been paralyzed by the regime's repression. We had lost. They had prevailed. Upon reflection, I wasn't surprised, but I was profoundly sad.

CHAPTER 40

BROTHERS AND ENEMIES

I met Muslim Brothers in the armed wing that was known as the Fighting Vanguard of the Brotherhood in the right corridor of C Wing, Floor 2.

In Tadmur Prison, I had only one opportunity to see and exchange signs with other prisoners over five years. I used to hear screaming and pleading from the nearby exercise yards, and this made me lose any sense of security. When I heard a human screaming, I turned into a tortoise searching in vain for its shattered shell.

In Sednaya, prisoners had the right to use their sight and even engage in a conversation normally, through speech.

Several of us went to Corridor Right of Wing C to get to know our neighbors. The effects of Tadmur were plain to see in their broken looks, emaciated bodies, and worn clothes, patched with any available fabric. In some cases, it was impossible to tell where the original fabric of the trousers and the patches began and ended.

It didn't take long to realize that we were interacting with three types of Brothers. There were the extremists, who, with their narrow worldview, wanted nothing to do with any person who claimed to be secular, a communist, or, worse, an atheist. Then there were Brothers who thought anyone opposing the regime, even if they were communists and atheists, had more of a conscience than men of religion who supported the regime. And finally there were the Brothers who landed in prison as some by-product of our country's conflict. These were mostly simple peasants in the wrong place at the wrong time, or impressionable people who joined the Brotherhood just because it was around them. They had no political knowledge or ambition, or any understanding that they were just being used. Now their greatest ambition was to get cigarettes.

I found myself automatically drawn to a prisoner named Muhammad, a bright-eyed man a little younger than me. We didn't ask each other which city we were from, only which prison. And when we found out we were both alumni of Tadmur, Muhammad asked, "Which cell were you in there?"

"We were in cell number one, and then we were moved to the clinic. After more of our comrades arrived, some of us were moved to the bathroom that was converted into a cell."

"It was good for all prisoners that they got rid of that bathroom."

I agreed. "It was torture, not a shower."

"What were you in for?" he asked. I crooked my finger. "And what crimes did you commit?" he inquired.

"I distributed pamphlets." He looked at me like I was going to elaborate, but I didn't. We laughed together at the triviality. "And you?"

Muhammad explained he was in prison accused of belonging to the Fighting Vanguard of the Brotherhood. I didn't want to start questioning him directly about the wave of violence that his organization had helped create. I was more interested in understanding the mentality of a young jihadi prepared to die or manufacture death.

"You don't seem like you're . . ."

"A murderer?" He laughed. "Don't worry. I never saw action, and I'm glad of it."

"So, why did you join?"

"At the time, I wanted to satisfy my God and believed He would reward me. Plus, I was young, and all my friends were joining."

"I suppose they let you open your eyes a few times at Tadmur."

"When the guards weren't around, of course. But not like you communists who had the run of the place."

"I suppose it looked like that to you. We'd been through the same experience as you, but the new governor changed the rules for us."

"Ah, the governor," Muhammad said, his tone changed. He fell silent.

"What about the governor?" I asked.

"One time he ordered our whole cell to open our eyes, and keep them open, on pain of punishment."

"Why?"

"So we could see how we could be tortured to death. Ahmad Tawir from Idlib was a good Muslim boy, not even eighteen. They tortured him until he was about to die, until there was no hope, and then brought him into our cell."

"Why?"

"So he could die in front of us."

"My God, what a barbaric —"

Muhammad interrupted me: "That was not the only barbaric incident."

"Another prisoner faced a similar fate?"

Muhammad seemed so anxious to continue telling me what he'd seen, as if to unburden himself of a heavy load.

"No, it was a colleague of theirs. A sergeant. They killed him right in front of our cell. A number of us could see what was happening through the space at the bottom of the door. Allah forgive me for watching. I wish I hadn't."

"But why did they kill him?" I had never heard of such a thing.

"This sergeant, Ahmad al-Siba'i, tried to reduce the level of abuse we received. He even tried to be comforting. I remember him once saying, 'May God relieve your troubles, young men.' That's all it took. Apparently, another soldier heard him saying this and denounced him."

"Wait a minute," I said. "How do you know his name?"

"Through that crack, I watched the governor point to this naked man covered in blood. And then the governor said to the soldiers from the disciplinary squad, 'We trusted your comrade Ahmad al-Siba'i, and he turned out to be a traitor. What is the punishment for a traitor?' As one man they replied, 'Death!' At a signal from the lieutenant colonel, they fell on him with their whips and clubs. It took two hours for him to die."

"Governor Barakat did this?" I asked.

"No, the bastard before him, Faisal Ghanim," and he spat.

His stories went on until curfew, and I thought I was done with them. But the next day Muhammad found me again. Smiling with his mouth, but not his eyes, he sat on the radiator in the hall and invited me to join him. I did so hesitantly, and there he talked in terrifying detail about the weekly executions in yard six. When I didn't want to hear any more, I leaned forward to stand, but Muhammad took my arm, and I reluctantly sat again. He seemed to have the need to unburden himself to someone outside the Muslim Brotherhood. After an hour, I changed the subject, to what I hoped was a more peaceful one.

"How did you patch your clothes?"

"We used bones to make needles. Sometimes we got leftovers of boiled chicken from the soldiers' mess. You could use one of the thighbones as a needle. A lot of time we used a nail that one of us got stuck in his foot while we were running barefoot in the exercise yard."

After three days of listening to Muhammad's stories, I saw him in the hall the next morning, but couldn't turn away fast enough to escape. While I honestly felt I needed to know the things he needed to tell me, I had had enough for the time being. But he caught up with me and began using me as his sounding board again. Among the new stories he told me was how they had used a single polyester thread they'd unraveled from a sock to divide up an egg. Sometimes into seven portions. And then he moved back to stories of executions in yard six.

"On some mornings at dawn the guards walked down the yard shouting for certain prisoners in different cells to prepare themselves."

"For what?" I asked. He didn't answer, and then I realized it was obvious.

"One day, when a person in our cell heard his name, he just got up, smiled, and seemed eager to settle his affairs. Others watched calmly as he performed the designated two rak'as, prostrating himself in prayer while facing south to Mecca. And then he bounced up and said his goodbyes, first to his actual brother who was in prison with him, and then he went about shaking hands with the rest of us. At the end he pointed to a man in his seventies. 'Abu Ahmad can have my share of the eggs,' he joked. When the cell door opened, he left us with a smile."

"Where did they take the bodies?" I asked in a choking voice.

"They were food for the desert." Then Muhammad took a close look at my face. "I'm sorry," he said. "I didn't want to . . ."

"None of us want to . . ."

Once again, I find myself on the shores of Lake Ontario attempting to lighten the load on my soul.

"Listen, waters of the world," I call over the expanse of water, "Muhammad told me the story of that bastard of a guard who called himself Fawwaz — the Winner. How he loved to amuse himself by breaking skulls. Actually breaking skulls! Muhammad, why did you tell me this story? In my dreams, even now, it's as if it's happening in front of me. How that son of a bitch put a Brother's head on the edge of a concrete step and then stomped on it with his boot, over and over again. How blood would run down on the ground, and if his victim still had breath, he'd take a boulder, and, with his psychotic eyes ablaze, finish the job. Muhammad, why? Why did you tell me this? How much more weight must my soul carry, Muhammad? Why did you involve me in all that ugliness and cruelty?"

"And Muhammad, I'll be very frank with you. I've never come to terms with the actions of the Muslim Brotherhood. I always saw in their call for the establishment of a religious state a fascist project. What else can you call ideological racism, a great deal of backward thinking, and brutal killing? But when I saw the ugliness of our jailers' naked repression, I didn't care how much I agreed or disagreed ideologically with this prisoner or that. I only saw human beings whose souls were violated and pushed to their lowest point, human beings who were subjected to brutal repression, starvation, and sickness, reducing them to creatures struggling instinctively to preserve their lives. Ideological evaluations at times like this are pointless."

"Waters of Kingston," I call across the waters. This time I'm not screaming. I almost have myself under control. Now, standing with my arms by my sides and an understanding smile on my face, I say, "When confronting unjust death there is only one important thing — and that is to preserve life."

And then, somewhat unburdened, I continue on my walk along the lakeshore, wondering if I will cross paths with the lady and her black dog. I don't expect to find her. Perhaps the coronavirus is keeping her at home. That's fine. I don't want her to lose her life. But I've been anticipating seeing her, because of an affection I've developed for this lonely soul, even though she'll never say anything to me, and I'll never say anything to her.

After getting to know our Muslim Brother neighbors, the Communist Labor Party, Local Sednaya Prison, Floor 2, Wing C, Corridor Left, held a meeting of the general council of all the cells. The issue at hand was to again offer as much aid as possible to the Brotherhood prisoners, since they weren't allowed visits from their relatives. The motion was passed by a large majority, and, unlike his predecessor, Governor al-Ish agreed. The resources committee was then charged with preparing clothes, food, cigarettes, soap, and cleaning products, and I was designated to visit the Brothers' wing to tell them of the gifts we wanted to offer. The inhabitants of eight of the cells thanked us very kindly, while the inhabitants of the remaining two cells refused to accept anything from communists. At one cell I extended my hand to a man with thin lips and hollow eyes. He looked to me like the most hardline of them.

"Jamal Saeed," I said, introducing myself. He ignored my outstretched hand and stared at me hard, trying to hide a hatred that actually caused his lips to tremble.

"I'll be brief," he said in a deep, parched voice. "We don't want your gifts."

"Think of them as a debt that you can repay when God blesses you," I said as warmly as possible. He looked disparagingly at me and turned away, putting an end to our brief interview.

Many of the Brothers began giving us their families' addresses and asked if we could find a way to get news to them. We passed their information on to our families, and they, in turn, took the trouble to give the Brothers' relatives something the regime refused, news that their loved ones were at least alive. Many of these families then sent homemade food, clothes, money, and even books for our families to pass on. And why not? In Sednaya we tried to be prisoners before anything else and, after a few years of generous cooperation, most inmates from all sides of the ideological divides were able to interact respectfully with others.

Once, I recounted how I was alone for months in a cell of Muslim Brothers, and that some of them tried to kill me. I was both Alawite and a communist, I explained, and either one was reason enough to execute me, let alone both together.

A young Brother from Sarmada said this didn't surprise him. "My brother is a communist who's made an alliance with the government. I was ready to kill him if I received such an order."

"And what if one of your superiors ordered you to kill him now?"

"After what I've learned in prison, I'd spit in my commander's face," he said. The cell went quiet at such a bold statement. And then the man continued in the tone of an old-time prophet — and keep in mind he said this in 1989 — "We've always been fuel for a battle where even the winner is a loser. And while we former enemies may be finding common ground for now, who knows what Syrians outside of prisons will end up doing to each other?"

CHAPTER 41

THE HOUSE HIGH ON A HILL

After my third and final release from prison in 1993, I spent a few late summer days helping my parents on the farm. That September I began preparing to pick up my studies at Damascus University where I left off. I was in the shade under the mulberry tree in the courtyard, packing my suitcase, when I looked up through the open gate to the road. There was Fadwa staring at me. She was pulling a complaining child along with one hand and supporting her back with the other, her large belly making her look as if she was about to give birth any moment.

Random buildings increased on the outskirts of Damascus. Many houses were built on this hill at the west of the city of Damascus.

"You're packing. Where are you going?" she asked without a hello.

"Damascus."

"Do you have a house there?"

"No."

"So stay here, near your mother."

"I'm going to try finishing university."

"University?" she laughed. "You're going to be a university student? Why bother? Graduates are more plentiful than watercress seeds, and they can't find jobs. They just play cards all day. An hour under this mulberry tree is better than any amount of time in a city."

"You're probably right," I said, and then we just stared at each other.

"Will you remember the people of the village when you go away?" she finally asked. Her eyes had become soft and sad, something I'd never seen before.

Here I am in Damascus — again. I'm looking for a place to live and work to pay my way. It's easier now than it was about sixteen years earlier, during my days in hiding. A friend, Abd al-Karim Darwish, offers to put me up. He also has something special for me. Before my last arrest, I was writing articles about contemporary cultural life in the Middle East. Abd al-Karim used to sell them through a friend, Omar, who had contacts with a number of magazines and newspapers outside of Syria. On my first day back, Abd al-Karim puts nine thousand Syrian pounds in my hand, my fee for six articles I wrote before going back to jail. That amount would keep a poor student alive for several months at university.

"And our friend Omar seems to want more," Abd al-Karim told me.

"Wonderful. Thank you," I said. "Do you think I could meet him?"

"We'll have to wait a while," he replied. "Omar was called in for questioning a few days ago. It's probably best we keep our distance, at least until we hear what's happening to him."

When Omar did get away from the authorities, he quickly fled the country. Such a disappointment. I had envisaged supporting myself by writing. Now I'd have to find a real job.

I visited some silk printers I'd worked with previously and continued creating designs for children's clothing. I drew thousands of butterflies, stars, laughing moons, birds, and smiling sunflowers. And then, not wanting to take advantage of my friend's generosity, I rented a room in the slum quarter officially called al-Nahda, but known locally as Bangladesh. If you live in a neighborhood like this, you can't be surprised when someone asks to borrow a loaf of bread in the evening or coffee in the morning. And you can't be surprised, or concerned, when they don't pay you back. Everybody here is poor and almost everybody helps others when they can.

My new home was one room built any old way, rough cement walls, uneven floor, and doors that squeaked. One of the two windows had no pane. It had been replaced with a sheet of blue plastic, the words *Bashayan Shoes* printed on it. The functional window looked out onto a narrow street crowded with houses similar to mine, and it was only seldom a vehicle would drive by, usually for emergencies. And with this window facing south, it was a good place to set up my makeshift desk of cement blocks topped with a sheet of used plate glass.

Among the characters in the quarter I found fascinating were two old men I would observe sitting across the road every afternoon, their heads resting in their hands. From what I could see, they exchanged silence more often than words.

Two weeks after school started, I was alone in my room after finishing three pieces of design work. It was late in the afternoon, and I hadn't left the house for three days. I was feeling in need of something outside of my room. I looked out the window. Not even the two old men were there to distract me. I looked over at the Swan edition of Shakespeare's *Antony and Cleopatra* lying on my foam mattress like a silent beggar ignored by all around him. Between its pages were lecture notes waiting for review. I sighed. And then I got up and took my jacket off its nail. I'd go for a walk. That's when a familiar pounding started on the apartment's metal door.

"Assalamu alaykum, hello, Jamal," I heard as I opened the door.

"Hello, Abu Nimr," I said to my landlord. He was an old potbellied man with gray hair and a thick mustache incongruously dyed jet black. And he always wore an old Cuban military jacket that was too small to close over his stomach. He always appeared a few days before the end of the month, to remind tenants to pay their rent, but this time he was early. Maybe he was bored too. He also always repeated advice on the care of his apartments.

"Some tenants think the apartment door is their enemy and slam it like they're at war," he repeated at least ten times. And he explained repeatedly how important it was to make sure the water in the sink was drained away properly. "You can't imagine the enormous losses I've suffered because of water damage," he'd complain. When he had gone through these and other admonishments, he'd then sit down without invitation and recount his acts of heroism in the 1973 October War. "My platoon commander told me I was the bravest fighter he had ever seen." This I'd heard at least twenty times, and so I proceeded to zip up my jacket, blocking his entrance. "Are you going out to get the rent money?" he asked, laughing.

"No," I replied, smiling politely and stepping into the hallway.

"Ah, you're going to see a woman? I know that look. Don't spend my rent money at al Marjeh." This was Damascus's brothel district, coincidentally right across the square from the Ministry of the Interior.

"No, sir," I said, locking the door.

"Hmmm. Not women?" he said, now sounding concerned for reasons other than rent.

"Abu Nimr, it's a whole week until the end of the month," I said. "Don't worry so much."

"But when I was your age . . ." He followed me into the street. "So where are you going?"

"To get some fresh air." I began to walk.

"Wherever your feet take you?" he asked, still following.

"Wherever my heart takes me."

He grabbed my arm. "No, no. Don't follow your heart, follow this," and he tapped his temple. I nodded and continued on my way. He didn't follow.

"Jamal. Goodbye," he called after me. I gave a dismissive wave without turning.

Not having a destination in mind, I took the first bus that came along.

Before my years in prison, Fadwa, buses had conductors you could exchange smiles with.

I put my ticket in the machine like the other passengers and got off and into the crowded streets at Bab Touma. The area was so crowded, as usual, and I decided to go to the Muhajirin quarter at the foot of Mount Qasioun. I walked in silence, speaking to nobody and nobody speaking to me. I bought a falafel sandwich from Fabian's takeaway shop and, like any hungry vagrant, devoured it while continuing to prowl the streets. As night fell, I walked partway up the mountain and sat on a wooden bench in Nirabin Park. Now that I was able to look out over most of Damascus, my eyes focused on all the illuminated windows in the thousands of homes and apartments. And finally a smile came to my face.

There are many houses here, Fadwa. Behind these myriad windows I have many friends. There is only one small problem. I haven't met them yet. But that's okay. One day doors will open, and I will no longer be a stranger in this city.

I returned to the house in Bangladesh, happy to have determined the cause of my malaise. My loneliness was only the phase of a young man getting his new life together. I had to work. I had to study. I was lonely. But in time, I would establish a personal life. And it was true. I made it true.

Lights indicate life behind the windows of the crowded city.

Throughout the 1990s I met many of those people living behind Damascus's windows, many becoming friends and even more. Among them was Rufaida, whom I eventually married. And I also got to know again dozens of people I'd known in prison, running into them in the street, in cafés, and some at university. One of the doors that opened to me was that of al-Tali'a Publishing House, where I began designing book covers. To design a cover, I first had to read the manuscript. Shyly, yet confidently, I offered my observations on the manuscripts to the director and owner, Marwan Saqqal, and was given the job of evaluating manuscripts. I began to stick my nose into other aspects of the business, doing copy and art layouts. This led to learning about budgeting for production and then overseeing printing. After about a year I became the official production manager, which gave me a steady income. I moved apartments many times, as income allowed — always poor places, but each one better than the last. Eventually I ended up renting a room in Assad al-Din, close to the city center and work.

I made friends both at work and at the university, but because of my time in prison, I was thirty-six and my friends were mostly in their twenties. But friends are friends, and I no longer walked the streets or took my meals alone. Some of us who loved art and literature began getting together to critique each other's work. We were even considering writing a film script together. And then one afternoon an intelligence officer from the dreaded Palestine Branch showed up at a place where I was working. He handed me a summons to appear at their local offices for questioning. Given the torture I had endured at their hands, I considered not responding.

But they know where I live and where I work, and they could arrest me if they wanted. Why have I been summoned? I no longer write political articles or belong to a political organization. Maybe they know I'm seeing friends who are still hiding from them. I'm not seeing them on political business, only to bring what food or money I can spare. After all, I was once in hiding and know what a wretched existence it is. But then, if they've been following me and know about these fugitives, why wouldn't they just arrest us all? Or maybe one of these friends has been arrested and told them about me. Oh my God, all this anxiety from a single sheet of paper.

I went to the branch, showed my summons, and a bored official showed me into a clean, windowless room. Its only furniture was two chairs and a table. The only adornment was a gold-framed photo of Hafez al-Assad hanging on the wall. While I waited for six hours, he was my only company — staring at me while I heaped blame on myself for some unknown transgression. My nervous tension silently grew into a boiling cauldron.

Were you right, Fadwa? Sitting under the mulberry tree would have been preferable to this.

Finally, a young interrogator entered. Not yet thirty, he looked as if he'd just come from the barber. He stood facing me. He looked as if he were trying to decide whether to intimidate or befriend me.

"Have you got more years to throw away in prison cells, Mr. Jamal?" he asked sarcastically. "What else do you want, man?"

"Sorry, can I go to the toilet?"

He guffawed. "Fighters don't piss!" Then he smiled and led me to a very clean lavatory. Why did I think it would be more like in the prisons?

Back in his office he leaned across the desk and spoke very earnestly.

"Listen, Jamal, really. I've only brought you here to warn you. I'm not even going to ask about those adolescents you try to entice with debates on literature and art. We know the arts are an umbrella for political activity." He paused, I suppose to see if I would object, but I didn't bite. He added scornfully, "Honorable fighter, we've learned from your kind how deep the relationship is between literature, art and politics." And then he sat back, waiting for me to comment.

"I'll tell you what you already know," I said slowly and calmly. "My discussions with friends about literature have no political goals. In fact, not even ideological ones."

"Oh, let's talk as friends," he said shifting in his chair. "Let me ask directly. Have you abandoned your illusions since the resounding collapse of communism?"

"You also know that I never for one moment sided with the communist regimes that fell with the Soviet Union."

"Perhaps. Who knows? Who cares? I just want you to understand how to keep away from dangerous situations. Concentrate on your studies — and your health. And if you need anything, you can of course contact me." He wrote a number on a scrap of paper and handed it to me.

I left the place in a quiet fury. I'd waited nervously for hours just to hear this bullshit warning? I threw the piece of paper into the first garbage container I came to, but I was able to muster up a bitter laugh.

At least they don't know about my friends in hiding.

When I told my university and work friends about my visit to the mukhabarat, we decided it was best to only get together one-on-one. In this respect, the regime had once again succeeded in destroying another piece of Syria's artistic and intellectual future, and the group was disbanded before I could learn the identity of the spy, or gossip, among us.

A few months after we were married, the doctor told Rufaida and me that our child was a boy. When we first watched and heard our son's heartbeat on an ultrasound scan, I felt my own heart begin to beat in time with his. That night, Rufaida and I began discussing names.

"Jawad. What do you think, Rufi?"

"We know so many people with that name."

"Hmmm. Sinan. The combination of the 's' and the 'n' makes the pronunciation easy and agreeable."

"No, impossible. His schoolmates will make fun of him. Sinan is the name of a squirrel in a cartoon."

"I didn't know," I said. "A squirrel?" and I pursed my lips and made a chattering noise. It's wonderful to hear your wife laugh.

When we grew weary of tossing names back and forth, we'd switch to the dream of owning a home. To me this was an impossible dream, but it made all too clear a very important reality. We were about to have a child. We needed to earn more money.

Several friends, without being prompted, also brought up the subject of us buying a home. But I just laughed.

"I'll give you all the money I have," I mocked, "and Rufaida and I won't eat until the end of the month. Even with all that, it would be a miracle if you managed to buy a hen coop in this city."

"That nonsense talk won't get you anywhere," al-Harith al-Nabhan said sternly. "You have to take the subject very seriously, Jamal! You and Rufi already spend half your income on rent. You must do whatever you can to borrow money so you have enough to buy a place. And then you pay it back in installments."

"Okay, so where will I get the loan from?"

"From us. We're your friends."

"But my friends don't have —"

"You're going to say we're all hard up, but that's not true. Some have savings we don't need right away. I can give you fifty thousand Syrian pounds as a long-term loan."

Rufaida did not have to be prodded to go house hunting, and within a few days we found ourselves standing in a little house in the Jadat Qudsaya neighborhood. While it certainly wasn't as bad as the slums that Abu Nimr owned, the area was quite humble. But that didn't matter to us. High up on a hill, about ten miles from the city center, this modest dwelling boasted a scenic view overlooking the Barada River and the Damascus-Beirut road.

Now knowing the exact amount we would need to buy a house, I contacted four friends and told them about the place. Not one of them hesitated to lend us what they could, all at no interest. Only a few days later, I found myself signing the contract. But no sooner had the pen left the paper then a reality became clear. My friends' lavish kindness now had me burdened with a substantial debt.

The place consisted of two rooms, as well as a large kitchen and good-sized bathroom with a tub. A bathtub was a luxury none of my apartments had. These rooms and amenities had doors opening out onto a tiled central courtyard with a chest-high wall running along the street. The wall also protected a large garden area with fruit trees. Friends brought their cars and helped Rufaida, me, and our unborn child move our belongings to the new home. Their eyes laughed with pleasure at both the structure and the view. We piled everything up in the courtyard, and then I insisted we didn't need help arranging the furniture. As thankful as we were to our friends, it was time for Rufaida and me to be alone. We carried the bed and bedding into one of the rooms, and then I suggested we leave everything as it was for now.

"Let's go to the cinema," I suggested. "My prison friend Ghassan Jaba'i is acting in the new film *The Extras* by Nabil Maleh." Rufaida laughed at the crazy idea, but then we tramped down the mountain to catch a minibus to the city center. And why not? We were doing better, and many of our friends obviously were doing better. When Ghassan appeared on the screen,

Ghamr and Taim play with water in the courtyard before we made it a living room.

I introduced him to Rufaida — "Look, it's Ghassan!" — then felt embarrassed, as the audience was completely silent.

The next morning, as we arranged our simple furniture, we were both so happy. I didn't even mind when Rufaida had me move furniture to one place, furrow her beautiful face in thought, and then have me move it to another. Again, why not? Never again would we be afraid of someone asking us for rent money we didn't have, and nobody could order us to vacate the house. I loved our little home on the hill. I loved its garden, where I sowed vegetables like my father on the farm, and there were already apple, olive, pear, apricot, lemon, and even pomegranate trees. Our property even had an old wire trellis with grapes growing on it. I expanded the trellis so that during the summer it created a pleasant shade over both the gate to the courtyard and door to the kitchen. And I planted a cypress hedge against the garden wall. As they grew taller, the shrubbery would keep down the dust from the road and make the courtyard more private.

"If our father planted that hedge, he would have put in more pomegranate trees than cypresses," my sister Khadija said with a laugh on her first visit.

I also liked the area because many nationalities and sects lived there. This created a more open-minded atmosphere. A half-mile below, the whole population in those neighborhoods were Sunni, while a half-mile above, it was all Alawite. But right here, in the middle, was just how I liked it.

One of the most pleasant things about home ownership is having friends visit. Sometimes we had gatherings of up to twenty people sitting in our courtyard. There we shared stories of our prison lives, laughing as if we were talking about events that happened to other people. We were engrossed in this conflicting idea: while the future appeared to offer us a modicum of upward mobility, if we minded our own business, Syrian society was becoming more suffocating. At the end of one evening's debate, as friends sipped on the last of their tea or beer, one quipped, "Why fault history for repeating itself? We must put the blame where it belongs. It's we humans who refuse to learn, and repeat our stupidities."

"So, what's to do about it?" a second friend asked.

The first friend looked at the second, smiled, shrugged his shoulders, drained his beer, and stood up.

"I have to work tomorrow."

On a pleasant evening in November 1999, Rufaida and I were sitting in our garden. We had just picked our vine's last bunch of grapes and were enjoying eating them slowly. This is when Rufaida reminded me of a wonderful letter I'd told her about quite some time earlier. It was one from Jamil Hatmal, sent while I was in the Citadel. An extremely warm, emotional letter, Jamil had signed it with the pseudonym Ghamr.

"Ghamr. A beautiful name," Rufaida remarked. "I hadn't heard it before."

"What do you think about calling our son Ghamr?" I asked.

"We've found a name," she said, beaming. "Even if the scan is wrong and we have a daughter, we'll still name her Ghamr." We never discussed the issue of the name again.

At the end of 1999, Hafez al-Assad was elected for the last time. When we former prisoners got together and discussed the tightening security, we felt our only useful response could be "nothing lasts forever," and then went on to talk about our personal plans.

While waiting for the birth of Ghamr, I was delighted to see the things Rufaida was preparing for him. She made matching curtains, a lace cover, and a mosquito net for his cradle. I smiled as it reminded me of the childhood stories of my mother's preparations for my cradle.

I was working harder than I'd ever worked in my life. Even though I felt constantly weighed down by debts, I didn't feel oppressed. Having the ability to provide for a family made me feel like a free man. In fact, I was energized. Among the many freelance jobs I took outside my regular job at the publishing house, I started providing graphic design for a children's TV station in Damascus. I also did a lot of book cover and layout work for a number of other independent publishers.

As pleased and proud as I was about my personal material progress within the dictatorship, the idealist inside my head was now in league, or perhaps conflict, with the pragmatic concerns of a father. In the scant time I had outside of earning a living for my family, I still kept an eye on what was going on in the wider world. I saw that the winds of change were blowing, and I held on to the hope that they might be positive. Old USSR satellite countries were becoming independent. The power of dictators such as Saddam Hussein in Iraq seemed to be on the wane. Perhaps these good winds would blow into Syria too. But even as it appeared that dictators were on their last legs, I was fearful of the wave of political Islam, which gathered momentum after the consolidation of the Islamic republic in Iran and the victory of the Taliban in Afghanistan. Now it was spreading its tentacles into many other countries, including Syria. Somehow, I could smell that same blood the old man had talked about after the massacre in Hama. Hafez al-Assad must have felt the same. At the end of the eighties and during the nineties, he maneuvered to pull the rug out from under the religious movement's feet. He established Institutes for the Memorization of the Quran, which still exist today, and among the pictures of him that invaded walls all over the country, more and more were showing him in clothes making him look like a Hājj, an elder who makes the holy journey to Mecca, the once-a-year pilgrimage also called the Hajj. Such insincere gestures seem to be a hallmark of dictators. Even in neighboring Iraq, al-Assad's enemy Saddam Hussein added the religious words, "Allahu akbar," God is great, to the Iraqi flag in Arabic. Written in his own hand, he had mistakenly added a hamzah to the word "Allah," a glottal stop that didn't belong. Even a child in third grade knew better. But nobody dared correct the error made by the mercurial dictator until after his fall.

CHAPTER 42

DAMASCUS SPRING AND
KHADIJA'S DEATH

I n December 1999, I read a surprising article in a Lebanese newspaper. It
was written by a close friend of the first al-Assad. Abdullah al-Ahmad
was a member of the Baath Party Regional Command. He pointed to the
need for reform in the Syrian media and the judiciary, emphasizing that we
needed a Syria like Spain after Franco, not Yugoslavia after Tito. If this wasn't
eye-opening enough, al-Ahmad also wrote, "I know as I write that I am dip-
ping my pen in my own blood, because I am from a nation that has made blood
lawful and prohibited ink." After his article came out, al-Ahmad wisely spent
many months in the Arab Emirates.

This article was widely shared and many who read it said they couldn't
believe their eyes. Al-Ahmad's boldness was interpreted in many different
ways. "Rebellion among the ministers," some mused hopefully. "Foreign
influence." "Another family squabble?" Some even went a step beyond hope
by foolishly suggesting that al-Assad had agreed to allow the editorial.

About six months after we'd moved house, and four months after the
article was published, Hafez al-Assad died. A lot of friends gathered in our
home that evening.

"Will Syria be like Spain after Franco?" I asked.

"Should be," an optimist said, adding, "at least, I hope so."

"Probably not," a pessimist warned. "But I hope so too."

"The future is full of probabilities," came another, "but we must hope."

In the midst of our anxiety, hope was a bright point that brought us together.

Bashar al-Assad, Hafez's son, became president on July 17, 2000. Three days later a memorial celebration was held to mark the forty days since his father's death. Greek Orthodox Patriarch Ignatius IV Hazim, Patriarch of Antioch and All the East, was one of the clergymen who spoke at the ceremony. But he was the only orator whose speech came anywhere close to being critical in his advice to the young president.

"We believe you wish the citizens to know that you will be a human being among other human beings, not the sublime and the elevated, nor, as some would have it, the divine."

Antun Maqdisi, the government official who published my book of short stories while I was in prison, penned an open letter to the new president in *al-Hayat* newspaper, again in Lebanon.

"Allow me first of all to congratulate you on the presidency, and also on the words contained in your statement — really promising words — 'respect for the opinion of the other and preference given to the country's point of view over that of the leadership.'" My old mentor then continued, "This is the beginning of a long road and, if we take it, we could gradually move from nomadism and tribal rule to the rule of law, and begin to enter the twenty-first century. To start with, the people need to regain confidence in themselves and in their government." He ended with, "And this will be no easy matter. It may need years of taking the opinion of the other into consideration, as you said, and then a shift in the people's status from that of subjects to citizens."

Antun Maqdisi, now eighty-six years old, was quickly fired from his post as director of the Department of Composition and Translation. But then, in a move that contradicted Maqdisi's firing, parliamentary member Riad Seif launched The Forum for Democratic Dialogue at his home in Damascus, inviting anyone who wanted to attend debates there. He also invited people all over Syria to form their own groups, to publish articles in newspapers, and to start discussion forums on the burgeoning internet. I followed news of meetings all over the country with great interest. I contributed anonymously in writing to the most popular forums, Suhair al-Atassi's and Riad

Seif's. But I didn't personally attend any meetings. Besides not wanting to be seen there by the mukhabarat, I was too busy working to pay off my debts and being a family man.

It was a very confusing time, as events appeared to be taking two contradictory paths. What became known as the Damascus Spring saw the new president releasing hundreds of political prisoners. Mezzeh Prison, long seen as a symbol of repression since our country became independent, was closed. Also a good sign, the new president was a graduate of the Faculty of Medicine at Damascus University and had spent some years living in London, completing a specialization in ophthalmology. On top of this, Bashir, born into an Alawite family, had married a Sunni woman. All these details fed the hope that maybe, just maybe, all the landmines of sectarianism and authoritarianism, planted in the community's memory during the bloody conflicts of the eighties, could soon be defused.

But then again, on the opposite path, anyone who followed the goings on of the government couldn't help but notice certain political maneuvers. On the very day that the elder al-Assad died, the People's Assembly voted unanimously to amend the constitutional age requirement for a president. It changed from forty years old to thirty-four, the younger al-Assad's age at the time. This wasn't in itself ominous, but the very next day Vice President Abd al-Halim Khaddam issued a decree promoting Bashar al-Assad from colonel to lieutenant general. This was followed by the Baath party electing Bashar as its secretary general and then putting him up as the only candidate in an election for president — an election he supposedly won with 99.7 percent of the votes. In a true democracy, all these posts are held by different people, all with much experience. In retrospect, or for cynics at the time, putting all this power in one person's hand could mean only one thing — enabling the succession of a dictatorship.

Though many in my circle, including the cynics, were aware of these government moves, to a person we foolishly retained hope. Personally, my mindset could be described as *almost* optimistic. After all, forums for political debate were active all over the country. People were signing their names to editorials. In cafés, drinkers of Turkish coffee and espresso, and even tea drinkers, were laying down their crossword puzzles and reading newspapers.

Hope was on full display for all to see. It was like the whole nation was holding its breath, awaiting the announcement of real political change.

In the final months of Rufaida's pregnancy, I had taken care to hide my worries about our debts and the state of our country. Now, only a few days before Ghamr's birth, I rested my hand on Rufaida's wonderfully large belly.

"Has our baby been moving much?" I asked, already an overly protective father.

"He hasn't stayed still since I woke up," she replied. And then Ghamr kicked my hand. I teared up.

"We'll do everything we can for him," I promised.

On March 3, at noon, in the year 2000, Ghamr was born. When the nurse presented him to me, he was sticking out his little tongue and making a fist. My mother-in-law asked me to recite the call to prayer in his ear. When I'd respectfully performed this ritual for her, she took him and laid him on the bed next to his mother.

As my heart grew increasingly attached to my son, my main thought was that I should do my best to keep him happy. I accepted any job, whatever the payment. After about a year and a half, I was getting ready to go out in the early morning, the last of my payments in my pocket. I was as happy as Sisyphus released from his rock.

Before I got out of the house, the phone rang, and I rushed to answer so Rufaida would not be awakened. I felt apprehensive about the phone ringing so early, and my instinct was right. On the line was my sister Khadija's husband, Munir Shabow. "Khadija is sick," he told me, "and we are at Al-Assad University Hospital."

"I'm coming. See you shortly," I said, and hung up the phone.

I woke up Rufaida and looked at Ghamr, who was still asleep.

"I have to go to Al-Assad University Hospital," I told my wife. "Khadija is ill. She's there."

"What's her illness?" Rufi asked me with sad eyes.

"I don't know," I said. "I'll tell you after I get to the hospital." I said goodbye and departed quickly.

During the next four months, as the disease of lupus ran its course through Khadija's body, friends were always at my side. But with all I still had to do, I felt the days needed to be ninety hours long. I visited my sister every morning and night, worked at al-Tali'a Publishing House, tried to finish the designs I'd promised others by their deadlines, and kept up with the events in my country.

Khadija died. We traveled to Kfarieh to bury her. I was so sad that a good woman, who had faithfully waited twelve years for her childhood sweetheart to be released from prison, should have this happen to her. And on top of that, she had delivered her own son just a few months before the diagnosis. My heart was broken. The mourning tent was visited by hundreds of people, many of them men I'd known in prison. I listened in miserable silence as a discussion began about how our country was standing at a crossroads. We didn't have long to wait to find out which path the nation would take.

Two months after Khadija's death, the intelligence services closed down all the discussion forums and arrested many of their organizers. I was so numb from work and grief that I wasn't even surprised. And when the novelist and publisher Nabil Suleiman was beaten up so badly he need hospitalization, I knew the Damascus Spring was over. A common tactic of the elder al-Assad was to beat up prominent people as a warning. Now the younger one was doing it too.

Another half year passed. The Damascus Spring had disappeared into history. I paid off all my debts, including Khadija's extra medical bills — something Rufi and I were pleased to take on. We were visiting my parents with Ghamr. After the loss of their daughter, he was a true joy for them.

But taking a few days off from work and not having it as a distraction, I felt my profound grief returning. I excused myself to take a walk through the village. It wasn't long before I saw her, and she saw me. We stopped a respectful distance apart and it was one of the few times nothing profane or spiteful came out of her mouth.

"Hello, Jamal."

"Hello, Fadwa."

We chatted for a while and then she brought up my sister's death.

"You have to forget," she said. "The sadness in your eyes won't raise her from the dead. They say the grief of the living disturbs the dead. Listen, is it true your wife is from Damascus?"

"Yes."

"And you own a house in Damascus?"

"Yes."

Fadwa sighed. It was like she was saying, "Oh well," and then she added with her old certainty, "Jamal, you will always be miserable."

"Why?"

"All the living are miserable."

"Is that the only choice we have?"

Fadwa just looked at me as if I didn't have the brains to understand.

CHAPTER 43

MINIBUS VISIONS ON THE ROAD
TO AND FROM THE HOUSE

On the way home from al-Tali'a to my new house on the hill, the public minibus I take every day drives along the Barada River for most of the way. As it passes below the landmark called "Idhkirini," or "Remember Me," many early memories flood my mind. The jagged rock formation rises almost thirty feet above the main way in Rabwa Park, the final shape at its pinnacle squared and flat, reminding me of a closed book. Some unknown person used to regularly repaint a sad message on it whenever it became faded from the sun and rain. Apparently, a man had originally written *Always remember me* before he killed himself by jumping off the edifice, and a woman had answered his message by adding, *I will never forget you.* And then she, too, threw herself off the rock. To me, the plaintive words, although susceptible to the weather, were seared inside the pages of the stony precipice.

This area of Damascus touches my heart more than others. This is because in the 1970s, when I was seventeen, I spent a number of afternoons as teenagers should, being light-hearted with friends. This included Widad, after I met her. Since I was in hiding, frolicking here offered a rare respite from my fears. I remember standing on top of the rock, spreading my arms like the wings of a bird. Widad giggled at my foolishness, and when I sat down we held hands and I ran my free hand over the sad words on the monolith's side: *I will never forget you.* Inspired just by touching it, I wrote a paranormal poem whose title translates to something like, "She Could Die but Not Forget." At some point while I was in prison in the 1980s, the park was taken over as part of the

LEFT: *Idhkirini, the suicide rock, or "Remember Me" rock, is connected with a tragic love story ending with the death of the lovers.*

BELOW: *Part of Barada River, which I watched almost every day.*

presidential palace grounds. And so, while the rock can still be seen from the highway, the words, like the names of the lovers, have been long forgotten.

In Latakia, there is also a rock known as "Lovers' Rock" or "Suicide Rock." And in the seaside area on the Mediterranean known as Raouche in Beirut, there, too, is a rock called "Suicide Rock" or the "Rock of Love."

There's obviously a connection linking suicide, love, and high rocks in these cities, and perhaps the whole of the Middle East. If Shakespeare had been from Damascus, he would have had Romeo throw himself from the Remember Me rock, with Juliet close behind. Now this rock and the surrounding green area of al-Rabwa remind me of Widad, the woman I'd once been in love with. But now, traveling home to my family, my relationship with Widad seems like some ancient writing that has been washed away by the rain and can never be rewritten.

Every time I met Widad after 1994, my mind traveled back to the young girl I used to know at the end of the 1970s. There was such a vast difference between the girl and the woman. The new Widad frequented my office at the publishing house, at first asking me if there was any work typesetting manuscripts, which I sometimes was able to give her. A few times she helped me find the extra work that helped pay off my house loans. And sometimes she simply showed up to share a cup of coffee or to borrow a small sum of money. I visited her home when she asked me to help her son, who was falling behind in his studies. But my few visits failed to stimulate in the boy any love for learning. In this he reminded me of Mustafa.

The one time she visited our home, she met Rufaida and eighteen-month-old Ghamr. When she began lighting up a cigarette in the house, I politely asked her to smoke in the courtyard.

"Even I smoke outside now," I said with a smile. "You know, the baby."

"If I'd known that, I wouldn't have visited you," Widad said, a sour look on her face. She meant it, but so did I.

On her last visit to my office in 2007, I learned that she and her first husband had gone into business developing an upscale residential subdivision. She had the title of Corporate Secretary and came to advise me to put my name down for one of the villas that they were going to build.

"What's the story?" I asked her suspiciously. "How did you get hold of land and building permits?"

"Why does that matter to you?" she replied firmly. "Don't complicate things. Do you want grapes, or do you want to kill the watchman?" An Arabic proverb, in this case meaning, do you want one of these villas or do you want to interrogate me?

As she left, she handed me a card with the address of her office, making me promise to at least visit. I visited her there just once and to my surprise found one of my friends, a writer of short stories, Nasir Muna, in the waiting room.

"Nasir, it's so good to see you," I exclaimed. "What brings you here?"

"Hello, Jamal. I work here. What about you?"

"I've come to have a look."

"Yes, you have an appointment with Umm Sami."

"How did you know?"

"She asked me to welcome you."

After Nasir and I had talked briefly about the state of Syrian short stories, Widad sent for me via the office intercom. I finished what I was saying about the late master of the Syrian short story, Sa'id Huraniyya, ignoring Nasir's nervous gesture that meant please hurry up and go in. But I knew what Widad was doing.

Finally in her office, I stood before businesswoman Widad, ensconced in her high-back chair behind a large desk. She didn't play her role badly, but I could tell she was playing. She indicated that I should sit in a chair facing a big television screen, and then she summoned one of her assistants and carried on an amiable conversation with him, which had nothing to do with our meeting. Was this nonchalance and wasting my time also to prove she was an important person now? As I watched the poorly designed promotional video, Widad explained the characteristics of the villa I would own when I bought into the scheme.

"So what do you think?" she asked, having rounded off her presentation with a summary of the cash payments I would be required to make.

I gestured toward the screen. "The video could have been better designed," I said.

A few days later, her brother Omar told me, "My sister's amazed that I'm still friends with a man who enjoys being poor."

"Who said I enjoy being poor?"

That was the last time I saw Widad. But over the next few years I read about her in the news. At first it was about the recently wealthy businesswoman and her battles with her husband. In a fit of pique, she actually invaded the home of her ex-husband and his new wife with soldiers she borrowed from her business partners. My storm of beauty had turned into an atomic bomb of destruction. And then she went after her second husband. In the end, poor Widad was charged, tried, and convicted for property development on land she didn't own. Government land, actually. The formal charges were trespassing on state property, investor fraud, and being involved in the corruption that plagued the country. Of course, the higher-ups in the regime pretended to fight corruption but were the most corrupt of all. This meant that Widad's partners in crime, senior intelligence officers and other influential personalities, saw their wealth and influence increase from the development scam. But they needed a fall guy — or girl — and Widad fit the bill.

My mind goes back to 1991, when I was released from prison for the first time. It was with some eighty others, as a way to soften the image of Hafez al-Assad just before an election. Then in 1994, when the president was pressured to release more prisoners who were never formally charged and convicted, what did he do? As usual, not what you would expect. After languishing in jail some for fifteen years, the remaining three hundred and nineteen communists in Sednaya, and fifty in other prisons, finally had charges brought against them. The judges of the Supreme State Security Court then swiftly and officially extended their time behind bars.

I am thinking of this during the minibus ride going home, and it prompts one of my regular flights of fancy, or what could be more accurately described as a waking nightmare. I had told myself often that I should put these memories down on paper, but I never got around to it. In finally writing this, I can see why I didn't. Many were truly subversive.

As I remember the obscene injustice of people being tried decades after they were imprisoned, I lean my head against the minibus's window, and my imagination takes over. I picture the country as a schizophrenic mother who eats her children and then cries for them. The country then turns its witch-like face to me and reproaches me, angrily professing she is innocent of bloodying her own children and the many tortures they were subjected to. She suddenly transforms herself and appears so tender, bending and kissing the scars left on her babes by the chains and whips. Then I picture the country in chains, with soldiers taking turns lashing her between the thighs, screaming that the general has ordered she should get pregnant and give birth to a miracle boy whose body cannot be pierced by bullets or burned by fire. As the soldiers continue to whip her, they demand of her stomach that it bear fruit so she can be happy and make the general and all of them happy too. "We must all be happy," they scream. But her face and her womb grow dryer and emptier. Her groans fill the air, and the people breathe in its pollution. Floggings continue and the stink of ulcerated sores and putrefying wounds continues to assault the nation's senses. The whole of the population becomes heavy-hearted without understanding the reason for their depression.

My imaginings seem so real that I spring up in my seat and fling open the minibus window. I'm trying to escape the fetid smell that has filled my imagination. I breathe in deeply as the outside air rushes in, hoping it will flush away the poisonous nightmare my head is concocting. I blink and try to distract myself by watching the trees along the side of the road. I study the water level in the Barada, now low in autumn. The resurgence of the river level is one of the reasons I rejoice in rain. Rain in Damascus seems to fall shyly — a soft, light rain that successfully tempts many to cleanse themselves under it.

I urge the minibus to eat up the miles so I can see my Ghamr and Rufaida. I miss them every day and have become more and more attached to my little house and family. I bring toys imported from China for Ghamr and a small gift for Rufaida, a coconut or a bar of chocolate or a bouquet of daffodils. Although the minibus is crowded, I feel alone. In my solitude, I talk to Ghamr as I imagine he will be as an adult.

"The first word you said was na'na', mint, I suppose because we used to walk around our little garden and I'd tell you the names of the plants. You know, son, one day in prison the soldier putting me in my cell was eating a sandwich stuffed with cheese and na'na'. As the smell of the sweet herb caressed my nose, I promised myself I'd eat cheese with mint when I finally got out of prison.

"And allow me to tell you another thing, Ghamr. Just like everybody else, I don't remember the day I was born. But I'll never forget April 29, 1991. That was the day of my rebirth and my first steps toward you. After many harsh years in prison, I walked out through the door of the interrogation branch all alone. It felt so strange, my feet touching the asphalt of a street that didn't end in a closed door or high wall."

Would it ever occur to anyone that the simple act of walking along a street unwatched could be a dream come true? Trees, blue sky, and clouds. I had just left a world totally populated by men, and so, to see women walking in public wearing lighter clothes because it's spring — normality. My eyes drank in the sights of the street as if they were drinking in freedom. Living free, without any of the philosophical pretensions I was wont to construct, I realize what all of those who have been imprisoned learn. Freedom is not a theoretical concept. It is something to live, practice, and enjoy to the utmost, something most civilians take for granted. And now I was out of prison. I was out of prison. I was free. Where shall I go now?

Wherever you want, Jamal.

I wanted to go to Bab Touma, al-Bazouriyah market, Nawfara Café, Nirabin Park, Kafarsousah, al-Rabwa, and al-Mezzeh all in one go. My soul was hungry for all of these places, for the city's streets, its parks, gardens, and markets. I think of a famous saying: "If all women were combined into one woman, I could kiss her and be content." I adapt it to, "If all places were combined into one neighborhood, I could visit it and be content."

But then the images of all the girls who had been in my young life appear in my head. I wonder what became of them. Zayn, who gave me the Seiko and with whom I'd clandestinely distributed revolutionary pamphlets. When we finished, we skipped along, giggling with our fingers entwined. She had broken it off with me here in Damascus because I lacked a future. A girl can only wait so long. The Seiko was now in my pocket, its clear crystal broken during the "welcoming" at Tadmur, its hands still stuck at two minutes to eleven. And then in the minibus I remember how I continued my memory tour. My feet had taken me to the front of the building where I lived before being arrested. Tears came to my eyes when I thought about Widad. We used to meet in the apartment on the first floor and have such wonderful times. But this was also where we'd had our quarrel, again about the fact that someone fighting the regime could never have a future. This should have been a clue about how Widad was changing. Not too many months later, I met Layla, who seemed like another girl attracted to would-be political heroes. I was arrested before Layla and I could become close, so she had no time to become disillusioned with me. But I visited her and her husband in 1991 on my extended memory tour. I went all the way to Latakia and spent fifteen minutes sharing a coffee with them before I left. I didn't want to cause any marital conflict. But in 1999 they gave Rufaida and me a generous wedding gift. They rented us a chalet by the Mediterranean in Latakia.

After I'd walked for some hours, I decided to take a taxi to my Uncle Khalifa's house in Qaboun. All I had in the right-hand pocket of my jeans was a fifty-lira note. I'd given two hundred and fifty lira to my friend Barzan Kurdi, who was released about twenty minutes before me. He needed to fly to Qamishli, where his family lived, in the northern regions of Syria. In the other pocket, next to the broken watch, was a red Clipper lighter, a gift from my friend Fadi al-Saghir, and a few cheap cigarettes stuffed into my shirt pocket. That's all I had with me, except for some writing stuffed into my shoes. The rest of my writing had been smuggled out by my sister Khadija with the help of a sympathetic guard. I left all my clothes for other prisoners.

When I got to my uncle's, I was shocked when the driver asked for forty-five lira. When I was arrested, it would have cost three.

"Isn't that too much?" I asked.

He gestured to a rectangular box with electronic numbers on it. "Look at the meter," he said. Taxis didn't have meters when I was arrested. I would soon learn that all life in Syria was now metered and measured.

I had five lira left when I got out of the taxi. I knocked on the door of my uncle's, but there was no answer. I knew it was totally by chance that nobody was home, but my years behind bars made it feel that this was just another door that wasn't going to open for me. This negative thought just kept looping around and around in my head. Finally, I ordered myself to abandon the unproductive conversation I was having with myself. I'd go to my cousin's house in the nearby quarter of Bustan al-Mahdi, one long bus stop away. I boarded the bus and waited for the conductor, but he didn't come, and the passengers were putting small tickets into a machine that made a *tik* sound as it clipped the ticket. *The conductor will come and I'll buy a ticket from him.* Then a man came strolling down the aisle, and all the passengers were holding up their tickets for him to see.

He looked at me. "Ticket please," he said.

"I don't have a ticket. The conductor hasn't been round yet."

He sighed like I was trying to get away with something and began writing up what I learned was a citation for not paying the bus fare. He held it out to me.

"Twenty-five liras please."

"I don't understand. Who are you, sir?"

"The inspector."

"I've only got five lira, and I don't know how to get a bus ticket."

"ID card please."

"I don't have one on me. I was told I need to get a new one."

"What? Are you some kind of idiot?"

"No. The fact is, I've just got out of prison today. Things have changed."

"Why were you in prison?"

"I was a political prisoner."

As if he had suddenly found himself next to a leper, the inspector took a quick step back. "You got what you deserved," he growled. And then, knowing that I couldn't pay, he grudgingly shoved the citation back in between the pages of his book and stomped away.

"The masses' kindly first reaction," I mumbled to myself. But I did see a lot of sympathy in the eyes of some of the passengers around me, or perhaps I saw what I wanted to see.

A passenger got off the bus at the same time as I did. I glanced behind and saw him watching the bus until it left, as if he didn't want anybody to see what he was about to do. Was I going to be robbed on my first day out of prison? What an irony. He trotted up to me, and I turned to face him.

"Brother . . . sorry, just a second please," he said.

"Yes, what is it?" The man held out his hand and I shook it.

"Thank God you're safe and well," he said, giving a common salutation. "But can you tell me, a relative of mine has been in prison for nine years, and we've heard nothing about him. Perhaps you've met him."

"Which prison is he in?"

"We don't know. Maybe the same as you?"

"What's his name?"

"Muhammad Rasmi al-Haffar. The Alawites put him in prison. He's a Muslim Brother like you."

I gave it some thought. *Where is this country heading?*

"I was arrested by the mukhabarat. I'm not from the Brotherhood, but I did meet some of them," I responded. "Unfortunately, not Rasmi al-Haffar. I hope you have good news of him soon."

As we parted, I realized why he had made sure nobody saw us talking. If Intelligence catches someone asking about prisoners, they, too, are arrested. As for me, I had also broken the rule by wishing this fellow's relative well.

When I reached home after the minibus journey, I lifted a laughing Ghamr high in the air as usual. And if I found him asleep, I'd kneel by him and shower his presence with the light that still shines from my eyes whenever I gaze upon him.

I grew to love my neighborhood. Though poor, it was a refuge far from the city center. I also loved the cooperation among its many different sects and ethnicities. Before the city provided water and electricity officially, neighbors worked together to illegally tap into the water and electricity lines at the bottom of the hill, allowing us to enjoy them for free. Well, except when an inspector gave us a certain little frown that meant it was time for a small bribe. When the city finally put in proper infrastructure, we began to pay monthly. And that was okay because I was happy. I was happy with my vegetables and trees and the visits from friends. I was happy with everything to do with my family's daily routines. With these I was content. But about the future for our country, I was secretly worried. I had personally survived what the regime had caused me to endure. But now whatever happened outside of our insular world, if things got worse, would affect my wife and my child's future as well.

CHAPTER 44

THE SYRIAN UPRISING

Two years and eleven days after the birth of Ghamr, and after the Damascus Spring had come to nothing, our little family grew. My son Taim was born. The only name we had come up with was Ayse, meaning existence, but my young university friends from the Institute of Dramatic Arts objected and suggested the name Taim, like Taim Hassan, a handsome student at the time, who became a very popular actor. Taim, meaning One Who Loves Greatly, was born with a very large head. He looked like a head with legs and arms attached. "He's all brains," my father joked, but soon he looked perfect. When Taim was about sixteen months old, he made up his own language. And I really think it was a language, because it didn't sound like a toddler's babbling. I shouldn't have laughed, but when he realized I didn't understand him and was perhaps making fun of him, he'd wrinkle up his face and protest loudly.

You know, I was familiar with the power that people have over others. First there was the authority of my father and my teachers, and later the influence of women I'd loved. I'd suffered the wrath of dictators and religious leaders, enduring the ferocity of their torture chambers and dungeons. I'd been handcuffed countless times. But in truth, even when it came to those who tortured me, I may have given them my screams, but I did not, not once, yield to them my soul. But Rufaida, Ghamr, and Taim? They had my soul and my heart in chains, and I submitted gladly to their authority.

As detainees I knew were released after serving their undeserved incarcerations, I visited those I could. Our group meetings became more frequent and at times we looked like retired veterans who found it necessary to socialize still. But as opposed to the days of our youth, our opinions now varied too much for us to come together in a single political party. Some had become liberals, some Arab nationalists, and others remained firmly committed to Marxism. There were even a few of us free thinkers. Our debates were extremely fierce, but that didn't spoil our personal relationships or put an end to our meetings. We had different attitudes towards the Iraq War, Hezbollah, the myriad religious groups and political parties. I was one of those who believed that potential explosions in our country could only be defused in a democratic civil state. This was a struggle that must be conducted through dialogue and civilized arguments beneath a parliamentary dome, not with bullets screaming in the streets and mothers wailing in graveyards. So, our debates didn't result in the formation of an organization of any sort. Instead our exchanges seemed more like reasoned but empty and ineffectual chatter that only existed in the scant snippets of the ethereal time we were borrowing, or the last wisps of smoke rising off the remains of a fire, now a heap of ashes. Less metaphorically, they were the last remnants of a dying political movement. And if what was happening in Syria wasn't enough to convince us, after watching the hijacked airliners destroy the Twin Towers in Manhattan and the smart bombs destroy so many buildings in Baghdad, we now understood how little a handful of people living in a poor neighborhood on the side of a mountain could do. It seemed to me we were like butterflies in fields of knives and guns. How could I feel any differently, and what could I be expected to do?

The cypress trees I'd planted grew and formed a protective fence round the house. I enjoyed walking with the boys down the hill and we had fun wandering in the markets. I devoted most of my time to taking care of my family.

Three main avenues ran along the side of the mound. On each, there were houses, stores, and kiosks. The boys always pulled me to the 4-U Super Market, a small grocery store. There Ghamr would buy a Snickers bar, his favorite, and Taim would buy a Kinder Surprise chocolate egg. The boys begged me to take them to New Boy, which sold licensed action figures from a children's TV channel. Hayel al-Salamouni was one of the two barbers at a small store, who cut my and the boys' hair for several years. He was so quiet and kind. Ghamr insisted that only Hayel cut his hair. "He is clean and nice, Dad," Ghamr told me. Hayel and his wife had been trying for years to have a child, and when the good news finally came, he was ecstatic. Abu Lateef, whose shop offered incredibly old and outdated merchandise, was a funny little man. Not at all hygienic, he smelled from wearing the same clothes all the time and had yellow teeth and fingers from smoking. He was very often sitting out front playing backgammon, and so, when I passed by with the boys, he'd always insist I stop. He'd smile his yellow smile, laugh, and then I'd cringe as he patted the boy's heads.

I bought frozen chickens from Abu Muhammad's kiosk. He was a short man, about thirty years old, with a red beard and a kind heart. I liked him, since he seemed so honest. I suggested many times that he stock frozen fish, too. "There are two other frozen chicken sellers here, but none with fish," I told him.

He would say: "Inshallah." Then the boys, bored, would take my hand and pull me away. Abu Muhammad would laugh at this as he waved goodbye.

Qudsaya, the town half an hour's walk from ours to the west, was controlled by opposition fighters. It was during this time when you could see many long beards with upper lips either clean-shaven or highly trimmed to give the same effect. This style was worn by radical opposition soldiers and Muslim fighters — a number of whom were also vendors at the market. A fellow known as al-Doumani was one of these. He was an extremely polite man, although he was the only vendor I knew who refused to barter and haggle. Despite this, I regularly bought most of my vegetables from him because of their quality. As he bent down to retrieve something from under his table, you would see his ever-present Kalashnikov rifle. I think that there were somewhere between fifty and a hundred of these religious fighters in the town. The Kalashnikovs could be seen on our street, in the stores owned by the militia members who supported the regime. At the time, neither side bothered us. But I could foresee that these rifles would be used one day and that our future would be stained with blood.

In 2003 the Iraqi dictator fell. A modern democratic civil state did not ensue. Instead there came a complex and naive sectarian quota system, which set Iraq up to explode periodically. Even the people in our little group could see this flaw. Many predicted it would end with the country's map being redrawn. During the short war that ended the era of military dictatorship there, we watched the satellite channels at home. One time, Ghamr was running around the room waving the pajama bottoms he'd stripped off as if they were a flag. As he ran, he repeated the cry of Saddam's supporters on television.

"Bush, Bush, listen well. We all love Saddam Hussein." "Bush, Bush, isma' zein. Kullna nuhibb Saddam Hussein." It rhymes in Arabic.

"I don't think even those shouting for him really like him," I told the boy.

"Don't you like him?"

"No."

"So why does the TV like him?"

The war in Iraq stimulated much debate in Syria, exposing the diversity of our population and the danger of tribalism. In March 2004, there was a soccer match between two Syrian teams, one from the city of Qamishli, and the other from Deir ez-Zor. Qamishli was a city mostly of Kurds, while the Deir ez-Zor population was such that it was known as an Iraqi city inside Syria. The fans from this team carried pictures of Saddam Hussein and shouted insults at the Kurdish fans. But Saddam had committed crimes of genocide against the Kurds, in particular in Halabja, where he used chemical weapons. Passions in the stadium quickly escalated.

"Bi-ruh, bi-dam, nafdiik, George Bush!" the Kurds chanted back. "Our soul, our blood, we'll sacrifice for you, George Bush!" George Bush and the Americans had been generous supporters of the Kurds, so they gave him the name Abu Azadi, the Father of Freedom.

Of course, the Syrian supporters of Saddam Hussein saw it much differently. The Americans had toppled their hero. Chanting support for Bush, the killer of Iraqis, was treasonous. Many of their kin had died during the American-led attack on Iraq. They shouted back across the stadium, "Bush, Abu Draat! Bush, Abu Draat!" — the Father of Farting. Fighting started in the stadium and spread like wildfire. Shots rang out and six Kurds were killed, among them three children. The Kurds insisted that both the other team's supporters and local police had been firing weapons.

There were demonstrations in parts of the cities where Kurds lived. Between our house and downtown Damascus was a poor Kurdish neighborhood called Wadi al-Mashaari', also known as Zurafa. There was a march there where protesters smashed some billboards and two phone booths. The next day I visited the quarter to meet with Kurdish friends, telling them how I thought it was shameful that citizens couldn't speak up for the victims simply as Syrians.

It was portrayed by the mukhabarat agents as a battle between Arabs and Kurds. We were all concerned with a question that required a practical answer: When will the battle be waged between those calling for a democratic civil state and the various agents of repression and despotism?

Late in 2010, when the revolution began in Tunisia, I literally cried with joy as I watched our television. The news footage showed lawyer Abdel Nasser Laouini going up and down a deserted street in the center of Tunis at dawn. The city was still under curfew, but he was animatedly waving his hands in the air and addressing the Tunisian people.

"Long live the great Tunisian people. No more killing, no more torture. Tunisia is free. The people are free. The criminal President Ben Ali has fled the country. Ben Ali has fled."

That day, we also saw Ahmad al-Hefnawi on TV. The gray-haired café owner turned activist was being interviewed in the streets. With tears in his eyes he put his hand on his cropped snow-white hair, crying, "We have grown old, we have grown old waiting for this moment," and then I, along with many other Syrians, went around waving our hands above our heads shouting the same phrase all throughout the country. "We have grown old waiting for this moment." As words written on a page, they may not carry much strength, but the videos are accessible on YouTube. Even if you don't understand the Arabic, the emotions, the relief, clearly come through. And so you may understand better how Syrians living under similar repressive circumstances would react emotionally. We wanted what they seemed to be on the verge of achieving.

At the start of the Egyptian revolution, I supported it. I rejoiced when I watched the chief of the Egyptian intelligence services, Omar Suleiman, bitterly announcing the resignation of his boss, President Hosni Mubarak. His face was flushed and angry, as if he were performing one of the most difficult duties of his career. I laughed at his disappointment and felt hope.

That evening, a debate was held in our house with visiting friends. We agreed that the fall of dictatorships was a necessary condition for getting rid of autocratic regimes, but insufficient in itself. It was just the beginning.

So, the big question was if this were the right time for Syrians to rise up too. As cowed and cautious as we were, we wanted what seemed to be happening in Tunisia and Egypt. Our first attempt occurred when some one hundred Syrians gathered in front of the Libyan Embassy in Damascus, expressing their support for the Libyan people. To begin with, the Syrian intelligence services made do with letting the crowd see they were around. Many thought they were there just to make sure things remained peaceful.

A teacher I knew told me that Intelligence had come to her school and asked that the basement of the school be cleaned and made ready, as they might have to use it as a shelter.

"A shelter or a prison?" I asked her.

She spread her palms and shrugged her shoulders. "Nothing would surprise me," she said. But still, we held on to our hope. We were ready for hope. But the mukhabarat were ready, too, with something quite different.

On day two of the demonstration in front of the Libyan Embassy, true to their nature, the mukhabarat attacked the crowd. They beat and detained many. My friend al-Harith al-Nabhan had a swollen face as a result of the blows he received.

On March 15, 2011, there was a spontaneous demonstration in al-Hariqa, a commercial district in Damascus. A traffic policeman insulted a man who parked his car illegally. A policeman berating a citizen shouldn't have caused such a reaction, but hope can be as powerful as a bomb. The hope that had been long suppressed in the breasts of Syrians now only needed a single spark to light its fuse. A crowd of two hundred quickly assembled and, seeing the single police officer as symbolic of the regime, exploded in anger. It was enough of an incident that the deputy minister of the interior hurried to the place and calmed matters by condemning the policeman's behavior. The demonstration broke up. But the government wasn't as accommodating elsewhere and had no intentions of making a habit of conciliation. Earlier in February in the city of Daraa, children wrote graffiti on the walls of their school: *Down with the regime* and *It's your turn now, Doctor*, referring to Bashar al-Assad, the one-time ophthalmologist. Atef Najib, the president's cousin and Daraa security chief, responded by jailing and torturing the twelve-to-fourteen-year-olds. Confronted by parents going out of their minds with worry, Najib purportedly told them, "Forget about your children and have others," adding, "and if you can't manage that, send your women to us."

This went on for weeks until, on March 18, a huge citywide demonstration of thousands of citizens was mobilized.

CHAPTER 45

HE DIDN'T LEAVE HIS GRAVE
TO BUY POTATOES

I covered my nose and mouth with my mask and used the hand sanitizer near the entrance to the Farm Boy supermarket near my new home in Kingston. All the customers were taking the same precautions because of the Covid pandemic. The shop assistant said something I didn't properly understand, as I'd left my hearing aid at home. You can't lip read when people are wearing masks. I guessed she was saying the shopping carts had been sanitized and so I nodded with a smile and began finding the items Rufaida had written on her list. Assessing a watermelon's ripeness, I tapped it up by my ear. This was a skill I'd learned from my father but, because of my hearing loss, I actually couldn't hear anything. Old habits die hard.

When I raised my head, I saw him. I put the melon in the cart and continued to stare in amazement. He not only resembled Tayyeb Tizini, a professor of philosophy at Damascus University, but appeared to *be* him. The same height, the same white hair, even the same haircut. He put some potatoes into a plastic bag as I watched. He was wearing a navy jacket and tie, the same color as the ones Tayyeb was wearing the last time I saw him. I don't know how fond the professor is of potatoes, but I think most Syrians eat them on a regular basis. I wanted to pull the mask off his face to see if the nose, mouth, and chin were the same too. Tayyib couldn't have possibly risen from his faraway grave in the city of Homs just to buy potatoes at a Farm Boy in the new world. The man vanished around the end of an aisle.

Still somewhat in shock, I contemplated speaking to the man. But being a shy, hard-of-hearing refugee, I began selecting tomatoes.

I first became familiar with the name Tayyeb Tizini in the 1970s. I read an article by him about viewing Middle Eastern culture in a scientific and objective way. The whole of our population had grown up subconsciously accepting our culture through a filter of repressive religion and deference to those "above us." For me, his writing was transformative. I got to know him face-to-face for the first time in the 1990s in my office at al-Tali'a. He visited me because of his interest in the Qumran Scrolls, also known as the Dead Sea Scrolls, and we had recently published a set of three books on the topic, all translated from French into Arabic. He came to buy them directly from us, but his writing had been such an important influence in my life that I insisted he accept them as a gift. We then discussed his own pet project, a book series — again based on his vision of looking at Arab culture through a scientific lens.

His series had the long academic title of *A New Vision of Arab Thought from Its Beginning Until Now*. It had been conceived as a twenty-nine volume series and had sold well when the first twelve volumes came out in the 1970s and '80s. But since ultra-conservative Islam was becoming a dominant influence across the Middle East, interest in modern thought — including Tizini's writing — had diminished. His publisher could no longer find financial justification to complete the project. It saddens me to think that when the professor died in 2019, he was known as the old man who cried during a lecture comparing Syria in the 1950s and Syria now.

On March 16, 2011, the day after a demonstration in al-Hariqa Square, I left home and headed for the city. I wanted to walk in the street where the demonstration had taken place. As I started on my way, I couldn't help but laugh inwardly at myself. Am I going there to catch an echo of the protestors' voices? They had chanted in unison their declaration that they could not and would not be intimidated into submission. "The Syrian people will not be humiliated!" was the chant heard on television broadcasts all over the Middle East.

Before I reached al-Hariqa, I met the journalist Abdul-Karim Aba-Zaid on al-Nasr Street. Never one for formality, he impatiently pulled at my arm.

"Let's go," he said. "Activists convinced the prisoners' families to hold a sit-in in front of the Ministry of the Interior. We have to be there."

We continued our conversation as we hurried toward the sit-in.

"How are things in Daraa?" I asked of Aba-Zaid's home city.

"Man, we're ruled by a bunch of thugs and criminals. Things are terrible. Since the kids were arrested, the whole city's been at a boiling point."

When we got to the edge of al-Marjeh Square, there was little sign of the sit-in. While the place was still bustling with cars and shoppers heading for the many stores, all that seemed left of the protest was a mop-up operation. Two men in civilian clothes were beating Professor Tayyeb Tizini on his white head with their black clubs. We, along with indifferent shoppers, watched as they dragged him along the ground and threw him into a non-descript car. Meanwhile, a group of mukhabarat stood pumping their clubs into the air in front of the ministry building, obviously jubilant about their success in breaking up the protest.

"God, Syria, Bashar, wa bass! God, Syria, Bashar, that's all!" they repeated over and over again.

Across the road, meanwhile, three more men with clubs were beating up a jean-clad youth who was desperately trying to protect his camera. As he finally raised both hands to protect his head, one of the thugs tore the camera away from him and smashed it on the ground with all his might. He then stomped on it with the heel of his boot until it lay shattered. Why I stayed and watched the mukhabarat clear out the rest of the square, I can't say. But after about fifteen minutes, when the square went back to its normal business, I looked around and Abdul-Karim was nowhere to be seen.

When I went home, non-Syrian television channels CNN, Al Jazeera, and France 24 were talking about the arrest of thirty-three people from the sit-in, mentioning Professor Tizini by name. Also arrested were twelve women, among them an engineer friend, Nahed Badawiyya. Suhair al-Atassi was also arrested. She was known for holding one of the more prominent National Dialogue Forums at her house during the Damascus Spring. Professor Tizini was released the same day, while Nahed and Suhair were the last to be released, a week later. Nahed later told me that the well-publicized call for a sit-in on social media meant that waiting for them in the square were a large number of intelligence agents. They monitor Facebook and Twitter too.

"And it's clear the mukhabarat had recently been on training courses," she said. "They were scattered all through the crowd and had clubs hidden under their clothes. The moment we held up photos of the detainees, the bastards pulled out their clubs, and while some started beating us, others grabbed the pictures and ripped them up. And those clubs weren't just for hitting. They double as electric stun batons. The brainwashing exercise seemed to have worked well on them. When some of us tried to talk to them reasonably, Syrian to Syrian, they just hit harder."

In those days, people chanting in protests against the regime and people attending rallies in support of the regime agreed on two words, God and Syria, but disagreed on the third. The protestors shouted, "God, Syria, freedom wa bass," and the loyalists said "Bashar" instead of "freedom." It's not unusual to find different combinations on Facebook, such as, "Bashar will die, but freedom never dies."

I left al-Tali'a Publishing House in 2009, two years earlier. I parted on good terms with all my colleagues there, especially the owner, Marwan Saqqal. As I got to really know him over the years, I saw how he was not only a sincere, dear man, he was also a wonderful study in contradictions. Aristocratic and yet a communist, totally secular and a believer in science, he was fascinated by Reiki therapy and the idea of opening universal energy pathways in the body. He was a vegetarian who loved meat, committed to drinking vinegar and honey every morning for his health, and he smoked forty cigarettes a day. I loved working at al-Tali'a, but the salary they could afford was no longer enough to support my family. And since the income of the majority of people was insufficient for even their basic needs, the publishing house wasn't doing that well. Believing that neither of us should be a burden to the other, I left.

I was able to secure a good job working for Asda'a, a public relations firm, doing translation and advertising.

Because Asda'a offices were in Latakia in Syria, and Dubai in the Emirates, my work was done by email from home. There my time was spent reading and working on a wide variety of high-end, first-world subjects: any news relating to modern marketing, local up-and-coming companies, international fashion seasons, all kinds of top-hundred personality lists, including *Forbes* Middle Eastern publications, and a host of similar magazines. The various skills I'd honed during my years in Marwan's publishing house allowed me this larger income, which enabled me, in turn, to give very small amounts of financial help to others, and to add equally small amounts to my family's savings. But working at home also allowed me to closely monitor what was going on during the unrest in Syria and other parts of the Middle East.

The situation in Daraa continued to deteriorate. On March 18, 2011, I was glued to the television, neglecting my work like most Syrians, watching video footage of the protests outside the Omari mosque in Daraa. Syrian television, which was entirely controlled by the regime, began to talk about unknown armed groups killing protestors. In reality, the mukhabarat had begun creating a militia made up of the unemployed soldiers and officers who had been laid off or were retired. These armed groups were euphemistically named Popular Committees, as if they were spontaneously organized by their members. But they were paid. They were also known as Shabbiha, meaning thugs. Employing such brutes allowed the regime to feign innocence when violence ensued. After all, a government couldn't be seen by the world to be killing their own citizens. But they were fooling no one.

To further distract from their malicious deeds, the intelligence services also spread ridiculous rumors about vehicles distributing suspicious food-stuffs and urged people not to have anything to do with them. But not a single Syrian I knew had seen these vehicles or received free food. What they did see, along with viewers all around the world, were the bodies of protestors, thanks to brave journalists, both official and citizen. The gunmen fired on protesters at the demonstrations and then, in turn, at victims' funerals. This sparked more demonstrations, which again were fired on, resulting in yet more people being killed.

Besides watching the Arab Spring unfold in Syria, Yemen, Libya, Egypt, and Tunis on satellite feeds, the internet allowed protestors to coordinate using Messenger and Skype. Syrians also began boldly publishing their views on Facebook, which became one of the most important social media platforms, especially after it was widely rumored to have played a role in the fall of the Egyptian president. Some say the Egyptian revolution happened so quickly because of a single picture. Khaled Saeed, no relation, was a young man beaten to death by Egyptian security services in Alexandria in June 2010. He wasn't even an activist, just the victim of a random police execution. His brother took a picture of Khaled's body lying in the morgue and put it on the internet. The image of his mangled and broken face was so horrible and so telling that it went viral. Subsequently a Facebook page called "We Are All Khaled Saeed" was set up.

During this time most of my friends were clearly spending too much time at their keyboards. As soon as I wrote on my "friends only" Facebook page, I'd see comments pop up, and when I commented on someone else's post, others replied to my comments just as quickly. It was the same for everybody. Some wrote impassioned full-length articles on the suppression of freedoms and about corruption. Facebook was also the most popular platform for pictures and video clips of events. Many images of martyrs killed in the demonstrations became historical icons. The joke went around that many dinners had been ruined, neglected on stoves, by women obsessively following events. Like most Syrian households, we, too, stayed up late into the night discussing the country's future while eating our burnt meals. When my father came to Damascus to be treated for gallstones, he expressed his admiration for the way my wife worked throughout the night. He thought she was doing translation, but the truth was, Rufaida was keen to discuss and learn about what was going on all over the country and the Middle East, and she was chatting with her virtual friends, and posting her poems and messages that expressed our aspiration for freedom.

And then at the end of March 2011 came the speech we were all waiting for. Even though we knew it was just a desperate dream, most Syrians still held on to the hope that Bashar al-Assad's exposure to science and modern thought might be enough to overcome that other impulse — his inherited right to be a despot.

I admit that I was very anxious when I turned on the TV to watch the speech.

The screen showed Bashar entering a packed parliament and being greeted by hundreds of his chosen members, all standing and clapping loudly to the refrain, "God, Syria, Bashar, wa bass!" They chanted it over and over as he made his way to the dais through the throng of sycophantic officials.

When the first part of the speech began, the president seemed to be conciliatory toward the citizenry, listing some of our just demands and making vague promises about the need for reform. Will he lead a real democratic change and let Syria start anew? I received an answer to my question immediately when he worked in mention of a treacherous conspiracy. Then, the president casually said something even more threatening.

"Eliminating discord is a national, moral, and legal duty," he said to his admirers, "and whoever is able to contribute to its destruction and does not do so . . . is a part of it." The parliament roared. The television image switched to packed crowds outside the parliament roaring their approval too. The president then borrowed the religious term "fitna," which means to lead someone astray, to sow sedition, civil strife, and discord. Speaking like a professor imparting wisdom to adoring students, he paused before scanning the hall, then gave a quote from the Quran. "Fitna is more serious than murder." He let that sink in, and then added, "Opposing fitna is . . . your legal duty." He ended his speech as if he were telling a parting joke, but his words were anything but. "And . . . if the fight is imposed on us," he said, shrugging, "we welcome it."

The speech came to an abrupt end. There would be no need for me to find a sacrificial bull, as no lamb of peace had been offered. Bashar made his way back through his adoring crowd, and they continued their roar: "God, Syria, Bashar, wa bass!"

Bashar had given his speech in such a calm manner that the end seemed anticlimactic. So much so that when the poet Eissa Mahmoud contacted me after it was over, he remarked sarcastically, "I thought he'd gone for a piss and would come back to finish."

The houses I visited had their televisions on constantly. People had stopped watching the soaps and now followed the news as it happened. Children protested at being deprived of their programs, and families who could afford it bought a second television so their children could watch their own channels, where the dose of religious stories had increased in keeping with the prevailing trend.

Demonstrators began to coordinate via Facebook pages, and groups appeared in neighborhoods and cities. Demonstrations habitually started on Fridays directly after the worshippers came out of the mosques, which had flourished after the 1980s due to the rising tide of religious activity and the regime's flirtation with it, making sectarian identities grow ever more prominent at the expense of national identity.

Live bullets causing a large number of fatalities at New Clock Tower Square in Homs put a stop to that day's sit-in, but this actually caused the brave citizens of the city to increase the size of their demonstrations. In fact, most cities saw their Friday demonstrations grow. In the early months these protests were given names like Friday of Dignity and Friday of Defiance. The regime forces were able to concentrate their efforts, suppressing the demonstrations in general while their electrified-baton-wielding thugs went through the crowds rooting out known activists. But I must admit, my experience with the authorities during all those years in jail, listening to Bashar's speech, having seen how our government was killing its own people, plus the fact that I now had the responsibilities of a family — all this limited my activities. I mostly stayed home and watched Syria's struggle from afar on foreign satellite channels. These foreign media outlets were also the only place that showed how many Syrian military officers and enlisted men were announcing their defection from the al-Assad regime. Lieutenant Colonel Hussein Harmoush, for example, announced his defection on a YouTube video. These were acts of bravery, as a soldier refusing to carry out orders to fire on civilians was considered guilty of high treason, the punishment being execution. Soon these defectors set up the Free Syrian Army in opposition. This was about the same time I began to hear the sound of live machine gun fire from our home on the hill. Of course, Rufaida and the boys, now eleven and nine, could hear it too.

My biggest challenge in keeping my family safe was rationalizing Rufaida's activism. She was full of enthusiasm and keen to participate in all forms of peaceful action. Along with other women, Rufaida went to different neighborhoods to give comfort and aid to those badly affected, whose family members had been killed and their homes ruined. In some neighborhoods, the only help these women could offer victims and their families was to recite the Fatiha — the opening verses of the Quran — which is usually recited at the beginning of all important events: births, weddings, and, in this case, deaths. Where they could, this women's brigade brought food, clothing, and medical supplies. Rufaida even went to al-Rahma Hospital to learn some basic nursing skills, in order to be more effective. She also attended leadership workshops, learning about international laws governing human rights and about founding civil organizations. She was tireless, leaving home early in the morning and not returning home until seven or ten hours later.

Although the regime continued to claim that the killers of participants in peaceful demonstrations were gangs of unknown conspirators, their aim was to use violence to continually break up the protests. Once, what was supposed to be a silent candlelit vigil turned into a brawl started by the government men. Rufaida and some friends tried to free a man who was being dragged away. She came home with a bruised shoulder from being clubbed. When she later went to Jalaa Park in the heart of the city to light candles at another silent vigil, I remember how she said goodbye to me and the boys. It was like it could be our last embrace. While the women were expecting the Popular Committee to assault them, that night their demonstration was only met by a counter-demonstration of the regime's men. Eyeing the demonstrators angrily as they marched by in force, the regime's men banged shoulders with the women while their contorted faces screamed the relentless pledge, "Our blood, our soul, we sacrifice for you, Bashar. Our blood, our soul, we sacrifice for you, Bashar."

But my fearless wife was not to be deterred. She tried to meet all demonstration detainees the moment they were released from custody and continued to take part in every protest she could. Her attitude reminded me of the way I was before being arrested those many years ago. Remembering this, and having lived the consequences, I became more and more upset when Rufaida put herself at risk. After watching her working on the computer one evening, I criticized the way she put so much trust in people she knew only through Facebook. She even invited some of these contacts to our home.

"Rufi, any member of the intelligence could claim to be an opposition activist. We don't need a Facebook conversation to give the mukhabarat an excuse to arrest us. Do good, but don't be seen." I continually exhorted, "Do good, but don't be seen." Still my darling continued to devote her immense emotional energy to a dream she still believed was within our movement's grasp. But as the level of violence increased, and armed fanatic militias were formed on the side of the opposition, my fears increased too, of violence and the deepening mire of conflict and the way weapons had come to have the last word.

CHAPTER 46

THE PRESIDENT WELCOMED WAR

W e could hear the chanting of demonstrators in Qudsaya Square loud
and clear at our house. Deep echoing cries of "The people want
the regime to fall" and "God, Syria, freedom, wa bass" seemed to split the
sky in two and reverberate up the side of the hill over and over again. A
few days later, when curiosity and worry convinced me to stroll around the
square, I could see the newly constituted Shabbiha had even reached our
part of the country. In town they were strategically stationed at the inter-
sections to observe the local residents' movements. Many of the Shabbiha
stared at me as I passed, as if they were searching my eyes for some inner
guilt to emerge and indict me.

Young people who'd taken part in the demonstrations visited us, and
together we'd sit and watch on Al Jazeera news about the countrywide protests. While I was certainly aware of how these young people had been risking
imprisonment or death, the possibility didn't seem to cross their minds, even
though they had seen many arrested and even killed. Convinced they were
making history and building the future, they were filled with euphoria and
spoke of the shining eyes of the other demonstrators, oblivious to the light in
their own eyes. But they discussed things in a way that made them seem more
like dreaming poets than rational politicians who could bring about difficult
reforms. Still, the complete disregard for their own safety seemed to partly
brush away the dust and rust that had accumulated around my soul. My opti-
mism did not go beyond the message that the playwright Saadallah Wannous

gave during World Theater Day in 1996, when he said: "We are doomed to hope." I sighed as I looked at the Syrian youth who were sitting in front of me and smiling. I thought about their willingness to make sacrifices, their future, and the future of my beloved country itself.

Demonstrations weren't always confined to Fridays. One Thursday afternoon in September 2011, as I was buying vegetables in Qudsaya Square, a demonstration started up, and I found myself in the middle of it with my bags of groceries. I saw men and women I knew there, neighbors, and suddenly, like in a dream, I was shoulder-to-shoulder in a huge throng, shouting along at the top of my voice with the rest, "Syria wants freedom! Syria wants freedom!" Luckily, the protest was short-lived and broke up before the Shabbiha had a chance to start firing on us. In the excitement of the moment, I had left my bags of vegetables on the pavement, and a young man with smiling green eyes approached me.

"Don't forget your vegetables, Hajji," he said, with the deference meant for a respected elder. If only he could see the fear and trepidation that was mixed in with the ecstasy those brief minutes of revolutionary zeal had rekindled in my heart.

"Thank you, my son."

Nothing about my appearance suggests I'm a Hajji except my newly graying hair, and I don't usually address young men as "my son." I took my shopping home and an hour later Rufaida returned from the Masakin Barza quarter, where she'd been delivering aid to a family displaced from Homs. I told her I'd seen a demonstration, but not that I'd taken part in it.

The Kurdish journalist Rustum Mahmoud used to visit us every Friday after the regular demonstration, and we usually had lunch together. One day he was accompanied by Gabriel Moushe Gawrieh, head of the Assyrian Democratic Organization. Gabriel, a sympathetic character with his bald head and captivating smile, talked to us about the Assyrians and gave us the broad outlines of his organization's program, whose aspirations we all shared. "This revolution seems like a big party where Syrians get to know one another. And I'm honored to meet the pioneers who went to prison ahead of us."

"Oh, please, Gabriel, prison is not a place to wish for," I said.

Gabriel laughed and put a hand on my shoulder. "Of course. Let's just say I hope we can soon celebrate the establishment of a state where everybody is free." I nodded with a weak smile. I felt so old.

After we'd finished eating and exchanging ideas, Gabriel gave Rufaida, the boys, and me our first lesson in writing Syriac. We have yet to get our second lesson. The man disappeared, and later we heard he'd been arrested. Gabriel wasn't released until June 2016.

By March and April of 2011, there were so many secular organizations active in the country: the Sun Group in Damascus; the Pulse Group for Syrian Youth in Homs and Aleppo; The Descendants of al-Kawakibi, also in Aleppo; and the Together for Syria Movement in Latakia and Tartus. We were able to keep in touch with these groups via Messenger.

Another secular leader of note during this time was Dr. Abd al-Aziz al-Khair. He again rose to prominence in the Communist Labor Party, having returned to political activism after ten years underground and thirteen years in prison. A great man, he even had the respect of his jailers. He was one of the few imprisoned medical doctors who was allowed to fulfill the obligations of his Hippocratic oath to all the prisoners, regardless of their affiliation. This ensured them more medical attention than they would have normally had. But now back in society, thugs from the Muslim Brotherhood tried to prevent the doctor from attending a conference of Syrian opposition groups in Cairo. They pelted him with eggs and stones in front of the Arab League building and set out to tarnish his image in all the media outlets they owned. The religious opposition sought to curb the secular opposition as much as possible, unless it agreed to be subordinate to them. As the religious element of the opposition grew in strength and audacity, they began to do things like burn down the stalls selling alcohol at the intersection in our neighborhood. They also occupied the beer factory on the Beirut road in the outskirts of Qudsaya on the way to the town of al-Hameh and destroyed the production equipment. Eventually, on September 21, 2012, the regime rearrested Dr. al-Khair. To this day, I don't know which prison he is in or if he is alive. The regime denies ever rearresting him.

In summer that year, Rufaida and I also got to know Amal Nasr al-Din and her husband, Adnan al-Dibs, both of whom had given up their time to work for democratic change and social justice. The couple's names weren't new to me. Amal had a history in the trade union struggle. Although the regime suppressed unions as well as political parties, Amal did what she could to help the cause of the workers. Adnan was still a member of my old Syrian Communist Labor Party. It was much smaller in 2012, but it remained somewhat active because of ultra-dedicated people such as Adnan and Dr. al-Khair.

And as if she wasn't already busy enough, Amal was also at the head of a secular, democratic youth group called Shams, the Arabic word for sun. Rufaida joined the group, and we were both invited to attend a meeting with a delegation from Aleppo. We took Ghamr and Taim with us to the meeting at their house in Jaramana, more than twenty-five miles from where we lived. We discussed the use of violence at length, from all different angles, and I agreed with those who thought being drawn into civil war would end up doing a great favor to the regime. Destroying a broad coalition of civil society was exactly what they wanted. Nonviolence was not the Aleppo delegation's preferred strategy, but we all agreed on the need to give aid to those displaced from their homes, neighborhoods, or cities. Some thought this might lead to an opening and, ultimately, victory. "After all," they said with conviction, "we're doing what's right." But the conclusion I'd already come to, although I was reluctant to say it out loud, was that charity was not something we were choosing from a list of possible actions. Demonstrating compassion was our *only* option.

When we got home, I found the lock of the front door broken and lying on the ground. Entering our home cautiously and then turning on the light, the first thing I realized was that our laptop was missing from its place on the dining table. Panic seized us. When the Syrian uprising started, I withdrew all our money from the bank and converted it into sixty-five hundred American dollars, our life savings. Rufaida had hidden the money in a clothes drawer. Now we saw a sign of impending disaster on the floor: a manufacturer's tag off a pair of leather gloves a friend had sent Rufaida from Montreal. The gloves were put in the drawer where the money was hidden, sixty-five green banknotes stuffed into a white sock in the second drawer. My face was pale with fear as she pulled open the drawer and reached in. Were we to become very poor again? I could feel Rufaida's relief as she pulled out the bulging sock and showed it to me. We exchanged a kiss and smiled.

At first I was afraid the mukhabarat had broken into the house and taken my computer, but I quickly abandoned that idea. They could enter any house any time they wanted and take me as well as my laptop. The mukhabarat don't steal gloves. They steal the ones who wear the gloves.

In 2011, all of Damascus got to know the woman with the red cloak. She held up a poster in front of the parliament building that read, *Stop the killing. We want to build a nation for all Syrians.* It was posted all over international media. Her name was Rima Dali, and she was arrested along with passersby who had tried to defend her. After their arrest, other people holding *Stop the killing* posters distributed flowers to passersby, and many of them were arrested too. Rima and others were soon released, but by mid-2012, prisoners were no longer released after days, weeks, or even months. Once again it was the case that those entering prison were lost and those finally coming out were newborns, like me, afraid of the world.

In August 2012 the Shabbiha arrested a friend, Zaki Cordello. He is a well-known playwright, theater director, and actor. They also arrested his son, Mihyar; his brother-in-law, Adel Barazi; and a friend, Ismail Hammoudeh. Since then the regime has refused to give their families any news of them. I mention them here not only because of the injustice but also because Syria lost a true theatrical innovator, who started a unique project in Syrian theater.

Toward the end of 2011, Bassam Jawhar visited our home. He was a former prisoner, arrested for being a member of the Communist Labor Party, and an army officer before his arrest. After his release he worked in a small shop in the city of Homs, and when the demonstrations started up there, he joined in enthusiastically. However, Sunni friends among the demonstrators advised him to leave the neighborhood. Because he came from an Alawite family, they said, he was at risk of being killed by opposition militants.

As Rufaida and I and other guests to our home listened intently, he told us, "At one rally, a demonstrator realized I was Alawite from my accent. Like someone from the mukhabarat, he grabbed hold of me and demanded, 'What are you doing in this demonstration?' I found myself surrounded by teenagers carrying knives. I told them my name and said I'd been in prison for more than a decade because of my opposition to the regime. The young man who'd accosted me now announced that I was one of the good Alawites, and the knives disappeared. The people in my mostly Alawite village had a different opinion of me being one of the good ones," the bewildered Bassam added. "Most of them believed all Alawites must be pro-regime, and so someone wrote 'The Traitor Bassam Jawhar' on the side of our house. Their attitudes hardened even more after my nephew, a university student in his final year, and my sister's husband, a man in his sixties, were both killed by opposition gunmen for being Alawite."

And then he added sadly, "It's all very complicated . . . and it got more so. Now it was the Alawites' turn to escalate the violence. They indiscriminately arrested three young Sunni men at a Shabbiha checkpoint and assassinated them in retaliation for the killing of my relatives. In the mourning tent, I was still treated with contempt by the Alawites of my village. They still insisted I was an ally of the Sunnis who murdered my own nephew and brother-in-law. My father advised me to leave, so here I am."

Bassam was right about the situation being complicated. It was also nonsensical, absolutely stupid, to those who had the ability to think outside their emotions. Despite the fact that there were more Sunni Shabbiha who supported the regime in Aleppo and Deir ez-Zor, the militia was still seen as an Alawite force — because most of the Shabbiha in the cities of Damascus, Homs, Latakia, and Baniyas were from Alawite families. But in most other places they weren't. Still, the practice of defining people according to their religious identity gathered momentum, and much of the public bought into this destructive attitude.

My worst fears that the war would take a sectarian turn and look like a conflict between Sunnis and Alawites were coming true. It also became obvious to me that the next step in Syria's descent into hell would be a parallel war pitting all Arabs against Kurds, while the separate Arab groups kept fighting among themselves. But I also saw how some benefited from a wartime environment. The government paid for the Shabbiha, who were just gangs whose main objective was stealing loot. Opposition forces, on the other hand, would work together to win an area from the regime, then fight each other over whose leader could become the local emir. And even when an emir rose to prominence, from either the pro- or anti-regime sides, some up-and-coming radical would plot to have his followers kill the new emir and take the number one position for himself.

These scenarios were happening on both sides, but sadly for the opposition, which had started as the Free Syrian Army under Lieutenant Colonel Hussein Harmoush, it transformed over time to something mostly manned by Muslim Brothers and other Islamic organizations. And to fund all this, and more importantly, to line the emir's pockets, the followers of these warlords committed crimes like kidnapping and extortion, murder for hire, gun running, prostitution of their defeated enemy's daughters, and more.

Pockets were lined, and, with great callousness, the emirs sacrificed their own men. ISIS held a portion of the country in which its oil fields lay, and they entered into a contract with al-Assad, the enemy, to sell the regime the oil it needed to keep its war machine running. ISIS fighters were dying — sold out by their own leaders.

All of us, citizens and radical fighters alike, weren't just doomed by our hope and delusions. We were doomed by those who possessed the most brutal weapons and the willingness to use them.

On the roads leading to the center of Qudsaya, the number of pro-regime checkpoints increased. This indicated to the fighters of the local opposition forces, like my vegetable seller al-Doumani, that the regime was closing in. Opposition forces began to exchange fire with government forces. Before I properly understood the developing situation, one day on my way to buy bread, I heard a bullet zip over me. Looking up I saw it had severed a taut black telephone wire, which then dropped onto my head. But I couldn't go back home without food. I hurried to the store and back home, realizing that at any moment, a bullet could find me. At night the darkness became a playground for bullets, and we'd all sit in our homes, away from the windows, wondering who was firing at whom. Was it a real battle, or terrorism practiced by the regime to let the residents of Qudsaya know what was in store for them?

One morning in summer 2012, I woke up and went out into our garden. Looking onto the street from the gate, I was surprised to see dozens of Shabbiha milling about, all neighbors who looked so different in their military uniforms with red armbands. Apart from three whom I knew to be of Sunni Circassian background, the rest were Alawite. As neighbors, I knew each and every one of them as good people. This included our shy neighbor

Semir, a construction worker. There was one man I hadn't seen before, a short, lively man in his fifties with a plaster cast on his arm. He seemed to be the militia leader and was shouting orders at his men. And when he was finished with that, he began to give orders to all the other, non-uniformed neighbors who, like me, were watching with curiosity from their gates.

"We will not be responsible for the death of anyone who comes out into the street," he cried. "Stay in your houses. Terrorists are infiltrating your neighborhood and these heroes will treat anyone in the street as an extremist." He paused for effect and added, "Understood?" He glowered at everybody and then sauntered away.

"What's going on?" I asked Semir.

"We're here to wipe out the terrorists in Qudsaya," he said nervously. "You'll see in half an hour. Keep the boys inside."

Huddled in our home, we heard a banging on our door. I went and there was an officer with a group of men holding a mortar and heavy boxes of ammunition. They wanted to climb onto our roof to fire down on west Qudsaya, since there was such a clear line of sight from there.

"No, please, my family is here. I don't want to draw fire on us."

Luckily, the officer didn't insist. It wasn't long before we heard helicopters overhead and then gunfire from small arms and medium weapons. The loudest noise was from the mortar that they ended up putting on top of a house owned by a member of the local Shabbiha. Apparently, regime soldiers poured into the downtown area, and opposition militants offered no significant resistance. Most of them had probably escaped the battle before it began, and there really hadn't been that many of them to start with. By midafternoon the battle for Qudsaya was over.

The whole of the following day we didn't hear a single shot, but standing on our roof we could see smoke rising from many houses and shops down below.

"Why did the Shabbiha have to do so much damage? There were so few opposition fighters," I wondered aloud to Rufaida as we watched. And if the damage done the day before wasn't enough, we saw with our own eyes the Shabbiha methodically looting buildings and then setting them on fire. In total, they put to the torch some twenty-five houses and fifty businesses. Overdoing the carnage showed the regime was serious about their slogan, "Al-Assad or we burn the country."

With houses and shops still smoldering below us, we then observed in disbelief as trucks loaded with stolen goods drove up the hill to the neighborhood where members of the Republican Guard, Bashar's private army, had homes. Many passed right by our house, and you could see the killers, arsonists, and thieves smiling and joking, acting as if they were coming home to their wives and children after an enjoyable sporting event. Having seen enough, I climbed down from the roof and went inside, while Rufaida stayed watching the scene below. A short time later some neighborhood women came to the door.

"Rufi is on the roof crying her eyes out," one said.

Suddenly a member of the local militia was standing in front of me. The women melted away.

"Is your wife in despair because terrorists are being wiped out?" he asked ominously. I stepped out into the street and saw Rufi standing defiantly on the roof, her face wet and angry.

"No, no," I said. "All the noise is just scaring her. I'll bring her down," and I left, not wanting to draw the attention of the militia to our politics.

"Make it quick!" the militiaman called.

"The militia is watching us," I said to Rufaida, pointing down to the soldier still watching us from the street. "We mustn't get arrested just because we can't hide our feelings. There are still useful things to be done. You've seen for yourself the hungry people you already deliver food to. It's even more important now. Yes, we must do all we can, but in a way that allows us to remain unseen. Do good, but don't be seen." And then I added for emphasis, "Imprisonment isn't an end in itself."

Finally back down on the ground, Rufaida looked at me again. "You and your old friends should be leading the opposition," she said.

I stared into her beautiful, accusing eyes. "To what end?" I asked.

She turned and went into the house. I was left remembering how enthusiastic I was when I was seventeen and began second-guessing myself. Had I become more cautious than I should be?

Members of the militia guarded the neighborhood at night. A group of them sat under the window of our new living room, the space in front of the two bedrooms that had been a courtyard when we first moved in. But through our hard work, we'd been able to afford to build a roof over it, transforming it into about 540 square feet of indoor living space.

Ghamr and Taim in the living room, which was a courtyard.

Rufaida and I have a big living room now.

Syrians in many areas of the country began to suffer from two different battles being imposed on them from opposite sides. The first was called the Battle of Liberation. This meant that when opposition fighters controlled a "liberated area," they were subjected to aerial bombardment from the regime, as well as bullets coming out of nowhere. The regime was also blockading the neighborhood, so food was difficult to come by. When food did get through, the men with guns seized it. Civilians got nothing. The second was called the Battle of Purification, which was when the regime's men drove out the opposition fighters and took control. During the "purification" and immediately after it, the Shabbiha ravaged the area, and looting became widespread. We found out later that the sellers of Qudsaya's stolen loot gave the markets they set up in neighboring Alsomariah insolent and derisive names like the Sunni Market, and Fruits of the Revolution Market, showing Alawite-led forces had overcome and defeated the Sunnis.

Two days after the storming of Qudsaya, I went down to the Jadat intersection, one of the main roads in and out of the community. There, sprawled at the side of the road, lay seven bloated and rotting corpses. A regime sniper wasn't allowing the bodies to be removed. It was a brutal measure meant to spread fear and hasten the subjugation of locals. The corpse closest to me was that of a man possibly in his fifties. On the ground,

Taim in front of a training place — the same place seven people were snipered. The area became very dangerous.

next to his hand, lay an old-fashioned doorknob. It was as if he were still trying to enter his home. Under that hand was a black plastic bag fluttering playfully in the breeze, a black flag of death.

Oh God, it's Abu Lateef!

The unkempt stall owner who liked to tousle my boy's hair and smiled with his yellow teeth was lying there bloating in the sun. His other hand was extended outward in the air, rigor mortis making it appear as if he'd just thrown the dice in a final game of backgammon. A stray cat crossed the road and looked dispassionately at the flies crawling over the bodies. And then the thought came to me. When I was a child, it seemed to me that covering the dead was not to hide the body, but to cover something called death itself. Seeing Abu Lateef and all the other monstrosities, I now knew differently.

These people were killed in the streets, some in front of their homes, by the snipers. But being inside was not a guarantee of safety. I learned that my red-headed chicken seller, Abu Muhammad, was killed inside his home. A stray bullet from one side or the other pierced his neck while he was sitting in his living room.

Over the next few weeks, photos started being posted on Facebook showing smiling fighters standing with one foot proudly on the corpses of their victims. A common caption below these photos was, "A dead pig." There were so many of these victorious-hunter pictures that it led to a glorification of military footwear. A female journalist was shown on a TV newscast kissing a boot she brought along especially for that purpose. Not long after, there was an unveiling ceremony for a statue of such a boot. It was an ugly, poorly sculpted piece of painted terra-cotta, a good three feet tall and garishly trimmed with silver-sequinned ribbon.

War is an amazing environment for the growth of moral decay.

The daily news that people shared online was further dispiriting.

"Regime snipers hunting people down in front of a communal oven killed barber Hayel al-Salamouni while he was riding home to his family on the back of a truck. He died instantly."

My boy's barber. A new, proud father.

"A religious opposition sniper went after a man who was accompanying his unveiled wife to the gynecologist. The man died, and his wife took bullets in both legs."

"There was a prisoner exchange last night. Opposition fighters returned a man kidnapped from the al-Arin neighborhood, so the seven al-Hameh bus passengers were released, along with their minibus and driver."

We had crossed the barrier of fear and found ourselves right where the regime wanted us. We were living squarely in a universe of terror populated with grotesque corpses lying in the streets where my children used to play.

Like many others, Rufaida and I and likeminded neighbors concentrated on where we could have an effect, securing food and shelter for people who had lost everything. Luckily, our home was just outside the area where bringing in food was forbidden. Some residents who were affected by this, and those whose homes were in the worst of the fighting, fled under heavy fire and had already spent their money to provide for their families. Some departed so quickly, they left their money behind. Others didn't have any in the first place.

CHAPTER 47

A CHECKPOINT BY BARADA RIVER

S ome months after the taming of Qudsaya, I was riding home in a minibus from a shopping trip in Damascus with my neighbors. Sitting in
the front passenger seat, next to the driver, I watched as we pulled off
the Beirut Road into a checkpoint right on the edge of the Barada River.
There was a cinderblock hut with a cement roof, an office where the soldiers could relax when they weren't busy. Or it could be used to carry out
detailed interrogations of suspicious people, and to call headquarters to
search computerized records for more information on them. On the walls
of the building were the posters spouting the threatening slogans that were
now everywhere, the most ominous ones being "Kneel or Starve" and
"Al-Assad or we burn the country."

We stopped behind another minibus, this one with a sign showing its destination was the town of al-Hameh. The regime had started a blockade of that
town, similar to what happened to west Qudsaya. Once again, they didn't
want any kind of aid coming in that could help the opposition fighters, and so
everybody was ordered off the bus for inspection.

The window by my seat was already open, so it was pleasant to feel the
cool breeze blowing off the river. But it also allowed me to see and hear
everything going on at the checkpoint. One by one I watched the passengers from the al-Hameh bus disembark with their possessions and huddle
together like sheep. The soldiers then began to search and question them,
pulling each out in turn from the flock.

I watched as one soldier with a prominent underbite approached a teenager whose mustache was just beginning to sprout on his upper lip.

"Stand up straight, animal," he ordered.

"I'm not an animal," the boy said.

The soldier smacked him hard on the face and then grabbed his arm and twisted it, forcing the boy to bend and turn. Then, with a practiced motion, the soldier slapped a handcuff on one of the youth's wrists and pulled the other behind his back, slapping on the other. The woman beside the boy began crying and pleading with the soldier.

"Please, brother, leave him alone, he's only young. God protect you and bring you back safe to your mother. Leave my son alone."

The soldier slapped the boy again. "He needs to be taught how to behave," he said, grabbing the chin of the boy whose lip was now bleeding.

Another soldier was searching a man who looked like an office worker in his thirties. Dressed in a dark gray sports jacket, a navy tie, and a white shirt, a loaf of bread rolled flat was found hidden under his shirt.

"What's this?" the soldier asked angrily.

"As you can see, a loaf of bread," the man said as calmly as he could.

"You know it's forbidden to bring food in."

"My pregnant wife needs food. Please, let me keep it, please. You're a decent man."

"Pregnant?"

"I swear to God she's pregnant."

"We're not responsible for people's sex lives," he said, as if he thought he was cracking a joke. And then with a smile, he threw the loaf into the river and carried on searching the man. From one pocket he took an envelope full of cash and from the other a mobile phone. He thrust the cash in the man's face. "What's this?"

"Money."

"Such a large amount? You're giving it to the terrorists."

"No, no. It's an advance I took from the company I work for. It's for my wife's hospital bills. She might need surgery."

"You're a liar. It's to finance terrorism." The soldier stuffed the money into his shirt pocket.

"I swear to God. Call my employer."

"Shut up!"

"I want to meet the person in charge here," the man said in a voice everyone could hear.

The soldier's eyes widened with anger, and he grabbed the man by his tie and yanked it down hard, forcing him to double over. And then he jerked him forward, forcing him to stagger toward the hut. As the man stumbled into the building, he was given a last kick to the neck, causing him to fall helplessly into the clutches of another soldier, who then slammed the door shut. The soldier with the money in his pocket now smiled and brushed off his hands, a job well done. He went back to the inspections.

A tall soldier wearing a black sweatband began interrogating an old man. The elder was bent over and wore a threadbare blue jacket reminiscent of the 1970s.

"What have you got on you, Hajj?"

"Nothing, nothing," the old man said. He was bent over with age, and it took effort for him to squint up at the soldier.

The soldier plunged his hand into the old man's jacket pocket and pulled out a small opaque bottle.

"What are these?" he said rattling it.

"Pills for my wife. She's got heart disease, high blood pressure, and even diabetes. Me, I just complain to God about my joint pain. I went to Damascus to get her pills. Old age is a journey, my son."

"Don't call me your son. You're taking medicine to the terrorists!"

"God forbid . . . what are you talking about?"

As the soldier opened the bottle and sniffed it, the old man craned his neck to look up at the younger man. "I kiss your feet," he begged. "I swear by God Almighty I don't have money to buy more pills for her. I swear I couldn't buy any for myself . . ."

The soldier threw the bottle into the river.

"Your pills want their freedom," another soldier said with a laugh.

"Maybe the frogs have high blood pressure," a third offered, pulling out another lamb from the flock.

The old man spread his palms and looked up at the sky.

"Oh God, take my soul back into your safekeeping," he said, tears falling from his eyes.

A sergeant came out of the hut and grimaced when he saw how a number of vehicles had driven off the highway and were lined up behind us.

"Allow that fucking minibus to go!" he shouted. "Lock the vehicles behind you, assholes." The commuters who had passed inspection, and hadn't annoyed the soldiers, were ordered back onto the al-Hameh minibus, which quickly drove off. The expectant father in the guard hut and the mother and teenager standing in the sun were all left behind. "The man complained that you took his money he needs for his pregnant wife," the sergeant said, his face close to his subordinate's. "Is that true?" he asked accusingly.

"What money are you talking about, sir?" the robber soldier asked, and then he smiled and winked. "They always accuse us, dirty terrorists." The sergeant smiled back.

Because my bus was going to an area already subdued by the regime, the soldiers just boarded our bus and checked our ID, looking closely between the pictures and our faces. As we drove off, I turned and saw the mother soothing the face of her terrified boy. He looked barely older than Ghamr.

Shortly after I arrived home, the phone rang. When I lifted the receiver, the angry voice of a man barked into my ear. "I'll teach you what it means to be sympathetic to terrorists. The time will come when you and your wife will long for death." And then the receiver was slammed down, leaving me with only the droning of the dial tone.

"Who was that?" Rufaida asked.

"A man making threats. His number didn't show up on the screen. Maybe he was from the mukhabarat."

"Why was he making threats?"

"He said we were sympathetic to terrorists."

There's this neutral look people have in their eyes when they haven't decided how to react to a situation. Rufaida and I were staring at each other in this manner when Ghamr and Taim came home for lunch.

We greeted them as they put down their school bags, and I looked at my wife. We silently agreed not to say what had just happened. As lunch was put on the table and we began our meal, we chatted to the boys about school and about the roadblocks they had to navigate on the way home. After lunch I put a question to the older Ghamr.

"There's a boy of your age. His parents have a car accident and don't come home. What would you advise him to do?"

"What's his name?"

"Deeb."

"I'd be upset for him but wouldn't say anything."

"Okay. Let's suppose your mother and I have a car accident and are taken to hospital and you don't know where we are. What would you do?"

"I'd look for you. And bring you food in the hospital."

"If I were you, I'd contact your grandfather's house and tell them my mother and father haven't come home. Do you know how to get there with your brother?"

"Of course I do."

"Good."

With the threatening voice from the phone still ringing in my ears, I tried to overcome my fear and prepare my little ones for terrifying possibilities I hoped would never happen.

CHAPTER 48

TELEPHONES RINGING,
PEOPLE DYING

I associate the ringing of a phone in the early morning hours with that distant dawn when we didn't have a phone. I was six. That's when I woke up
to hear my cousin Bahir's distressed voice speaking to my mother from just
a few feet away, from the thin, handmade mattress my brother Kamal and I
were sleeping on. My only other sibling at the time, Asmahan, six months old
then, was sleeping next to my parents' mattress in the family cradle originally
made for me.

"She's dead, Auntie. Kawthar's dead," Bahir said. Kawthar was my beautiful twenty-year-old cousin.

Because we were all sleeping in the same room, I could see my mother
jump to her feet. She stood confronting Bahir, as if defiantly ordering him to
take back such despicable words would make them untrue. "What are you
saying?" she shouted. I had never seen her near hysterics.

I got out of bed and stood beside my mother, rubbing my eyes. My head
swiveled between her and Bahir as they talked. I felt Kamal, three years my
junior, take my hand as he watched.

"The bus hit her, Auntie," Bahir explained. "It killed her."

I'd never seen a bus in my life and imagined it was a kind of wild animal,
like a hyena or a wolf.

My mother and father rushed to my uncle's house less than half a mile
away. Mama held Asmahan close to her, and my brother and I followed, our
little legs pumping furiously in the early morning dawn. I was curious to see

my first dead person, but it didn't happen. The women were crowded around the coffin, wailing and crying, and my mother joined their noisy commiseration. Kamal started crying too. I tried to make him stop, but when this failed, I joined in.

At dawn in the middle of April 2011, I received an anonymous message on my cell phone: "Regime soldiers have opened fire on the sit-in in Clock Square in Homs. Dozens killed." The next morning the foreign news agencies also talked of dozens of civilians killed and of blood still staining the square. I then received a message from Syriatel, the telecommunications company owned by Bashar al-Assad's cousin Rami Makhlouf. This news feed assured me that the watchful eye of the security services would protect the country from those conspiring against it. Milad Salim, a friend from Syria Pulse, the secular relief movement, told me the number of deaths was going up after the battle due to the lack of available blood for transfusions. Or, more accurately, a lack of empty blood bags for taking the life-saving gift to wounded victims. Anyone trying to bring in medical supplies was arrested at government checkpoints for attempting to give aid to the enemy. Blood bags were now considered to be more dangerous than weapons or illegal street drugs.

The phone rang at dawn on July 30, 2011. My brother-in-law, Emil, was on the line.

"I'm sorry to wake you up, Jamal," he apologized.

"Who died?" I asked bluntly. Emil seemed taken aback for a moment.

"May you live long," he said. He added softly, "It's your brother Kamal. He'll be buried today."

I sat bolt upright. "But . . ." I didn't know what to say next. Perhaps it was an expression of helpless protest against the power of death. My brother-in-law waited as the word hung in the air. "We'll be there," I said.

I hung up the phone and looked into Rufaida's large, beautiful eyes. I could tell she was expecting the worst. When I told her about Kamal, she burst into tears and held on to me as if, once again, it was our last embrace.

We sat in the kitchen, Rufaida preparing breakfast before our journey to Kfarieh, and me sipping coffee, smoking — and remembering. Suddenly

I was back in my father's orchard when I was seven and Kamal was four. Together we were collecting stones to make a small hill under the lowest branch of the single peach tree in my father's orchard. I stood on the mound and picked a peach, offering it to Kamal. But he refused the fruit, insisting he must pick one for himself. And so we collected more stones, and soon he was standing on tiptoes, twisting a ripe peach away from its branch all by himself. His face beamed and at that moment he looked like the happiest and proudest creature on earth.

He can't remember any of that now.

My aunt said that the souls of the dead remember all the little details of their lives and hover above those who love them. I liked the idea, and it made me smile, but I didn't believe it. Death seemed to me an impertinence and one of the worst laws of the universe. But Kamal himself had once told me, "Life is just a road to death. All our roads lead there."

A few days earlier, my sister Asmahan had phoned to say my brother had been taken to hospital with pains in his chest and shortness of breath. They didn't know what the problem was, and neither did the doctors. But he was young and strong, the call had come in the afternoon, not the early morning, and Asmahan asked me not to be anxious, so I presumed he'd be home in a couple of days. Then I'd go and visit Kamal while he convalesced, and, like so many times before, we'd sit together under the mulberry tree and play chess. And like so many times when we'd challenged each other to a game before, our mother would come out with food and expect us to stop playing. But we would wave her away, insisting on silence. And as always, she'd complain that brothers who didn't see each other often should be talking, not staring wordlessly at a board.

"Mama, please. Not now," one of us would say, and she'd go back into the house in a huff.

Kamal and I were about even in our ability to play the great game, and we took our wonderful, ongoing rivalry very seriously. It was only after one defeated the other that we would start speaking and smiling at one another again. And then we'd have to coax our mother back out with the food.

"Mama, I'm so hungry, Mama," Kamal called the last time we played out this script.

"I think he's dying of hunger, Mama," I shouted, laughing. "Hurry."

Mama appeared with the food, feigning anger at first, then she kissed us both, and we all sat together and ate. Now none of this could happen. Kamal was dead. But death is never satisfied. It eats us all.

The doctors said my brother died of pneumonia, but to this day we don't know how he got it. But during those days many others were dying too. Shots fired directly into crowds of demonstrators and the aerial bombardment of towns and cities were turning death into a routine occurrence. Mass deaths from shooting and bombing were more serious than my brother's death, but I mourned for Kamal in a different way, with a sorrow linked to something deep within me. I hadn't made a hill of stones to pick a peach with anyone but him.

I took a last sip of my coffee and stubbed out my cigarette as Rufi put breakfast on the table. And then I suddenly thought of my friend al-Harith al-Nabhan. He was another comrade who had done a lot of prison time and was going to visit me that evening. And so I contacted him to tell him I wouldn't be at home, explaining I had to go to the village to attend my brother's burial.

"Wait for me, I'm coming with you," al-Harith replied.

We went in his car to the village and arrived before my brother was buried. I looked at Kamal, expecting that by some miracle he would greet me. He seemed annoyed by the white gauze over his head and face. The miracle didn't happen, and we lowered him into the grave. We threw earth on him and left him alone, as we always do with our dead, and we went back home. The next day I asked my father about the peach tree. He said it had died long ago.

I usually came back to Kfarieh with the family twice a year, at Eid and summer vacation. This would be the third time this year I'd see my remaining siblings. Khadijah, my second mother, had died of lupus, so with Kamal now gone, there were just eight of us. Asmahan, who had lived underground for eleven years, now owned an optical store with her husband, Emil. Ahmad and Yousef, the twins, still looked so alike and insisted on playing tricks on my father, since he couldn't tell them apart. Mahmoud, the tallest, was always so calm. Iyad, the practical one, loved dogs. He's always had one. My little sister, Rosa, the beauty, and Fedil, the most handsome of us brothers. We were all there.

"There are seven. The death took Khadijah and Kamal, prison and exiles took you," my mother told me on the phone.

Demonstrations continued all over the country, but travel between cities was no longer safe. I stayed in the village for a week, receiving people who came offering their condolences. We also talked anxiously about our concerns for the country, everyone trying to answer the question, "Where are we going?"

"I can't support violence," I said. "Even though I think we should understand its causes and consequences."

"So how would you respond to shots aimed at your heart?" challenged my friend Rami.

"Jamal preaches satyagraha, nonviolent resistance in a jungle of weapons," Sami teased. "Death in the manner of Gandhi or Martin Luther King."

"John F. Kennedy had an arsenal and was no pacifist," I argued, "but he couldn't defend himself."

"Nonviolence . . . that's a utopian idea," Rami said disparagingly.

"It's better to have a utopian idea than blood on your hands," I continued to protest.

"History isn't made with morals and good intentions," Sami said, now serious.

"So . . ." I commented, "if politics lack morals, let us bring morality into politics. Why do people separate the two? Why do they consider this separation normal?" This mini-diatribe garnered me looks that suggested I was being naïve in the extreme.

"This discussion is futile," concluded Sami.

But even though I couldn't properly describe the reasons to my friends and other mourners, my rejection of violence grew more intense after the regime massacred more of its own citizens in Homs, Baniyas, and the countryside around Damascus. And the number of deaths increased as more people took part in demonstrations. The scenes shown on satellite channels of people in handcuffs lying in al-Bayda Square in Baniyas were ones among many that made clear to the world the extent of the regime's barbarity. Some people began wanting us to issue a call to arms, but I didn't agree with them. I had been subjected to violence for more than a decade in prison and I realized that to take revenge would make me like one of the barbarians. I remember that whenever I did have violent fantasies against this guard or that officer, I'd lie in my cell and think of Nelson Mandela. As a boy my grandfather's honesty made the villagers respect his word; they went to him to resolve disputes.

"Being moral makes you the winner," he repeated to his sons and grandsons.

Putting aside that I was becoming more pacifist, even from a pragmatic perspective we had to reject a call to arms, not because I didn't want those bastards in power to be sentenced, but because the opposition fighters, who were supposed to be fighting for us, were actually preying on us. On the other hand, it was clear to me that the regime was too strong to resist militarily, with its equipment, an organized army, and its militias, like the Shabbiha, unless the soldiers refused to carry out the orders and moved to the other side to protect the demonstrators.

In the early morning of August 4, 2013, I once again woke to the sound of the phone ringing. I picked up the receiver, expecting news of death. My friend, the poet Talal Salim, was on the other end.

"Please, my whole family . . . my father, my mother, my brothers, my wife, my children . . . all of them."

"Talal, calm down. What's going on?"

"All killed or kidnapped. Armed men attacked the summer home in the village. Jamal, I'm telling you, all of them. There's not one left."

"How do you know?"

"He called me. He called. I'm in Damascus and was getting ready to go to work. He said all of them . . . all of them."

"Calm down, Talal. Who called you?"

"My brother, Maher. He told me my father and two brothers were killed. They even killed my blind aunt, Nesiba. And they kidnapped my wife, Awatif, and my children — Loujain, Hanin, Jawa, Wajd . . . they were kidnapped from the village. And they were taken by our own opposition fighters. Please, maybe you could find somebody in the opposition leadership to help free my children. I'm going to Latakia in a few minutes to be closer. Maybe I can find out more."

"Talal, be careful. Keep in touch. Let me know immediately if there's any news."

When I hung up the phone, Rufaida was standing beside me, her face again showing she expected the worst from another early morning call. I explained and she began to sob. Rufaida cries if the wind flattens flowers in the garden, so you can imagine her reaction to the death and kidnapping of friends.

I got to know Talal when his first collection of poems, *Let's Sit in the Rain*, was published by al-Tali'a. The book's happy title told you everything about the man. His wonderful poems caught my attention, and our friendship began. Al-Tali'a published two of his books. He had a little shop in Damascus, where he sold makeup and perfume, and an old family summer house in the village of Balluta, about ten miles from my parents. He invited us there in summer 2010, and our families got to know each other. Like many other properties in the area, his house had a small apple orchard out front, and I felt quite content and familiar walking about. Apples I knew. Back in Damascus, Talal used to visit me from time to time, and we talked mostly about Arabic poetry.

I sent the following long text on Messenger to a number of opposition activists and leaders about Talal's family and others, describing the crimes perpetrated by opposition forces who were supposed to be protecting the people. I got word that the message was forwarded many times, so it was widely circulated.

"The battle to liberate the coast, or the Battle of Aisha, Mother of the Believers, is a series of crimes against women, children, and old men. What happened in this battle is no less despicable than the crimes of the regime. The missing are still being counted, but the number includes more than one hundred women and children, and the death toll is more than two hundred, including more than sixty women, about twenty elderly men, and fifteen children. I hope we can work together for the release of the kidnap victims, including the children of the poet Talal Salim — Loujain, Hanin, Jawa, Wajd — and his wife, Awatif."

The next morning, in a report broadcast on Al Jazeera, a photo showed opposition fighters helping an old woman. Talal told me later that this woman was found slaughtered only several feet away from where she was photographed.

The Al Jazeera satellite channel also showed a short video of opposition leader Brigadier General Salim Idris walking through agricultural land in a village in the Sahel Mountains. With this peaceful scene as his backdrop, he spoke about the battle to liberate the Sahel, the Mediterranean coastal region. He gave assurances to the local people that the Free Syrian Army would not violate their honor as the regime's army had done. Because I'd heard what happened from those fleeing the area, and from the relatives of the dead and kidnapped, the man seemed merely to be a media shield for the crimes carried out by the opposition fighters who were not under the control of the Free Syrian Army. Many had presumed the different groups would work under the central command of proper military officers, but the ex-regime officers ended up as just another competing faction. Over time, officers and enlisted soldiers who did have the country's best interests at heart were killed by their former colleagues in the military or their potential allies, joined one of the extremist groups, or fled for their lives. Lieutenant Colonel Hussein Harmoush, who organized the Free Syrian Army, fled to Turkey. But he was mysteriously kidnapped from inside Turkey after a meeting with Turkish intelligence and handed over to Syrian intelligence. He was most likely executed, but nothing is confirmed.

Atrocities continued on the other side of the conflict as well. Only seventeen days after Talal's phone call, hundreds of Syrians in the Ghouta area, just east of Damascus, were asphyxiated after the regime attacked them with chemical weapons. Among the dead were many children. After the attack, the regime agreed to a UN resolution to dismantle their chemical weapons facilities and hand over any remaining supplies under a joint American-Russian plan. But they didn't shy away from continuing to use every other weapon at their disposal to attack their own cities, towns, and villages. The regime used rockets, aircraft, helicopters, artillery, and tanks. They also let loose the resources and manpower of their own Shabbiha militias, militias from allied countries, and international jihadist groups. Many of these were not natural allies of al-Assad, but saw working with him as a stepping-stone to achieving their own long-term aims.

These militias came from all over the Middle East and beyond. On the regime's side, there were the Shia Hezbollah from Lebanon, Shia militias from Iraq like the Abbas Brigade and Asa'ib Ahl al-Haq, the Fatemiyoun Brigade from Afghanistan, the Zainabiyoun Brigade from Pakistan, and the Iranian Revolutionary Guard. They all came to Syria under the pretext of protecting the "holy shrines of the family of the Prophet," meaning the graves of the sons and grandsons of Ali ibn Abi Talib, and claimed through their slogans to be taking revenge for Hussein Ali ibn Abi Talib, the grandson of the prophet Muhammad, who was killed fourteen centuries ago.

Against the regime were al-Nusra Front, a branch of al-Qaida in Syria, and Daesh. There were also a number of miscellaneous Islamic organizations, supported by Turkey, Saudi Arabia, or Qatar.

And then local and supposedly pro-Syrian militias were created, all opposing both the regime and the militias from other countries. Their goal was to overthrow the regime and then establish an independent Islamic state, not under the control of outsiders. Interestingly, they were able to attract many of their fighters from a number of nations in Europe, the Americas, Asia, and elsewhere. Many of these recruits believed their own governments were complicit in anti-Islamic policies, and a great percentage of them had personally felt victimized by these prejudices at home.

But whoever any of these people were and wherever they came from, they all carried arms and began establishing different sorts of government in the areas they controlled. These were so-called caliphates, such as the city of Raqqa, some neighborhoods in east Aleppo, and some in east Ghouta, close to Damascus. I became convinced that my country was in the hands of competing savage predators, who were allies one day, enemies the next, and attracted each other like flies to a wound.

But when it came to kidnapping people for money, they were all much the same. Our opposition fighters had demanded huge sums from Talal for the release of his children, money he didn't have. In one of the telephone bargaining sessions, Talal asked to speak to his daughter Hanin.

"What's the point?" he heard Hanin say in the background. "Tell Dad that Mom and Loujain are dead." When Talal heard Hanin say his wife and older daughter were gone, he began to scream in sorrow. And those soulless beasts on the other end only used his distress as a lever to extort what they wanted from him. But there was no way he could beg, borrow, or sell what he had to meet their demands. His remaining three children were kept hidden somewhere in the northern hills of Syria until three years later, when two were released in a prisoner exchange. It took another year for Hanin to make it back into her father's arms in a similar trade.

During that time the regime's Russian helicopters started dropping barrel bombs — cylinders filled with explosives, shrapnel, oil, or chemicals — on schools, hospitals, and neighborhoods. It was a relatively cheap but effective weapon, especially as the opposition didn't have any air power to counter their attacks. This is when I no longer had the slightest hope that my country was on its way to join the modern era. What I could see was that we citizens were all destined to be fuel for a civil war, helping international players fulfill their own power-play aspirations, and the smaller regional warlords to profit by convincing their followers to kill, rape, steal, and extort for them.

CHAPTER 49

MY FAMILY ALMOST KIDNAPPED

Every time I looked at Ghamr and Taim, I pictured that our country had been transformed from my old vision of the schizophrenic mother killing her children to a dreadful ghoul purposely kidnapping people for sale and misuse. I boiled like a volcano when the boys were late home from school or from the karate club at the crossroads. It was a hobby that gave them some sense of childish joy, but I was a father in a country at war.

To get to school, the boys took a minibus that picked them up at the house and took them right to their classes. But the fighters didn't distinguish between homes and schools, civilian adults or children. They had no respect for anything that wasn't them.

After all, they killed the chicken seller Abu Muhammad when he was sitting on a chair at home.

And sometimes Ghamr and Taim would be late because of the roadblocks.

The soldier manning the roadblock might insult and beat them, like they beat the boy going to al-Hameh with his mother. What's the use of going to school?

"I'm not sending them to school tomorrow," I'd finally shout at the ceiling, and then I'd hear the door opening and I'd rush over and kiss my sons, smiling at them with my eyes still glistening with tears.

When we heard the sound of gunfire, at first Taim hid in our bed and pulled the cover over his head. As time went on, and there came to be different kinds of bombs producing a greater range of explosive sounds, Taim grew accustomed to noise and began recognizing what ordinance was being employed. He grew bolder, going outside to see where the action was, often climbing up onto the roof of our house or that of the abandoned building close by. Afraid he could become a target for snipers, I always ran after him and forced him to come back inside. Our older son, Ghamr, reacted differently to the sound of the fighting. He sat playing with his Xbox hour after hour, hardly flinching as the air and ground shook around him. His only outburst came when the electricity was cut off. But being a planner, he'd always have his PlayStation Portable charged and ready.

One night in 2013 a terrific explosion rocked our house like an earthquake. The chair I was sitting on careened around the room, the ceiling light swung back and forth like a pendulum, and the windows shattered in the house next door. Taim woke up and went to go outside to see what was happening, but I stopped him. Ghamr came toward me, holding back tears, his lips trembling.

"Dad," he begged, "you have to find a place for us to live away from these explosions." That's when I looked around and saw that Taim had disappeared. "At school they said the safest place to be during shelling is the bathroom," Ghamr added.

"Go there with your mother. I'll get Taim."

As the sounds of shelling and explosions began to move into the distance, we ended up sitting in the living room, where I kept Ghamr close to me. But then I reached for my laptop and, with my son watching, I searched online for the contact information of ICORN, the International Cities of Refuge Network, an agency that connects writers and artists at risk with sponsors in other countries. As we continued to hear the sounds of explosions echo up the hill, I emailed them to ask if they could secure a place of shelter for me and my family, describing what had been happening the last while.

The next afternoon, with the night's chaos behind us, we were all sitting in the garden when we saw that one of Taim's cats had given birth to four kittens. She seemed to sense the danger around her family and was carrying her babies to a hidden spot. We watched in fascination as, one by one, she took her precious offspring in her mouth and disappeared under the thick branches of a yellow jasmine bush. We looked at each other and my children's eyes seemed to ask, "Am I worth less than one of those kittens?"

I resigned from my job with Asda'a. They were a very good employer, but with everything going on around us, fighters roaming the streets, me needing to watch over the boys, dealing with frequent power blackouts, I wanted my time to be more flexible. Meeting Asda'a's deadlines, although they were always reasonable, might distract me from responding quickly to an emergency. And honestly, I had lost all enthusiasm for writing where the prime objective was to praise every international trend in fashion and promote the best of multimillion-dollar modern corporations, restaurants, and cafés. These could only be seen in places such as Dubai and Abu Dhabi, and I simply couldn't relate to such things anymore, especially with Syrians dying and disappearing daily. Instead, I began translating the book *Postwar: A History of Europe Since 1945*, by British historian Tony Judt. It is a huge book of more than 450,000 words. I signed a lump sum buyout contract and was paid in installments. Fortunately, payment was in US dollars, and a friend living near the publisher in Beirut agreed to pick up the money. He could then get it to me in such a fashion that I would keep it all. This was the only way my family could eat. In Syria the banking system was rigged so that all money transfers being converted into Syrian pounds allowed the regime to take 70 percent of each transfer's value. They claimed the conversion rate they set was to keep the currency stable, but that was just an excuse. It's changed since then. Now the regime steals only half.

Having a more flexible timetable also allowed me to become more active in local relief efforts. But I kept this to myself and a few seasoned neighbors who had been through similar experiences with the regime. These were people I knew could keep a secret under pressure. Even though Rufaida had been criticizing me for not being active locally, I decided it was best that she not know the extent of what I did, in case she was ever interrogated. I was following my own advice, "Do good, but don't be seen" — in this instance, not even by my own wife. Sometimes, when I had more donations in hand than I could disburse at the moment, I would pass them on to Rufaida. When she asked where they came from, I'd just nod with a smile and walk away. This was a discipline I'd learned from being part of a banned political party and also from having to keep secrets in jail, even under torture.

One day I went to the town of Qudsaya for shopping with my niece. Raghad was a lovely, innocent child of ten. Her dark piercing eyes and bright smile were framed by an equally beautiful mane of black wavy hair. Raghad didn't wear a hijab at the time.

Over a year, since the regime attacked, the number of long beards in Qudsaya had again increased and, over time, as they became more confident, the hair on their upper lips decreased, so that they had an identifiable jihadi appearance. Raghad and I were wandering, hand in hand, when we stopped at the vegetable stall, where I'd been buying produce since my previous favorite, al-Doumani, had disappeared. When I saw the new vendor approach me, I waved and happily called out to him.

"Assalamu aleykum. I don't see the tomatoes."

"Aleykum assalam. You will find them, inshallah," he said with a smile, and then he looked at Raghad. His smile vanished. It was obvious he didn't like the idea that Raghad's hair wasn't covered.

"Is she your daughter?" he asked seriously.

"No, she is my niece," I replied. He nodded.

"We must do what satisfies Allah," he said and turned away abruptly. While he was gone to fetch more tomatoes, I looked under his bench, to check the Kalashnikov was where he usually hid it. The fellow returned, still scowling, with a fresh box of tomatoes.

"You were asking for these," he said

"Yes, thanks."

When we got home Rufaida could tell something was bothering me.

"Raghad, Ghamr, Taim, would you like to water the flowers and feed the cats in the garden?" I said, and when the children went out, I explained to Rufaida what had happened and how I thought the religious extremists were becoming more confident and aggressive.

"You're over-cautious. I never have any trouble in the market. Nobody's ever bothered me."

"Rufaida, you can't be too careful. The town has changed; they want women to wear hijab in their area. It is a kind of ID now. Without hijab they think you're Alawite or a spy, or a stranger who has to be watched."

"The other month I asked a fighter I know if I should be worried about helping displaced people there and he gave me his number. He said to phone him right away if I have any trouble. And, Jamal, I have to go there to look after the refugees. There are more than ever."

"Rufaida, things change in a dramatic way," I said. "Rufi, please . . ."

That was the last time I went to Qudsaya Square, but I couldn't change my wife's mind.

A few days later, Rufaida took Ghamr and Taim to Qudsaya. She wanted to buy vegetables and deliver some relief money to a displaced woman whose home had been burned down in another town. Waiting for them, I was a toy in the hands of anxiety. I couldn't concentrate on my translation work. I jumped up and went out when I heard the front gate slam. Though Rufaida and the boys were there, I didn't feel reassured. Rufi's eyes were restless, and the two boys seemed troubled.

"What's happened?" I asked.

"We have a story to tell," Rufaida answered with a sad voice.

I made Turkish coffee and sat with Rufaida in the kitchen. We were silent for a while. She was so sad.

When I couldn't wait anymore, I asked again, "What happened?"

"I was giving the aid money to the woman near Qudsaya Square, and over her shoulder I noticed a young man with a black keffiyeh. He was standing in front of the Rizma store, watching us," Rufaida explained. "I sensed he was staring at my uncovered hair. He thought I was Alawite, I guess." She lit a cigarette and had a sip of coffee.

"And then?" I asked.

"I could see his eyes following the woman's hand as she hid the envelope in her handbag. And as she left, he continued to watch her." Tears sprang to Rufi's eyes, but she continued: "Then he passed close by me and muttered a few words in my ear."

"What did he say?" I asked, apprehensive.

"He said, 'I ask God to end your life today.' Then Taim said, 'Mama, there's more than one man watching us.' The man started backing away slowly. I turned around and saw another guy staring hard at me and the boys. 'He started to walk toward us,' Taim told me, 'and the one who spoke to you

Samira Khalil with Rufaida during the wedding party at Rufaida's house. Samira Khalil is currently missing after being abducted in Douma in December 2013. Her husband confirmed that she was kidnapped by Jaish al-Islam militia.

signaled for him to wait.' Jamal, I looked at them and I almost went crazy. Suddenly, all I could see in my mind were Samira and Razan."

Samira Khalil and Razan Zaitouneh were good friends of ours who were kidnapped with Wael Hammada, Razan's partner, and Nazem Hammadi in December 2013, only five months earlier. No one has heard from them since.

"And then I took the boys and rushed back to the bus. When I looked back at first, they seemed to be following us," Rufaida said. "But halfway to the bus stop, they disappeared. I think they decided to go after my client and the money. At the bus stop, my phone rang, and it was her number. But all I could hear was street noise. Jamal, do you think she's been kidnapped, and those guys have my cell phone number now?"

"It's possible," I answered.

"You were right, Jamal," Rufaida continued. "Things are getting worse. What kind of trauma would the boys have if they were kidnapped or saw their mother kidnapped in the street? I feel so guilty having exposed them to that."

We later found out that when Rufaida's client realized she was being followed, she hurried back to her building and called somebody. But she redialed Rufaida by mistake. This meant the religious radicals didn't have Rufaida's cell phone number. Luckily, we didn't pay a lot for this lesson; those two armed men were either incompetent or it was their first attempt at kidnapping and theft. But we couldn't depend on such luck the next time.

"We have to be more careful," I said calmly, wiping Rufaida's tears. She nodded.

That night, I couldn't sleep, and I sat in the garden with my tobacco.

Kidnapping had become so normalized that offices had been opened in Homs to coordinate the release and exchange of kidnap victims, the corrupt owners charging a commission for their services. Ugly thoughts spun around in my head. What if one of my family was taken? Whether the kidnapper was a supporter of the regime or an opponent, or just a gang member whose only concern was money, we wouldn't have found anyone to defend us, except our comrades, whose only strength lay in their morals and ideas, which had become objects of ridicule for those who carried arms.

What's keeping me and my family in this country? I wondered. I thought of the continual threats from the mukhabarat on my cell phone. Am I going to stay here until one of us is kidnapped or arrested? I must secure a place of refuge before the axe falls. I don't want to be sitting in a prison cell thinking about what my two little ones are going through and being tormented by a longing to see them.

The next morning, Rufaida and I took steps.

CHAPTER 50

PASSPORTS AND VISAS

I n 2011, Rufaida and I had Facebook accounts. Mine was available only to friends, while Rufaida's was quite public. This was an issue she and I had discussed more than once since she was being blatantly critical of the regime. But even with my precautions, in 2011 I found myself almost paralyzed with fear, waiting for intelligence agents to break into my house and take me away.

"Jamal, are you a fool?" a friend had asked me earlier that day.

"What do you mean?"

He explained that he had watched in horror as my name and Facebook page, along with a post I had written about the crimes of the regime, were broadcast on Al Arabiya TV, a Saudi-owned station in Dubai. Apparently, a Facebook friend copied and pasted one of my "private" posts and sent it to them. But the mukhabarat didn't appear. At the time, there were millions of Syrians on Facebook, and so I guess the regime couldn't watch every Facebook user.

This is probably why Rufaida and so many others supposed that posting their criticisms of the regime on Facebook was a reasonable risk. At the time, most Syrians believed we would be the next country to get rid of their authoritarian regime, as the people of Tunisia and Egypt had done. By 2013, the hopes of peaceful civilians in Syria for reform had faded.

During the first year of the Syrian revolution, and because of the critical posts Rufaida was writing back then, a Syrian businessman had sent us both Facebook friend requests, to connect formally, so we'd see each other's posts and could exchange information and ideas. We never responded because of the suspicions we had about him. He was the son of a long-serving former government official whose name opened many doors for him. For me, that meant he was part of the whole machine of corruption, the reason we ignored his requests for several months.

However, while I was still working at al-Tali'a Publishing House, I saw how this man had given grants to a few Syrian writers and poets so they could have their works published. Some even published with us. Rufaida also learned through her relief work that he was sending aid to families who had been displaced and helping get supplies to areas the regime was trying to starve out. He also sent money to support a private non-faith school in an area controlled by the opposition in Aleppo. He even made public pronouncements calling for Syria to become a true democracy. As for his political ambitions, he said perhaps he might become a member of parliament, but that was all. Despite all this seemingly benevolent largesse, he was still suspect to me. But I guess it wasn't a ruse, as word came that this businessman had fled the country and declared his opposition to the regime. His old childhood friend, Bashar al-Assad, had put out a warrant for his arrest and soon after, in mid-2013, the Anti-Terrorism Court sentenced him to death. His substantial properties in Syria were confiscated. His private home was handed over to a Lebanese journalist who created huge amounts of propaganda on behalf of Bashar and his cronies. And so, finally, Rufaida and I accepted this fellow's invitation to become friends on Facebook. He and I then had several online conversations. During these chats he didn't deny that he had benefited in his work from his father's position, and in fact he repeated this openly on his own Facebook page. He also wrote defiantly that he would be willing to be tried in a fair court in a future free Syrian state.

Rufaida, Ghamr, and Taim had their kidnapping scare about a year after my first conversations with my new Facebook friend. This prompted Rufi and me to request an online video meeting with him, and it was during this conference that we asked him directly if he could help us get out of Syria. He said he could help us go to Dubai, so we asked if he could guarantee us jobs there and schools for the boys. I understood from him that I would be able to work at the Orient Research Centre and Rufaida could have a job as a translator at Northern Logistics. Plus, there was a well-developed education system in Dubai for the boys. Now we had a new and potentially insurmountable problem. I didn't have a passport.

While working as a production manager at al-Tali'a Publishing House, I applied for a passport. I wanted to go to book fairs, and visit cities like Cairo, Beirut, Baghdad, Casablanca, and others. Shortly after I submitted that request, the Military Investigation Branch in Latakia summoned me. Though I assumed it would be a routine thing, I was nervous approaching the building of a government agency where I had been violently treated. Nevertheless, I went to the place where I'd been imprisoned. There was no sign to say that it was a military establishment, but there were barriers known as Czech hedgehogs, made of heavy steel, that prevented the potential attack of any vehicle. And a huge picture of Hafez al-Assad above a heavy front door.

I tried to calm myself as I approached a sulking soldier with a plump body and big head. His shape reminded me of a strong mule. I told him that I had been summoned to the branch and gave him the paper when he requested it. He entered a small room near the main gate and used the phone. After about two minutes, a young man who was his complete opposite came. He was slim, elegant, and seemed very calm.

"Are you Jamal?" the slim guard asked with a smile.

"Yes." I smiled too.

"Follow me, please."

We stopped at a polished wooden door with a sign on it that read Branch President. The young soldier opened the door a crack.

"Jamal Saeed, sir," he said.

"Ah, wonderful. Bring him in."

That voice reminded me of him, the barbarian officer I had met before.

As the door to the office swung open, I saw Abd al-Muhsin Hilal. He had been promoted to brigadier general. I hadn't seen his face since I was a prisoner in the military investigation branch 235 about fifteen years earlier, when he was a colonel.

I was counting my little stones when I was isolated in cell number nine. I was just finishing the seventh pile of one hundred stones while taking stock of my inventory. When I heard the key click into the lock of the door, I pushed the stones under the very thin mattress of my small cell.

It's not lentil soup time. What do they want?

The door opened.

"Number nine. Come on," the soldier ordered. "Colonel Abd al-Muhsin Hilal wants to see you."

The soldier grabbed the Spanish bracelet from his belt.

"Your hands behind your back," he ordered.

"That won't be necessary," a voice said. That's the first time I saw the face of Colonel Hilal. We looked at each other. He stood there straight and relaxed, hands behind his back. His civilian clothes were expensive, but he was not elegant. His hair and mustache were neatly trimmed, with just the smallest hint of gray hair making him look distinguished. The soldier took his place by the wall and kept watch. "Jamal Saeed?" the colonel asked, making sure he had the man he wanted.

"Right, I'm Jamal Saeed," I answered, trying to keep calm and prepare for what hardship might come.

He stepped forward. "I know that you are a hero, and I like heroes," he whispered. "Number nine, I heard that you are a smart hero. Help me, please: are you Jamal or number nine?" He smiled. I could see that he was holding a three-foot-long wooden stick. "You have to answer. Who are you?" he said, louder. He raised the improvised cudgel over his head and smashed it down on my shoulder. "Are you dumb? I'll make you sing like a nightingale." My shoulder muscles spasmed.

He continued hitting me hard on my thighs, hands, and back.

When I said, "My name is Jamal," he continued beating.

"This is for number nine," he said, panting. "We can't hurt Jamal the smart hero." Was this entertaining to him? What I know is that I was in pain and had more pain ahead. The last blow of the plank was on my temple and I heard the thud on my skull. I screamed. He kicked me on the back, and I fell into my cell. My forehead hit the wall and I heard him order the guard, "Lock the chalet and let the hero relax."

A few days later, I was called out of the cell around noon. I was handcuffed and taken from my cell in the basement to an office on the first floor. My bruises were just starting to fade. The soldier squeezed my arm harder and walked me in, stopping in front of a very neatly organized desk. "The hero again! Ahlan wa sahlan," Hilal welcomed me. "Your beard needs to be shaved," he said with a laugh.

"So, number nine. Tell me about the printing and distribution of anti-government literature you were engaged in."

"I haven't been involved in printing against the government," I said.

"Let us begin." He started picking out the hairs of my beard with silver pliers, then he began to mash the skin of my neck between its jaws. He smiled more widely when my tears rolled down.

"Number nine. Tell me about the printing of anti-government literature you've been engaged in," he asked politely again.

"I . . . I . . . didn't . . ."

He went behind me and pressed the tip of my index finger between the pliers' jaws.

"Tell the truth. Don't lie," he shouted and clamped my nail harder.

The pain was unbearable. I fainted.

When I woke up, I was no longer in his office. The soldier was pouring water on me, and Hilal was hitting my face and neck with a piece of iron. Water mixed with the blood from my nose and the wounds of my face.

He asked the soldier to take me back to chalet nine and asked me to think hard about the printing details he needed to know.

The last time I saw Abd al-Muhsin Hilal in jail, I was again handcuffed and walking down the cellblock corridor with a guard. I was being taken to the dentist. As we passed Hilal, he stopped us.

"Where are you taking the hero?" I could tell he saw that my cheek was swollen.

"He's got a bad tooth, sir. He's going to get it pulled by the dentist."

"A dentist? No. I'll help him." Suddenly, he punched me over the swelling with all his might. I screamed, but he kept punching me all over my face. Repeatedly he beat me. He didn't stop until blood was streaming from both my mouth and nose. "Well, he's not as strong as I thought," he said sarcastically. "Take him to the doctor."

His eyes hadn't changed. He was now a bit heavier, his face lined, and his slightly graying hair and mustache were now dyed a dark black, an affectation of many older, powerful men in the Middle East. And now here he was, a brigadier general in charge of a whole branch, and here I was, once again standing in front of him, powerless. This wasn't some low-level functionary. He had asked specifically to see me. There could be only one reason.

"Come in, smart hero. Come in. Please, sit down."

I walked in slowly and took a seat in front of his desk. The only time I looked away from his eyes was to instinctively check the top of his neat desk for the silver pliers, which were thankfully absent.

It would be wise not to prolong this discussion.

He picked up my application and held it before me. "So, number nine, I see you're very successful in publishing. A manager," he added, sounding impressed. "Do you like your work? Do you see yourself doing it for a long time? And your parents still work their farm. Wonderful. I always wanted a farm." He paused. I nodded. "Why do you want a passport?" he asked.

"To travel, like other people."

"You're not like other people."

"I need to go to book fairs outside of Syria."

"Ah. Are you going to France?"

"I'll go if the need arises."

"And you'll meet Youssef Abdelke, Hala Abdullah, and Fatima Ladhkani?" he asked. These were old comrades who had escaped the country.

"I'm more likely to meet them than Jacques Chirac," I replied, trying not to sound too sarcastic.

"Great, great. If you want a passport, no problem." He paused; I suppose waiting for me to smile. But I had already decided there was no way I would agree to anything this man proposed. "No problem at all," he repeated. "You just must promise me that you'll give me a report on their activities in France."

I stood up. "I don't want a passport," I said.

"Jamal, sit down, sit down," he ordered. "Don't be in a rush. Emotion won't help you get a passport."

I sat and glowered across the desk, unable to stop the images of what he had done to me years earlier. Hilal then looked down, opened a newspaper with a snap, and began to read. We sat in silence for several minutes, him calmly reading his paper and me looking around at the furniture. I presumed he was hoping I'd cool off and would think better of his offer. Then he'd have another informer. But I knew a passport was not worth the price he would extract from me. After a while, he looked up, assessed me, and sighed.

"You can go now," he said. "But I'll keep this on file . . ." he added, waving my application.

After that I didn't even attempt to apply for a passport. Now, fifteen years later, I really needed one. But if I did apply, the best outcome I could hope for was to get one in five months, while the more likely scenario was that I would be arrested. This is what happened to a friend, Ibrahim Musa. To this day I still don't know if he's been released, alive or dead.

I was in the office of a friend of mine, Abu Yamin, who was a wholesale supplier of men's clothes. Occasionally, I went to help translate international business correspondence for him. While we sat at his desk having coffee afterwards, I told him about my passport dilemma.

"You can get a passport," he said with a laugh. "This is not a problem, my friend. Money solves all problems in this country. Do you understand what I'm saying?"

"Money doesn't fix political detentions."

"We're talking about solving problems, not performing miracles." He laughed again.

I needed three passports, for me and the boys. Rufaida had obtained a passport four years earlier. I watched my friend pick up his phone. He then looked over at me and winked.

"Mr. Murad," he said as somebody answered, "I need something from you. Please come to my office right away," and then he hung up. "An immigration officer will be here in quarter of an hour."

Before the fifteen minutes were up, a young man wearing a gray tracksuit arrived. Abu Yamin greeted him, introduced him to me, and then left us in his office, closing the door with a click. The young man shook my hand and then looked at his watch, to show that he didn't have a lot of time.

"How can I help, Uncle?" he asked.

"I want a passport for myself and one each for my two children, as soon as possible."

"Each will cost you thirteen thousand Syrian pounds," he said without hesitation. That would be about three hundred American dollars total at the time. "You'll get them two days after you and your sons have signed the papers, supplied government photo IDs, and brought proper photos to attach to the documents." And then he added with a smile, "Payment is in advance."

"My sons aren't yet fourteen, and so don't have ID cards."

"Not a problem. Just take photocopies of their pages in your family identification document." This is a common Syrian document, a booklet about the size of a passport. As a new family member is born or marries into the family, they are added by hand to the book and receive an official stamp. There are four slots for wives and twenty for sons and daughters. I knew a man who needed two of these booklets.

"Fine, I'll bring you the cash, documents, and photos tomorrow," I said. "Is three p.m. okay?"

"That's perfect, Uncle. Bring the children, too, so they can sign their applications or have fingerprints taken if they can't write properly. Don't forget the photos, and tell the photographer they're for passports."

His instructions complete, the young man hurried off, looking like he still had a full day's schedule of friendly graft and extortion ahead of him.

The following day I returned to Abu Yamin's office with Ghamr and Taim. I gave the young man, still in the same tracksuit, a thick envelope of cash, the documents, and the photos. He zipped open his fleece jacket and took from an inner pocket more official-looking documents. We signed where he indicated, and then he put the papers safely back where they had come from.

When he returned two days later, he opened the zip of the very same gray jacket and took out our three new passports, all freshly minted with our pictures and official stamps.

Even though this was a serious situation, I couldn't help thinking that his jacket seemed to be an official but little known branch of the Department of Immigration and Passports. If you knew somebody, you could get what you wanted — if you had the cash.

That same day, we sent an email to our new businessman contact with photos of the front pages of our passports and personal information. A few days after that, we received an email response with four attachments. There was a UAE tourist visa for each member of my family. Again, even though this was now a life and death situation, I couldn't stop myself from thinking that businesspeople all over the Middle East must know people in tracksuits too.

CHAPTER 51

THE ROAD FROM DAMASCUS

I 'm home alone, sitting and staring at my email page on our home computer. The boys are at school, and Rufaida has gone to help a pregnant woman who has fled from Homs. She can't stop helping internal refugees. I stare at what's on the screen, and I'm having an unexpected reaction. The airline tickets have just arrived, and they somehow feel like an unexpected punch in the gut, even though I was fully aware that they were coming.

The decision to leave was the logical conclusion of a reasoned discussion. But now that it's a tangible reality, the tickets showing up means in a very few days we're really going to leave Damascus, travel to Beirut airport, and then at 6 p.m. on June 20, 2014, we'll board an Emirates flight to Dubai. But these tickets also seem like a confirmation of my defeat, the defeat of my generation. Of all who have been unable to build a country where a person is neither killer nor victim. The men with guns have defeated us. And now I am putting my defeat into practice. I stand up and look away from the computer and around at the house that has been my constant companion and refuge, a symbol of all our hard work to build a life. And here I am, abandoning its walls and furniture. For a moment I lose my equilibrium, and I reach out to the table steadying myself.

I'm falling apart!

I'm discarding everything I've done in my life, just throwing it away, and soon I'll be a man without a history. I'm being ejected from it. My past no longer belongs to me. The war has eaten it up. I'm an old tree being uprooted from its soil. But damn it all to hell, I can't be of less value than one of Taim's cats. I have to get away from this season of death.

Calm down, calm down, man. Take your history with you and protect gentle, kind, intelligent Ghamr and precocious, perceptive Taim. Here, they could be kidnapped and humiliated. Rufaida too. And you could be disfigured by war, turned into a madman in a prison cell or, like so many, wandering the streets, zombies bereft of their families, hopes, and dreams. Such lost relics of humanity are everywhere now. And so what good are the walls of your house if they can't protect you?

I look at the books that grace the two large library shelves in the living room. In the attic are boxes full of more books. Almost a thousand of them in total. My father called the books the silent teachers. And when I was poor, I bought many of them instead of food. Now I'm abandoning them. On the table is Tony Judt's book *Postwar*, the one I'm translating into Arabic. That project will be delayed, and next to it is the first part of Chekov's collected works in Arabic. Before our decision to leave, I'd put a bookmark at the first page of the short story "Vanka," for Rufaida to read. Afterward, I thought we'd discuss it some evening, as we have with so many other pieces of literature. But Vanka will have to wait.

I'm so nervous and confused, I walk around the house laughing at myself as I quickly take in everything, things that I'm leaving and don't want to forget. Our desktop computer, tables, chairs, couches, beds, drawers full of the detritus of life, and even the black landline telephone. When it rings lately, I am slow to pick it up. This is because in recent days I've received increasingly frequent and substantial threats from the mukhabarat. The thought of them takes me back to the stink of the cells in intelligence branches, and I'm jolted back to seeing our new plan through. We are going to escape. But what if they arrest me at a checkpoint? A good number of those leaving have been arrested on the way to Beirut. But the risk has to be taken, to save Ghamr and Taim from the consequences of this hellish civil war, a war whose duration nobody can predict. I feel my relationship with the house, the stones, the people, the river, the greenery of Rabwa Park and Idhkirini, the Remember Me rock, all of it being shattered. A mass of contradictions and conflicts, I am desperate not to see myself as defeated.

It's pointless having this debate and letting yourself fall apart. You're going to leave, you're going to protect your children. The world is more than this kingdom

of suffering, or maybe that's the way it is everywhere . . . but some woes are easier
to bear than others. Calm down, calm down, calm down. Time passing by is life,
so don't let pain and suffering take it over. Save your children. Do something for
your children. Save them.

The world is full of contradictions, and so am I. I don't want to stay, and I
don't want to go. I can't bear defeat, yet there's no way I can win. But there's
no time for these sophistries. These things I'm living through are eating away
at my soul. The important thing now is that we go somewhere safe.

We decided to not even make one last trip to Kfarieh to say goodbye
to my family. Some former prisoners I know, Munif Mulhim and Youssef
Abdelke, were stopped and arrested between Damascus and Latakia. I don't
want to join them. A phone call to Kfarieh will have to suffice. Then I laugh
out loud as I wonder what the difference is, whether I'm arrested on the way
to my parents or to Beirut. I can't even say why I think it's funny, but I laugh.

Now I have to decide how we're going to travel to Beirut. I had heard about
Abu Anas, who lives nearby. He is a tall man, bald, and very calm. Apparently,
he uses his car as a source of income, transporting passengers between Beirut
and Damascus since the beginning of 2012. I asked Shahin Ahmad, a relief
worker I'd met, about him.

"Abu Anas, he's cunning as a fox," Shahin said, "and knows how to buy
his way through the checkpoints. I hear he can be trusted."

I showed up at the driver's house, and after a few words at the door, Abu
Anas invited me in for Turkish coffee, although he checked both ways down
the street before closing the door.

"How much for the trip to Beirut airport, and what will the drive be like?"
I asked.

"Are you leaving?"

"Yes."

He talked as if he already had the job, describing how between here and
Beirut we'd pass through twelve checkpoints, the roughest being the one
controlled by the Fourth Armored Division of the Syrian Army.

"Now, I want twenty-seven thousand Syrian pounds for myself," about
one hundred US dollars at the time, "and if you don't want us to stop for long

at the checkpoints, it's going to cost you more," he said, rubbing his fore-finger against his thumb. "Barteel. Bribes. That will be, oh, probably another eighty-one thousand pounds total — for all the checkpoints." I could see him eyeing me, to see my reaction to the mention of so much money. And then he laughed when I didn't flinch. "The income from a checkpoint in Syria is larger than any Syrian factory's income nowadays."

I tried to laugh at his levity, but I was too focused on understanding the details. "So, Google Maps shows it's less than sixty miles from our house into Lebanon and to the Rafic Hariri Airport. Can we make it in good time?"

He answered as if I were a child asking a foolish question. "I understand Google Maps about as well as I understand al-Idrisi's maps," he said with a laugh. Al-Idrisi was a famous twelfth-century geographer when Arabs were making the most advanced maps in the world. "Jamal," Abu Anas continued, "you can't think of this trip in miles. With traffic jams and checkpoints, it must be measured in hours. It's usually seven hours to the airport." And then he added proudly, "With me and my Bride, it will take a maximum, a maximum of five."

"Your bride?"

He laughed again. "That's my car."

"I've agreed with Abu Anas that we will leave here at ten in the morning on June 20," I told Rufaida, Ghamr, and Taim when I got home. That was two days away.

"No, Baba," shouted twelve-year-old Taim. "Why do we have to leave?" I'd never seen him so angry.

"Don't you see what we're going through?"

"So what? Other people are going through the same thing."

"Taim, I might be arrested, your mother might be arrested, and you or your brother might be kidnapped. You almost were."

It was ironic that I was trying to convince Taim when I didn't want to go myself, even though I knew rationally that we had to. Leaving, to my mind, was an admission of defeat.

"We're leaving because we're cowards," Taim shouted back. "I'm not coming with you."

I looked at my son and didn't respond to his outburst. My heart ached at how this war was robbing him of a normal childhood. Besides having become addicted to the adrenalin rush of the war around him, Taim had begun his first, sweet infatuation with a girl in his class. So I didn't say anything and endured watching him mope around the house, not meeting my gaze for the rest of the day and the next. Rufaida and Ghamr were more composed than Taim and I. They seemed to know it was the sensible thing to do. The next day we packed six suitcases with our clothes and only half a dozen books, including a book I'd given to Rufaida early in our courtship — a collection of poems by Mahmoud Darwish, *It Is a Song, It Is a Song* — and the anthology in which Ghamr's poem was published when he won first prize for poetry at the age of nine. And then I handed Rufaida our photo albums.

This is all we have left of our country.

I watered the garden one last time, my way of saying goodbye.

Keep on living, delicate flowers.

And I tightened up the screws of a shutter that kept on coming loose every few months, a regular bit of maintenance that had become a habit.

I suppose I'll develop new habits.

The Bride arrived on time and Abu Anas crammed five of our six suitcases in the white Nissan's trunk. I took the last and placed it on the front seat where I would sit.

We then exchanged tearful farewells with the friends who would be the first to look after our house, at no cost. This arrangement suited all of us, as their house was in a less secure neighborhood.

And then we all got into the car and took a last look at the structure we had built into a home. Something inside me wished the journey would be aborted for reasons outside my control, at least some event that wouldn't end up with us arrested. And then I remembered the cat protecting her kittens and took heart. I turned and looked at my family in the back seat. Taim was crying silent, bitter tears, while his brother sat motionless, looking into nothingness. I think I said something to Rufaida.

"We mustn't look back. If one of us is arrested, the other must carry on with the journey. If we're both arrested, I'll give the cash to the boys, and Abu Anas will take them back to your parents in Damascus."

Or perhaps I was saying it to myself.

And then began the stomach-churning anxiety of more than a dozen checkpoints.

The first al-Safsaf checkpoint on the road between Qudsaya and Damascus went smoothly. The guards just accepted a box of tobacco hidden beneath the passports that Abu Anas handed them. It was the same with the second checkpoint, after the Bride skirted around the main part of the city and began her journey toward the Lebanese border.

The third checkpoint was different. It took over an hour. Even though Abu Anas had slipped a good bribe into one of the passports, he and my family had to stand out in the bright June sun while a sergeant and his enlisted men tossed our luggage to the ground and rifled through it. But they eventually closed the bags and even put them back into the trunk before tersely ordering us to leave.

About a half an hour later Abu Anas brought the white Nissan to a halt behind a long line of cars. He turned and put his arm on the back of the front seat.

"This is the Fourth Armored Division checkpoint," he said, "the worst one. Even though they demand a bigger share in the bribes, they are harsher. They behave as if they're taking revenge on the people leaving. They arrest passengers on the slightest suspicion and sometimes invent reasons to arrest them."

I don't think Abu Anas intended to add to my anxiety but just wanted to show that he was an expert on this route and also to warn us.

I looked at the scene in front of me. Soldiers, all dressed in camouflage fatigues, were walking among the cars, brandishing their Kalashnikovs. I became increasingly tense inside and prepared myself to talk as little as possible, and not react impulsively to anything. This was going to be difficult. My anxiety was like a noose winding itself slowly round the neck of my soul.

I turned to the back seat and saw that Rufaida and the boys looked much calmer. This helped replenish my strength until it was our turn for inspection.

"Get out of the car and bring your things with you," a tall, pimply-faced soldier ordered, motioning to us with the barrel of his Russian-made automatic assault rifle.

The first time I was arrested, a soldier with pimples said almost the same thing to me.

I get out of the car with the one suitcase. My family exits, too, their faces and body language stoic. The soldier points with his gun for me to put my bag down at the back of the vehicle, and then I stand with my family in a line watching the goings on. Abu Anas opens the trunk and hands our passports to the sergeant, tapping the top passport, which I can see has a thick wad of bills in it. The sergeant doesn't react, but just motions for his two men, their arms bulging with muscles. They take the suitcases out of the trunk, literally throwing them to the ground. The fabric of one case rips and its metal springs pop out, twisting in a coil as if they are the intestines of a murdered creature. The soldiers scatter our clothes around as they look for something or nothing at all. Again, we are standing in the sun, showing no emotions and not moving a muscle. The soldiers look the most contemptuous as they throw our few books onto the tarmac. And finally, when their battle is over and they've defeated our shirts and photo albums, our suitcases look like violated and exhausted maidens.

The sergeant comes over and stands close to my face, opening up the first passport. I can see the money is gone.

"Are you Jamal?" he demands. It sounds more like an accusation, as if he is really asking, "Are you the one we should arrest?"

"Yes, I'm Jamal," I reply, as neutrally as possible.

"Father's name?"

"Saleh."

He opens another passport and looks at my wife's face, then gives the passports back to Abu Anas, telling him to get moving. Rufaida begins repacking our belongings with her customary tidiness, arranging things so they fit in the bags neatly, putting everything back in its place. I stand watching, my insides trembling, my temporary calm evaporated.

Rufaida, this is no place to be neat and tidy, on a road planted with soldiers who take delight in bullying suitcases. And what's the point of being neat when the bags will be checked again?

"Yalla, yalla!" I shout. "Come on, let's go!"

I'm sitting in the front seat, the Bride gently rocking me back and forth as it drives cautiously along the poorly maintained motorway. I close my eyes, ashamed of my outburst. Now hidden in my own darkness, the drive along this road reminds me of my many long, restless nights in prison cells, nights that seem never-ending. It is like the endless night that sixth-century poet Imru' al-Qays addressed.

"O long night, will you never disperse to reveal the dawn, although dawn won't bring anything better?"

Abu Anas passed easily through the fifth and sixth checkpoints without luggage searches. Those soldiers just came and leaned into the window, silently staring at our driver, expecting their barteel. At one, the bribe was inside Taim's passport. After reading the name on the document, and taking the bill, the soldier smiled at my younger son.

"Goodbye, Taim," he said, and the Bride whisked us away.

At the seventh checkpoint, Abu Anas and I went to the back of the car and watched as a single soldier looked inside the trunk. He didn't disturb any of the cases, and then Abu Anas gave him my passport only with the money in it, expecting us to go through quickly again.

"Give me them all," the soldier demanded.

Oh no, this is when it happens.

Abu Anas handed all the passports to the soldier and when he opened mine and realized he had already been holding the passport with the money in it, he simply pocketed the cash and returned the other documents unchecked. He smiled and tapped the Bride's backside. "God go with your wheels."

As we drove the next fifteen minutes to another checkpoint, I was feeling profoundly and emotionally drained, but I tried to remind myself that our potential lot was better than most.

We are a small detail in the history of Syria, and many events have brought it to its current state. We are four out of millions of Syrians who have been kicked out of their houses and some out of their country. In any case, this is preferable to the grave or prison. We might become the lucky ones.

There's a long queue of vehicles at the next checkpoint. It includes a concrete building on which is painted one of the regime's constant threats, this one in near perfect diwani script. The calligraphy reminds of the hand-written signs in the library at al-Qala'a prison. The sad face of their author, Abu Khaldun, flashes in my mind, replaced by the image of him all aflame and crashing down the steps. The sign reads, "Al-Assad or we burn the country."

Soldiers with Kalashnikovs come and take our passports.

"That building is known as the computer room," Abu Anas says, making conversation as we begin to wait. To lighten the mood, I suppose. "They take the passports and run a name search to find out if anyone is wanted by the authorities." Now my stomach goes into violent spasms, and I have to swallow back bile. I look away, fighting the fear and nausea. Arrest seems a likely possibility here. "The computer is an amazing invention, isn't it?" Abu Anas adds, trying to engage me.

"It certainly is," I say, gagging and forcing back bile that had made it up into my mouth.

Think, Jamal, think!

I watched the soldier who took our passports walk toward the building, but instead of going in, he stopped, pulled out a cigarette, and began to smoke, our passports still in his other hand.

"Abu Anas," I said. "Maybe ask them to speed up their inspection of our passports so we could catch our flight."

He scratched his head for a moment then opened the car door and beckoned to one of the Kalashnikovs. The young soldier came over and Abu Anas got out.

"This family might miss their flight," he said, slipping some more cash into the soldier's hand. The soldier leaned into the car and looked at me with a sarcastic smile.

"Where are you traveling to?" he asked.

"Iran," I replied.

The younger soldier walked off; my eyes remained fixed on him. He walked up to the fellow on the steps, said something I couldn't hear, and patted his pocket. The first soldier, cigarette dangling from his mouth, looked over, disinterested, stared at me, and then handed the passports to his partner in bribery.

A minute later we were passing the four parked vehicles in front of us and were on our way. I took a deep breath, trying to relax, but remained tense. It was still quite possible the road ahead would lead us into a basement cell with blankets smelling of urine and mold. The Bride passed through two more checkpoints, and, again, it didn't take more than a barteel to get us through. And then we drove up to the eleventh checkpoint. With soldiers standing around him, and while we were still a good 150 feet away, there was a sergeant staring calmly right through the windshield at me. We locked eyes. I felt like prey coming directly into his hunting ground. My stomach cramps grew more violent when we slowed down and the sergeant walked around to my side of the car. He even opened the door for me. When I went to take out the single suitcase, he motioned for me to leave it.

"Open the trunk, please," he said to Abu Anas. "Come," he said to me pleasantly. This man somehow reminded me of Brigadier General Hilal. I stood as he took out one suitcase at a time, opened each, and then slowly, neatly, and methodically went through its contents. When he finished, he made a show of closing the last with a snap, and then he replaced it in the trunk. He closed the trunk and turned to me.

"Where are you going?" he asked.

"Russia," I answered. He looked interested.

"Really? Did you wire your money ahead or do you have it with you?"

"What would you do if you were me?" I asked, and he laughed.

"I'm asking the questions," he said, his eyes cold above his smile.

That's when Abu Anas stepped forward and forced a bigger bribe than intended into the officer's hand. The sergeant looked at it. "Carry on, Nissan," he said.

"It looked like things were about to get complicated," Abu Anas said gravely as we drove away.

"Shukran," I said, putting a hand to my stomach. When we were some way away, a thought came to me, and I had to ask: "Why have they set up all these checkpoints?"

"No one really knows except the mukhabarat and the Lord," he said, his sense of humor returning.

Here we were, in front of the last Syrian checkpoint. This is where I was to get the first stamp in my new passport, an exit visa, paying a fee for the privilege. More than a hundred people were waiting in front of the Department of Immigration and Passport building. Abu Anas turned to me.

"You want to avoid the computers again?" I nodded. "This means paying them a bigger bribe. I'll use the excuse about missing the plane again." He put out his hand. "Thirteen thousand pounds." About fifty US. I didn't hesitate to give it to him.

He disappeared inside the building, and we waited. I looked up at the sky, but the clouds didn't inspire any movies in me. I took another deep breath, trying to relax. Here we were. We'd left home four hours ago and traveled twenty-two miles, and it'd been the longest twenty-two miles I'd ever traveled in my life. Finally, after about twenty minutes, Abu Anas emerged from the building waving the passports in the air and doing a sort of happy dance as he returned to the car.

We passed through the border, but I couldn't relax. It was the first time I had ever been out of Syria. A short distance away, in front of a building whose sign read *Lebanese General Directorate of Security* was a long lineup of more than two hundred Syrians. They were waiting for entry visas. The whole family got out of the Bride and joined them. Once again we were standing under the June sun, which, in the middle of the afternoon, was now fierce. Abu Anas had gone to fetch forms for us and to pay the entry fees. While waiting, I looked back the short distance to my country. There I again watched the lizards, birds, butterflies, and flies going back and forth across the invisible border. They did it without papers or official stamps, and the first hopeful smile of the day came to my face. Perhaps we would become like them in the days to come, wandering over the planet without stamps, seals, papers, roadblocks, and men with guns . . . and without fear. Over half an hour later I found myself in front of an arrogant and obviously xenophobic Lebanese official.

"What's the reason for your visit to Lebanon?"

"We're just in transit to the airport."

"So you won't be staying in Lebanon?

"No."

"So, you've wrecked your country and now you're off to destroy others?"

"Sorry, I don't understand."

"Nothing."

He stamped the passports and gave me another suspicious look. I didn't respond. I told myself I'd forfeited the right to argue or fight. Now my only right is to silence.

Back on the road, Abu Anas now drove his Bride at full throttle.

"Forty-five minutes to the airport," our now happy driver chirped.

We had an hour and a half before we had to board our flight, so there was plenty of time. Finally, I felt my body relaxing. I cracked open the window and took in a deep, cleansing breath. Even the air felt and smelled different. I smiled back at my family, who all tried to smile too. And then I remembered Hani Ahmad, a friend who lived in Beirut. We had agreed on Messenger the day before that we would meet and visit for a while at the airport. If we didn't make contact, he would let our family back home know that there was a problem. I brought his number up on my phone and was just about to phone when Abu Anas's phone beeped, announcing a text message. He fumbled for his phone as he drove and squinted to read.

"*Tfooh!*" he said, almost spitting. I stared at him wide-eyed, my own phone still frozen in the air. "There's been an explosion on this road at Dahr al-Baydar," he said. "It's impassible for now. We'll have to go around."

"Will we make our plane?" Rufaida asked.

"We have to drive up into the mountains and back in on another road. It's four times the distance, but it's still possible." He sped up and pulled his Bride hard to the right as he turned onto another road at the first intersection and headed north toward the Bekaa Valley. This is twenty-nine miles from Beirut in the wrong direction.

On the way, we passed different villages. They were segregated much like our own. "Here they're Sunnis," Abu Anas said, again trying to distract us from worrying. "This is a Christian area. Druze on the other side. We'll pass Shia neighborhoods on the road to the airport."

I called Hani and told him we were delayed and might not have time to meet him.

"I'll pick you up in Brummana," he said. "Meet me at the pizza parlor."

After an hour of clear, quick driving, I had allowed myself to half doze off, letting the scenery outside my window wash over my dropping eyelids. That's when I felt Abu Anas stamp on the brakes. I looked in front of me, and to my horror there was a long queue of cars.

"A Lebanese checkpoint?" Abu Anas said with some surprise.

"We don't need any more of those," I shouted desperately.

I felt a familiar hand on my shoulder. "Jamal," Rufaida said calmly.

But even Abu Anas seemed concerned. "There are hardly ever roadblocks on this road. It's probably because of the bombing. Let's hope the checkpoint isn't manned by Hezbollah."

"Smile," Abu Anas said as we got to the front of the line, and it must have worked. After a quick look at our bags in the Bride's trunk, we were waved on. But now, even as we arrived in Brummana and saw our friend Hani smiling and waving at us, my stomach couldn't be convinced to relax again.

"Put your things in my car," he said. "I promise to get you to the airport on time, and we can visit while we drive." Abu Anas was delighted, as this would save him time, but all the same, he asked for more money, saying he had paid more in bribes than planned, and the extra miles were costing him in gas and maintenance. I gave the man what he wanted.

I saw the boys eyeing the pizza parlor.

"Hani, do we have time for Rufi and the kids to eat?"

The children and Rufaida ate their slices of pizza with gusto, but I couldn't face a mouthful. We'd been in Lebanon for just over an hour, and our plans had already gone bad twice. Who knew what would befall us next? The moment the meal was finished, I insisted we go. It was after 4:30 p.m. On the way to the airport, as if fate were giving us a last poke, we saw pictures of Bashar al-Assad along the highway. They were put up by Hezbollah, along with graffiti, glorifying him as a great leader. We got to the airport on time, and Hani accompanied us as far as he could inside the terminal. I said goodbye to my final contact with Syria, apologizing for being poor company.

Going through security, while all our papers, passports, and visas were inspected, I was a mixture of sad and anxious, still expecting Syria to reach out and grab me, but we were soon walking toward the departure gate.

Here I am. I'm fifty-five years old and have just left Syria for the first time. And now I will shortly board a plane for the first time, too, more than a hundred years after the invention of the aircraft.

Our economy class seats were what we had booked, but all the same, I was disappointed. I thought they would be like the airline seats I'd seen in magazines. But it was a trivial disappointment. When I sat down in the plane, I felt just a bit more relaxed, smiling as I watched the boys with their noses pressed to the windows. And as we took off, this is when my whole body finally unclenched and my hunger returned with a vengeance. When they brought the food, I devoured my meal, and Rufaida, seeing this, offered me hers. I consumed it with relish, and then asked for more. A stewardess with a kind face covered in light brown freckles promised to bring me another meal. But I didn't see her again until we disembarked at Dubai airport.

CHAPTER 52

DUBAI

My family and I landed at Dubai airport after midnight. We were the last off the plane and followed instructions and arrows to a queue at immigration control. My first impression of Dubai was formed when we got to the head of the line and stood in front of two desks. At one, a male official sat in a white robe, a jubba. At the other was a female in a black dress. Her head cover was pushed back to reveal an obvious fondness for dyed-blond hair, cosmetic surgery, and excessive amounts of makeup. As we stood waiting in front of them, the man adjusted the ghutra covering his head and carried on talking to his co-worker.

"Assalamu alaykum," peace be upon you, I said a little louder than I normally would, my voice showing more than a hint of irritability. Although I was elated to have completed our escape, a long day squeezing through checkpoints and then taking a first plane ride caused me to be both physically and mentally exhausted. I just couldn't control my emotions, something very out of character for me. But the cross note in my voice didn't seem to concern this fellow. He ignored my greeting and carried on determinedly with his conversation. I took out my phone and decided it was as good a time as any to make this call. Our sponsor and employer in Dubai continued his help by providing the name of Ziyad Abu Sayf, a young Syrian who would rent a flat for us in Dubai.

"Hello, sorry to call so late," I said, a little louder than necessary. "We're still in the airport. I don't know when we'll get out. It depends on the airport officials. We're waiting to have our passports stamped."

Speaking about Taha Hussein's project of democracy, modernization, and liberalization in Jebel Ali Club.

The man at the counter looked at me out of the corner of his eye but still carried on talking to his colleague. I saw Rufaida give me a look, like she was worried I was going to cause a problem. Finally, he stopped his conversation and turned toward me.

"Hello. Welcome," he said with official politeness.

I handed over the passports and entry visas. He began stamping and writing on them with a pen bearing the Cartier logo. Meanwhile, his highly adorned associate had us take turns standing on a specific spot to perform eye scans. I had read about this new technology.

And just like that, we four were in the global system.

Around two o'clock in the morning on June 21, 2014, we emerged from the airport with our luggage. Staying for long in the open air isn't recommended during summer in Dubai. We felt as if an enormous hair dryer were blowing hot, sticky air at us. I called Ziyad again.

"Hello. We're out of the airport."

"Welcome. Thank God you're safe. I'll wait for you in front of the building. Take a taxi and give him the address. I've just sent a text."

We headed for a big Toyota at the taxi stand. A Filipino-looking driver got out, and we loaded the cases into the trunk together.

"How are you?" I said to him in Arabic.

He replied with a pleasant smile, making it clear he didn't know our language. The only thing he said the whole way was "Address please?" in English.

I read out the text message: "Saba 3 — Cluster Q — JLT," and showed him the screen.

The man nodded his head, smiling, and in about half an hour we were in front of the building. After greeting us, Ziyad, a young blond man from Damascus, guided us into an elevator. It began to rise.

"How was Damascus when you left?" he asked with a yawn.

"There are more checkpoints —"

"I know, I know," he interrupted, another yawn escaping.

I realized he was just making conversation and not particularly interested in an answer. As we now stood in silence, watching the numbers ding higher and higher, I took another look at the sleepy Ziyad. He had his jacket collar turned up and behaved as if he were trying to be an Arab version of Brad Pitt. Inside the flat he took a card from a drawer in a television table. On it was the name of the telecom company and the password for the Wi-Fi. Commending us for already having a smartphone, he took his leave with a Syrian expat farewell.

"We will all return one day and celebrate the fall of the criminal."

I looked through our luxurious apartment's windows. They took up most of the wall of the room facing the main street. Far below us, bright lights illuminated the wide thoroughfare and the neighborhood around it. It made me realize how dark the streets back in Damascus were at night. Before I slept, I wrote a brief email to a group of friends in Syria.

"In a little while, and for the first time in my life, I will lay my head down outside of Syria's borders. We are twenty-seven floors above the ground in a rented condominium in Dubai."

Over the first few days, we arranged meetings with Syrians who were Facebook friends. Hasan Abd al-Rahman, who had left Syria at the beginning of the 1980s, came to visit and drove us to Mall of the Emirates, a huge shopping mall in Dubai. There we bought a laptop and acquired Emirati numbers for our phones. Hasan was very generous with his advice, and it was always

The family in our apartment in Dubai.

accurate, about how working in Dubai was different, the eccentricities of its culture, and, most importantly, about school for the boys. With his help and that of others like him, everything went well. We were advised how best to get around and where to shop. We received suggestions about the jobs available to us. I wrote to Marianne Hovdan from ICORN, with whom I had been corresponding about possible immigration. I let her know I had arrived in Dubai, and she wished me a pleasant stay and told me to keep in touch. I was glad that many Syrians living in the Emirates took the time to visit us, bestowing upon us their advice and much-needed affection. Among them were the actor and director Maher Salibi and his wife, Yara Sabri. She, too, was a well-known Syrian actor whose Facebook page was filled with demands for the names of detainees and their release. She also posted celebratory announcements when anyone got out. Then there were Imad Tawila, who had been the director of distribution at the publishing house I worked at for so long; Fahim Shariqi, a man from my village who had also been imprisoned for years by the regime; and Azza Gharibeh, a Sky News presenter working for France 24 Television. We participated in expat meetings organized by Samir Sa'ifan, the economist; Nabil Maleh, the Syrian film director; and many others, including professors, doctors, engineers, and various professionals in search of safety from the regime. Everybody was keen to guide and show us what we should do to help ourselves and the boys settle and succeed.

It didn't take me long to find out that a hybrid form of English was the dominant language in Dubai. You could hear British and American accents, Indian, Pakistani, Filipino, and Arabic; all of the respective languages branched out into various local forms of communication while still maintaining some of their own words and character. A Filipino cashier might say, "Bibty-baib," which I learned was "fifty-five," and when the Indian taxi driver said "sida sida" in Hindi, it was somehow clear that it meant "straight on." People understood one another not only by mashing words from different languages together. Body language was also a recognized part of communication in this extravagant city.

All I can see from my balcony is an incredible number of tower blocks and the lush gardens surrounding them. There is nothing of the desert evident in this modern picture, that is, except for the heat, which isn't dry like the deserts of our Levant. Here the air is stiflingly humid. Neither is there any sign of oil wells or pumps. All that appears before me are artificial lakes, meadows, green trees, and tower blocks. The official name of the area we live in is Jumeirah Lakes Towers, but everybody just refers to it as JLT. It seems to me the Dubai government is obsessed with abbreviations and English superlatives. When I worked for Asda'a back in our little home on the hill, I translated more than one article about "the largest," "the most enormous," "the longest" — any number of world-class things for which someone could claim bragging rights. And many of these things are installations right here in Dubai: the Dubai Mall, the Burj Khalifa, the artificial archipelago called Palm Jumeirah, the dancing fountains, and the Miracle Garden.

On the roof of our building there was a swimming pool and a hot tub. (At the age of fifty-five, I used a hot tub for the first time.) There were never more than a handful of people in the pool, and Rufaida, the boys, and I usually met three other people there, an Iranian woman, her mother, and her daughter. We had conversations about repression in Iran and Syria, the hijab becoming compulsory under Khomeini, the project to Islamize this region and the world, and the efforts by America, Iran, and Saudi Arabia to get rid of the Soviet-controlled regime in Afghanistan, agreeing to support the

Mujahideen there. We talked about the works of Persian poets as diverse as the fourteenth-century Hafez, and Forough Farrokhzad from the mid-twentieth century. The hot tub was also a place to discuss Iranian novels, our children's schooling, and different Persian and Syrian dishes. Oddly, although I introduced myself when we first met, and we shared hours of discussion, they would never tell us their names.

Because we entered Dubai on visitor visas, we couldn't start working as quickly as we had been promised. Luckily, Rufaida was able to do translation work online before she could officially begin the job she had lined up with our sponsor. My job at the Orient Research Centre also ran into a snag. I was told it was due to lack of space in the office, but I think it was because everyone else working there had a PhD, while I had only an undergraduate degree. But then I also had the chance to get a research job at Northern Logistics, too, thanks to our Facebook friend. Most of the research I did there was related to the history and current circumstances of Islamic political organizations after the founding of the Muslim Brotherhood in 1928 in Egypt, and the current conflict in Syria. Having steady jobs helped us feel relatively settled. In record time, the boys managed to overcome the difficulty of studying entirely in English.

Often I came home to find business cards and pamphlets beside our apartment door or pushed underneath it. On them were pictures of nearly naked women in poses some photographer thought enticing. Written on the cards were advertisements announcing how these women were ready to perform "massages" in "the comfort of your home." All you had to do was call. One of my new friends assured me the sex trade took various forms here, and the word "massage" was a euphemism for sex. As I listened to him, I thought about the pictures of women that accompanied the reports I was currently reading on my computer screen at the office. The women in the advertisements, while definitely being exploited, had it better than the Syrian and Iraqi women who fell into the hands of jihadists.

The young women on the business cards had smiling faces, the smiles of their profession. Meanwhile, the faces of the Yazidi women on my computer were despondent as they were offered for sale in the markets set up by Daesh. Comparing the two forms of slavery, I was reminded of my saying that I was happier being doused in freezing and then hot water than having my bones broken. And I felt I was looking through my computer screen into the souls of the Syrian women kidnapped by Jaysh al-Islam, the Islamic Army, who were then placed in iron cages on the roofs of buildings. This was done to use them as human shields, to stop the regime from dropping barrel bombs on them. These women's faces revealed a resignation to a fate that is hard to imagine.

And I listened to the stories of brave women in videos, openly speaking about how they had been raped in the basements of the regime's intelligence services, perhaps rooms I had occupied during my own harsh interrogations. I felt as though I were suffocating as images on my screen showed the devastation caused by countless barrel bombs dropped from helicopters on Aleppo. I read about al-Tawba prisons, "repentance" prisons, the first thing Jaysh al-Islam builds and quickly fills when they conquer an area. Then there were the reports of the theft of international humanitarian aid, stolen from warehouses and rerouted by every faction to their own militias and militaries, depriving the starving population in Ghouta.

I read a report of a woman who was no longer able to leave the town of Douma, where she was trapped with her two children. She had to secure a large sum of money in order to pass through the regime checkpoint that divided the area controlled by the opposition from that of the regime. When she finally did get through, bereft of money, she had to somehow avoid being raped at an opposition checkpoint.

In contrast to this anarchy, Dubai is a precisely drawn city. It's like the illustrations in a futuristic graphic novel. Here you will find the cleanest streets in the world. The buildings in the JLT development gleam as if they were built just a month before our arrival. The trees in the gardens are cultivated to live in this terrible heat. Around the artificial lakes, workers stand supervising the watering, drop by drop it seems, and they immediately pick up the leaves as they fall on the ground, keeping the area perpetually spotless. Dog owners will find free plastic bags for their dogs' droppings, something I'd not seen before. The whole of Dubai, inside and out, seems like a large, clean hotel that welcomes some guests — if they have the means.

Rufaida and I got to know the malls of Dubai and stood with the crowd to see the fountains whose water was programmed to dance to both Eastern and Western music. We strolled in Ibn Battuta Mall, named after the famed

Moroccan scholar and explorer. I imagined how amazed he would be, if he were still alive, as he walked around the indoor shopping bazaar named after him. In my mind, I watched him writing in his journal, "You see such a wealth of goods in this astounding place. Among the strangest are the transparent boxes, where written in excellent calligraphy on each are the names of charitable societies. It is into these that the people of the city drop their own money. It's unbelievable that the general population, and not just the sultan of this place, has such an excess of wealth to spread." And it's true. I would say that the whole of Dubai's excessive opulence can be summed up in the following phrase: If you joked with a waiter in Dubai and asked for bird's milk, he would respond, "Which bird's milk would you prefer, sir?"

Rufi fulfilled her second dream in Dubai. Her first was to get rid of her hijab, which she had already done on our wedding day. The second was to drive a car. She acquired a driver's license and bought a white Honda Accord on credit.

The first time Rufaida went out without her hijab was on our wedding day.

Dubai is slippery underfoot for expatriates. You don't know when the place will turn its back on you and refuse to renew your residency. It could happen because of some scheme you are unaware of, or something you've done without realizing it. In Dubai, companies come into being and others collapse, and you can lose your job at any moment. You might wake up one day to find the company you work for has gone bust, suddenly stranding you without food or shelter. The city changes its expatriates like a spoiled trophy wife changes designer shoes. Nobody knows who Dubai will keep and who it will kick out, or when. UAE laws don't allow expatriates to obtain permanent residency or citizenship. Therefore, after our initial relief about escaping Syria and feeling settled, Rufaida and I became aware that our future in Dubai was unclear. We began to realize that, if we were unable to get better-paying jobs, the day would come when we would be unable to support our sons through university — and their futures had been the driving factor in our escaping Syria. But worse, if we lost our jobs, we literally wouldn't be able to pay our rent or buy food. Moreover, because there is no social safety net for people caught in this dilemma, we could end up in a refugee camp. The real possibility of this began to manifest itself after about a year. The company we worked for seemed to be running into difficulties. Often, we'd receive only part of our salary and the rest was delayed. Although it was paid soon after, I saw this as a bad sign. Making me more nervous, I read that 250 Syrian workers were fired from an oil company and the government refused to renew the residency of some.

In the midst of this anxiety, an email arrived from ICORN:

Dear Jamal Saeed,

My name is Elisabeth Dyvik, and I am a colleague of Marianne here at ICORN. Today we have some potentially good news for you.

Through a partner organization, PEN Canada [. . .], we have secured an offer of sponsored relocation to Canada as refugees for you and your immediate family (wife and children). This offer is not from an ICORN member, but we trust the hosts and the offer to be serious and well-funded.

We are aware that you and your family are safe in Dubai for the moment, but we still thought you would consider this offer of permanent, safe relocation.

The offer comes from a group called the Kingston Writers' Refugee Committee. They have secured funding and all the formalities to be able to bring you and your family to Canada as sponsored refugees.

[. . .]

If this offer is of interest to you, we will put you in direct contact with the good people of Kingston.

Elisabeth Dyvik
Programme Director, ICORN

Elisabeth sent the names of the members of the sponsors committee, the one organized by Ray Argyle.

Rufaida, the boys, and I gathered around the laptop and read and reread the email together. This time I was happy to move. Dubai had looked to me, from the very first moment, like the official who took scans of our eyes at the airport and wore excessive and expensive makeup to conceal any true intentions. Once again, Taim was upset.

"Every time we make friends," he complained, "you move us."

"Taim, you'll find friends wherever you go."

"You're just saying that . . ." he said, resigned.

We started gathering information about Kingston. It was the first time I'd heard of it. I blamed myself for such a lack of knowledge of geography. We searched on Google for information about the city and our sponsors. Looking at photos from there, I remembered the day I despondently climbed Mount Qasioun and saw the lit windows of the city but could not see the people living behind them. However, a spark of positive thinking had forced me to tell myself that, in time, many of these hidden people would become friends. I just hadn't met them yet. And it happened. Back then, I was seeing the windows of Damascus. Now I was looking at more faceless windows, but of a city half a world away, on Google Earth. And so again I told myself, just like I did years ago, and just like I had just told Taim, you will make friends there. You just haven't met them yet.

I had to fill out numerous government application forms. These required me to remember lots of information, like the dates of birth of my siblings, the innumerable addresses of houses where I'd lived, cities I'd traveled to outside Syria, and my education from primary school to university. At the age of fifty-seven, I was summarizing the whole of my life in brief sentences. It reminded me of the forms filled out during every transfer to a new jail. During our correspondence, Ray sent me a presentation by Jeremy Lucyk, entitled "Understanding Syria," which focused on the outcome of the 1916 Sykes–Picot Agreement, in which Britain and France arbitrarily divided up the larger area previously referred to as Syria, planting the seeds for the misery that grew and blossomed over the next century.

I wrote to Ray: "I think many factors have combined to push millions of Syrians out of their country as refugees. I suggest I start writing about that under the title *Out of Syria*." Then I began to think about writing a book on the history of Syria and its formation as a political entity after the First World War and its independence after the Second World War. I began gathering documents in Dubai but didn't have time to begin the project. After that, I thought of writing about my own experience, as a small detail of Syrian history and the suffering of its people. And I began to write about the history I had seen, heard, smelled, touched, and sensed and whose different flavors I had tasted.

Not long after submitting our finished applications, we were invited to the Canadian embassy in Dubai. There, we met a smiling young man in his thirties who asked us a lot of questions and politely requested access to our Facebook and WhatsApp accounts. He made it clear that he would be gathering information about us over the next few months "in the interests of Canadian national security." It seemed obvious to me that this friendly guy was from the Canadian intelligence services.

Finally he asked: "Do you have any questions or anything you'd like to add?"

"I hope we can travel to Canada in June 2017," I replied. "By then we will have gotten together some money so we can manage things better, the boys will have finished the school year, and we won't need to renew our Dubai residency papers. And we would like to first encounter Canada at its warmest, in the summer."

The man smiled. "Unfortunately," he answered, "we are not the ones who decide travel dates. But I do hope you get what you want."

We didn't get what we wanted, exactly. The embassy informed us that we had to travel to Canada before the end of December 2016, much sooner than anyone expected. When I told Ray we would have to leave Dubai before the end of December, committee members quickly rented an apartment and sent us photos of it, inside and out. It was on the top floor of an older three-story walkup. In Dubai we read the address and took a Google Map walk along the street where the apartment was located. Not long after that, on December 28, 2016, at 9:55 a.m., my family and I were sitting in the center of the back row of the Emirates Airline Airbus A330-800 heading for Toronto Pearson International Airport. These had been the last seats available.

When we exited the gate of the airport, we found a group of our sponsors waiting for our arrival, holding up a sign welcoming us. Ghamr and Taim waved their hands and smiled.

CHAPTER 53

THE UPSIDE-DOWN
COFFEE CUP OF GOD

As my mother's chattering friends streamed through the doorway into our home's courtyard, she flung the piece of laundry she was scrubbing into the washbowl, quickly dried her hands, and enthusiastically added her voice to the friendly chorus of new arrivals. These gatherings were spontaneous affairs, always a welcome break for the hardworking village women of Kfarieh.

Their cheerful exchanges were punctuated by bursts of laughter and my almost seven-year-old self couldn't work out how they managed to talk and understand the heaps of words being created by so many at the same time. Personally, I was just hoping they didn't notice the new patch on the knee of my trousers, and I thought if I kept looking at it, the patch would somehow disappear.

My mother gave an extra-warm welcome to Umm Yusuf, who'd just arrived from Beirut, and then hurried to make Turkish coffee for her guests. I sat with them and forgot about the patch on my knee, as it didn't seem any of them cared about it.

When my father drank coffee, he enjoyed it, pausing for a while between each sip, raising the cup calmly from the saucer. But the women drank their coffee quickly, as if it were something they had to get through. Then they would turn their cups upside down on the little saucers as if that were the whole point of the exercise. And while they waited for the remaining dark coffee grounds to dry on the inside of their cups, they exchanged tales of their troubles: children, livestock, the state of their land, and the state of their husbands. And then they'd move on to pregnancy, childbirth, and menstruation, referred to as the monthly habit, which seemed like a bad habit to me. I listened to their remarks and the resounding laughter accompanying them.

"We wake at dawn before the cattle and go to bed after them, and we hardly rest during the day."

"I hope I don't come back as a donkey after I die."

"Do you think the life you're living now is better than a donkey's?"

"We heard that you doze off when your husband starts his nightly plowing."

"Yes, and I ask him to put my clothes back as he found them!"

When I laughed, they realized I understood what they were saying, and Zayna, who was dressed in her husband's faded blue jacket, asked me to leave. But Umm Walid held me tight and gave me a kiss. "I like the clever ones," she said.

Personally, it hadn't occurred to my younger self that cleverness was required to understand what they were talking about.

"When we have fun like this, I feel like we're stealing time and should be doing it in secret," my mother said.

"Even the cows and donkeys get a siesta or a short break," remarked Umm Walid.

Sitting in the courtyard, around a table made of sycamore wood, they talked and whispered together, each topic ending in an explosion of laughter. They made fun of everything, including themselves, and it was only at times like this, when my mother was together with a group of women, that I saw her so unreservedly happy.

And then came the main event. When the remains of the coffee had dried on the inside of every cup, it fell to Umm Yusuf to read one after another and tell each woman her future. I was fascinated by her predictions, listening intently as she calmly stared into each cup while turning it around in her fingers. It amazed me how she read the symbols formed by the dried dark grounds.

Umm Yusuf told my mother that she would have something joyful to celebrate after three signs. I furrowed my brow. Did this mean three days, weeks, months, or years? *God alone knows*, I thought. And there was also the image of a snake in her cup. "The snake is an enemy stalking you," she told my mother and then glanced at me and added, "but you will escape from its evil intentions."

To our neighbor Umm Samir, she said, "Look at that bird on the rim of the cup. You'll set off on a long journey shortly."

A few days later, Umm Samir died.

Umm Yusuf told Umm Walid that she could see a big fish in her cup, and that meant she would receive great wealth. Umm Walid clapped happily at this, and then made a dismissive gesture at such unlikely news. After the last cup had been read, the women started saying they were late with the bread, that it had been left to rise for too long and the dough must be getting sour. They left hurriedly to complete what remained of the day's work, or what my maternal aunt Umm Ahmad described as their "never-ending tasks."

My mother returned to scrubbing the clothes in the washbowl, and I went off to the part of the village called Dulud. This consisted of four adjoining houses, three of them belonging to my maternal uncles and the fourth to my grandfather. This row of houses was next to an ancient holm oak. It was so large I thought it must be the first tree to have appeared in the world, and underneath it there was a huge rock with a smooth, flat surface.

"That rock is the empty bed of a thirty-three-foot-tall angel sent by God to watch over Dulud," my aunt Umm Ahmad had told all of us kids. "Then God recalled the angel, and, being so busy, the Almighty forgot to send the guardian angel of Dulud back to his post on the rock." Whenever she told this story, she laughed and asked God's forgiveness.

Taking the place of the angel, I lay on the rock, enjoying the shade of the overhanging branches and gentle breeze. I gazed at the clouds moving through the sky, and after what I had just witnessed at my mother's coffee party, it was as if I were discovering the skyscape through new eyes. Suddenly, I realized what the sky really was. It was God's coffee cup turned upside down after He'd finished drinking. The clouds were the remains of the coffee, staining the blue ceramic background of God's enormous upside-down vessel. And then I was overcome by another revelation. It struck me like a thunderbolt. What if *I* could read the signs in Allah's upside-down cup? I could become a prophet and know what God ordained for all people, trees, livestock — everything. This cup looked very different from the little coffee cups on our shelf. Ours were called Romeo and Juliet cups because of the picture of a girl and boy dressed in clothes quite unlike ours. These cups, which Umm Yusuf had turned around in her fingers, foretold the future of the people who'd drunk their contents.

But His divine cup would answer my many questions with real details. For when I'd ask Jaddi a question that was burning in my brain, often he'd answer this or that query with the phrase, "It is because of God's wisdom." But now I would see for myself all the wisdom and hidden mysteries that ordinary prophets and elders such as Jaddi apparently did not aspire to know. I would be able to see what was going to happen to God and the entire cosmos after reading three or four signs. Yes, if I learned to read the Lord's coffee cup, I would become the greatest prophet of them all.

Try as I might, I guess I just didn't have the patience required to become even a minor prophet. No matter how long I lay there, I failed to understand a single divine mystery. But I did develop into a skillful player of clouds. Joining forces with the wind, I saw in the western arena of the sky my very own Hollywood. In my mind, it was I who wrote film scenarios, formed characters from clouds, and told them how to act and what to say. I saw mythical creatures, like horses roaming the sky with three legs or sometimes seven, with small kindly heads, holding a dozen moons in their mouths instead of bouquets of roses. I liked moons better than flowers and, in my imagination, had the horses scatter them all around Barbara on my behalf. In the clouds I also saw the shadows of dead people I knew, such as my father's grandmother Badra. She was in the sky just as she was on Earth, dancing like a poplar tree released from her chains, surrounded by tall trees that sang and applauded her dancing. I spent many long hours enchanted by these sights.

I began playing with clouds whenever they appeared and wherever I was. Often, my mother thought I couldn't hear her when she called me in for lunch. But I did hear her and was annoyed because she was distracting me from being totally focused as storyteller, director, and audience for the sky cinema I named The Lord's Tales. And she was annoyed in turn because I didn't answer straight away and obliged her to call me many times. She explained my behavior by saying that I had a condition from my father's family, who had moments when they didn't hear or see and seemed to be living in another world.

I can't remember how many attempts I made to read God's coffee cup, or how many movies I watched in that vast screen in the sky. But I haven't forgotten how some of those movies portrayed many of my wishes at the time: Barbara's and my victory over her grandmother, what would have happened if Haifa and I had not been found in the cave or I hadn't been banished from my uncle's house because of Layla and Abu Suhayl. And I remember the stories where I envisioned relieving my mother of her never-ending housework, where she could do it in one minute and then enjoy life. I watched our neighbor Umm Samir rising from the dead, my grandfather managing to kill Azrael, and then his resounding laughter as his voice echoed throughout the whole of Syria, "Nobody will die from this day forth!"

My grandmother Umm Hassan had another way of reading clouds. I learned from her how to identify a very specific cloud, one that she called the Haddadeh fish. I saw this cloud when Rufaida and I were going back home after weeding and watering the thirty-square-foot plot of land we signed up to tend at the Lakeside Community Garden in Kingston.

"Look! The Haddadeh fish!" I said to her. Like my childhood self, my wife didn't hear, or maybe she wasn't interested. She carried on driving without knowing what I was talking about. *Perhaps she doesn't care*, I told myself, and went on silently observing the cloud that looked like a big fish. I wished grandmother Umm Hassan could shake off her shroud and the dust from her grave. If she could, I would tell her how the cloud she had taught me to identify more than half a century earlier was now above me in Kingston, half a world away from Kfarieh. And then I remembered a discussion we had.

"You are on the road to being seven years old," she told me.

"Does age have a road?" I asked.

"Of course."

"Will I get older more quickly if I run along it as fast as I can?"

"No. Time is what moves, never changing its pace. We can change where we live, but not how old we are." And then she explained more by telling me something of her life. "My father went to Buenos Aires when I was a child. They told us he married there and I have sisters in that country. My father's age wouldn't have been any different if he'd stayed here or gone away. I don't know when he died. A man came with a necktie and a hat like the one your uncle Jabr wears. He told us that my father had died in the American city of Boston, but he didn't tell us when or how. The man went away, and we didn't know how to get in touch with him. I'd like to see my sisters before I die." That's when my grandmother broke off her story and pointed at a long cloud in the fiery sunset sky. "Do you see that long cloud?"

"The one that looks like a fish?"

"Yes, very good. This is the Haddadeh fish. When it appears, it means tomorrow will be rainy."

Before we reached home, Rufaida asked me if I'd said something about fish. I assured her that I'd said something about clouds. She thought I was making fun of her, so I hurried to clear up the misunderstanding and told her about the Haddadeh fish. Then I added, "We have sky, sun, and clouds everywhere, and so it makes me realize how the Earth is one single country torn apart." My wife congratulated me on my brilliant insights, and I laughed, going along with her sarcasm.

In Tadmur Prison, when I was some twenty years past my seventh birthday, I received a bouquet of roses that my sister Khadija had wrapped in a page torn from a local newspaper. On one side was part of an interview with Hafiz al-Assad, president of the republic, in which he denied the existence of political prisoners in Syria. On the other side was an article with an illustration of Hadad, the Syrian god of storms and rain. He is the spirit who roams the sky in a chariot pulled by bulls. Hadad whipping the clouds causes them to rain, and the roaring of his bulls is the thunder that shakes the earth. In his left hand, he carries arrows that become lightning. In my cell, I stared at the picture of the god crowned with ears of wheat. And even though I was an avowed atheist, I prayed to this ancient god of my homeland for one time only.

"O lord god, why are you holding this whip? I pray you put down your whip and your arrows. We don't need more waste and devastation."

The sky let me down a few times. Once, when I came out of prison for the third time, and later when my sister Khadija died. During those days, the sky was a never-ending blue desert, arid and empty of both life and hope. I don't find the sky in Kingston arid or empty. There are always clouds to be interpreted, and today I'm trying to read God's upside-down coffee cup to know the future of my two sons, Ghamr and Taim.

For myself, though, it seems that I have already arrived at what they call the future.

CHAPTER 54

THE WORLD KEEPS TURNING . . .
SO DO WE

On the plane to Toronto, en route to Kingston, I remember how I used to follow the planes passing over our village until they disappeared from sight. When my father said that people travel in these planes, I thought he was joking.

"How can a machine the size of a goose carry people?" I laughed.

My father explained that airplanes are large but because they are so far away, they look small to us.

"Where do planes go?" I asked.

"To other places in the world."

I raised my finger and drew a circle in the air, pointing to the mountain-tops all around us that appeared to be joined to the sky. "Isn't this the world?" I said.

"Behind those mountains are faraway countries. Different countries. Son, the world is divided into our country and different countries."

I didn't know the meaning of the word "different."

"Different countries are the countries planes go to," I said to my brother Kamal, but he wasn't interested.

I was seven years old when I announced to my mother, "I'm going to go to faraway countries . . . the different ones!"

"How will you get there?" she asked.

LEFT: *Ray Argyle and Larry Scanlan were among our sponsors who came from Kingston to pick us up as we left the Toronto airport.*

BELOW: *Rufaida with a group of our sponsors who welcomed us at the airport: Pamela Paterson, Larry Scanlan, Ray Argyle, and Tarek Hussein, who is shaking hands with Rufaida.*

On the sign in the top photo:

الأستاذ جمال سعيد والعائلة
اهلا وسهلا بكم في كندا
Welcome to Canada
Jamal, Rufaida, Ghamr & Taim

"I will ask a plane to let down a rope for me."
"But planes don't let down ropes!"
"So how do people fly?"
"Planes land on the ground, and people get in and out of them."

"I'll ask the plane to land in front of our house," I said.

"But why do you want to go away? You haven't told me yet!"

"Grownups beat children here," I said, and my lips quivered.

My mother stopped wrapping vine leaves round rice and looked at my face with concern.

"What's happened?" she asked.

"My uncle asked me to bring him a box of matches to light his cigarette when he was playing cards," I answered, the tears rolling down my cheeks. My voice began to shake. "He hit me because I forgot. My uncle's strong. I couldn't defend myself."

Trying to hide her own tears, my mother advised me to remember when I was asked to do something, but to run to her when strong people threatened me.

"But they might hit you too."

My mother took me in her arms. "Stop crying," she said. "And don't be afraid."

"You stop crying. You first."

Now, fifty years later, I'm going to Canada, fleeing from the guns that destroy everything in their path. These days, Baba, the world is divided into our country where bombs destroy the houses and burn the trees, and the rest of the world.

My mother and father left our home in the village because of the bombing. Regime aircraft were shelling the village of Salma, which overlooks our village; then, on October 10, 2014, some houses in Kfarieh were hit by shells fired by the opposition. One struck our neighbor Zahra Swaid while she was picking olives, and she died. On November 10, exactly a month later, our village was bombed again by forces opposing the regime. I was in Dubai when my mother told me that another neighbor, Rabia, had taken refuge in our house with her baby girl. Since it was a house where a dissident who had spent many years in prison had grown up, she figured it couldn't possibly be a target for other opposition activists. Just as Rabia arrived, a bomb fell on the new tiled roof of our veranda. Falling tiles hit the baby on the head, and she died in her mother's arms. My own mother suffered minor injuries to her

*A bombing at the family home
caused a hole in the new tiled roof
of our veranda.*

hand from the shrapnel. The irony was that Rabia's house was left unscathed. That day my mother and father fled to my sister's house nearby.

"Our father is worried," my sister told me on Skype, "always looking to either side of him like a chick that's fallen out of its nest and doesn't know what to do next."

My father couldn't bear being away from home and decided to return. "It's more comfortable to die at home," he said.

I don't always understand my father's philosophy of life. I realize that life is more or less comfortable depending where you are, but death has the same taste, or no taste at all, wherever it occurs.

I called from my house in Dubai to tell my family I was on the move again.

"Where are you going?" my mother asked.

"To Canada."

"Things are hard here, son, and now they'll get harder because we may never see you again."

"No, Mama. We'll definitely see one another again!"

My father said in a sadly confident tone, "We will not see you in this generation, my son. Only if my grandfather comes back."

My father's grandfather traveled to Buenos Aires before the outbreak of World War I, and the family never heard from him again.

Rufaida was looking forlorn. "We won't lose touch with them," I assured her. "It's not so difficult or expensive to talk to everyone on Messenger or Skype." She nodded and smiled. Her smile was like a boat floating on a sea of bitterness.

In the aircraft, I watch the screen in front of me and see the blue line indicating the plane's route. We will travel 6,888 miles.

I look at Rufaida, Ghamr, and Taim, each absorbed in their dreams, fears, and memories, and surrender to my own dreams and fears.

We entered Canada from its sky. It was night. I didn't have a window seat, so I was unable to see our new country from above, but all airports in the world have the usual employees, documents to be stamped, and luggage. I take the documents given to me by a kindly official in uniform: permanent residency and certificates for one year of federal health insurance for each of us, Taim, Ghamr, Rufaida, and me, and a little red case to put these papers in.

A number of our sponsors were waiting for us, holding up a welcome sign with our names on it. I recognized Ray Argyle and Pamela Paterson.

ABOVE: *My father died a year and a half after I arrived. With his death, he emerged from the tunnel of depression he'd entered after the deaths of my sister Khadija and my brother Kamal, and rested in his grave like so many others.*

LEFT: *On the wall, behind my mom, the three photos of the absentees were hung; Kamal and Khadijah passed, and I was displaced.*

Before I left, I'd seen a photo of Ray on the internet and watched a video in which Pamela talked about her book. During our brief meeting at the air-port, after we'd all exchanged hugs, I was struck by Lawrence Scanlan's witty remarks and Tarek Hussein's sense of humor and appealing Egyptian accent.

When we went out into the street, I felt as if I'd suddenly stepped into a freezer. A few steps, and we and our luggage were in a heated van, heading for Kingston. The apartment we'd seen photos of in Dubai wasn't ready yet. Its walls were still getting a fresh coat of paint, so we lived in Ray and Deborah's house for ten days.

I first met Kingston in her dress of snow. I was looking out the window and addressing the new city as if that's all there was to it, while in fact it was also inside the house, embodied in Ray and his wife, Deborah, who fed us and made us comfortable, not to mention Morig the dog, who helped me overcome my fear of dogs. When I was eight a vicious dog bit me. Its owner said it was my fault because I'd run away from it, and from that day on I was terrified of dogs. When we arrived at Ray and Deborah's house, Morig greeted us in her own way, and Rufaida tried to take my share of the welcome as she knows I'm not crazy about dogs. For some unknown reason Morig insisted on sitting next to me, and in the end we became friends.

On the first night in Kingston, Rufaida and I woke up at two in the morning. Our bodies were not accustomed to the new time zone. I called my family via Messenger to reassure them that we had arrived and all was well. Their sun had risen hours earlier.

"What does this Canada look like to you?" my mother asked.

"Whiter than the bags of Canadian flour you made our clothes from! There's a thick blanket of snow covering the roads, trees, and rooftops."

In the morning, snow continued to fall in Kingston, casting its flat unvarying color over the city, indifferent to all. In Damascus people celebrate snow, having snowball fights and laughing together. Perhaps Damascus takes this opportunity to celebrate when there are so many people in the streets and alleys. Rufaida still loves zaatar with olive oil on snowy days. For our first breakfast Deborah gave us pastries like fatayir that Canadians call pancakes, and this was the first time I tasted maple syrup. Ray and Deborah enveloped us in smiles and questions and kind remarks, while I looked at Ghamr and Taim, trying to work out whether they were accepting their new world. To Rufaida I said, "There will be enough snow here for you to have zaatar with olive oil. I think we'll be able to get it here."

I look out the window. There are no children in the streets — in fact, nobody at all. From time to time I see a man or woman walk by with a dog sniffing the smells of the dogs who've been there before him. No shops or cafés in sight. Cities, like people, have different features.

We spent the last night of 2016 at a New Year's Eve party at Tarek and Pamela's house, getting to know our sponsors. My first problem was poor hearing. I was ashamed (and still am) to keep asking people to repeat what they'd said. I tried to read lips and often ended up avoiding conversations. I felt embarrassed when I laughed at a joke I didn't understand or nodded my head, pretending to know what people were saying. It wasn't easy to get to know English here. It was so different from the English I'd learned to read, but not speak, at Damascus University, and the few times I'd listened to English classes on the BBC weren't enough to give me confidence now. This almost made me cut myself off from everyone. I told myself to do something and began attending English classes at KEYS Job Centre, but I could only hear or understand a little of what my teacher Hal was saying. "Exile from language is real exile," I used to repeat to myself in silence. Eight months later, with Ray's help, I acquired a hearing aid, which made me less fearful of interacting with Canadian friends and better able to understand the range of accents.

The apartment we moved to was close to the city center, the boys' school, and various services, but it was old and couldn't compare in terms of spaciousness and cleanliness to the apartment we left in Dubai. All the same, it was a safe refuge equipped with everything we needed.

One day, when I was talking to my mother on Messenger, I wanted to cheer her up by showing her a view of the snow. It had the opposite effect.

"It's a disaster, my son," she cried. "Will the snow rot your bones and the bones of your wife and children?"

"No, not at all. Look, I'm not shivering!"

"You should have learned more about Canada before you went. How are you finding it?"

After a brief pause, I responded with a phrase I would repeat often: "Winter is cold in Canada, but people's hearts are warm." Then I added, "And the houses are warm too."

"May God fill people's hearts with compassion for you, and God be with you in your exile."

"You are in greater need of the Lord's help. Here bombs don't fall on people's heads and people don't live without water or electricity, and there's no poverty as dark as the poverty created by war. People aren't killed for reasons they have no control over, such as coming from one sect or another. And they aren't imprisoned for having a different opinion from the ruler's."

After the conversation with my mother, I felt that I'd been addressing myself as much as her, perhaps making a statement on behalf of Canada and grieving for Syria.

I came to know the Mess Studio in the basement of St. Andrew's Church, where all drawing materials are available free, and went back to my old hobby of painting. I was a child again, loving to play with colors. In that studio I sold my first painting, of lilacs, for a hundred dollars. It was my first income in Canada.

When we'd been in Canada for ninety-eight days, our sponsors held a party for Rufaida's fiftieth birthday. It was to be a surprise for Rufaida, and we started exchanging emails with the title "the white lie." We went to the house of Lory and his wife, Myungja, who initiated the idea to celebrate Rufaida's day. When we entered the house, everyone was hiding in the kitchen, including Ghamr and Taim. As we walked into the living room, they all jumped out, shouting "Surprise!" Rufaida's eyes filled with tears. She felt she had a family in Canada now.

Suddenly she saw our sons. "How did you get here?" she cried. "I thought you were with your friends."

I was so happy to see tears of joy on Rufaida's cheeks. This time we were celebrating her birthday thousands of miles away from the bombs that fell indiscriminately on people, trees, roads, and houses.

Before we left Syria, I could never relax until the boys came home safe from school each day. In Kingston I was worried they wouldn't get to school on time. They both studied day and night, and I wanted to do everything to encourage them. I was proud of what the teachers told me about them at a parent-teacher meeting at their school, the Loyalist Collegiate and Vocational Institute. And I was really happy when the boys' friends started visiting our apartment. It made me see that Ghamr and Taim belonged to a world less harsh than mine when I was their age.

If my father had come to Canada, he would have been astonished to see that houses don't have fruit trees in their gardens, and most don't even have vegetables. He would wonder why the people of Canada were wasting the sun, water, and soil, and why they grow grass, not for their livestock to graze, but to cut with machines, so it can grow and be cut again. My father used to dig up rocks and stones and replace them with good soil so he could grow more trees and vegetables. He'd be surprised to know that North Americans care about dogs and cats, and allocate part of their household budgets to them, far more than they care about goats and sheep that would increase their income.

My father never did come to Canada. He died a year and a half after I arrived. With his death, he emerged from the tunnel of depression he'd entered after the deaths of my sister Khadija and my brother Kamal, and rested in his grave like so many others. I walked the streets of Kingston feeling like a real orphan. I didn't want my sons to see my tears or my grief, so I shed those tears outside, but my grief didn't leave me and go back east to Syria. It came home with me.

I received condolences from friends in all different parts of the world, including Syria. Syrians' Facebook pages have turned into walls where death notices are pasted and condolences received. My Canadian friends consoled me too. They came with bouquets of flowers and cards with kind messages of sympathy. I talked to them about my father and told them how I'd seen him kissing a plant of his one summer. Syrian friends in Kingston held a mourning ceremony where they served the customary bitter coffee and dates and recited the Fatiha prayer.

Many friends who have been mentioned in this book have died. This includes Jaffan al-Homsi, Abd al-Karim, Musab Nabhan, and Salman Ismail. They died young, in a country where there were shortages of food and medicine and where different types of weapons were all over the streets. I sometimes think they'll be there to welcome me when I visit Syria. At such moments, I don't imagine they'll rise up from their graves, but that they never died. When I think of returning to Syria, I don't think of visiting my father's grave, but rather of him receiving me with open arms under the mulberry tree in front of the house.

If my mother were sitting with me on the balcony of my apartment on College Street, she would look in surprise at the old women wearing lipstick. She would call out to them cheerfully, "Maybe it's too late, ladies. Lipstick might have been more use when you were younger."

"We think differently," one of them would say. Then she would hold out a lipstick to my mother and say, "This color would suit you," and my mother would laugh. I picture my mother talking to them in their language, telling them a thousand and one tales about her ten children, eighteen grandchildren, and life and its troubles in her different world.

"Wow!" they would say, and "Incredible!" and ask to know more.

Month thirteen is a difficult month for the new arrivals. The sponsorship period has ended, and the budget is about to run out. I must find a job. Ray noticed what was happening to us and helped me get a grant to start writing this book. Rufaida worked with Mary Campeau, a lively woman in her seventies, in a real estate office, then moved on to a post at a job center that provided services to refugees. She also acquired part-time work as an interpreter for Arabic-speaking refugees. She'd go with them to doctors, lawyers, or government agency appointments. After her contract with the job center came to an end, she embarked on a Syrian food catering business. We worked together on it and were able to provide enough income, but we were exhausted. Rufaida also worked as a medical courier driver and continued work as an interpreter when required. But finding me a regular job was not easy, and we entered the usual vicious circle: to get a job you need experience, and to get experience you need a job. For a time our primary income came from Rufaida's work and from me extending my grant. Ray introduced me to the writer Sharon McKay, and within an hour she and I had agreed to work together on a novel for children. It was released in 2020 under the title *Yara's Spring*. It's about the civil war in Syria, as experienced by a Syrian girl who ends up in a refugee camp in Jordan. Since I couldn't land a regular job to help pay the bills, I started holding Arabic calligraphy workshops at a local arts center and offered private Arabic classes at home. I also became an after-school mentor to a wonderful young man with Down's syndrome, and we would walk through the streets of Kingston singing, "We hate cold, we love summer." Before the Covid pandemic hit, I gave lectures on Middle Eastern art and culture at a seniors' center and enjoyed the way my students were so engaged and interested.

I cried for joy when Ghamr was awarded a full scholarship from the University of Toronto to study engineering, and again when Taim obtained a prestigious Loran scholarship. Now the boys are both over eighteen, standing on the edge of the family nest, poised for flight. Soon they will take off to build their own nests. Here there is nothing to fear about them growing wings. There's plenty of room to fly.

There are no cats in the roads here like those strays that roamed Jadat Qudsaya. Taim's cat, who stayed in Damascus, didn't need anyone's help to take her kittens to safety, but I needed the help of organizations and friends I didn't know to take my children to a safe place. For this I am grateful, and I hope to be worthy of the help they gave me.

We moved to a clean, more modern house on Ellesmeer Avenue. It is a source of joy to Rufaida that I no longer strew my papers, laptop, keys, wallet, and coffee cups over the dining table, as I have an office in the basement of the new house, with a couch and a bed where I can take a siesta when I work long hours. Some of our friends decided to have what they call here a "house-warming" for us. Larry Scanlan and his wife, Ulrike Bender, having heard my stories about apples, decided to present me with an apple tree for our new backyard. However, the agency that rented the house to us didn't agree to us planting it, because most people don't take good care of trees and because it might attract raccoons, and therefore, the tree might cause problems. I imagine my father looking completely astonished and asking, "Did I hear right?

Can a tree cause a problem? Does the earth know any creature more innocent than an apple tree?"

Larry told me I could plant it near his cottage in the country, but the onslaught of the pandemic prevented me, so Larry planted it for me and sent a photo of it in an email. I read Larry's name and felt immense gratitude and looked at the picture of the tree as if it were my daughter. I also adopted a baby apple tree in a community vegetable garden, with the agreement of the management. I gave the tree my mother's name, Najeebah, and I've been taking care of it for two years now.

I'm standing on the shore of Lake Ontario again. The winds are getting stronger and the waves surge and dance together, then fade to nothing on the shore. The sky is a great blue dome over the whole world. I remember God's inverted coffee cup and Umm Yusuf reading the future in the coffee cups of my mother and her friends. Clouds race each other in the vast western sky, and I hear the sounds of the wind and the waves. Images from news bulletins crowd into my head: apple orchards, olive groves, fields of wheat, all burning and the smoke rising up into the sky and the peasants' faces just a single, long, drawn out, dried-up scream of misery.

"Awwwwwwww!" I howl over the lake again, trying to drive out the pain overwhelming me.

Listen! This howling is no use to anyone. Sending sums of money back home, however small, is better than howling. But I need to free my soul from this screaming.

I decide to visit my tree in the garden near the lake. I love this child of mine. When I arrive, I look at Najeebah. Her leaves are like emeralds, fluttering playfully in the breeze. I kiss her gently. I don't consider kissing trees a sign of madness. I begin walking round the tree. Heavy rain falls and as it waters my tree, it seems to me that it is watering all the trees in the world. My clothes are drenched and drops of water run over my hair and down my face. I smile and walk faster round the tree. Najeebah will grow and give people her fruit.

My father used to rejoice when it rained, describing it as sky music to make the earth happy. Hurrah! Life wins. Najeebah dances to the rhythm of the sky music. I dance as I circle the tree. Galileo jumps from the magazine my Uncle Jabr gave me, dancing round the tree and shouting, "E pur si muove."

I dance with the echo of his cry and with my uncle's ghost. If Fadwa could see me now, she would say I'd gone mad. I dance with my teacher Nazeer and the ants that didn't fall off the basketball. I'm smaller on the Earth's surface than a single ant on the basketball. All the same, I am at one with the universe, and I'm growing and feeling that the Earth is turning inside me, along with the pain and scars of my homeland, but also with great hope. Here beside Najeebah I feel safer. I spin round in the halls of the future with enough time and space to dance. In my homeland, sadly, time still looks like prisons and graves and bombing raids. The world we roam through is full of weapons, famines, borders, passports, and asylum seekers. But the world that turns in my heart is like a warm house, open to all, an amazingly beautiful world that keeps turning, and turns its back on passports and borders and bloodshed and famine and all the suffering that people endure.

We visited City Hall in January 2017, a few days after our arrival, and met Chris Wyman, the nice crier, on the steps near the front door.

In 2017 we met kind Sophie Kiwala, an Ontario MPP at the time, at City Hall.

Rev. Joan Hughes, a retired United Church minister, is one of our sponsors.

ACKNOWLEDGMENTS

It goes without saying that I owe Rufaida, Ghamr, and Taim immense gratitude, always. A special thanks to Ghamr and his friend Kallandra Moor for proofreading my English.

My sincere thanks to Pen Canada and the International Cities of Refuge Network (ICORN) who helped me move to Canada, where I can write without fear.

My sincere thanks to my sponsors from the Kingston Writers' Refugee Committee: Ray Argyle, Wayne Myles, Larry Scanlan, Deborah Windsor, Lory Kaufman, Barbara Bell, Joan Heaton, Rev. Joan Hughes, Pamela Paterson, and Tarek Hussein, who not only contributed to bringing us to a safe haven but took care of the details of daily life in our new home and did their utmost to relieve the pain of exile for myself and my family.

I am deeply grateful to Ray Argyle not only for his fatherly care for my family, but also because he did as much as he could. I began writing this book in English, with considerable help from Ray. He discussed and wrote the broad outlines with me. At the same time, Ray introduced me to the amazing writer Sharon McKay. Deep thanks to Sharon, who was so generous and kind when we worked together writing *Yara's Spring*.

After writing the first three chapters of this book in English, I was convinced that I was much better able to write in Arabic, at which point Lory Kaufman suggested I compose in my mother tongue and find an English translator for the book.

Special thanks to Lory, together with Ian Baines, for their support in help-ing me find a translator. Lory had a notable role in providing great support in achieving this book; he enthusiastically helped with editing and corre-sponding with the people who helped me build this book. I am so grateful for everything he has done.

I noticed while searching the internet that Catherine Cobham had translated the works of several major Arab writers, and Canadian friends admired her translations. I contacted her and asked her to translate some sample chapters to present to an agent, and when I read her email saying she would translate these sample chapters "for Syria," I had tears in my eyes. While working on the book, she checked the chapters after the ini-tial round of editing and offered some important observations. Catherine was not only a translator, but also a reader and critic who had a part in the construction of this book, and for that I would like to express my greatest appreciation.

Writer and editor Lawrence Scanlan volunteered to edit the chapters of this book before I sent the first draft to the publisher. In Arabic, there is an expression that means "He took care of every detail of the writing." The literal translation is, "He revised every word from first to last cover." Of course, Larry did not revise every word, but he did read some chapters sev-eral times, and he always edited the chapters sent to him as quickly and precisely as possible and made very important observations in many places. Larry never said no when I needed his help. I'm extremely grateful to him.

My sincere thanks go to Frances Itani who was always generous with her time and advice, and who connected me with the wonderful literary agent Chris Casuccio of Westwood Creative Artists. Chris showed great care in his dealings with me, was very helpful with his advice on the traditions and legal-ities of publishing in Canada, and soon found a publisher for *My Road from Damascus*. I would particularly like to thank him.

I am most grateful for the precious trust shown by Michael Holmes, whose words made me cry tears of joy. Along with everyone at ECW Press, Michael made me feel that this establishment was not only my family in the field of writing and publishing, but also my close friends in my new home-land. Many thanks to Shannon Parr; I'm grateful for your kindness, Shannon. Thanks to Jessica Albert, Emily Ferko, Aymen Saidane, Elham Ali, Claire

Pokorchak, and the staff at ECW Press, who are all are so kind. Many thanks to Steph VanderMeulen, whose perceptive reading was so helpful.

Special thanks to Yousef Abdelke, who gave me the permission to use his art for the cover, and many thanks to the designer, James Jones.

My thanks and gratitude to the Canadian organizations whose financial aid played a major role in giving me time to work on this book: the Foundation for the Advancement of Canadian Letters (FACL), the Ontario Arts Council, the Canada Council for the Arts, and thanks also to the Kingston Writers' Festival for its support.